About Philosophy

About Philosophy

ROBERT PAUL WOLFF

University of Massachusetts

PRENTICE-HALL, INC., Englewood Cliffs, New Jersey

Library of Congress Cataloging in Publication Data

WOLFF, ROBERT PAUL.
  About philosophy.

  1. Philosophy—Introductions. I. Title.
BD21.W64   100   75–15739
ISBN   0-13-663377-3

Printed in the United States of America.

10 9 8 7 6 5 4

Prentice-Hall International, Inc., London
Prentice-Hall of Australia, Pty. Ltd., Sydney
Prentice-Hall of Canada, Ltd., Toronto
Prentice-Hall of India Private Limited, New Delhi
Prentice-Hall of Japan, Inc., Tokyo
Prentice-Hall of Southeast Asia (Pte.) Ltd., Singapore

ACKNOWLEDGMENTS

Confucius, *The Wisdom of Confucius*, edited and translated with notes by Lin Yutang. Reprinted by permission of the publisher, Random House, Inc. Alexis de Toqueville, *The Old Regime and the French Revolution*, trans. by Stuart Gilbert. Copyright © 1955 by Doubleday & Company, Inc. Reprinted by permission of Doubleday & Company, Inc.

Erik H. Erikson, *Childhood and Society*, 2nd ed. Copyright 1950, © 1963 by W.W. Norton & Company, Inc. Reprinted by permission of W.W. Norton & Company, Inc.

Sigmund Freud, *The Future of an Illusion*, trans. by W.D. Robson-Scott. Reprinted by permission of Liveright Publishing Corporation and The Hogarth Press. Copyright 1955 by Liveright Publishing Corporation.

Immanuel Kant, *Groundwork of the Metaphysic of Morals*, trans. by H.J. Paton (New York, Harper & Row, 1964), pp. 94, 98–100. Reprinted by permission of the publisher.

Immanuel Kant, *Immanuel Kant's Critique of Pure Reason*, trans. by Norman Kemp Smith. Reprinted by permission of St. Martin's Press, Inc., and Macmillan, London and Basingstoke.

Søren Kierkegaard, "Preface" in *Philosophical Fragments or a Fragment of Philosophy*, 2nd ed., originally translated and introduced by David Swenson. New Introduction and commentary by Niels Thulstrup, translation rev. and commentary trans. by Howard V. Hong. Copyright © 1936, 1962 by Princeton University Press; Princeton Paperback, 1967, pp. 3–7; Notes to Preface 1st. ed., p. 97. Reprinted by permission of Princeton University Press.

Norman Malcolm, "Scientific Materialism and the Identity Theory" from *The Journal of Philosophy*, Vol. LX, 22 (October 24, 1963). Reprinted by permission of the publisher and the author.

Herbert Marcuse, *One-Dimensional Man*. Copyright © 1964 by Herbert Marcuse. Reprinted by permission of Beacon Press.

Michael Oakeshott, *Rationalism in Politics and Other Essays*, pages 1, 2, 3, 7–8. Copyright © 1962 by Michael Oakeshott. Basic Books, Inc., Publishers, New York. Reprinted by permission of Basic Books, Inc. and Methuen & Co. Ltd.

Plato, *Gorgias*, © 1952 by the Liberal Arts Press. Reprinted by permission of the publishers, The Bobbs-Merrill Company, Inc.

Plato, *The Republic of Plato*, trans. by F.M. Cornford, 1941, by permission of the Oxford University Press, Oxford.

Theodore Roszak, *The Making of a Counter Culture*. Copyright © 1968, 1969 by Theodore Roszak. Reprinted by permission of Doubleday & Company, Inc.

Saint Anselm, *Saint Anselm: Basic Writings*, trans. by S.N. Deane. Published by Open Court Publishing Company, La Salle, Ill., 1966. Copyright © 1962 by Open Court Publishing Company. Reprinted by permission of the publisher.

Saint Thomas Aquinas, "Summa Theologica" from *Basic Writings of Saint Thomas Aquinas*, ed. by Anton C. Pegis. Reprinted by permission of the publisher, Random House, Inc. Copyright 1945 by Random House, Inc.

J.J.C. Smart, "Materialism," from *The Journal of Philosophy*, Vol. LX, 22 (October 24, 1963). Reprinted by permission of the publisher and the author.

P.F. Strawson, *Individuals: An Essay in Descriptive Metaphysics*. Reprinted by permission of Methuen & Co., Ltd.

"Supporting Evidence for the Theory of the Steady State," © 1970; and "Headlong for the Breakthrough . . ." © 1968, *Science News*. Reprinted by permission from *Science News*, the weekly news magazine of science and the applications of science. Copyright 1970 and 1968 by Science Service, Inc. Edward Westermarck, *Ethical Relativity*, © 1932 by Kegan Paul, Trench, Trubner & Co., Ltd. Reprinted by permission of the publisher, Routledge & Kegan Paul, Ltd.

ILLUSTRATION CREDITS

Page   2 Courtesy Vatican Museum, Scala, New York/Florence.
       14 Courtesy the New York Public Library Picture Collection.
       23 S. Maria Novella, Florence, Scala, New York/Florence.
       27 Courtesy New York Public Library Picture Collection.
       33 Drawing by Lorenz; © 1960 The New Yorker Magazine, Inc.
       35 Courtesy The Granger Collection, New York.
       38 Courtesy New York Public Library Picture Collection.
       57 Courtesy The Bettmann Archive, Inc.
       69 Drawing by R. Taylor; © 1957 The New Yorker Magazine, Inc.
       78 Courtesy The Bettmann Archive, Inc.
       92 (left) Courtesy The Bettmann Archive, Inc.
       92 (right) Courtesy Brown Brothers, Sterling, Pa.
      102 Courtesy The Granger Collection, New York.
      104 (left) Courtesy Calogero Cascio/Photo Researchers, Inc.
      104 (right) Courtesy Wide World Photos, Inc.
      111 Courtesy Photo Guillimette.
      114 Courtesy Giraudon, Paris.
      116 Drawing by W. Miller, © 1969 The New Yorker Magazine, Inc.
      117 Courtesy Brown Brothers, Sterling, Pa.
      135 Courtesy United Press International, Inc.
      150 Courtesy Vatican Museum, Scala, New York/Florence.
      152 Drawing by W. Miller; © 1968 The New Yorker Magazine, Inc.
      169 Courtesy Culver Pictures, Inc.
      171 Courtesy The Phillips Collection, Washington.
      175 Courtesy Sovfoto. Photo by Belyakov.
      176 Courtesy Spanish National Tourist Office.
      177 Courtesy Martha Swope, photographer.
      181 Courtesy University of California, San Diego.
      188 Courtesy The Granger Collection, New York.
      191 Courtesy The Granger Collection, New York.
      193 Courtesy New York Public Library Picture Collection.
      194 Drawing by Stevenson; © 1960 The New Yorker Magazine, Inc.
      224 Courtesy New York Public Library Picture Collection.
      226 Courtesy John Hart and Field Enterprises, Inc.
      253 (left) Courtesy Chateau Versailles. Scala New York/Florence.
      253 (right) Courtesy New York Public Library Picture Collection.
      260 Courtesy The Bettmann Archive, Inc.
      274 Courtesy NASA.
      281 Courtesy John Hart and Field Enterprises, Inc.

Contents

9 An Ending and—Perhaps— A Beginning

LIST OF BRIEF SELECTIONS INCLUDED IN TEXT

Preface

This book is the outgrowth of two decades of teaching. I faced my first philosophy class in the fall of 1955, when I was a graduate student not much older than my students. Because I was young, it was easier then for me to put myself in their place and try to see philosophy through their eyes, as an entirely new experience. As the years have passed, I have grown older, but my students remain the same age. So the gap between us widens, and I must work harder each year to recapture their perspective. Long familiarity with the problems and methods of philosophy has led me to take them too much for granted. Again and again, I must remind myself that philosophy is a special way of looking at life, a way that is *natural*, but not therefore obvious. And should I forget this fact, my students will very quickly remind me!

In this introduction to philosophical problems, theories, and personalities, I have tried always to keep the student's point of view central. I imagine my reader to be intelligent, naturally curious, but sceptical. He or she is willing to listen to new ideas, but not to accept them merely on the authority of an author or teacher. My job is to present philosophy as an activity that sensible, intelligent people would *want* to engage in. It is not enough for me to explain what the great philosophers said in a clear, uncluttered way. I must also help my reader to understand *why* they said it, why they felt compelled to think about their moral, scientific, religious, or logical problems as they did.

In writing this book, I have had the help of a great many men and women, and it is a pleasure to have the opportunity to acknowledge my debt to them. My first thanks must go to the several thousand students who have listened to me, argued with me, learned from me, and taught me over the past twenty years. Some of them have become teachers of philosophy themselves; others are craftsmen, lawyers, clerks, doctors, politicians, policemen, and I know not what else. But all have helped me to become a better teacher. I hope their voices echo in these pages.

Several of my colleagues at the University of Massachusetts answered my questions and corrected some of my misconceptions in one or another of the branches of philosophy touched on in this book. First among them is Professor Robert J. Ackermann, an extraordinarily gifted and widely learned man whom I am fortunate to count as my friend. Professor Mary Sirridge guided me through some of the complexities of the philosophy of art, a field in which she is an expert and I am a novice.

The single most important source of assistance was Ms. (soon to be Dr.) Karen Warren, who devoted several months to invaluable research and background work on every chapter of the book. To say that Ms. Warren was my "research assistant" entirely fails to do justice to the nature and magnitude of her contribution. Ms. Warren is, by the common agreement of my colleagues, far and away the most successful teacher among all the graduate students who have come through the Philosophy Department of the University of Massachusetts. Her research for me included beautifully clear analyses of key issues in each field of philosophy, as well as the more conventional mustering of sources and biographical details. Her own teaching skill enabled her to lay out the material for me so that I in turn could present it in what I hope is a coherent and comprehensible manner. I quite literally could not have written this book without her aid.

Robert Paul Wolff
Northampton, Massachusetts

About Philosophy

SOCRATES was tried by the Athenians on charges of "impiety" and "corrupting the young of Athens," but it seems clear that his real "offense" was opposition to, or even lack of sufficient support for, the leaders of the newly restored democratic regime. Socrates had associated with the aristocratic families which overthrew the first democracy, and his disciple, Plato, was a member of one of the powerful families which ruled Athens for a while before the restoration. Since an amnesty had been declared, it was legally impossible for the rulers to prosecute Socrates for political offenses, so they trumped up the religious accusations and enlisted a religious fanatic, Meletus, to bring charges against the seventy-year-old philosopher.

Socrates could have fled from Athens before the trial, conviction in which could carry a death sentence. Even after his conviction, he could have proposed banishment as an alternative to death, and the Athenian jury of 501 citizens would almost certainly have accepted such a compromise. But Socrates was convinced that he had done Athens no harm by his philosophical questioning. Indeed, he insisted that he had, by his activities, been a benefactor of his native city, and so as an alternative to the death penalty demanded by the prosecution he proposed that Athens pension him off as a respected citizen.

The Athenian rulers, trapped by Socrates' uncompromising integrity, were forced to carry out the sentence of death, though they would probably have been all too happy to allow their prisoner to escape before the execution. One month after the trial, following a long night of philosophical discussion with his friends, Socrates drank the poison hemlock prepared for him by his jailers, and died.

What is Philosophy? 1

When I was a student, one of my professors told us about the conversations he would strike up in the club car on the train from Boston to New York. A group of men would gather around the bar, and each in turn would introduce himself, saying a few words about the line of work he was in. One would announce himself as a lawyer, a second as a traveler in ladies' apparel, a third as an engineer. When it was my professor's turn, he would say, "I am a philosopher." That, he told us, would always bring the conversation to a dead halt. No one knew quite what to say to a man who described himself as a philosopher. The others were too polite to ask, "What does a philosopher do?" But the announcement always cast a pall over the gathering. Eventually, he took to saying, "I am a teacher." That went over all right, and so long as no one asked what he taught, they could get on to more congenial topics, such as the prospects for the Red Sox, or the weather.

What *do* philosophers do? Oddly enough, that is a question philosophers have been asking for as long as there has been a discipline called philosophy. Indeed, as we will see a bit later on, "What do philosophers do?" is probably the most common philosophical question! But all this sounds like double talk, which is just what makes people nervous about philosophy in the first place. You all know what a doctor does; you know

3

what physicists, historians, composers, and sanitation engineers do. Most of you probably even have some sort of idea of what microbiologists do. But philosophers are something else again. Philosophers ask questions—odd questions, like "Could my whole life be a dream?" and dangerous questions, like "What right does the government—any government—have to tell me what to do?"

The best way to find out what philosophers do is to take a look at one of them, and on anybody's list, the natural first choice must be the most famous philosopher of all time, SOCRATES. Socrates was born in 469 B.C. to a stonemason and a midwife in the Greek city-state of Athens. As far as we know, he spent his entire life in and about Athens, serving his time in the army at one point, taking his turn in the government at another. He was a rather homely man in a society that prized manly beauty, and though he was hardly poor, he seems to have managed on much less money than his friends and disciples had. Athens itself was a city of 130,000, busy and prosperous by the standards of the time but small enough so that everyone who was anyone knew everyone else. In his youth, Socrates studied the scientific theories a number of original thinkers had developed in the preceding several centuries, but he soon became convinced that the most important and puzzling subject was man himself. He developed the practice of going into the public squares and meeting places of Athens to cajole, goad, or draw his fellow townsmen into discussions about how men ought to live their lives. (In the Athens of Socrates' day, it was taken for granted that women would play no role in these discussions, or indeed in any other public business.) Socrates was quick-witted, clever, and tenacious. He had a knack for asking hard or embarrassing questions that forced others to think a good deal more than they really wanted to. Because some of the people he quizzed were important politicians and famous teachers, it was fun to watch him trip them up—so long as you weren't one of those made to look foolish. So a number of wealthy young men gathered around Socrates as a band of disciples and as a sort of permanent audience. Sometimes he talked with them, quizzing them in the same way and forcing them to examine their own lives; sometimes they watched as he took on a local bigwig or visiting personage.

If this practice of asking questions were all there were to Socrates' life, we would never have heard of him 2400 years later, and we certainly wouldn't think of him as the first and greatest of all philosophers. But three things transformed Socrates from a local curiosity and general pain in the neck into the patron saint of philosophy and one of the great figures of Western civilization.

The first thing was an accident. Among those who followed Socrates was a brilliantly gifted, wealthy young man named Plato. Plato was only twenty-eight when his teacher died, but he was deeply, permanently affected by his relationship with the aging Socrates, and many years later he began to write his Dialogues, playlets in which the style and personality of Socrates were captured, transformed, and elevated into works of great art. Most of what we believe about Socrates comes to us from these Dialogues, including most importantly our conception of Socrates' techniques of questioning. Scholars still debate how much in the Dialogues is Plato's artistic invention and how much is accurate historical portrayal. But there can be no question that the essential style belonged to Socrates himself.

The second thing that happened was not really an accident, though it may seem so at first glance. The rulers of Athens decided that Socrates was more than an annoyance; he was becoming a threat to their political security. So they trumped up some charges against him and put him on trial. Socrates could have plea-bargained, in effect, and gotten off with a punishment of exile, which would have put him safely out of Athens without making him a martyr. But he chose instead to defend himself and his life without excuses or apologies. He had done nothing wrong, he insisted, and now that he was seventy, Athens should be thinking of giving him a pension rather than threatening to put him to death. In the end, Socrates forced the government's hand, and a sentence of death was handed down. Even then, he could probably have escaped from jail with the help of his friends, but he stayed and took the poison his jailors gave him. And so he became the first martyr to philosophy. It is easy to second-guess the Athenian rulers and conclude that they could have spared themselves a lot of trouble by handling the case a bit more skilfully. But Socrates' persistent questioning of established doctrines and received opinions really was a threat, not only to the government but also to the lifestyle of the families who ruled Athens. In a way, the accident is not that Socrates was put to death at the age of seventy, but rather that he had been permitted to go on for so long before those in power landed on him.

The third and most important reason for Socrates' immortality is no accident at all, but the very essence of his life and calling. Witty though he was, irreverent though he could be, annoying though he certainly became, Socrates was deadly serious about his questioning. His death only confirmed what his life had already proved—that for him, the relentless examination of every human action and belief was more important than survival itself. As Socrates said at his trial, "The unexamined life is not worth living," and by drinking the poison, he showed that he would rather die honorably in the cause of that principle than flee in dishonor to some foreign refuge.

Each of us makes countless decisions which affect our lives and the lives of those around us to some degree. Many of the decisions are of very little importance, such as whether or not to go to the movies, where to have dinner, or what to wear. A few of the decisions are truly momentous —whom to marry, what career to pursue; and for some of us, caught up in a war or facing a personal tragedy, our decisions may literally determine life and death. Socrates believed in his own time (and I think he would still believe if he were alive today) that these decisions must be questioned, examined, and criticized if we are to live truly good and happy lives. Most of us make even the most important decisions without really asking ourselves what principles we are basing our choices on, and whether those principles are truly worthy of our respect and commitment. When war comes, young men go off to fight and die with hardly more than a passing thought about whether it is ever morally right to kill another person. A student spends ten years of his or her life working to become a doctor, simply because mom and dad always wanted it. A man and a woman drift into marriage, have children, buy a house and settle down, and only twenty years later does one of them ask, "What am I doing here?"

Socrates had a theory about how each of us ought to examine his life, subjecting it to critical analysis and questioning. This theory, on which he based the special style of teaching and philosophizing that has come to bear his name, rested on four basic principles:

1. The unexamined life is not worth living. To be truly human, and thereby truly happy, each man and woman must subject his or her own life and convictions to critical testing.

2. There are objectively valid principles of thought and action which must be followed if we are to live good lives—lives both happy and just. It isn't true that every person's way of life is as good as every other's. Some people are unjust, self-indulgent, obsessed with worthless goals, estranged from their fellows, confused and blind about what is truly important and what is beneath notice, terrified of shadows, and incapable either of living or of dying with grace and dignity. Such people need to find the truth and live in accordance with it.

3. The truth lies within each of us, not in the stars, or in tradition, or in religious books, or in the opinions of the masses. Each of us has within him, however hidden, the true principles of right thinking and acting. In the end, therefore, no one can teach anyone else the truth about life. If that truth isn't within you, you will never find it; if it is within you, then only relentless critical self-examination will reveal it.

4. But though no one can teach anyone else about the fundamental principles of right action and clear thinking, some people—call them

teachers, philosophers, gadflies—can ask questions that prod men and women to begin the task of self-examination. These teachers may also be able to guide the process, at least in its early stages, because they have been over the same ground themselves and know where the pitfalls are.

From these four principles, it follows that philosophy consists of a process of question and answer, a *dialogue* between two people, one of whom is seeking rational insight and understanding, the other of whom has already achieved some measure of self-knowledge and wishes to help the novice. The dialogue begins with whatever beliefs the student brings to the quest. If he thoughtlessly repeats the traditional moral sayings of his society, then the philosopher will try to force him to question those sayings; if he takes up the position that everything is relative, that nothing is true or valid for all men (a stance many students adopt at about the time they leave home and cut loose from their parents), then the philosopher will try a different line of questioning. The end point of the journey is always the same: wisdom, rational insight into the principles of thought and action, and thus a happier, more integrated, more worthwhile life. But the starting points are as many as the students who make the journey.

Socrates discovered that each journey to wisdom has an enormous obstacle blocking the road. Modern psychoanalysts call the roadblock "resistance," but a simpler way of putting it is that no one wants to admit that he needs to learn. Certainly the politicians and public figures with whom Socrates talked didn't think of themselves as in need of further wisdom. They were quite convinced they already knew how to run the state and how to order their own lives. Socrates had to discover a trick for getting inside their defenses so that he could make them see—really see—that they were not yet truly wise. What he did was to invent a verbal form of judo. The basic trick of judo is to let your opponent's force and momentum work for you. Instead of launching a frontal attack, you let him swing or grab, and then you roll with his motion so that, in effect, he throws himself on the mat. Socrates achieved the same effect in his debates by means of a literary device called "irony." Although this is a book about philosophy, not literature, it might be worth taking a few moments to explain how irony works, so that we can see what Socrates was trying to accomplish.

Irony is a kind of speech or communication that assumes a *double audience*. When a speaker makes an ironic statement, he seems to be directing it at one group of people. This group is called the first, or superficial, audience. But in reality, he is directing his remarks at a second audience, called the real audience. His statement has a double meaning, and the trick of the irony is that while the first audience only understands the superficial or apparent meaning, the second audience understands *both* meanings. This second audience knows that the first audience has misunderstood, so the irony becomes a private joke between the speaker and the second audience—a joke at the expense of the first audience, which never suspects a thing. The whole complicated relationship is portrayed in the drawing below.

For example, suppose a young man calls for his date at her parents' home. The parents are very strict, and insist that their daughter be home early. They think she is obeying their rules to the letter, but unknown to them, she is actually having an affair with the young man. As the couple leaves, supposedly to go to the movies, the mother says, "Now dear, be good!" They go to the man's apartment and make love. When they return, the mother is waiting up. "Were you good?" she asks. "Oh yes," the young woman says with a secret look at her date. "I was good. I was very good!"

The young woman is speaking ironically. The mother is the superficial audience, and the young man is the real audience. The apparent meaning, which the mother understands, is that her daughter has been a "good girl," has been chaste. But the real, secret, ironic meaning is of course that she has been "good in bed," good at making love. The remark is a private joke between the couple at the mother's expense.

The young woman is speaking *ironically.* The mother is the superficial audience; the young man is the *real* audience.

When Socrates strikes up a conversation with a self-important, self-confident, but really rather ignorant man, he does not try a frontal attack, arguing directly against his opponent's false beliefs. That would simply lead to an impasse, in which each participant would be asserting his own convictions and neither would engage in critical self-examination. Instead, Socrates says, with a deceptively modest air, "Of course, I don't know anything at all, and you seem to be very wise indeed, so perhaps you would be so good as to enlighten me." His opponent, thinking Socrates means literally what he says, gets all puffed up with his own importance and pontificates on goodness or justice or truth or beauty or piety. Then Socrates goes to work on him, pretending to be puzzled, asking politely for clarification, poking away at just those places in his opponent's position that are most vulnerable. After a while, the poor man is thoroughly deflated. Embarrassed by his inability to give coherent, defensible answers to Socrates' apparently humble questions, he finally reaches the rather painful conclusion that he doesn't know what he thought he knew. Now, and only now, can Socrates help him to set out on the path to wisdom, for as Socrates so often insists, the first act of true wisdom is to admit that you are ignorant.

When Socrates says that he himself is ignorant, he is speaking ironically. In fact, he is uttering what students of literature call a "double irony." In the first place, he is having a private joke with his followers, at the expense of the man with whom he is debating. His opponent thinks Socrates is really being deferential, that Socrates actually wants to sit at the great man's feet and learn great truths. But of course Socrates means that he is "ignorant" of those great "truths" just because they are false, confused, and not worth knowing. We have all met someone who thinks he is an expert on some subject when in fact he doesn't know beans about it. "Tell me more!" we say, and sure enough he does, not realizing that we are kidding him.

At a deeper level, which Socrates' own followers sometimes don't really understand, Socrates genuinely means that he is ignorant, in the sense that *he* doesn't have a truth to teach any more than his puffed-up opponent does. The disciples think that Socrates knows what truth, beauty, justice, goodness, and wisdom really are, and they expect that just as soon as he has deflated his opponent, he will teach them. But Socrates believes that every man must find the truth for himself, and so his followers cannot shortcut their journey by learning the truth from Socrates any more than they could by observing the mistakes and confusions of Socrates' opponents. In this deeper double irony, we, the readers of Plato's Dialogue, are the real audience, and both Socrates' opponent *and* his disciples are superficial or apparent audiences.

This *dialectical* method of argument, as it has been called, serves a

First
Audience

I am
ignorant

SOCRATES

Third
Audience

Second
Audience

First, or superficial audience, thinks Socrates
is humbly confessing inferiority to him.
Second audience (Socrates' followers),
realizing Socrates is making fun of first audience,
laughs at first audience. Third audience
(the reader) laughs at first audience,
smiles at second. Third audience realizes
both that Socrates is making fun of first
audience *and* that Socrates' own followers
don't realize the true meaning of his statement.

theoretical purpose as well, for Socrates (or Plato, we don't know which) holds that the key to wisdom is the distinction between things as they appear or seem to us and the reality that lies behind them. Just as the world of the senses is merely an appearance of the true reality to be grasped by reason, just as the apparently true opinions of the mob conceal the genuine truth, so too the superficial meaning of an ironic statement is the apparent meaning which hides the deeper, real meaning intended for the real audience. Thus, the structure of language mirrors the structure of reality. Throughout this book, we shall encounter philosophers who have struggled with this notion that language, thought, and being, have parallel structures, so that by analyzing one we gain insight into the nature of the others.

We have talked enough about Socrates and his debating tricks. It is time to see him in action. The following passage comes from the most famous of Plato's Dialogues, the *Republic*. Socrates and some friends have been having a discussion about the nature of *justice*, by which they mean the fundamental principles of right and wrong. Several suggestions have been made, which Socrates has disposed of without much trouble, and now a young, very excitable, and very bright member of the party jumps into the debate. He has been listening to the others impatiently, barely able to control himself, and finally, he butts in and offers his own definition of justice, or right. Thrasymachus, as the young man is called, is no push-over for Socrates, and in a sense their debate ends in a deadlock. In this passage, however, we can see how Socrates uses Thrasymachus' own impetuosity and self-confidence to trip him up, just like a judo master who allows his opponent to rush at him headlong, and then with a flip of the hip tosses him on his back. Notice the ironic modesty with which Socrates turns aside Thrasymachus' blunt attacks, each time gently showing him that he has not yet thought clearly or deeply enough. The contrast between Socrates' inner quiet and Thrasymachus' tempestuousness is also intended by Plato to teach us a lesson, for he, like Socrates, believed that the truly wise man possesses a tranquility which the ignorant cannot achieve.

> Listen then, Thrasymachus began. What I say is that "just" or "right" means nothing but what is to the interest of the stronger party. Well, where is your applause? You don't mean to give it me.
>
> I will, as soon as I understand, I said. I don't see yet what you mean by right being the interest of the stronger party. For instance, Polydamas, the athlete, is stronger than we are, and it is to his interest to eat beef for the sake of his muscles; but surely you don't mean that the same diet would be good for weaker men and therefore be right for us?

You are trying to be funny, Socrates. It's a low trick to take my words in the sense you think will be most damaging.

No, no, I protested; but you must explain.

Don't you know, then, that a state may be ruled by a despot, or a democracy, or an aristocracy?

Of course.

And that the ruling element is always the strongest?

Yes.

Well then, in every case the laws are made by the ruling party in its own interest; a democracy makes democratic laws, a despot autocratic ones, and so on. By making these laws they define as "right" for their subjects whatever is for their own interest, and they call anyone who breaks them a "wrongdoer" and punish him accordingly. That is what I mean: in all states alike "right" has the same meaning, namely what is for the interest of the party established in power, and that is the strongest. So the sound conclusion is that what is "right" is the same everywhere: the interest of the stronger party.

Now I see what you mean, said I; whether it is true or not, I must try to make out. When you define right in terms of interest, you are yourself giving one of those answers you forbade to me; though, to be sure, you add "to the stronger party".

An insignificant addition, perhaps!

Its importance is not clear yet; what is clear is that we must find out whether your definition is true. I agree myself that right is in a sense a matter of interest; but when you add "to the stronger party," I don't know about that. I must consider.

Go ahead, then.

I will. Tell me this. No doubt you also think it is right to obey the men in power?

I do.

Are they infallible in every type of state, or can they sometimes make a mistake?

Of course they can make a mistake.

In framing laws, then, they may do their work well or badly?

No doubt.

Well, that is to say, when the laws they make are to their own interest; badly, when they are not?

Yes.

But the subjects are to obey any law they lay down, and they will then be doing right?

Of course.

If so, by your account, it will be right to do what is not to the interest of the stronger party, as well as what is so.

What's that you are saying?

Just what you said, I believe; but let us look again. Haven't you admitted that the rulers, when they enjoin certain acts on their subjects, sometimes mistake their own best interests, and at the same time that it is right for the subjects to obey, whatever they may enjoin?

Yes, I suppose so.

Well, that amounts to admitting that it is right to do what is not to the interest of the rulers or the stronger party. They may unwittingly enjoin what is to their own disadvantage; and you say it is right for the others to do as they are told. In that case, their duty must be the opposite of what you said, because the weaker will have been ordered to do what is against the interest of the stronger. You with your intelligence must see how that follows. . . .

Now, Thrasymachus, tell me, was that what you intended to say—that right means what the stronger thinks is to his interest, whether it really is so or not?

Most certainly not, he replied. Do you suppose I should speak of a man as "stronger" or "superior" at the very moment when he is making a mistake?

I did think you said as much when you admitted that rulers are not always infallible.

That is because you are a quibbler, Socrates. Would you say a man deserves to be called a physician at the moment when he makes a mistake in treating his patient and just in respect of that mistake; or a mathematician, when he does a sum wrong and just in so far as he gets a wrong result? Of course we do commonly speak of a physician or a mathematician or a scholar having made a mistake; but really none of these, I should say, is ever mistaken, in so far as he is worthy of the name we give him. So strictly speaking—and you are all for being precise—no one who practises a craft makes mistakes. A man is mistaken when his knowledge fails him; and at the moment he is no craftsman. And what is true of craftsmanship or any sort of skill is true of the ruler: he is never mistaken so long as he is acting as a ruler; though anyone might speak of a ruler making a mistake, just as he might of a physician. You must understand that I was talking in that loose way when I answered your question just now; but the precise statement is this. The ruler, in so far as he is acting as a ruler, makes no mistakes and consequently enjoins what is best for himself; and that is what the subject is to do. So, as I said at first, "right" means doing what is to the interest of the stronger.

Very well, Thrasymachus, said I. So you think I am quibbling?

I am sure you are.

You believe my questions were maliciously designed to damage your position?

I know it. But you will gain nothing by that. You cannot outwit me by cunning, and you are not the man to crush me in the open.

Bless your soul, I answered, I should not think of trying. But, to prevent any more misunderstanding, when you speak of that ruler or stronger party whose interest the weaker ought to serve, please make it clear whether you are using the words in the ordinary way or in that strict sense you have just defined.

I mean a ruler in the strictest possible sense. Now quibble away and be as malicious as you can. I want no mercy. But you are no match for me.

Do you think me mad enough to beard a lion or try to outwit a Thrasymachus?

You did try just now, he retorted, but it wasn't a success.

PLATO, *The Republic*

II   I told you that Socrates spent some time when he was young studying the theories about the nature of the universe which had been developed by other Greek thinkers during the 200 years before his own time. The Greek word for world or universe is *kosmos,* so we call the study of the nature of the world *cosmology.* The study of man and the study of the cosmos are the two great branches of philosophy, and there is no division more fundamental in philosophy than that between the philosophers who study the human experience and the philosophers who speculate about the order

Ancient cosmology.

of the entire universe. (Later on, we shall see that some philosophers have tried to unite the two in a single theoretical framework, but that is getting ahead of our story.)

The Greeks, like all cultures and peoples, had their religious myths about the creation of the world and the origins of their civilization, but some time roughly 600 years before the birth of Christ, a number of men began to search for a more rational, more factually well-grounded theory of the composition, order, and origin of the world. Some of these early scientists—for that is what they were—flourished in a city-state named Miletus on the coast of what is now Turkey, in the eastern Mediterranean. They are known as Milesians, after their home town, and they appear to have been the very first philosophers in what we are calling the cosmological tradition. For various reasons, only bits and pieces of what they wrote still survive, and most of what we know about them must be learned indirectly from what other ancient writers say about them. They are little more than names to us today, but perhaps it is worth telling you their names, for we owe them an intellectual debt almost too great to calculate. There was *Thales*, usually spoken of as the very first philosopher of all. Thales was what we today would call an astronomer; the story is told that while walking one evening with his eyes turned to the stars, he fell into a well, and thereby created the myth of the absent-minded professor. But it is also said of him that by using his superior knowledge of the weather, acquired by his astronomical studies, he managed to corner the market in olive oil and make a fortune. Following Thales were the Milesians *Anaximander* and *Anaximenes*, who expanded and developed speculative theories about the basic components of nature and their order. Their names are strange, and we have long since lost almost all of what they wrote and said, but as you study your physics, chemistry, or astronomy, or watch a rocket lift off for yet another space probe, you might just give them a thought, for they started Western civilization on its scientific journey.

The theories of the ancient cosmologists seem odd to modern readers. When we look behind the surface detail, however, we can see some surprisingly modern ideas. The fundamental problem of the Milesians was to determine the basic stuff or component matter from which all the variety of things in the world were composed. The four categories into which they divided all things were earth, water, air, and fire. Thales claimed that at base everything in the universe was water; earth, air, and fire were simply forms of water, or water in other guises. Anaximenes, by contrast, said that everything was air. Now all of this sounds quaint and very peculiar, but suppose that we say solid instead of earth, liquid instead of water, gas instead of air, and energy instead of fire. Then we have the theory that everything in the universe is solid, liquid, gaseous, or some form of energy, and that isn't a bad guess at all! What is more, the search for some underlying element that simply *appears* in one or another of these forms has a distinctly modern ring to it. The nineteenth-century theory of the atom, for example, told us that ninety and more elements found in nature could really be reduced to differing arrangements of three basic building blocks: neutrons, protons, and electrons. The theory of subatomic particles has become much more complicated since that simple model of the atom was proposed, but the Milesian search goes on today for the building blocks of the universe.

The second great theme of the Milesians and their successors was that natural events were to be understood by appeal to natural forces, not by appeal to the actions of the gods or the interventions of some non-natural forces. The keynote of these early philosopher-scientists was that nature is natural, and in their speculations and observations, they showed remarkable shrewdness and good sense. For example, water seems to turn into ice (a solid) when it is very cold, and into steam (a gas) when it is very hot. Solid things (such as iron) which are very solid indeed, actually melt when made hot enough. All of this suggests that there is some underlying stuff which takes on different forms under different conditions.

Here is a short passage from a philosopher who lived very much later in the ancient world, but whose attention to the evidence of his senses is typical of the cosmological frame of mind. Lucretius was a Roman philosopher and poet who lived in the first century before Christ, nearly five centuries after the Milesians. He defended a cosmological theory called atomism, according to which everything in the universe, including even man's spirit, is composed of little bits of matter called atoms, which are so small that they cannot be seen by the naked eye (another surprisingly modern doctrine!). As you can see, Lucretius uses a variety of familiar observations to prove that despite appearances to the contrary, all things are composed of tiny, indestructible atoms which themselves have no parts and are absolutely solid.

Now mark me: since I have taught that things cannot be born from nothing, cannot when begotten be brought back to nothing, that you may not haply yet begin in any shape to mistrust my words, because the first-beginnings of things cannot be seen by the eyes, take moreover this list of bodies which you must yourself admit are in the number of things and cannot be seen. First of all the force of the wind when aroused beats on the harbours and whelms huge ships and scatters clouds; sometimes in swift whirling eddy it scours the plains and straws them with large trees and scourges the mountain summits with forest-rending blasts: so fiercely does the wind rave with a shrill howling and rage with threatening roar. Winds therefore sure enough are unseen bodies which sweep the seas, the lands, ay and the clouds of heaven, tormenting them and catching them up in sudden whirls. On they stream and spread destruction abroad in just the same way as the soft liquid nature of water, when all at once it is borne along in an overflowing stream, and a great downfall of water from the high hills augments it with copious rains, flinging together fragments of forests and entire trees; nor can the strong bridges sustain the sudden force of coming water: in such wise turbid with much rain the river dashes upon the piers with mighty force: makes havoc with loud noise and rolls under its eddies huge stones: wherever aught opposes its waves, down it dashes it. In this way then must the blasts of wind as well move on, and when they like a mighty stream have borne down in any direction, they push things before them and throw them down with repeated assaults, sometimes catch them up in curling eddy and carry them away in swift-circling whirl. Wherefore once and again I say winds are unseen bodies, since in their works and ways they are found to rival great rivers which are of a visible body. Then again we perceive the different smells of things, yet never see them coming to our nostrils; nor do we behold heats nor can we observe cold with the eyes nor are we used to see voices. Yet all these things must consist of a bodily nature, since they are able to move the senses; for nothing but body can touch and be touched. Again clothes hung up on a shore which waves break upon become moist, and then get dry if spread out in the sun. Yet it has not been seen in what way the moisture of water has sunk into them nor again in what way this has been dispelled by heat. The moisture therefore is dispersed into small particles which the eyes are quite unable to see. Again after the revolution of many of the sun's years a ring on the finger is thinned on the under side by wearing, the dripping from the eaves hollows a stone, the bent ploughshare of iron imperceptibly decreases in the fields, and we behold the stone-paved streets worn down by the feet of the multitude; the brass statues too at the gates show their right hands to be wasted by the touch of the numerous passers by who greet them. These things then we see are lessened, since they have been thus worn down; but what bodies depart at any given time the nature of vision has jealously shut out our seeing. Lastly the bodies which time and nature add to things by little and little, constraining them to grow in due measure, no exertion of the eyesight can behold; and so too wherever things grow old by age and decay, and when rocks hanging over the sea are eaten away by the gnawing salt spray, you cannot see what they lose at any given moment. Nature therefore works by unseen bodies.

LUCRETIUS, *On the Nature of Things*

Cosmological speculation goes on today, as it did 2500 years ago. From the earliest times, philosophers have been actively involved in the experi-

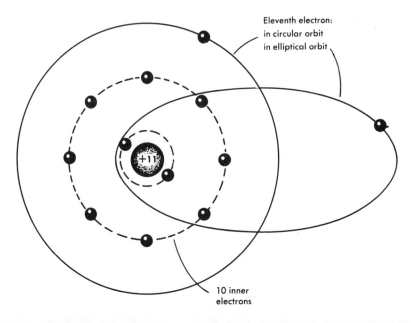

Eleventh electron:
in circular orbit
in elliptical orbit

+11

10 inner
electrons

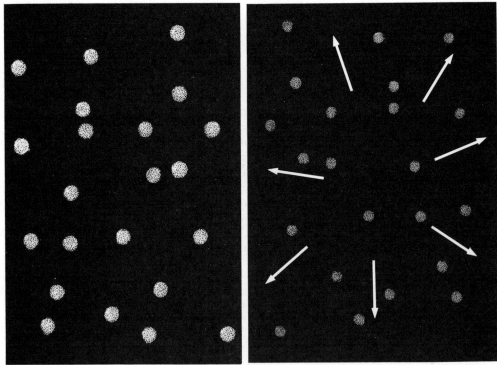

Modern cosmology.

mental and theoretical advances of what today we call science. Indeed, it is difficult to say just where hard science leaves off and speculative, philosophical cosmology begins. Thales himself, for example, was said to have discovered a method for measuring the height of the Egyptian pyramids, by waiting until the precise hour of the day when a body's shadow was equal to its height. Anaximander devised an instrument known as a gnomon, a rod whose shadow permits us to calculate the direction and height of the sun. The great fourth-century B.C. philosopher Aristotle, pupil and follower of Plato, virtually invented the science of formal logic, and made significant contributions to what we would today call taxonomy. Plato's school of followers, the Academy, did important work in the branch of mathematics known as solid geometry. Two thousand years later, René Descartes, the French philosopher and scientist, invented analytic geometry (which we still study in school today) as a tool for analyzing and giving expression to his theory of the nature of the material universe. His successor, Gottfried Leibniz, invented a version of the differential calculus as part of his dispute with Descartes about the nature of matter. In our own century, the logicians and philosophers Bertrand Russell and Alfred North Whitehead established the modern discipline of mathematical logic with their monumental *Principia Mathematica*. Throughout the entire course of Western civilization, philosophical speculation, scientific experiment, and pure logical and mathematical theorizing have advanced together, often in the writings of the same men, sometimes in the very same works. The philosophical enterprise begun by the ancient Milesians has borne splendid fruit, both in an expanded scientific understanding of nature and in a refined conceptual sophistication about those original questions of the nature and order of the cosmos. Before leaving our discussion of this great tradition of philosophical thought, let us read a few selections of modern cosmology. The first deals with the microcosm—the unimaginably tiny bits of stuff from which all else in the universe is compounded. These speculations, we may imagine, are the lineal descendants of the ancient atomistic theories of Democritus, Epicurus, and the Roman Lucretius. The second deals with the macrocosm, the universe as a whole, and specifically with its origins. It traces its lineage to the inspired guesses of the Milesians and their followers.

In this century it has been possible to describe the atom as a hard core surrounded by orbiting electrons; and then the atomic nucleus appeared as a composite of neutrons and protons held together by a short-range force much stronger than the electric force which would tend to push them apart. Both these concepts are easy to visualize.

But with the elementary particles, including neutrons and protons, physicists just don't know what the underlying causes of behavior are.

On the other hand, they have discovered more than a hundred particles, many of them created in high-energy accelerators and existing for only a fraction of an instant. They have catalogued them and classified them according to their mass, their electric charge, the way they spin, and various other qualities.

They have found that some of the particles can be organized in groups of eight or ten with similar properties. But understanding, as well as explanations of inconsistencies in the groupings, remain elusive.

One promising concept, which however hasn't yielded very good numerical results, is that the particles that are subject to the strong force binding nucleus are made up out of each other, so that none of them is fundamental.

The basis for this theory, called the bootstrap hypothesis, comes from the way forces are applied between particles. Physicists found they could describe electromagnetic forces by saying that charged particles exchanged another particle, called a photon, and by this means exerted electromagnetic force on each other.

The strong forces are also exerted by exchanging particles other than photons. What the bootstrap theory suggests is that any strongly interacting particle can serve as the means of exerting strong forces between two others. When two particles exert a strong force, they create another, producing a bound system; and that system, according to the theory, is the created particle.

Another theory, easier to visualize but extremely unlikely to be more than a mathematical tool, is the . . . quark model, which holds that the particles are made up of combinations of two or three different kinds of sub-particles.

Developed by Dr. [Murray] Gell-Mann, the quark hypothesis predicts the grouping of particles into already observed sets of eight and ten.

Science News

Cosmology attempts to deduce the history of the universe from astronomical observation. Its great difficulty is that the events concerned take millions or billions of years to work themselves out, and it is therefore hard to observe the history in progress and be exactly sure what one is seeing.

Modern cosmologists are left with two general classes of theory: the so-called big bang or cosmic fireball and the steady-state or continuous creation theories.

In the middle 1960s radio astronomical observations provided evidence that was taken as very dramatic support for the big-bang theory, and the buildup of data became so convincing to many cosmologists that they were ready to bury the rival steady-state theory. Recent observations in infra-red light, which have been possible only in the last few years, give proponents of the steady-state ammunition to strike back.

The difference between the two theories rests on the density of the universe. If the universe has been expanding for any length of time, everyone agrees there must have been a time when it was very small, and the question is: Did it then have the same amount of matter as it has now?

If it did, then the pressure temperature and density were beyond anything imaginable today. This is the cosmic fireball and its physical conditions suggest that it must have exploded and thus given the impetus for the expansion now seen.

The other side says that this did not happen. The matter in the universe was always as dense as it is now, and therefore there was never a hot high-density state. This requires that matter be added as the universe expands. It can be continually created out of nothing or pumped in from some realm beneath the universe, possibly through galaxy centers. . . .

The source of matter for galactic expansion . . . could be some kind of continuous creation or pumping-in process at the centers. Some of the matter is annihilated at or near the source; some survives to build up the galaxy.

Acceptance of this idea immediately raises the problem of antimatter. According to currently accepted laws of particle physics, when matter is created, so is an equal amount of antimatter.

There is no observational evidence for any large amounts of antimatter in the visible universe. On the other hand, there is no observational evidence against its presence. An antistar would look precisely like a star, so there is no way to tell. . . .

Meanwhile the evidence on which the proponents of the big-bang theory based their jubilation a few years ago remains, though its interpretation is more and more questioned. Radio astronomers had found a background of radio waves whose spectrum corresponded to a perfect thermal radiator or blackbody at a temperature of three degrees above absolute zero (SN: 7/5, p. 9). Existence of such a blackbody background is a prediction of the big-bang theory, and the discovery seemed to be evidence for it.

There are other possible interpretations of this radio spectrum, although the blackbody is the simplest. Extension of the observations into the infrared was eagerly awaited since it was in this range that the background's blackbody character should show up unmistakably.

The infrared observations so far have not been happy for the blackbody enthusiasts. The first of them showed background infrared fluxes, which, if they were thermal, were hotter than three degrees. These could be explained away as the background plus something else . . .

The battle between the rival cosmologies is far from over, but with the advent of infrared observations it is becoming clear that the steady-state theory, over which some cosmologists were reading funeral orations a few years ago, is very much alive again.

Science News

One final point before we move on. Thales, Anaximander and the rest are called "philosophers" in dictionaries of biography or histories of Western thought. But if you look up Murray Gell-Mann in *Who's Who,* you will find him listed as a physicist. Why is it that cosmological questions are investigated by scientists today, although they were investigated by philosophers 2000 years ago? Is this just what labor unions call a "jurisdictional dispute" or has some important theoretical change taken place here?

The most common answer to this question is that "philosophy" used to include just about everything that men and women did by way of systematic, reasoned investigation of the heavens, the earth, or man. In the writings of Plato, Aristotle, and the other ancients we find discussions which today would be labeled physics, mathematics, astronomy, biology, psychology, economics, political science, sociology, anthropology, theology, and even engineering. Over the past two millennia, one after another of these branches of human knowledge has pulled itself together, broken off from "philosophy," and established itself as an independent discipline with its own rules of inquiry, objects of investigation, and theoretical framework. Philosophy today, according to this way of looking at things, is what remains after all the intellectual children have left home. Roughly speaking, that reduces philosophy to conceptual analysis plus some armchair speculation on whatever the other sciences haven't laid claim to yet.

There is another view, however, which seems to me to be a good deal closer to the truth. Philosophy, it holds, is the systematic reflection of the mind upon the criteria of right thought and right action which it employs in all of its activities. On this view, there is a "philosophical" component to virtually everything we do. Political scientists (and politicians too), scientists, artists, economists, and astronomers all need to reflect on the nature of their enterprises, and the people officially called philosophers are simply those among us who concentrate their attention on this self-critical or reflective side of man's intellectual undertakings.

III   Although the study of man and the study of the cosmos are the two great themes of Western philosophy, it must not be supposed that they developed in an unconnected way. Philosophers are, above all else, seekers after unity. Where human experience presents a manyness, they seek the underlying oneness. In the long history of Western thought, philosophers

To medieval thinkers, as God ruled
the world, so the king ruled society,
and reason in each individual ruled the passions.
The art of that period reflects
this hierarchical view of the universe.

have tried two basically different strategies for bringing the philosophy
of man and the philosophy of nature into some interconnected whole.

The first strategy was tried by some of the earliest philosophers, among
whom were a group known as Stoics. The Stoics claimed that the natural
world exhibited a rational order which could be explained by appeal to
the existence and operations of a power of reason, which they called *logos*.
(We get our word *logic* from this term, and also the word ending -ology,
meaning "study of.") In the cosmos, this logos was often identified with
what we today would call God, but it could also be identified with the
power of reason in each human being. Therein lies the principle that
bridged the gap between the study of man and the study of nature, for the
very same fundamental logos or rational order which made itself known in
the order of the planets, the succession of the seasons, and the regular
behavior of natural bodies in space and time also exhibited itself in man's
capacity for logical reasoning, in his ability to control his passions by the
power of his understanding, and in the proper order and arrangement of
men and women in a stable, just, and rationally ordered society. Man's
power of reason was said to be a "spark" or fragment of the divine Logos

23

which informed and governed the universe. Eventually, this ancient Greek doctrine was taken up into the theology of the Christian, Jewish, and Muslim religions, and became the basis for much of the religious theology that flourished in the Middle Ages.

After studying cosmology as a youth, Socrates turned away from it, convinced that the proper study for man was his own nature. But if the Stoics were correct, then a philosopher could study man and nature together, for the same principles that explained the arrangements of the heavenly bodies would, properly understood, also explain how men should live their lives within a well-ordered set of social arrangements.

The unifying doctrine of the Stoics gave rise to one of the most important philosophical ideas in Western thought—the idea of *natural law*. God, or the power of Reason, created the universe in accordance with a rational idea of the proper form and order of its organization. On the cosmic level, this conception determined the existence, nature, and relative positions of the stars, the sun, the moon, and the earth. At the social level, this same idea determined the appropriate hierarchy of classes and statuses from the king or emperor down to the lowliest serf. Within each individual human being, the same idea determined the relative order and importance of the rational, passional, and appetitive elements of the soul. Man was unique in the natural order by virtue of his possession of a spark of that logos or reason, for it permitted him at one and the same time to

For almost five centuries, Rome ruled a vast empire stretching from Great Britain through what is now Western Europe, entirely around the shores of the Mediterranean Sea, and deep into northern Africa and the Middle East. Marcus Aurelius (121–180 A.D.) was one of the most remarkable men to hold the exalted position of Emperor. He was both a gifted and successful general, winning many battles against the barbarian tribes who repeatedly attacked Rome's border provinces; and also a wise and thoughtful philosopher, learned in the writings of the Greeks and his Roman predecessors, and without illusions about the fleetingness of the power and glory which were his as emperor. During the second century after the birth of Christ, the empire persecuted the followers of that Eastern prophet, and Marcus, despite (or perhaps even because of) his commitment to Stoicism, carried forward these persecutions. It was not until more than a century later, with the conversion of the emperor Constantine, that Christianity ceased to be the object of official attack, and became instead the established religion of the Roman Empire.

understand the grand plan and also to live his own life freely and responsibly in conformity with it.

Among the greatest of the ancient Stoics, strange as it may seem, was a Roman emperor who ruled from 161 to 180 A.D. Marcus Aurelius combined great skill as a general and ruler with a contemplative nature. His reflections on the universe and man's brief stay in it have come down to us in the form of a series of meditations. Following are a few selections which convey the themes and something of the flavor of his thought.

> Constantly regard the universe as one living being, having one substance and one soul; and observe how all things have reference to one perception, the perception of this one living being; and how all things act with one movement; and how all things are the co-operating causes of all things which exist; observe too the continuous spinning of the thread and the contexture of the web.
>
> The intelligence of the universe is social. Accordingly it has made the inferior things for the sake of the superior, and it has fitted the superior to one another. Thou seest how it has subordinated, co-ordinated and assigned to everything its proper portion, and has brought together into concord with one another the things which are the best.
>
> All things are implicated with one another, and the bond is holy; and there is hardly anything unconnected with any other thing. For things have been co-ordinated, and they combine to form the same universe (order). For there is one universe made up of all things, and one God who pervades all things, and one substance, and one law, one common reason in all intelligent animals, and one truth; if indeed there is also one perfection for all animals which are of the same stock and participate in the same reason.
>
> To the rational animal the same act is according to nature and according to reason.
>
> MARCUS AURELIUS, *Meditations*

Thus, the first strategy devised by philosophers for uniting the study of man with the study of nature was the Stoic doctrine of natural law. The second strategy was worked out 2000 years later by a brilliant group of seventeenth- and eighteenth-century philosophers in the British Isles and on the continent of Europe. We shall be taking a close look at some of their theories in Chapter Seven when we talk about the branch of philosophy known as the "theory of knowledge." In this introductory look at the nature of philosophy in general, we ought nevertheless to try to form some preliminary idea of what they were doing, for their ideas and their writings have been among the most influential in the entire literature of Western thought.

The key to the new strategy was a very simple, very powerful idea: The universe is vast, and ten thousand generations would be too short a time to say everything that can be learned about it; but every single fact, every theory, every insight, guess, hypothesis, or deduction is *an idea in the mind of man*. So instead of turning our eyes outward to the universe, let us turn our eyes inward to the nature of the human mind itself. Let us study *the way in which* men know, rather than *what* they know. The universe may be infinite, but the mind is finite. What is more (these philosophers thought), though the universe is infinitely varied, the human mind is everywhere and always exactly the same. (They hadn't yet heard of evolution, or the variation in conceptual frameworks from culture to culture.) Instead of writing many books on cosmology, physics, psychology, politics, morals, and religion they needed to write just one book on the powers, capacities, forms, and limits of the human mind. So during the seventeenth and eighteenth centuries, we find titles like the following cropping up in the philosophical literature: *An Essay on the Human Understanding*, by the Englishman John Locke; *Principles of Human Knowledge*, by the Irishman George Berkeley; *A Treatise of Human Nature*, by the Scotsman David Hume; and the greatest of them all, *A Critique of Pure Reason*, by the Prussian Immanuel Kant.

Now, it might look at first glance as though these philosophers had simply taken Socrates' advice to forget about the study of nature and seek instead a knowledge of man. But that would be a mistake, for the British empiricists (as Locke, Berkeley, Hume, and their lesser compatriots are called) and the continental rationalists (Descartes, Leibniz, Kant, and their fellow philosophers) had got their hands on a wholly different way of doing philosophy. Socrates never imagined that we could learn something about the natural sciences by studying man. He simply thought that the search for the just and happy life was more important than speculation about the elements of the universe or the origin of the order of the heavenly bodies. The British empiricists and continental rationalists, by contrast, thought they had found a device for combining the study of man and the study of the universe in one single philosophical enterprise. If they could learn *how* men know—whether it is by looking with their eyes, touching with their hands, and listening with their ears, or whether it is by reasoning with their minds and ignoring the evidence of their senses, or perhaps whether it is by some combining of what the senses tell us with what reason tells us—if philosophy could study the process of knowledge rather than getting all tangled up in the details of particular bits of knowledge of this and that, then maybe philosophy could give us some very general answers to such questions as, Can men know anything at all? How much can we know? Can we know about things that happened before we were born, or somewhere else in space? Can we know that things *must* happen the way they do, or must we simply say, "This happens, and

David Hume

DAVID HUME (1711–1776) was one of those precocious philosophers whose greatest work was done early in life. Born and reared near Edinburgh in Scotland, Hume attended Edinburgh University, where he studied the new physics of Isaac Newton and the new philosophy of John Locke. When still a teen-ager, Hume conceived the idea of developing a full-scale theory of human nature along the lines of Newton's revolutionary theory of physical nature. After what seems to have been some sort of mental breakdown, Hume went to France to rest and recover, and while there he wrote his first and greatest book, the monumental *Treatise of Human Nature*.

Hume went on to become an extremely popular and successful essayist and man of letters. His six-volume *History of England* established his reputation as the first major modern historian. Nevertheless, his sceptical doubts about religion and his attacks on the metaphysical doctrines of his continental and British predecessors earned him many enemies. One of his most brilliant works, twelve *Dialogues Concerning Natural Religion*, were only published after his death. His friends, including the economist Adam Smith, persuaded him that the book was too controversial, and might permanently damage his reputation.

As you can see from the portrait of Hume, the lightness and quickness of his mind was entirely hidden by the lumpishness of his appearance. Nature often plays such tricks on us!

then this . . ." and let it go at that? Can we know about things we can't see or feel, like atoms, or the unconscious, or even God? Can one man know for sure that there are other men in the world with him, and not just bodies that look like men? Can I, myself, be sure that the whole world isn't simply my dream? All these questions, and many more besides, might be answered by a systematic study of the human mind itself. In this way, the study of nature would be combined with the study of man, not through a theory of universal logos or intelligence, as the Stoics thought, but through a theory of how men know.

One of the best statements of the new strategy is to be found in the introduction to David Hume's great work, A *Treatise of Human Nature*. Hume was a Scotsman, born in 1711. The *Treatise*, in three volumes, was published in 1739 and 1740, when Hume was not yet thirty years old! There are three important points to notice in the following passage from Hume's *Treatise*. First, as we have already remarked, the basic idea of

Hume's strategy is to turn the multiplicity of sciences and fields of study into a unified examination of human nature and the mind's power of knowing. Second, Hume thinks that he shall have to study "the nature of the ideas we employ," for it is from those ideas that we form whatever judgments we wish to make in physics, religion, politics, or morals. And finally, Hume says, he shall have to examine "the operations we perform in our reasonings." In Chapter Seven, we shall see that this distinction between the nature of our ideas, on the one hand, and the nature of our reasonings with our ideas, on the other, is an important weapon in the strategy of the new theorists of knowledge.

Reading selections from the works of the great philosophers is a bit like watching videotape replays of great football stars. Since we know who made it to stardom, it is easy for us to spot their greatness from the very first. But let us have a little pity for the poor book reviewer who was handed an anonymous work entitled *A Treatise of Human Nature* and told to write a brief review of it in a few weeks. Here is what one nameless unfortunate had to say about Hume's *Treatise*, in a literary journal rather imposingly called *A History of the Works of the Learned:*

> . . . a Man, who has never had the Pleasure of reading Mr. Locke's incomparable Essay, will peruse our author with much less Disgust, than those can who have been used to the irresistible Reasoning and wonderful Perspicuity of that admirable Writer.

Poor Hume was so upset by the negative reviews of the *Treatise* that later in life he disowned it, saying that it was merely a first effort of his youth. How many of us, I wonder, would recognize the greatness of a new book of philosophy within months of its publication?

It is evident, that all the sciences have a relation, greater or less, to human nature; and that, however wide any of them may seem to run from it, they still return back by one passage or another. Even *Mathematics, Natural Philosophy,* and *Natural Religion*, are in some measure dependent on the science of MAN; since they lie under the cognisance of men, and are judged of by their powers and faculties. It is impossible to tell what changes and improvements we might make in these sciences were we thoroughly acquainted with the extent and force of human understanding, and could explain the nature of the ideas we employ, and of the operations we perform in our reasonings. And these improvements are the more to be hoped for in natural religion, as it is not content with instructing us in the nature of superior powers, but carries its views further, to their disposition towards us, and our duties towards them; and consequently, we ourselves are not only the beings that reason, but also one of the objects concerning which we reason.

If, therefore, the sciences of mathematics, natural philosophy, and natural religion, have such a dependence on the knowledge of man, what may be expected in the other sciences, whose connection with human nature is more close and intimate? The sole end of logic is to explain the principles and operations of our reasoning faculty, and the nature of our ideas; morals and criticism regard our tastes and sentiments; and politics consider men as united in society, and dependent on each other. In these four sciences of *Logic, Morals, Criticism,* and *Politics,* is comprehended almost everything which it can anyway import us to be acquainted with, or which can tend either to the improvement or ornament of the human mind.

Here then is the only expedient, from which we can hope for success in our philosophical researches, to leave the tedious lingering method, which we have hitherto followed, and, instead of taking now and then a castle or village on the frontier, to march up directly to the capital or centre of these sciences, to human nature itself; which being once masters of, we may everywhere else hope for an easy victory. From this station we may extend our conquests over all those sciences, which more intimately concern human life, and may afterwards proceed at leisure, to discover more fully those which are the objects of pure curiosity. There is no question of importance, whose decision is not comprised in the science of man; and there is none, which can be decided with any certainty, before we become acquainted with that science. In pretending, therefore, to explain the principles of human nature, we in effect propose a complete system of the sciences, built on a foundation almost entirely new, and the only one upon which they can stand with any security.

DAVID HUME, A *Treatise of Human Nature*

The new study of the mind's capacity for knowing came to be called *epistemology,* from the Greek for the study or science (-ology) of knowledge (*episteme*). It was not to be merely descriptive, like psychology, however. Its purpose was to settle some ancient philosophical disputes by finding out what men could legitimately claim to know, and what they could not claim to know because their claims carried them beyond the limits of the powers of the mind. This *critical* dimension of the new strategy extended across the entire spectrum of philosophical investigations, as the passage from Hume's *Treatise* indicates. In a brief excerpt from Immanuel Kant's *Critique of Pure Reason,* you can get some sense of what a dramatic challenge the new critical epistemology was to established ways of thinking.

We often hear complaints of shallowness of thought in our age and of the consequent decline of sound science. But I do not see that the sciences which rest upon a secure foundation, such as mathematics, physics, etc., in the least deserve this reproach. On the contrary, they merit their old reputation for solidity, and, in the case of physics, even surpass it. The same spirit would have become active in other kinds of knowledge, if only attention had first been directed to the determination of their principles. Till this is done, indifference, doubt, and, in the final issue, severe criticism, are themselves proofs of a profound habit of thought. Our age is, in especial degree, the age of criticism, and to criticism everything must submit. Religion through its sanctity, and law-giving through its majesty, may seek to exempt themselves from it. But they then awaken just suspicion, and cannot claim the sincere respect which reason accords only to that which has been able to sustain the test of free and open examination.

IV From the very beginning, philosophers have been objects of suspicion and even ridicule. Socrates was satirized in a play by the brilliant comic poet Aristophanes as a man with his head in the clouds who talked in a crazy fashion about nonsensical matters. We have already seen that the very first philosopher, Thales, acquired the reputation of being absent-minded. Usually, philosophers are accused of quibbling about questions so divorced from any genuine human concern that only someone unfit for real life would make his living worrying about them.

Needless to say, I don't think this caricature of philosophy has much truth in it; otherwise, I would hardly have spent my own life thinking about philosophical questions. But it is not hard to see how the notion has gained popularity. Suppose that I say to you: Four is two plus two. Four is also three plus one. Therefore two plus two is three plus one. All right, you would answer. Perfectly reasonable. If A is B and A is C then B must be C. Right? Fine, I go on. Socrates is wise, and Socrates is ugly. Therefore Wisdom must be Ugliness! Now right there, you know you have been had. Something has gone badly wrong.

Here's another one. Yesterday, I remembered seeing a friend of mine, but after thinking about it for a moment, I realized I must have been remembering a dream, because my friend has been in Europe for two years. Last night I dreamed that I was the king of Persia, and at the time it was so real I could fairly smell the incense and hear the court musicians! It would seem that sometimes, when we think we are awake, we are really dreaming; and some of the things we think we actually remember doing are just recollections of dreams. So maybe everything I see, touch, smell, and hear is a dream. Maybe my whole life is a dream, and I have never been awake. Well, there you are again! I start out with some perfectly reasonable premise and end with a conclusion so wild that only a philosopher would take it seriously.

Peculiar puzzles and strange counterintuitive conclusions have been popping up in philosophical books ever since the days of the ancient Milesians, but somehow the arguments of the British Empiricists and the

Continental Rationalists in the seventeenth and eighteenth centuries contained more really puzzling statements than was usual even for philosophers. Somewhat in reaction to their way of doing philosophy, a gifted Austrian mathematician and philosopher named Ludwig Wittgenstein developed a new and extremely controversial theory of what philosophical problems are and what we ought to do about them. Wittgenstein (1889–1951) suggested that a philosophical problem is a sort of cross between a logical confusion, a grammatical mistake, and a neurosis. Philosophers start off using language in a perfectly proper way to talk about the world, and then they formulate a question or propose a thesis which *sounds* all right but is really odd in some way. Instead of realizing that they have gone wrong, however, they press right on, drawing more and more bizarre conclusions, obsessed with the seeming plausibility of their own words.

For example, it makes perfectly good sense to ask, How high is the Empire State Building? How high is the moon? But it makes no sense to ask, How high is up? That is just a child's joke. Well, it also makes perfectly good sense to ask, was that a dream or did I really see my friend?

LUDWIG WITTGENSTEIN (1889–1951) was born in Vienna, and spent his formative years in Austria. He wrote virtually all his philosophical works in German, but his principal influence has been on English and American philosophy, where he is probably the single most important philosophical thinker of the twentieth century. After early training in engineering, Wittgenstein turned to mathematical logic, under the influence of the work of the Englishman Bertrand Russell. Eventually Wittgenstein came to Cambridge, England, where he spent much of his adult life.

His highly original research in logic led Wittgenstein to a theory of language, truth, and meaning which he set forth, in a laconic and distinctive style, in his *Tractatus Logico–Philosophicus*. This was the only philosophical book published by Wittgenstein during his lifetime, but he wrote great quantities of philosophy which appeared posthumously. Later in life, he thoroughly reversed his own earlier theories, and set forth a new account of language and meaning in his *Philosophical Investigations*. Wittgenstein was an intense, brooding man who made so deep an impression on his students and colleagues that even now, a quarter of a century after his death, there are many distinguished English and American philosophers who still consider themselves his disciples.

Am I dreaming now, or am I really the king of Persia? But perhaps it *doesn't* make sense to ask, Is my whole life a dream? That question *looks* sensible enough, but then, so does How high is up?

Wittgenstein proposed that philosophers treat their problems as symptoms of a conceptual disorder rather than as subjects for investigation and debate. Whenever we come upon someone who is really mesmerized by a philosophical problem, we ought to try to relieve him of his distress by dissolving the problem, by showing him where he went wrong and how he can get back onto the path of talking ordinary common sense. These two statements from Wittgenstein's book, *Philosophical Investigations,* capture the spirit of his approach:

> My aim is: to teach you to pass from a piece of disguised nonsense to something that is patent nonsense.

> The philosopher's treatment of a question is like the treatment of an illness.

The second statement suggests that philosophers ought really to be in the business of putting themselves out of business! If philosophical puzzles are like illnesses, then the sooner we cure the people who have come down with a bad case of philosophy, the sooner there will be no philosophy left to cure. Odd as it may seem, Wittgenstein is not the only great philosopher to claim that his philosophy would put philosophy out of business. Immanuel Kant thought roughly the same thing, and so, in a way, did Karl Marx, as we shall see.

V   Philosophy is a reflective self-examination of the principles of the just and happy life, says Socrates. Philosophy is a study of the universe, its origins, elements, and laws, say the ancient cosmologists and their modern descendants. Philosophy is a search for the rational principles that bind the universe and man's life together into a single, logical whole, say the Stoics and many others. Philosophy is a critique and dissection of the mind's power to know, say the epistemologists of the seventeenth and eighteenth centuries. Philosophy is a conceptual disease of which we should be cured, says Wittgenstein. It would seem that there couldn't be five more dissimilar conceptions of philosophy imaginable. On second look, however, we see that they all have something in common. They all say philosophy is something you *think about,* not something you *do* something about. Philosophers are dreamers, popular opinion has it, even if they don't think that all of life is a dream. Philosophers sit in their cozy studies, or in their ivory towers.

*"I may be a philosopher, George, but I say,
if we didn't __belong__ on top,
we wouldn't __be__ on top."* *

Philosopher in his ivory tower.

Strange as it may seem, the most devastating criticism of philosophy as mere do-nothing talk that anyone has ever written was authored by, of all people, Plato! You will remember that Plato came from a wealthy and powerful Athenian family, and the normal thing for the son of such a family to do was to go into politics, to participate in the public life of Athens. Roughly in middle life, Plato was faced with a hard choice: whether to go on with his philosophical studies, gathering around him the group of followers and fellow thinkers with whom he had been spending his time; or to give up philosophy and take his natural place in the affairs of his city-state. Plato had already begun to write the Dialogues for which he is famous, and so in one of them, *Gorgias*, he talked about the problem indirectly. The Dialogue is really three arguments between Socrates and a series of opponents (a bit like an elimination match). A famous teacher and lecturer, Gorgias, has come to town, bragging that he can give a public speech on any subject his audience wants to hear about. Socrates takes him on, and suggests that Gorgias explain to them what *rhetoric* is. The discussion becomes a more general examination of the nature of the good life, and as we might expect, Gorgias is no match for Socrates. Very quickly, he gets tangled up in his own definitions, and Socrates has little trouble throwing him verbally to the mat. Then one of Gorgias' disciples, a young man named Polus, steps in. He isn't really any brighter than Gorgias, but he is full of self-confident enthusiasm, and he manages a few tussles with Socrates before he too is thrown. Now the real antagonist steps forward. He is a gifted young man named Callicles, with a quick wit, a sharp mind, and much of the same impatience that we saw

*Drawing by Lorenz; © 1960 The New Yorker Magazine, Inc.

at the beginning of this chapter in Thrasymachus. The remainder of the Dialogue is a knock-down, drag-out match between Callicles and Socrates, and Plato puts so many good arguments into Callicles' mouth that we cannot really say either man is the final winner. During one of his several long speeches (Callicles tends to talk too long, not answering Socrates' questions), Callicles ridicules Socrates for spending his time philosophizing instead of engaging in grown-up and manly pursuits, such as politics. Dramatically, this passage is an attack by Callicles on Socrates, but because Plato wrote both sides, he is really arguing with himself about what he ought to do in his own life. As you know, Plato decided to continue talking and writing philosophy, but it is a part of his greatness that he can give such witty expression to the opposing point of view.

> Here, then, you have the truth of the matter. You will become convinced of it if you only let philosophy alone and pass on to more important considerations. Of course, Socrates, philosophy does have a certain charm if one engages with it in one's youth and in moderation; but if one dallies overlong, it's the ruin of a fellow. If a man, however well endowed, goes on philosophizing throughout his life, he will never come to taste the experiences which a man must have if he's going to be a gentleman and have the world look up to him. You know perfectly well that philosophers know nothing about state laws and regulations. They are equally ignorant of the conversational standards that we have to adopt in dealing with our fellow men at home and abroad. Why, they are inexperienced even in human pleasures and desires! In a word, they are totally innocent of all human character. So, when they come to take part in either a private or a public affair, they make themselves ridiculous—just as ridiculous, I dare say, as men of affairs may be when they get involved in your quibbles, your 'debates.' . . .
>
> But the best course, no doubt, is to be a participant in both. It's an excellent thing to grasp as much philosophy as one needs for an education, and it's no disgrace to play the philosopher while you're young; but if one grows up and becomes a man and still continues in the subject, why, the whole thing becomes ridiculous, Socrates. My own feeling toward its practitioners is very much the same as the way I feel toward men who lisp and prattle like a child. When I see a child, who ought to be talking that way, lisping and prattling, I'm pleased, it strikes me as a pleasant sign of good breeding and suitable to the child's age; and when I hear a little lad speaking distinctly, it seems to me disagreeable and offends my ears as a mark of servile origin. So, too, when I hear a grown man prattling and lisping, it seems ridiculous and unmanly; one would like to strike him hard! And this is exactly the feeling I have about students of philosophy. When I perceive philosophical activity in a young lad, I am pleased; it suits him, I think,

and shows that he has good breeding. A boy who doesn't play with philosophy I regard as illiberal, a chap who will never raise himself to any fine or noble action. Whereas when I see an older man still at his philosophy and showing no sign of giving it up, that one seems to me, Socrates, to be asking for some hard knocks! For, as I said just now, such a man, even if he's well endowed by nature, must necessarily become unmanly by avoiding the center of the city and the assemblies where as the Poet says, "men win distinction." Such a fellow must spend the rest of his life skulking in corners, whispering with two or three little lads, never pronouncing any large, liberal, or meaningful utterance.

PLATO, Gorgias

Among philosophers themselves, the greatest modern critic of philosophy as mere armchair contemplation was Karl Marx. Marx, as the saying goes, needs no introduction. He, Einstein, and Freud are probably the three most influential thinkers to have lived and worked in the West in the past two centuries, and when one considers the numbers of human beings who live in societies that are at least officially "Marxist," he prob-

"Storming the Arsenal": wood engraving depicting the revolutionary outbreaks in Berlin, 1848.

ably can claim precedence even over Einstein. (There seems to be something special about speaking German as your native language! All three of these great men wrote in German, and there are dozens of others—Kant, Hegel, Max Weber, Max Planck, etc.,—who did also.)

You all know Marx as the founder of communism, as a leading theoretician of the economic and political theory of socialism, as the co-author (with Friedrich Engels) of a famous pamphlet, *The Communist Manifesto*, and as the author of a huge, important, not-very-much-read book about Western capitalism and socialism entitled *Capital*. But probably very few of you know that Marx began his career as a philosophy student, and that his doctoral dissertation was actually devoted to a critical study of one of the ancient cosmologists, an atomist named Democritus who lived roughly at the same time as Socrates.

All the philosophers we have talked about and read in this chapter, and just about all the philosophers we will be talking about and reading in the rest of this book, believed that the mind can discover significant truths about man or nature by thinking hard enough, by observing the evidence, reasoning about first principles, analyzing concepts, and criticizing the mind's power of reasoning itself. Some of those philosophers were rich and powerful men (such as the emperor Marcus Aurelius); others were in what we would today call the middle or upper middle class, such as Professor Immanuel Kant. A few lived lives of either voluntary or enforced poverty (the ancient philosopher Epicurus actually tried to get by on the equivalent of five cents a day). All were men, because until the twentieth century, philosophy has been almost exclusively a man's activity. But none of them thought that his wealth, power, social class, sex, or status had any *essential* connection with his philosophy. David Hume cared a great deal about his literary reputation, and he struggled to write books that would win popular acclaim, but he would have thought it mad to suggest that his position in society as an educated man of modest means bore any significant relationship to his theory of knowledge. And though the emperor Marcus Aurelius meditated a good deal on the fleetingness of his power and wealth, he certainly didn't think that there was any connection between the imperial politics of Rome, the slave base of the Roman economy, and his Stoic doctrine of the universal rationality of the cosmos.

Marx challenged all of this with *two* fundamental theses which were aimed at exposing the inadequacy of all previous philosophizing. The first thesis goes by the rather formidable name of *dialectical materialism*. We shall have a good deal more to say in Chapters Three and Four about Marx's materialist theory. The key notion from it which we need here is Marx's claim that we can only really understand the religion, art, jurisprudence, or *philosophy* written in a society at some time by seeing it in its relationship to the economic organization of that society. This claim directly contradicted the usual philosophical assumption that philosophy could be understood solely in terms of its own concepts and arguments. Thus Marx claimed that, to understand Plato's abstract theories of Being and Becoming, you must begin with an examination of the slave economy of Athens. To understand the ethereal beauties of St. Thomas Aquinas' metaphysics, you must take a look at the feudal system of land tenure in medieval Europe. To grasp the true significance of the philosophies of Locke, Berkeley, Hume, Descartes, Leibniz, and Kant, it is first necessary to study the rise of the new capitalist order within the old remaining feudal economy of early modern Europe.

Marx did not deny that ideas could have important effects in the real world of the economy and the state, but he emphatically denied that ideas were the prime moving forces in either history or the universe, and he just as emphatically denied that the realm of ideas could be treated as separate from the day-to-day world of work, production, buying and selling.

Marx's second thesis was in its way more revolutionary still. After all, if they believed in the first thesis, philosophers would have to change the sorts of things they study, but they could still go on *studying*. His second thesis was that philosophers must give up merely reasoning about man, nature, and the universe. They must get up, get out, and *do* something about the world. Thought unconnected with action, he held, is purposeless, empty, or as he would put it, "abstract."

A good way to end this opening chapter is to quote Marx's most famous remark about the relationship between philosophical thinking and practice. As you work your way through the remainder of this book, it might be worthwhile to turn back from time to time and reread that remark, for it stands as a permanent challenge to the entire philosophical enterprise. Here is Marx's challenge:

> The philosophers have only *interpreted* the world, in various ways; the point, however, is to *change* it.

IMMANUEL KANT (1724–1804) was born, lived out his life, and died in the provincial city of Königsberg. Kant's early studies were concentrated in the areas of natural science, mathematics, and philosophy. At the University of Königsberg, he learned the philosophical theories of Leibniz, as they had been interpreted by a widely-read German philosopher, Christian Wolff. After graduating from the University, Kant took a number of jobs as a tutor to children in the houses of Prussian aristocrats. Finally, he returned to the university to become what was called a *privatdozent*. This meant that he was licensed by the university to offer lectures, which the students could attend. But he was not paid by the university; instead, he had to collect fees from the students. The more popular he was, the more money he made! For more than a dozen years, Kant lectured as much as twenty-one hours a week on virtually every subject imaginable, from mathematics and logic to geography and history. Finally, in 1770, he was appointed to the position of Professor of Logic and Metaphysic.

Kant was already well known throughout Germany for his writings on physics, astronomy, and metaphysics, but his important work was still far in the future. For eleven years, from 1770 until 1781, he published virtually nothing. All that time, he was struggling with fundamental problems of human knowledge. Finally, in 1781, there appeared the book that was to revolutionize all philosophy: *The Critique of Pure Reason*. In the next ten years, book after book flowed from his pen. After the *Critique*, Kant published the *Prolegomena to any Future Metaphysics* (1783), *The Groundwork of the Metaphysic of Morals* (1785), *Metaphysical Foundations of Natural Science* (1786), *The Critique of Practical Reason* (1788), and the *Critique of Judgment* (1790).

Kant continued writing and revising his theories until finally, at the age of eighty, shortly after the start of the new century, he died. Though he had never left his native Königsberg, his mind had spanned all time and all space, and he had left an indelible mark on the thought of his civilization.

Ethics 2

Irwin Edman, a well-known early twentieth-century Columbia University professor of philosophy, is said to have stopped a student on the street one day. "Excuse me," Edman said. "Can you tell me whether I am walking north or south?" The startled student replied, "You are walking south, Professor." "Ah, good," Edman replied. "Then I have already eaten lunch."

Well, it isn't much of a joke, and it has been told of half the professors in America, but it does capture the popular impression of philosophy professors as rather unworldly characters, out of touch with the real world —people, as American businessmen are fond of saying, who have "never met a payroll."

Immanuel Kant is the greatest philosopher to live and write since the ancient times of Plato and Aristotle; he is the first great philosopher in modern times (after the end of the Middle Ages) to make his living as what we would call a professor of philosophy; and he is also about as close as any great philosopher has ever come to the standard caricature of the professor. Kant is said to have lived so regular and retiring a life that the townspeople of Königsberg, his lifelong home, could set their clocks by him as he went by on his daily walk. One would expect a professorial

39

type like Kant to make contributions to such abstruse technical fields as cosmology, metaphysics, or the theory of knowledge, and so he did. But it is rather surprising to discover that Kant also wrote profound, powerful, and deeply moving books on the problems of morality. Despite the uneventful regularity of his own private life, Kant was able to confront and grapple with the great issues of duty, right, justice, and virtue which have troubled men's souls since the ancient times recorded in the Old Testament. The contrast between his outer life and his inner thoughts serves as a reminder to us that the greatness of a philosopher's insights cannot readily be measured by the external excitements of his life or times.

Kant was born on April 22, 1724 to a north Prussian family of modest means in the port city of Königsberg on the North Sea. Two centuries earlier, Luther had turned Central Europe upside down with his Reformation of the Catholic Church, and out of Luther's challenge to the institution of the papacy and to the rituals of medieval Christianity had sprung a number of Protestant sects. Kant's family belonged to the sect known as pietism, an extremely individualistic form of Protestant Christianity which rejected the mystery, ritual, and ceremony that the Catholic Church had interposed between the ordinary Christian and his God. Pietism emphasized the direct, inner relationship of the individual worshipper to God. It placed a strong inner conscience and a stern self-control at the center of its religious doctrine. Kant's mother was particularly devout, and it was universally said of him that he owed both his religious faith and his overpowering sense of moral duty to her influence.

For Kant, the central question of morality was not, What should I do? This he firmly believed was perfectly well-known to every decent man and woman, whether a peasant or a professor. As he remarked at one point in his moral writings, the truths of ethics had been known for thousands of years, so that a moral philosopher could hardly expect to discover something *new* in ethics. Rather, Kant saw the real moral problem in the way that most Puritans and other individualistic Protestants did, as the constant struggle to do what we know is right in the face of temptations and distractions. The soldier who knows that his duty requires him to stand fast even as his fear tempts him to run; the businessman who knows that he should give honest measure for honest measure in the marketplace, but nevertheless secretly wishes to tilt the scales in his own favor; the good husband who knows that his marriage vow is absolutely binding but feels the temptation of adultery—these and others like them are the men and women Kant has in mind when he writes on moral questions.

Kant was a student of the new science of Newton as well as a deeply committed Pietist. He saw a fundamental conflict between the scientific explanation of natural events, which emphasized their subordination to causal laws, and the moral assumption that man was free to choose his actions and hence morally responsible for what he did. How could we demand that man resist temptation and hold to the moral law if his every action was merely another causally determined event in the universal natural order? How could we conceive of man as a free, responsible being and yet also acknowledge his place in the system of events and objects studied by science?

Equally important to Kant, how could we prove, absolutely and without the slightest room for doubt or uncertainty, that the fundamental moral beliefs shared by all right-thinking men were true, and not merely public opinion? As we saw in the first chapter, Kant insisted that even religion and morality submit to the spirit of *criticism*. The simple peasants and proud professors of north Prussia might believe that they knew the truth about ethics, but until they could produce a valid proof of their beliefs, they would have no argument to offer against the skeptic, the relativist, the doubter who said that all opinions were equally good or even that there was no truth about ethics to be known at all.

Kant had some ideas about how to handle these two problems. He thought that he could work out a philosophical truce between ethics and science that would give each its rightful place in the totality of man's knowledge; at the same time, he hoped to provide a proof of the fundamental principles of ethics. In this way, he would bring all the parts of his own life and work into harmony with one another. In his philosophical system, there would be a place for the devout faith imparted to him by his mother, a proof of the moral maxims he had grown up with and which to his death he never doubted, and a conceptual framework for the great new achievements of science and mathematics which so dominated the intellectual world of his day and to which he devoted so much of his own life and work. Kant's struggle to achieve a harmonious accommodation among his scientific interests, his moral convictions, and his religious faith was a model for many later struggles by other philosophers. Today more than ever, science seems to encroach upon religion and morality. New developments in behavioral psychology threaten our age-old belief in man's moral freedom. Though many philosophers have challenged Kant's solution, few would deny that he saw deeply into the problem and forced the rest of us to face up to it as philosophers.

II   Having read this far into a chapter on ethics, some of you may have the feeling that you don't quite recognize the subject as one that you can relate yourself to. Perhaps Kant knew perfectly well what was right, but many of *us* are filled with doubts. Furthermore, you may want to say, his single-minded emphasis on duty, on conscience, on doing the *right* thing, misses the real flavor of much of our thinking about how to live our lives. The fact is that although this book contains only one chapter called Ethics, there are many quite different sorts of problems that have been discussed under that name since the time of the ancient Greeks. There is hardly enough room in a single chapter, let alone in one book, to talk about them all, but at least *three* are important enough to demand some extended examination.

Kant has already introduced us to the first reason that people worry about what is called Ethics, namely a desire to discover an absolutely certain, irrefutable proof of the moral principles which we are already convinced are true. This proof serves two purposes: first, it answers the skeptic, who denies that there are any moral truths at all; and second, it answers the relativist, who says, in effect, "Everyone's opinions are as good as everyone else's."

A second reason why people worry about ethics is that sometimes we get into situations in which we want to do the right thing but really don't know what it is. For example, a woman may find that she is pregnant, and feel that to have a baby will simply turn her life inside out. Perhaps she wants to continue her studies in order to prepare for a career; perhaps the pregnancy is the result of a casual affair with a man whom she does not love; perhaps she and her husband already have as many children as they want and feel they can care for. Should she have an abortion? Part of her tells herself that abortion is morally wrong; another part tells her that to have the baby would be wrong. She wants to do what is right, but she just doesn't know what *is* right in the situation.

Or a young man wants to leave home and start a life of his own, despite his parents' pleas that he remain with them and care for them. On the one hand, he feels love for his parents and a debt of gratitude and loyalty for all the years they have given him. On the other hand, he knows that this is his only life, and that it is wrong for him to sacrifice it to the needs or demands of his parents. Again, he wants to do what is right, but he does not know whether he really has an obligation to stay at home, and if he does, for how long.

In philosophy, cases such as these are sometimes called "hard cases." They are real-life moral dilemmas in which ordinary moral opinions are either hopelessly contradictory or else just confused. Many philosophers have sought some method or rule by which we could decide hard cases, either by a process of moral reasoning or even by a sort of calculation. Genuine confusion rather than temptation is the motivation here, and frequently the emphasis is less on an absolutely rock-solid *proof* of things we already believe than it is on some genuinely new insight into an otherwise unsolvable dilemma.

But the oldest tradition of ethical reflection in Western thought has nothing to do with rights and duties, temptations and their denial, hard cases and tortured choices. For Plato, for Epicurus, for the ancient Stoics, and for countless philosophers since their time, Ethics has been concerned with the definition, analysis, search, and achievement of the Good Life. Our stay on this earth is brief, the years pass faster and faster as we grow old, and all too soon we are forever dead. As we grow up and grow old, how shall we live our lives? What set of precepts, what style of inner feelings and outer relationships, what set of commitments will make us truly happy during the short passage of our lives? Should we strive to pile wealth upon wealth? fulfull our talents? aim for power and fame? retire to quiet contemplation? taste every experience, pleasurable or not, before death comes? Can reason and philosophy even help us in this choice? Or is the life of the mind itself just one path among many, and not the happiest at that?

Sometimes, when we say that someone lived a "good life," we mean that he or she experienced a great deal of pleasure—ate, drank, made merry. As the Italians say, such a person lived "la dolce vita," the "sweet life." But just as often, we mean that the life was one of virtue, of service, of honor and dignity, that it was a life in which there was goodness. Many philosophers deliberately preserve this ambiguity because they believe that a truly happy life must also be a virtuous life, a life of goodness. Plato is perhaps the philosopher most often associated with this claim, and we shall read something by him on the subject later on in this chapter. But many other philosophers have, in one way or another, made the same claim, among whom are such unlikely bedfellows as Confucius and Karl Marx.

Here, then, are three reasons for thinking about ethics—or better, three searches which are usually grouped under the heading "Ethics": the search for absolutely certain, universally valid first principles of conduct that can stand against the challenges of the skeptic and the relativist; the search for a method or process of reasoning to help us in deciding hard cases and other real-work moral choices; and the search for the good life, the life that combines virtue and happiness in true human fulfillment. Most of the remainder of this chapter will be devoted to a deeper examination of these three approaches to the subject of ethics.

III   When we are very little, our parents stop us from doing things we shouldn't —hitting baby brother, eating paint, touching a wall plug—by physically pulling us away and saying "No!" in a loud, firm voice. You can't have a philosophical discussion with a two-year-old, as I was forced very quickly to recognize with my own two sons. As we grow older, we internalize those

"No's" in the form of some set of rules, or norms, some conception of what is right and wrong. For a very long time, we simply accept these rules as given, a part of the world just as trees and tables, our parents and friends are a part of the world. Pretty early on, of course, we discover that not everyone abides all the time by the rules that our parents have taught us, but we can handle that fact, conceptually, by means of the category "bad." "Why can't I hit my brother? Tommy does." "Because it is wrong. Tommy is a bad boy, and I don't want you to be a bad boy like him."

So we grow older, with a more or less coherent moral code as part of our mental equipment. There are bad guys, naughty children, villains, criminals, but they are the "others," the ones who aren't nice, the sort of people *we* don't want to be like.

Then, one day, somewhere, there comes the great shock. It may be when we are still children, or when we go away to college, or when we move from a tight little homogeneous neighborhood to a big, heterogeneous city. It may simply be something we see on television. But all of a sudden, we encounter a whole group of people who seem to be good, decent, respectable, law-abiding, and upright, except that they call good what we call bad! We think it is good to fight for our country, and they think it is wicked. We think homosexuality is evil, and they think it is a perfectly acceptable lifestyle. They think abortion is a sensible technique for rational family planning and population control, and we call it murder.

This discovery, in whatever form it comes, is a genuine shock. The problem doesn't lie in the realization that some people do bad things. Ever since we saw Tommy hit his brother, we have known that. The real problem is that these people doing "bad" things and living by the "wrong" rules are *good* people. They are responsible; they are respected by their friends and neighbors. They may even be held up to children as models of virtue. And yet they do bad things! A man comes home from a war in which he gunned down two hundred women and children in a defenseless village, and he is paraded along Main Street as a hero. A mother and father refuse to allow their baby to receive medical treatment, the baby dies, and they are praised in their church as pillars of rectitude. A governor calls out the National Guard to shoot striking prison inmates, and he is immortalized in marble in front of the state capital.

If it is unsettling to encounter men and women within our own society whose moral codes differ markedly from our own, think how much more unsettling it is to discover whole cultures or civilizations in which what we call virtue is despised as vice and what we condemn as wicked is celebrated as noble! Even a study of the history of the literate civilizations of the East and the West provides countless examples of this sort of variation in moral beliefs. When the anthropologists' experiences with nonliterate cultures are added to our stock of information, it begins to appear that there isn't a single rule, precept, or moral belief that has been accepted by decent men and women everywhere. War? Torture? Child murder? Adultery? Suicide? Theft? Lying? Every single one has been condemned by some cultures and accepted, approved, or even praised by others.

There are basically three ways in which a philosopher can deal with the troublesome problem of the variation in moral codes from person to person, group to group, and culture to culture. The first way is to deny that the variation exists, despite appearances to the contrary. The second way is to admit that the variation exists, and conclude that there are therefore no universally valid moral norms applicable to all persons in all places at all times. The third way is to acknowledge the variation, but insist nonetheless that some moral principles are true and other supposed principles are false, no matter how many people believe them. Those who take this last route then do their best to provide some sort of proof for the principles they believe to be valid.

How can philosophers possibly maintain that there is no real disagreement about norms and moral principles, when the evidence of personal and cultural variation is all around them? Essentially, their tactic is to argue that when two people or two cultures seem to disagree about what is right or good, they are *really* only disagreeing about some of the facts of the case. If they could settle that disagreement, then it would turn out that they actually make the same moral judgments. For example, the Christian Scientist, like the nonbeliever, wants what is best for his sick child. But he firmly believes that the body is not real, and that salvation depends upon holding firm to that belief. So for him to consent to an operation for his child would be as irresponsible (on his assessment of the facts) as for another parent to give a diabetic child all the candy he wants. To take another example, the culture that condemns abortion may believe that the fetus is already a person; the culture that approves abortion does not think the fetus is a person until after it is born. Both condemn murder, defined as the wilful killing of a person, but they disagree on the factual question of whether abortion is murder.

A number of philosophers have taken this line, including the Scotsman David Hume whom you encountered in Chapter One. Anthropologists have actually carried out cross-cultural surveys of norms in an effort to discover any constants. Although it does appear that the ban or taboo on incest is very widespread, the effort has essentially been a failure. There aren't any broad moral principles of justice, charity, equity, or benevolence which can be discovered in the moral systems of all cultures. (There is a much deeper question which we have not touched on yet. Even if there *were* universally accepted norms, what would that fact prove? Does everybody believing something make it right? Don't we need some justification for our moral convictions which goes beyond saying, "Everybody agrees with me?" This problem troubled Kant a great deal, and a bit later on in this chapter, we shall see how he tried to deal with it.)

The second response to moral disagreement—the denial of objective, universal moral norms—has actually been relatively rare in the history of Western ethical theory, but it has had its defenders from the time of the ancient Greeks to the present day. Strictly speaking, there are two different forms of this position; the first, which can be called *ethical skepticism*, denies that men can have the slightest certainty about questions of the right and the good. Sometimes the ethical skeptic says that words like "right," "good," "ought," and "duty" just don't have any meaning; sentences containing them are a bit like incantations or cheers of approval or perhaps just plain gibberish. Because the very words we use to make moral judgments have no meaning, our moral judgments can hardly be called true or false, valid or invalid. At other times, the ethical skeptic contents himself with saying that no valid argument can be found for any particular moral principle. If I doubt that murder is wrong, you cannot find an argument that will prove to me that it is. If I can't see why I should help another person when he is in distress, there is no way it can be demonstrated to me that I should. Philosophers who take either of these lines frequently think that science and scientific language are the models on which we should base all of our knowledge. They point to the nondescriptive character of moral statements (they don't tell us how things are; they claim to tell us how things ought to be). They contrast the orderly experimentation and examination of data in the sciences with the haphazard, intuitive, unfactual character of moral disputes. Sometimes they suggest that moral arguments really come down to disagreements over matters of taste, and as the old saying has it, *de gustibus non disputandem est* (there is no disputing in matters of taste).

The *ethical skeptic* is sometimes joined in his fight against objective moral principles by the *ethical relativist*. How often, in a bull session, have we heard someone say, "Oh well, it's all relative!" Sometimes that means "Everyone *has* his own opinion." Sometimes it means "Everyone *is entitled* to his own opinion." But sometimes it means "Everyone's opinion is true for him, even though it may not be true for someone else." As a student said to me once in class when I asked whether he thought that Hitler had been wrong to kill millions of people in death camps, "Well, it wouldn't be right for me, but I guess it was right for him."

Among the modern defenders of ethical relativity, Edward Westermarck stands out by virtue of the thoroughness with which he has maintained the position against the whole field of possible opponents. Westermarck, who taught philosophy in Finland and sociology in England, wrote several books explaining and arguing for the doctrine he called "ethical relativity." The following passage states his position in extremely strong terms, for he goes beyond mere skepticism concerning the objective validity of moral judgments. In this excerpt, he is prepared to stake out the stronger claim that there *cannot be* any proof of the validity of moral principles. Notice that in developing his argument, he relies heavily on the claim that moral judgments are based on feelings rather than on observations and experiments. In effect, Westermarck concludes that although the sciences of psychology, sociology, and cultural anthropology can exist—sciences which describe the moral attitudes and emotions actually experienced by people—there can be no "science" of ethics.

EDWARD WESTERMARCK (1862–1939) was a Finnish philosopher and anthropologist whose principal works appeared in English. Westermarck's professional career spanned the period during which modern anthropology came into its own, and in his writings on moral philosophy, he made imaginative use of the materials on alternative value systems collected by cultural anthropologists in their studies of primitive societies.

I have thus arrived at the conclusion that neither the attempts of moral philosophers or theologians to prove the objective validity of moral judgments, nor the common sense assumption to the same effect, give us any right at all to accept such a validity as a fact. So far, however, I have only tried to show that it has not been proved; now I am prepared to take a step further and assert that it cannot exist. The reason for this is that in my opinion the predicates of all moral judgments, all moral concepts, are ultimately based on emotions, and that, as is very commonly admitted, no objectivity can come from an emotion. It is of course true or not that we in a given moment have a certain emotion; but in no other sense can the antithesis of true and false be applied to it. The belief that gives rise to an emotion, the cognitive basis of it, is either true or false; in the latter case the emotion may be said to be felt "by mistake"—as when a person is frightened by some object in the dark which he takes for a ghost, or is indignant with a person to whom he imputes a wrong that has been committed by somebody else; but this does not alter the nature of the emotion itself. We may call the emotion of another individual "unjustified," if we feel that we ourselves should not have experienced the same emotion had we been in his place, or, as in the case of moral approval or disapproval, if we cannot share his emotion. But to speak . . . of "right" and "wrong" emotions, springing from self-evident intuitions and having the same validity as truth and error, is only another futile attempt to objectivize our moral judgments. . . .

If there are no moral truths it cannot be the object of a science of ethics to lay down rules for human conduct, since the aim of all science is the discovery of some truth. Professor Höffding argues that the subjectivity of our moral valuations does not prevent ethics from being a science any more than the subjectivity of our sensations renders a science of physics impossible, because both are concerned

with finding the external facts that correspond to the subjective processes. It may, of course, be a subject for scientific inquiry to investigate
the means which are conducive to human happiness or welfare, and
the results of such a study may also be usefully applied by moralists,
but it forms no more a part of ethics than physics is a part of psychology. If the word "ethics" is to be used as the name for a science,
the object of that science can only be to study the moral consciousness
as a fact.

EDWARD WESTERMARCK, *Ethical Relativity*

Westermarck himself would agree that Immanuel Kant is the strongest
opponent of the ethical relativist position. A major aim of Kant's philosophical efforts was to provide an absolutely solid, totally universal proof
of the validity of that moral principle which he considered the foundation
of all ethics, the principle which he called the *categorical imperative*. Kant
was well aware that there were serious ethical disagreements among philosophers on particular questions of moral judgment, though he was not so
impressed as Hume had been by the systematic cultural differences which
appeared to divide "cultivated" peoples. But Kant was extremely concerned about the lack of solid foundations for even those ethical beliefs
which were more or less broadly agreed upon. In a number of profound
and very difficult treatises on ethics, Kant undertook to lay those foundations.

Saying just a few words about Kant's philosophy is like saying just a
few words about quantum mechanics or the theory of relativity! Nevertheless, some of the key notions of Kant's moral philosophy can be understood pretty well without plunging into the depths of his argument,
and in the remainder of this section, I shall introduce you to those notions
through a combination of my exposition and Kant's own words.

Kant first set out his moral philosophy in a little book called *The
Groundwork of the Metaphysic of Morals* (a rather imposing title). He
intended the book to be just an introduction to his theory and shortly
thereafter he published another, longer work called *A Critique of Practical
Reason*. But as often happens, the short "introductory" book took on a life
of its own, and today it is widely viewed as the finest statement of Kant's
position.

The aim of *Groundwork* is to discover, analyze, and defend the fundamental principle of morality. As you know, Kant didn't think he had discovered a *new* principle, and he liked to say that his categorical imperative
was nothing more than a philosophically more precise statement of the old
Golden Rule: Do unto others as you would have others do unto you.
Here is the way in which Kant revised and restated that rule:

Act only on that maxim through which you can at the same time will that it should become a universal law.

That doesn't *look* much like the Golden Rule, but Kant thought it contained the same basic notion, which is that we ought to put aside our own private interests and act instead on the basis of rules that would be equally reasonable for all moral agents to adopt as their own. "Do unto others as you would have others do unto you" doesn't mean "Go ahead and steal from your neighbor so long as you don't squawk when he steals from you." It means something more like "Treat other people with the same respect and dignity that you expect to be treated with." As we shall see, the idea of human dignity plays a central role in Kant's moral philosophy.

There are three ideas that lie at the heart of Kant's ethics. If we can understand something about each of them, we can form at least a preliminary notion of his theory. The ideas are first, that man is a rational creature, capable of thinking about the choices he faces and selecting among them on the basis of reasons; second, that man has an infinite worth or dignity which sets him above all merely conditionally valuable things in this world, that he is what Kant calls an end-in-himself; and third, that man, as a rational end-in-himself, is the *author* of the moral law, so that his obedience to duty is not an act of slavish submission but an act of dignified *autonomy*. Man as rational agent, man as end-in-himself, and man as autonomous—these are the basic building blocks out of which Kant constructs his proof of the categorical imperative.

When Kant asserts that men are rational agents, he means more than merely that they are capable of making judgments about the nature of the world, or inferences from one set of propositions to another. A rational agent is a person who is capable of *moving himself to act* by reason. David Hume, like many other philosophers, had thought that reason was incapable of moving men to action. Hume argued that *desire* moved men to act; reason could merely point out the most efficient path to the goal that desire chose. So Hume said, in a much-quoted passage, that "reason is, and ought only to be the slave of the passions, and can never pretend to any other office than to serve and obey them" (*Treatise of Human Nature*, Book III). Kant replied that if we are to make any sense at all out of man's condition as a creature capable of choice and deliberation, we must acknowledge that he can be moved by *reasons*, not merely by *desires*.

If Kant is right that men can be moved by reason, then it makes sense to ask whether a man has acted wisely or foolishly, whether he has reasoned consistently in his choice of ends and means. It makes sense, also, to ask whether in his reasoning he has taken special account of his own particular wishes and interests, or instead has limited himself only to reasons which would be compelling reasons for any person who found himself in the same circumstances. In short, it makes sense to ask whether he has acted *rationally*.

This notion of "reasons good for all rational agents" is a difficult one to grasp. Perhaps one way to get some idea of Kant's meaning is to compare a moral agent to a mathematician doing a geometry problem. Suppose the mathematician is trying to show that the square of the hypotenuse of a right triangle is equal to the sum of the squares of the other two sides (the so-called Pythagorean Theorem that some of you studied in high school). Now, the first thing he does in developing the proof is to draw a triangle, and because every triangle has to be some size and shape or other, the particular triangle the mathematician draws will be some particular size (maybe 4½ inches by 6 inches by 7½ inches), and it will also be some particular color (depending upon the color of the paper he draws it on), and so forth. But of course he isn't supposed to pay any attention to the actual size and color of the triangle. They are there, all right, but he is supposed to ignore them. The only thing he is allowed to count in his proof is the fact that the triangle has a right angle in it. If our

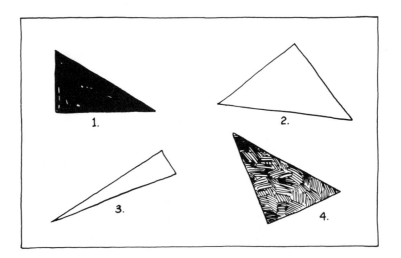

All four triangles have three angles and three sides, though they differ in color, shape, and size. When mathematicians prove geometric theorems, they ignore the irrelevant differences, and make reference only to the properties on which their arguments are based.

imaginary mathematician constructs his proof by using only the fact that his triangle is a right triangle, then his conclusions, when he gets them, will apply to *all* right triangles, not just to the one he actually drew.

In the same way, Kant claims that moral agents, when they reason about what they ought to do, should ignore all the particular facts about their own interests, special desires, individual circumstances, and so on, and concentrate just on those facts which hold for *all* rational agents as such. If they do that, he says, then the conclusions they come to will be valid for all rational agents, not just for themselves. In short, their conclusions will be universal laws, not just personal rules. Kant uses the word "maxim" to mean a personal rule on which we actually base our decisions. So he is telling us that when we make our decisions, we, like the mathematician, should restrict ourselves to rules, or maxims, that could just as well serve any rational agent. In other words, he tells us to restrict ourselves to maxims that could serve as universal laws. That is what he is trying to say in the categorical imperative: Act only on that maxim through which you can at the same time will that it should become a universal law.

If we do succeed in acting in a genuinely rational way, Kant says, we show ourselves to possess a dignity that sets us above everything else in the world. Indeed, the statement that moral agents, as persons, have an infinite worth or dignity, is, according to Kant just another way of saying what has already been said in the categorical imperative. Here is the famous passage in which Kant develops the notion that man is an end-in-himself. Difficult as Kant's argument is, I think you will be able to see in it something of the grandeur and profundity which made Kant so great a moral philosopher:

> Now I say that man, and in general every rational being, *exists* as an end in himself, *not merely as a means* for arbitrary use by this or that will: he must in all his actions, whether they are directed to himself or to other rational beings, always be viewed *at the same time as an end*. All the objects of inclination have only a conditioned value; for if there were not these inclinations and the needs grounded on them, their object would be valueless. Inclinations themselves, as sources of needs, are so far from having an absolute value to make them desirable for their own sake that it must rather be the universal wish of every rational being to be wholly free from them. Thus the value of all objects that can *be produced* by our action is always conditioned. Beings whose existence depends, not on our will, but on nature, have none the less, if they are non-rational beings, only a relative value as means and are consequently called *things*. Rational beings, on the other hand, are called *persons* because their nature already marks them out as ends in themselves and consequently imposes to that extent a limit on all arbitrary treatment of them (and is an object of rever-

ence). Persons, therefore, are not merely subjective ends whose existence as an object of our actions has a value *for us*: they are *objective ends*—that is, things whose existence is in itself an end, and indeed an end such that in its place we can put no other end to which they should serve *simply* as means; for unless this is so, nothing at all of *absolute* value would be found anywhere. But if all value were conditioned then no supreme principle could be found for reason at all.

If then there is to be a supreme practical principle and a categorical imperative, it must be such that from the idea of something which is necessarily an end for every one because it is an *end in itself* it forms an *objective* principle of the will and consequently can serve as a practical law. The ground of this principle is: *Rational nature exists as an end in itself*. This is the way in which a man necessarily conceives his own existence: it is therefore so far a *subjective* principle of human actions. But it is also the way in which every other rational being conceives his existence on the same rational ground which is valid also for me; hence it is at the same time an *objective* principle, from which, as a supreme practical ground, it must be possible to derive all laws for the will. The practical imperative will therefore be as follows: *Act in such a way that you always treat humanity, whether in your own person or in the person of any other, never simply as a means, but always at the same time as an end.*

I. KANT, Groundwork of the Metaphysic of Morals

Hume had described reason as the "slave" of the passions, subservient to their direction. Kant is the sworn foe of such slavery, as he was of slavery in the political realm. If my reason is the slave of my passions, then I forfeit the dignity that I possess in virtue of being an end-in-myself. There is no honor in subservience to passion, anymore than in subservience to a king or emperor. In the inner life of each man and woman, as in the public life of the State, honor is to be found only in submission to self-made laws. The citizen of a republic, who makes the laws to which he bows his head, loses no dignity by his obedience, for he is obeying only himself when he abides by the law. His obedience is an act of responsibility rather than of servitude.

The same principle, Kant thought, holds true within the individual soul. When reason bows to passion, it forfeits its claim to honor and dignity. But if reason can itself legislate the laws to which it submits; if reason can itself write the categorical imperative that binds it, then it will preserve its freedom in the very act of submission. To give laws to oneself is, following the Greek, to be *auto-nomos*—giver of law to oneself—in short: autonomous. The principle of the autonomy of reason is, Kant says, yet another version of the categorical imperative. In the following passage, Kant develops this notion of autonomy. Do not be surprised if you find this bit of text hard going. Kant is difficult to understand even in his easier writings, and this statement about autonomy is one of his chewiest bits of argument.

> This principle of humanity, and in general of every rational agent, *as an end in itself* (a principle which is the supreme limiting condition of every man's freedom of action) is not borrowed from experience; firstly, because it is universal, applying as it does to all rational beings as such, and no experience is adequate to determine universality; secondly, because in it humanity is conceived, not as an end of man (subjectively) but as an objective end—one which, be our ends what they may, must, as a law, constitute the supreme limiting condition of all subjective ends and so must spring from pure reason. That is to say, the ground for every enactment of practical law lies *objectively in the rule* and in the form of universality which (according to our first principle) makes the rule capable of being a law (and indeed a law of nature); *subjectively*, however, it lies in the *end*; but (according to our second principle) the subject of all ends is to be found in every rational being as an end in himself. From this there now follows our third practical principle for the will namely, the Idea *of the will of every rational being as a will which makes universal law.*
>
> By this principle all maxims are repudiated which cannot accord with the will's own enactment of universal law. The will is therefore not merely subject to the law, but is so subject that it must be considered as also *making the law* for itself and precisely on this account as first of all subject to the law (of which it can regard itself as the author).
>
> Imperatives as formulated above did, by the mere fact that they were represented as categorical, exclude from their sovereign authority every admixture of interest as a motive. They were, however, merely *assumed* to be categorical because we were bound to make this assumption if we wished to explain the concept of duty. That there were practical propositions which commanded categorically could not itself be proved, any more than it can be proved in this chapter generally; but one thing could have been done—namely, to show that in willing for the sake of duty renunciation of all interest, as the specific mark distinguishing a categorical from a hypothetical imperative, was expressed in the very imperative itself by means of some determination inherent in it. This is what is done in the present third formulation of the principle—namely, in the Idea of the will of every rational being as *a will which makes universal law.*
>
> Once we conceive a will of this kind, it becomes clear that while a will *which is subject to law* may be bound to this law by some interest, nevertheless a will which is itself a supreme law-giver cannot possibly as such depend on any interest; for a will which is dependent in this way would itself require yet a further law in order to restrict the

interest of self-love to the condition that this interest should itself be valid as a universal law.

Thus the *principle* that every human will is *a will which by all its maxims enacts universal law* would be *well suited* to be a categorical imperative in this respect: that precisely because of the Idea of making universal law it is *based on no interest* and consequently can alone among all possible imperatives be *unconditioned*. Or better still if there is a categorical imperative (that is, a law for the will of every rational being), it can command us only to act always on the maxim of such a will in us as can at the same time look upon itself as making universal law; for only then is the practical principle and the imperative which we obey unconditioned, since it is wholly impossible for it to be based on any interest.

We need not now wonder, when we look back upon all the previous efforts that have been made to discover the principle of morality, why they have one and all been bound to fail. Their authors saw man as tied to laws by his duty, but it never occurred to them that he is subject only to *laws which are made by himself* and yet are *universal*, and that he is bound only to act in conformity with a will which is his own but has as nature's purpose for it the function of making universal law. For when they thought of man merely as subject to a law (whatever it might be), the law had to carry with it some interest in order to attract or compel, because it did not spring as a law from *his own* will: in order to conform with the law his will had to be necessitated by *something else* to act in a certain way. This absolutely inevitable conclusion meant that all the labour spent in trying to find a supreme principle of duty was lost beyond recall; for what they discovered was never duty, but only the necessity of acting from a certain interest. This interest might be one's own or another's; but on such a view the imperative was bound to be always a conditioned one and could not possibly serve as a moral law. I will therefore call my principle the principle of the *Autonomy* of the will in contrast with all others, which I consequently class under *Heteronomy*.

I. KANT, *Groundwork of the Metaphysic of Morals*

Having set forth three key principles: (1) the rationality of man's will, (2) the infinite worth of man as an end-in-himself, and (3) the self-legislating, or autonomous, character of reason, Kant now pulls them all together in the notion of a society of moral agents, all of whom govern their actions by reason, all of whom are ends-in-themselves, and all of whom are autonomous. He calls this society a *kingdom of ends*, and we can imagine it as an ideal community of upright, responsible, rational men and women who base their actions on universally valid laws which they autonomously lay down for themselves. It is a community that lives according to the categorical imperative. In our last passage from Kant, we see all of these themes united:

In the kingdom of ends everything has either a *price* or a *dignity*. If it has a price, something else can be put in its place as an equivalent; if it is exalted above all price and so admits of no equivalent, then it has a dignity.

What is relative to universal human inclinations and needs has a *market price*; what, even without presupposing a need, accords with a certain taste has a *fancy price* (*Affektionspreis*); but that which constitutes the sole condition under which anything can be an end in itself has not merely a relative value but has an intrinsic value— that is, *dignity*.

Now morality is the only condition under which a rational being can be an end in himself; for only through this is it possible to be a law-making member in a kingdom of ends. Therefore morality, and humanity so far as it is capable of morality, is the only thing which has dignity. Skill and diligence in work have a market price; wit, lively imagination, and humour have a fancy price; but fidelity to promises and kindness based on principle (not on instinct) have an intrinsic worth. In default of these, nature and art alike contain nothing to put in their place; for their worth consists, not in the effects which result from them, not in the advantage or profit they produce, but in the attitudes of mind which are ready in this way to manifest themselves in action even if they are not favoured by success. Such actions too need no recommendation from any subjective disposition or taste in order to meet with immediate favour and approval; they need no immediate propensity or feeling for themselves; they exhibit the will which performs them as an object of immediate reverence; nor is anything other than reason required to *impose* them upon the will, nor to *coax* them from the will—which last would anyhow be a contradiction in the case of duties. This assessment reveals as dignity the value of such a mental attitude and puts it infinitely above all price, with which it cannot be brought into reckoning or comparison without, as it were, a profanation of its sanctity.

What is it then that entitles a morally good attitude of mind to make claims so high? It is nothing less than the *share* which it affords to a rational being *in the making of universal law*, and which therefore fits him to be a member in a possible kingdom of ends. For this he was already marked out in virtue of his own proper nature as an end in himself and consequently as a maker of laws in the kingdom of ends—as free in respect of all laws of nature, obeying only those laws which he makes himself and in virtue of which his maxims can have their part in the making of universal law (to which he at the same time subjects himself). For nothing can have a value other than that determined for it by the law. But the law-making which determines all value must for this reason have a dignity for the appreciation of which, as necessarily given by a rational being, the word 'reverence' is the only becoming expression. *Autonomy* is therefore the ground of the dignity of human nature and of every rational nature.

IV How shall we deal with those terrible situations in which we want very much to do the right thing but simply cannot figure out what it is? Sometimes, there are two different and conflicting things, both of which seem right in the situation. Sometimes the situation is such a tangle that we are just at a loss. The source of our uncertainty is not temptation, or skepticism, or relativism, but the genuine moral difficulty of the case itself. One of the most ancient attempts to deal with such hard cases, and also to lay down a rule for action which will always tell us what we ought to do, is the moral philosophy which these days goes under the name of *utilitarianism*. In this section, we are going to take a look at several varieties of utilitarianism, see what the theory says and how it works, and also consider some serious objections to it.

Utilitarianism is simply the rule that we should always try to make as many people as happy as possible. Indeed, it is sometimes called "the greatest happiness principle" for this reason. The cosmologist Lucretius was a utilitarian, and so was the man whose teachings he followed, Epicurus. In the modern world, the most famous utilitarian, generally credited with establishing the doctrine as a serious contender in moral philosophy, was the eighteenth-century Englishman Jeremy Bentham.

Bentham argued that however people may appear to use the words "good" and "evil," we all really just mean "pleasant" or "pleasurable" when we say "good," and "painful" when we say "evil." More good is better than less, which is to say that more pleasure is better than less. And of course, less pain is better than more. The only good reason for doing anything is to increase the amount of pleasure that human beings experience, or at least to reduce the amount of pain. What is more, pleasures and pains can, in a manner of speaking, be added to and subtracted from one another. I can ask myself, Which gave me more pleasure: the good movie I saw last week, or the mediocre movie I saw last night plus the really good pizza I had afterward? I can also ask myself, which will be more painful: three dentist's visits now, complete with drillings, or a toothache followed by an extraction followed by the annoyance of a missing tooth later? If the mediocre movie plus the pizza gave me more pleasure, then the next time I have to choose between a good movie and no pizza, or a mediocre movie and pizza, I ought to take the mediocre movie plus pizza. And more seriously, if the dentist's visits, bad as they are, add up to less pain than the rotting of my tooth, then I ought to go to the dentist even though I don't want to, because the only rational thing to do is to minimize the total amount of pain in my life.

Bentham announced the doctrine now known as utilitarianism in a book entitled *Introduction to the Principles of Morals and Legislation*,

56

Jeremy Bentham *

JEREMY BENTHAM (1748–1832) was the founder of the ethical doctrine now known as utilitarianism. He began his long life during the reign of King George II, and died in the year of the Reform Bill that extended the franchise to virtually all of middle-class England. He lived through the American Revolution, the French Revolution, the Napoleonic Wars, and the rise of parliamentary government in England, and nearly survived into the reign of Queen Victoria. He was the godfather of John Stuart Mill, the son of his friend and colleague James Mill. John Stuart was, in his own turn, the godfather of Bertrand Russell, the great English philosopher who ended his own long and distinguished life by leading the British campaign for nuclear disarmament in the 1960s. So in three generations of great English philosophers, we move from the mid-eighteenth century world of wigs, carriages, and kings, to the mid-twentieth century world of jets, nuclear weapons, and popular democracy.

Bentham's primary concern as a philosopher was with legal and social reform. The law in the eighteenth century was a crazy quilt of precedents, quibbles, hanging offenses, and rank injustices. Several of Bentham's books were devoted to the attempt to sort things out and find some rational system of principles to put in place of the tangle that had grown up over so many centuries. He hoped that his simple, intuitively appealing principle of utility—the Greatest Happiness of the Greatest Number—would serve as the basis for a thoroughgoing reform of the law.

first printed in 1780 and formally published in 1789. Here is a selection from the opening chapter. Notice the complete identification of pleasure with good and pain with evil. This is the heart and soul of Bentham's utilitarian doctrine.

Nature has placed mankind under the governance of two sovereign masters, *pain* and *pleasure*. It is for them alone to point out what we

* In his will, Jeremy Bentham left his whole estate to the University of London provided that his remains be present at all board meetings. The University stuffed his body, shown above. The head here is wax, but the actual head, preserved in the tradition of South American head hunters, lies between his feet.

ought to do, as well as to determine what we shall do. On the one hand the standard of right and wrong, on the other the chain of causes and effects, are fastened to their throne. They govern us in all we do, in all we say, in all we think: every effort we can make to throw off our subjection, will serve but to demonstrate and confirm it. In words a man may pretend to abjure their empire: but in reality he will remain subject to it all the while. The *principle of utility* recognises this subjection, and assumes it for the foundation of that system, the object of which is to rear the fabric of felicity by the hands of reason and law. Systems which attempt to question it, deal in sounds instead of sense, in caprice instead of reason, in darkness instead of light.

But enough of metaphor and declamation: it is not by such means that moral science is to be improved.

The principle of utility is the foundation of the present work: it will be proper therefore at the outset to give an explicit and determinate account of what is meant by it. By the principle of utility is meant that principle which approves or disapproves of every action whatsoever, according to the tendency which it appears to have to augment or diminish the happiness of the party whose interest is in question: or, what is the same thing in other words, to promote or to oppose that happiness. I say of every action whatsoever; and therefore not only of every action of a private individual, but of every measure of government.

By utility is meant that property in any object, whereby it tends to produce benefit, advantage, pleasure, good, or happiness, (all this in the present case comes to the same thing) or (what comes again to the same thing) to prevent the happening of mischief, pain, evil, or unhappiness to the party whose interest is considered: if that party be the community in general, then the happiness of the community: if a particular individual, then the happiness of that individual.

The interest of the community is one of the most general expressions that can occur in the phraseology of morals: no wonder that the meaning of it is often lost. When it has a meaning, it is this. The community is a fictitious *body*, composed of the individual persons who are considered as constituting as it were its *members*. The interest of the community then is, what?—the sum of the interests of the several members who compose it.

It is in vain to talk of the interest of the community, without understanding what is the interest of the individual. A thing is said to promote the interest, or to be *for* the interest, of an individual, when it tends to add to the sum total of his pleasures: or, what comes to the same thing, to diminish the sum total of his pains.

An action then may be said to be conformable to the principle of utility, or, for shortness sake, to utility, (meaning with respect to the community at large) when the tendency it has to augment the happiness of the community is greater than any it has to diminish it.

A measure of government (which is but a particular kind of action, performed by a particular person or persons) may be said to be conformable to or dictated by the principle of utility, when in like manner the tendency which it has to augment the happiness of the community is greater than any which it has to diminish it.

The crucial step in Bentham's argument is his move from the total pleasure and pain experienced by one person to the total pleasure or pain experienced by all the members of the community taken together. This is the device which permits Bentham to extract a moral principle from his theory. The point is that whenever I do anything at all, my action has effects which impinge on the lives of other people. Sometimes I cause them pleasure, sometimes I cause them pain, and sometimes of course I cause some of them pleasure and others pain. For example, if the young man we mentioned earlier decides to stay at home with his parents rather than leave and set out on his own, he will probably cause himself pain and his mother and father pleasure. That is just why he doesn't know what to do! If his staying at home caused his parents pain too (they, after all, might want to live their own lives), then the decision would be an easy one for him.

Whenever we face hard choices, Bentham tells us, we can translate an impossible moral dilemma into a problem of addition and subtraction. For the young man, the choice is between staying home with his parents and leaving. He adds up all the pleasure and pain (negative values for pain, of course) that anybody in the situation will experience as the result of his staying, and compares it with the total pleasure and pain that everyone will experience as a result of his leaving home. He then chooses the alternative with the highest positive total (or, if it is one of those "least of evils" situations, the alternative with the smallest negative total). For example, suppose that the young man desperately wants to leave home. Then we can assume that he will suffer great pain if he must stay, and he will gain great pleasure if he goes. Let us also assume that his parents would like him to stay at home, but they are not dead set on it. They will manage all right if he leaves. Now we have great pain plus moderate pleasure on the side of staying, and great pleasure plus moderate pain on the side of going. Obviously, this adds up to a decision to go.

A great many objections can be raised to utilitarianism, and I am about to raise several of the more serious ones. But before we start chopping this theory down, it is worth taking a few moments to look at its very considerable strengths. In the first place, utilitarianism assumes that everyone wants to be happy, and it is hard to argue with that. But even more important, utilitarianism explains happiness in terms that everyone

TO MARRY OR NOT TO MARRY
A UTILITARIAN CALCULATION

IF I MARRY	UNITS OF PLEASURE
1. A secure sex life	+ 1000
2. But no playing the field	− 300
3. The joy of children	+ 700
4. The expense of children	− 500
5. Companionship in old age	+ 400
6. Responsibilities, ties, burdens	− 600
THE UTILITY OF MARRYING	+ 700

IF I DON'T MARRY	UNITS OF PLEASURE
1. Freedom to enter new relationships	+ 500
2. Loneliness	− 300
3. No children, no grand-children	− 800
4. But no responsibilities	+1000
5. No ties to hold me in one job, one place	+ 400
6. But no roots, no one who really cares whether I live or die	− 500
THE UTILITY OF NOT MARRYING	+ 300

+700 IS GREATER THAN +300, THEREFORE: I DO

According to Bentham, the rational man or woman will choose
the alternative which offers the greatest total of pleasure.
Does anyone ever make an important decision this way? Would you?

can understand. It doesn't say that happiness is oneness with the infinite, or self-fulfillment, or the integration of adult roles with childhood ego formations, or what have you. It says that happiness is pleasure, unhappiness is pain, and the more pleasure or the less pain the better.

Nor does utilitarianism demand strange, painful sacrifices from its believers. Kant believed, for example, that we should keep our promises and tell the truth no matter who got hurt. That is a dark saying, fraught with potentiality for terrible choices where lives are lost or hideous pain inflicted simply because someone will not violate an absolute moral rule. But Bentham says nothing of that sort. By all means lie, he says, if the total pain produced by the truth is greater than that produced by the lie. Make sure to add in the side effects of the lie, such as the likelihood that the next time you tell the truth it won't be believed. But when all those long-term, short-term, direct, and indirect effects have been calculated, then just choose the course promising the greatest happiness for the greatest number of people.

The most impressive strength of utilitarianism is its ability to transform seemingly impossible problems of moral deliberation into manageable empirical problems of investigation and addition. To see what that means, imagine that we lived a long time ago in an agricultural society which had not yet discovered geometry. Each year, as the flood waters from the river receded, it become necessary to divide up the land again for the spring planting. The plots all had to be triangular (owing to some religious belief, we may suppose). The high priest would stake out each family's lands, and then the arguing would begin over whose plot was bigger, and who had been slighted in the dividing up. The wise men would gather, great deliberations would ensue, with much prayer and meditation, and in the end no one would really be satisfied with the high priest's decisions. Now just think what it would mean, in such a society, for someone to discover the simple geometrical theorem that the area of a triangle is equal to one-half the base times the height! All those moral and religious disputes would be dissolved in an instant into a process of calculation. The royal surveyor would just measure the bases of the family plots, multiply by their heights, (the plots, not the family's), and then make adjustments until each family had the same area. It would put the royal moral philosopher and the royal priest out of business!

Well, Bentham had hopes that his greatest happiness principle would do the same for the modern wizards who, in his own society did the job of the ancient priests and moral philosophers—namely the judges and lawyers. He believed that rational legislators, with the principle of utility to guide them, could replace the hideous tangle of laws and punishments of the English common law with a single reasonable schedule of punishments designed to produce the greatest happiness for the greatest number.

Where the legislators lacked enough facts to make a sensible decision, instead of digging around in their law books for precedents and corollary cases, they could go out and collect some facts to settle the matter. Here is another selection from Bentham's *Principles* which shows how he hoped to use the Greatest Happiness Principle in practice:

1. The general object which all laws have, or ought to have, in common, is to augment the total happiness of the community; and therefore, in the first place, to exclude, as far as may be, every thing that tends to subtract from that happiness: in other words, to exclude mischief.

2. But all punishment is mischief: all punishment in itself is evil. Upon the principle of utility, if it ought at all to be admitted, it ought only to be admitted in as far as it promises to exclude some greater evil.

3. It is plain, therefore, that in the following cases punishment ought not to be inflicted.

1. Where it is *groundless*; where there is no mischief for it to prevent: the act not being mischievous upon the whole.

2. Where it must be *inefficacious*: where it cannot act so as to prevent the mischief.

3. Where it is *unprofitable*, or too *expensive*; where the mischief it would produce would be greater than what it prevented.

4. Where it is *needless*: where the mischief may be prevented, or cease of itself, without it: that is, at a cheaper rate. . . .

CASES WHERE PUNISHMENT IS UNPROFITABLE

These are,

1. Where, on the one hand, the nature of the offence, on the other hand, that of the punishment, are, *in the ordinary state of things*, such, that when compared together, the evil of the latter will turn out to be greater than that of the former.

Now the evil of the punishment divides itself into four branches, by which so many different sets of persons are affected. 1. The evil of *coercion* or *restraint*: or the pain which it gives a man not to be able to do the act, whatever it be, which by the apprehension of the punishment he is deterred from doing. This is felt by those by whom the law is *observed*. 2. The evil of *apprehension*: or the pain which a man, who has exposed himself to punishment, feels at the thoughts of undergoing it. This is felt by those by whom the law has been *broken*, and who feel themselves in *danger* of its being executed upon them. 3. The evil of *sufferance*: or the pain which a man feels, in virtue of the punishment itself, from the time when he begins to undergo it.

This is felt by those by whom the law is broken, and upon whom it comes actually to be executed. 4. The pain of sympathy, and the other *derivative* evils resulting to the persons who are in *connection* with the several classes of original sufferers just mentioned. Now of these four lots of evil, the first will be greater or less, according to the nature of the act from which the party is restrained: the second and third according to the nature of the punishment which stands annexed to that offence.

On the other hand, as to the evil of the offence, this will also, of course, be greater or less, according to the nature of each offence. The proportion between the one evil and the other will therefore be different in the case of each particular offence. The cases, therefore, where punishment is unprofitable on this ground, can by no other means be discovered, than by an examination of each particular offence; which is what will be the business of the body of the work.

2. Where, although in the *ordinary state* of things, the evil resulting from the punishment is not greater than the benefit which is likely to result from the force with which it operates, during the same space of time, towards the excluding the evil of the offence, yet it may have been rendered so by the influence of some *occasional circumstances*. In the number of these circumstances may be, 1. The multitude of delinquents at a particular juncture; being such as would increase, beyond the ordinary measure, the *quantum* of the second and third lots, and thereby also of a part of the fourth lot, in the evil of the punishment. 2. The extraordinary value of the services of some one delinquent; in the case where the effect of the punishment would be to deprive the community of the benefit of those services. 3. The displeasure of the *people*; that is, of an indefinite number of the members of the *same* community, in cases where (owing to the influence of some occasional incident) they happen to conceive, that the offence or the offender ought not to be punished at all, or at least ought not to be punished in the way in question. 4. The displeasure of *foreign powers*; that is, of the governing body, or a considerable number of the members of some *foreign* community or communities, with which the community in question, is connected.

JEREMY BENTHAM,
An Introduction to the Principles of Morals and Legislation

Utilitarianism has probably had more words written about it than all the other moral theories put together. It is a clear, simple, natural-sounding moral philosophy, and it has a thousand things wrong with it as a theory! That is a perfect formula for a philosophical argument. Two sorts of objections turn up over and over again in philosophical discussions. First, critics say that although utilitarianism looks clear and simple, it is actually so confused that we can't tell exactly what it says. And second, these same critics argue that, even after we have decided what utilitarianism says, we find that it tells us to do things that most of us would consider deeply immoral. Let us take a look at both of these objections.

What does utilitarianism say? Very simple: maximize happiness. But what exactly does that mean? The most natural answer is, add up all the pleasure experienced by all the people in the world, subtract all the pain they suffer, and that is the total. Then anything that increases the total is good, anything that decreases it is bad, and if two actions promise to increase the total, the one that offers a bigger increase is just that much better. What could be clearer?

Ah well. A little philosophy teaches us that a trap very often lurks in even the simplest-looking statement. If *total* happiness is all that counts, then a world with a *billion* marginally happy people will be morally better than a world with a *million* extremely happy people. The point is that if the very happy people are only five hundred times happier than the marginally happy people, then one billion times the small happiness in the first world will be a bigger total than one million times the tremendous happiness in the second world. Something is obviously wrong with that conclusion. In an already overcrowded world, it makes no sense to go on increasing the population as long as each additional person can be said to experience a slight balance of pleasure over pain. Surely Bentham wasn't merely arguing for a population explosion.

So maybe what he really meant was to maximize the *average* happiness experienced by the people already on this earth. That makes a good deal more sense. A world of a million very happy people is obviously preferable to a world of a billion marginally happy people, because in the first world, the *level* of happiness—in other words, the average—is higher. And it is the level of happiness we are really interested in.

But once again, serious problems arise. Suppose we can make some people very happy indeed by making other people miserable. That isn't an implausible hypothesis at all. Slavery is a social system which lays the burden of work and suffering on one group—the slaves—so that another group—the masters—can lead easy, comfortable lives. (So is capitalism, but we shall get to that in the next chapter.) Is Bentham really in favor of slavery?

Bentham has an answer, of sorts. His principle, he claims, calls for "the greatest happiness of all those whose interest is in question." Because everyone (even a slave) is somone whose interest is in question, it follows that utilitarianism calls for the greatest possible happiness for everyone, not just the greatest happiness for the slave-owners, or the capitalists, or the rulers. Now the trouble with this interpretation of the Principle of Utility is that on closer examination, it turns out not to be any sort of rule at all. The proof for this is a trifle technical, involving as it does the mathematical theorem that in general two or more independent functions cannot be maximized simultaneously. But the real point—if that last sentence hasn't caused you all to close your books—is rather simple.

Sometimes, life offers me a way to make everybody happier at the same time, and obviously when a chance like that comes along, I take it. Too often, life offers me a way to make everybody unhappier at the same time, and if I have any sense at all, I stay away from chances like that. But most of the time, what I do will make some people happier and other people unhappier. Remember the young man trying to decide whether to leave his parents? His first choice, to stay home, makes his parents happier and him unhappier. His second choice, to leave, makes him happier and his parents unhappier. There just isn't any way to make all of them happier at the same time. That is precisely why it is a hard case. Now, we don't need Bentham to tell us what to do on those rare occasions when we can make everyone happier simultaneously. But utilitarianism is supposed to give us a rule, a method, for handling just the hard-to-decide cases in which one person's happiness has to be balanced off against another person's unhappiness. Plausible as "the greatest happiness for the greatest number" sounds, it doesn't work out in practice to be a rule that is going to settle any hard cases for us.

Suppose we go back therefore to the notion of the greatest average happiness. (Notice, by the way, that if you keep the population stable, greatest average happiness is exactly equal to greatest total happiness, so that is probably what Bentham had in mind.) How does that stand up as a rule for deciding what to do? At least it is unambiguous; if we have enough information to predict the outcomes of our actions, then we can add up the pleasures, subtract the pains, divide by the total population, and get some sort of average. But now we run into the second sort of objection to utilitarianism—namely that it tells us to do things that seem immoral.

Once again, the problem is making some people suffer so that others may be happy. Let me sketch out a bizarre example that will help to make this point. Suppose Americans, like the ancient Romans, positively enjoyed watching people being tortured. (Naturally, such an assumption is totally contrary to the real facts, because American taste in movies, television shows, and novels shows that we are all kindly, peace-loving, sympathetic creatures who hate the sight of violence!) Now Bentham will obviously believe that torture is an evil to the person who suffers it, for torture is painful, and pain is evil. But the pleasure that a group of sadists get from watching the torture is good, for pleasure, says Bentham, is good. So for a utilitarian, torture can be justified if and only if the total pleasure produced outweighs the total pain produced, including side effects, long-run effects, and so forth. What is more, if torture produces, in total and on balance, greater happiness than any other alternative open to us, then it is the positively right thing to do, according to utilitarianism.

We shall therefore institute a new TV show called "Torture of the Week." This is a live show in which real victims really do get tortured. (Sadists get little or no pleasure from watching simulated torture.) The victims are simply snatched off the street by force (no one except a masochist is going to offer himself as a victim, and real sadists don't enjoy watching masochists undergo torture). According to utilitarianism, if there are enough viewers who are ecstatic at the sight of this torture, then their pleasure must outweigh the pain suffered by the victim. And if no other show on television has anything resembling its high ratings, then we can assume that putting on the torture show is not only justified, but positively morally obligatory!

Just to handle an obvious objection, let us also assume that a board of social psychologists concludes that the torture show does not increase the probability of violent crime in the society. Indeed, it may even decrease such crime, by offering an outlet for sadistic desires. In short, assume that from any point of view, this torture show meets the criterion of the Principle of Utility.

What is wrong with this proposal? Don't tell me that there aren't enough people around who would enjoy the show. The point of the example was to show that according to utilitarianism the show *would* be right if there *were* such people in America. Besides, we could always increase the pleasure product by beaming the show overseas so that sadists all over the world could watch it. And don't tell me that the pain of the victim's suffering outweighs the pleasure of millions of sadistic viewers. That is just plain implausible, and what is more, I can always adjust the total torture inflicted on the victim downward until the pleasure of the viewers outweighs it.

No, what really convinces me that my proposal is immoral (and I suspect many of you feel the same way) is that society has *no right* to make one man or woman suffer for the mere amusement of others. This is one of those cases, something inside me says, where adding up pleasures and pains is the wrong way to find out what we ought to do. If America's sadists have to suffer the pain and frustration of losing their favorite show, then so much the worse for them!

We have opened up a very large and complicated subject with this appeal to the notion of *rights*, and a few words can only begin to indicate some of its ins and outs. Nevertheless, let's explore it for a bit, just to see what makes Bentham's pleasure-pain calculus seem such an inadequate expression of our moral convictions. To begin with, we must not go overboard and say that society never has the right to derive benefits from the suffering of one of its members. Leaving aside obvious but controversial cases like wars, we can simply recall that every time a major bridge or tunnel is built, several workmen lose their lives. It may seem callous when we put it into words, but all of us employ a rough utilitarian calculation in judging the social desirability of large-scale public works. We try hard to minimize the loss of life in heavy construction, but we refuse to bring it to a dead halt simply because we know that men lose their lives on the job. If a project is going to cost hundreds of lives, we will probably veto it. If only a few men are likely to be killed, we will give it the go-ahead. Aren't we weighing one man's life against the convenience of the motorists who will use the bridge? How does that differ from weighing the pain of the victim against the pleasure of the sadistic viewers?

Well, one answer is that the construction men choose voluntarily to work on the bridge, knowing that it is a risky job, whereas the torture victim is forced into his role. That certainly is part of the difference, for I imagine we would take a *somewhat* different view of the show if we knew that the victims were volunteers.

But there still seem to be other differences. The motorist benefits from the suffering of the construction worker, to be sure. But that suffering isn't the object of his pleasure. The sadist, on the other hand, takes pleasure in the victim's pain. Now, it seems to me that there are some pleasures that are evil in and of themselves. They are bad pleasures, pleasures which people should not have; and pleasure taken in the pain of another person is one of those evil pleasures. So the torture example suggests, at least to me, that Bentham's original assumption was wrong. Not all pleasures are equal, save for quantity or intensity. And "good" does not simply mean "pleasant." So when we perform Bentham's social arithmetic, adding up pleasures and pains in order to evaluate a social policy, we most certainly ought not to put the sadist's pleasure on the plus side. He doesn't have a right to that pleasure, and if it is to be weighed at all, it ought to be put on the negative side with the pains. (Needless to say, there may be some pains which ought to go on the positive side! As you can see, this subject gets more and more complicated the deeper into it you go.)

It may even be, as Immanuel Kant thought, that there are some considerations more important than pleasure and pain—considerations of justice and freedom. Kant would argue that the torture show degrades both the victim and the viewers, that it treats them—in his famous phrase—as means merely and not as ends in themselves.

But when all is said and done, when examples like my torture show have been brought forward to refute utilitarianism, when the unclarities in the very meaning of the principle have been exposed to view, there still remains a natural appeal of Bentham's theory that will not go away. In

the next chapter, when we meet John Stuart Mill, Bentham's most famous
follower, we shall try once again to discover the kernel of truth that seems
to lie inside the moral philosophy of utilitarianism.

V   The Greeks spoke of the search for the principles of the good life. The
Romans had a phrase, *mens sana in corpore sano*—a sound mind in a
sound body. Psychoanalysts today talk about an integrated ego. Marx
wrote of "alienation" and a future of "unalienated labor." The idea is
essentially the same in each case, even though the emphasis, the underlying theory, or the viewpoint differs. For ages, men and women have been
seeking for a style of life and spirit that achieves a wholeness, an integration, an authenticity of mind and body, of reason, passion, and desire.
These days, the search is left to psychologists and the religious, at least in
England and America, but in the tradition of Western thought, it is philosophers who have given the most sustained and thoughtful attention to
the search for the good life.

Everyone who has reflected for even a short while on the problem of
achieving an integrated, fulfilled, virtuous life agrees that the key to a
solution lies in the discovery of the proper internal order of the self itself
(what the Greeks call the "soul" or *psyche*). And needless to say, there
are almost as many theories about the precise nature of that desirable
inner order as there are writers on the subject. But on one fundamental
issue, the philosophers of the good life divide into two distinct camps.
One group, which includes Stoics like Marcus Aurelius, claims that inner
peace and harmony can be achieved regardless of the character of the
society in which we live, regardless of the external circumstances of peace
or war, tyranny or justice, health or disease. The other group emphasizes
the interplay between the individual personality and the larger society,
claiming that not even a wise man can be truly happy save in a truly just
and virtuous society. In this latter category we find Plato, Aristotle, Karl
Marx, and such modern psychological theorists as Erich Fromm and Erik
Erikson. You have already had an opportunity to read a bit of what
Marcus Aurelius wrote about the good life. In this last section, we shall
explore the view of Plato and others that the inner harmony of the self
must be integrated with a proper order of society before a truly good life
can be achieved.

In philosophy, we return to the same great books again and again. In
Chapter One, you read a selection from an early section of Plato's immortal dialogue, the *Republic*. Now we shall jump ahead more than a
hundred pages to the point at which Plato pulls together the long argument he has been developing. The official subject of the *Republic* is a

*"I roamed the world trying to find myself,
and then I came home and discovered happiness
right here in my own back yard."**

Not all successful businessmen feel their
lives have been wasted!

search for a definition of "justice," a word to which Plato gives a broader
meaning than we do today. Plato suggests two analogies or comparisons
as aids in discovering the nature of justice, or true morality. The first
analogy is between the soul (i.e., the personality) and the body. He argues
that we can speak of a healthy body and also of a healthy soul, of a diseased body and also of a diseased soul. Health of the body rests on a proper
harmony or order of the bodily elements, and health of the soul in like
manner consists of the correct ordering of the psychic elements. In this
Dialogue, Plato distinguishes three functional parts of the soul. (I say "in
this Dialogue" because Plato didn't really have a fully worked out theory
of psychology, and in other Dialogues he divided the human personality
up in other ways. Don't just memorize "the parts of the soul in Plato"—
Try to see what he is driving at, and put his thought into your own
words if you can.) The three elements are reason, or the power to deliberate, compare alternatives, suppress unwise impulses, and make sensible
choices; the "spirited element," or the aggressive, warlike, wilful part of
one's personality; and appetite or desire. Each of these elements has a role

*Drawing by R. Taylor; © 1957 The New Yorker Magazine, Inc.

69

to play in the healthy, virtuous soul, but each must learn its proper function and perform it willingly and in harmony with the other elements. Reason must rule, governing the spirited element and directing its aggression in wise, nondestructive ways. The healthy, necessary appetites must be regulated by reason and satisfied in the proper proportion and to the appropriate degree. Too much indulgence of one or many desires may produce superficial and short-lived pleasure, but in the end it causes inner conflict and unhappiness. A well-integrated soul is a smoothly functioning whole in which each element performs its proper function and all together maintain balance, health, and true happiness.

The second of Plato's analogies is between the individual soul and the society as a whole. Just as there are several elements in the soul with special functions and a just order of subordination to one another, so there are several classes of citizens in the society with special functions and a proper social relationship to one another. The wisest citizens must rule in society, as reason does in the soul, for they possess at one and the same time the knowledge of what is truly good for the society and the rational self-control to resist the temptation of harmful desires.

In this passage from the *Republic*, Socrates is summarizing his argument. Thrasymachus and most of the others have dropped out of the conversation, and there remain only two young men, Glaucon and Adeimantus (in real life, Plato's older brothers). They are really yes-men for Socrates, and so the passage is a dialogue in name only.

And so, after a stormy passage, we have reached the land. We are fairly agreed that the same three elements exist alike in the state and in the individual soul.

That is so.

Does it not follow at once that state and individual will be wise or brave by virtue of the same element in each and in the same way? Both will possess in the same manner any quality that makes for excellence.

That must be true.

Then it applies to justice: we shall conclude that a man is just in the same way that a state was just. And we have surely not forgotten that justice in the state meant that each of the three orders in it was doing its own proper work. So we may henceforth bear in mind that each one of us likewise will be a just person, fulfilling his proper function, only if the several parts of our nature fulfil theirs.

Certainly.

And it will be the business of reason to rule with wisdom and forethought on behalf of the entire soul; while the spirited element ought to act as its subordinate and ally. The two will be brought into accord, as we said earlier, by that combination of mental and bodily training which will tune up one string of the instrument and relax the other, nourishing the reasoning part on the study of noble literature and allaying the other's wildness by harmony and rhythm. When both have been thus nurtured and trained to know their own true functions, they must be set in command over the appetites, which form the greater part of each man's soul and are by nature insatiably covetous. They must keep watch lest this part, by battening on the pleasures that are called bodily, should grow so great and powerful that it will no longer keep to its own work, but will try to enslave the others and usurp a dominion to which it has no right, thus turning the whole of life upside down. At the same time, those two together will be the best of guardians for the entire soul and for the body against all enemies from without: the one will take counsel, while the other will do battle, following its ruler's commands and by its own bravery giving effect to the ruler's designs.

Yes, that is all true.

And so we call an individual brave in virtue of this spirited part of his nature, when, in spite of pain or pleasure, it holds fast to the injunctions of reason about what he ought or ought not to be afraid of.

True.

And wise in virtue of that small part which rules and issues these injunctions, possessing as it does the knowledge of what is good for each of the three elements and for all of them in common.

Certainly.

And, again, temperate by reason of the unanimity and concord of all three, when there is no internal conflict between the ruling element and its two subjects, but all are agreed that reason should be ruler.

Yes, that is an exact account of temperance, whether in the state or in the individual.

Finally, a man will be just by observing the principle we have so often stated.

Necessarily.

Now is there any indistinctness in our vision of justice, that might make it seem somehow different from what we found it to be in the state?

I don't think so.

Because, if we have any lingering doubt, we might make sure by comparing it with some commonplace notions. Suppose, for instance, that a sum of money were entrusted to our state or to an individual of corresponding character and training, would anyone imagine that such a person would be specially likely to embezzle it?

No.

And would he not be incapable of sacrilege and theft, or of treachery to friend or country; never false to an oath or any other compact; the last to be guilty of adultery or of neglecting parents or the due service of the gods?

Yes.

And the reason for all this is that each part of his nature is exercising its proper function, of ruling or of being ruled.

Yes, exactly.

Are you satisfied, then, that justice is the power which produces states or individuals of whom that is true, or must we look further?

There is no need; I am quite satisfied.

And so our dream has come true—I mean the inkling we had that, by some happy chance, we had lighted upon a rudimentary form of justice from the very moment when we set about founding our commonwealth. Our principle that the born shoemaker or carpenter had better stick to his trade turns out to have been an adumbration of justice; and that is why it has helped us. But in reality justice, though evidently analogous to this principle, is not a matter of external behaviour, but of the inward self and of attending to all that is, in the fullest sense, a man's proper concern. The just man does not allow the several elements in his soul to usurp one another's functions; he is indeed one who sets his house in order, by self-mastery and discipline coming to be at peace with himself, and bringing into tune those three parts, like the terms in the proportion of a musical scale, the highest and lowest notes and the mean between them, with all the intermediate intervals. Only when he has linked these parts together in well-tempered harmony and has made himself one man instead of many, will he be ready to go about whatever he may have to do, whether it be making money and satisfying bodily wants, or business transactions, or the affairs of state. In all these fields when he speaks of just and honourable conduct, he will mean the behaviour that helps to produce and to preserve this habit of mind; and by wisdom he will mean the knowledge which presides over such conduct. Any action which tends to break down this habit will be for him unjust; and the notions governing it he will call ignorance and folly.

That is perfectly true, Socrates.

Good, said I. I believe we should not be thought altogether mistaken, if we claimed to have discovered the just man and the just state, and wherein their justice consists.

Indeed we should not.

Shall we make that claim, then?

Yes, we will.

So be it, said I. Next, I suppose, we have to consider injustice.

Evidently.

This must surely be a sort of civil strife among the three elements, whereby they usurp and encroach upon one another's functions and some one part of the soul rises up in rebellion against the whole, claiming a supremacy to which it has no right because its nature fits it only to be the servant of the ruling principle. Such turmoil and aberration we shall, I think, identify with injustice, intemperance, cowardice, ignorance, and in a word with all wickedness.

Exactly.

And now that we know the nature of justice and injustice, we can be equally clear about what is meant by acting justly and again by unjust action and wrongdoing.

How do you mean?

Plainly, they are exactly analogous to those wholesome and unwholesome activities which respectively produce a healthy or unhealthy condition in the body; in the same way just and unjust conduct produce a just or unjust character. Justice is produced in the soul, like health in the body, by establishing the elements concerned in their natural relations of control and subordination, whereas injustice is like disease and means that this natural order is inverted.

Quite so.

It appears, then, that virtue is as it were the health and comeliness and well-being of the soul, as wickedness is disease, deformity, and weakness.

True.

And also that virtue and wickedness are brought about by one's way of life, honourable or disgraceful.

That follows.

So now it only remains to consider which is the more profitable course: to do right and live honourably and be just, whether or not anyone knows what manner of man you are, or to do wrong and be unjust, provided that you can escape the chastisement which might make you a better man.

But really, Socrates, it seems to me ridiculous to ask that question now that the nature of justice and injustice has been brought to light. People think that all the luxury and wealth and power in the world cannot make life worth living when the bodily constitution is going to rack and ruin; and are we to believe that, when the very principle whereby we live is deranged and corrupted, life will be worth living so long as a man can do as he will, and wills to do anything rather than to free himself from vice and wrongdoing and to win justice and virtue?

Yes, I replied, it is a ridiculous question.

PLATO, *The Republic*

Plato's insight into the human condition, although profound, was by no means unique. Halfway around the world, in the already highly developed civilization of China, very similar ideas were becoming a part of the intellectual currency of educated men. The greatest of the Chinese sages, Confucius, actually died ten years before Socrates was born. In these few short selections from his sayings, we find a conception of the harmony between the well-ordered individual and the well-ordered society which Socrates would have welcomed, had he been able somehow to communicate with his fellow philosopher from distant culture.

The principles of the higher education consist in preserving man's clear character, in giving new life to the people, and in dwelling (or resting) in perfection, or the ultimate good. Only after knowing the goal of perfection where one should dwell, can one have a definite purpose in life. Only after having a definite purpose in life can one achieve calmness of mind. Only after having achieved calmness of mind, can one have peaceful repose. Only after having peaceful repose can one begin to think. Only after one has learned to think, can one achieve knowledge. There are a foundation and a superstructure in the constitution of things, and a beginning and an end in the course of events. Therefore to know the proper sequence or relative order of things is the beginning of wisdom.

CONFUCIUS, or K'ung Fu-tse, (c. 551–479 B.C.) is the greatest moral teacher of the classical Chinese tradition. He died ten years before Socrates was born, and though there is no evidence of any connection between classical China and classical Greece, the similarities in their teachings is striking. Like Socrates, Confucius focuses his attention on the achievement of an inner emotional balance or order, in which reason gently guides the passions. Inner psychic order is then reflected in an outward poise, maturity, and balance which is the mark of true happiness. The deeply conservative leaning of Confucius' thought has led Mao Tse-tung and the Chinese communist regime to attack his reputation and reject his teachings.

The ancients who wished to preserve the fresh or clear character of the people of the world, would first set about ordering their national life. Those who wished to order their national life, would first set about regulating their family life. Those who wished to regulate their family life would set about cultivating their personal life. Those who wished to cultivate their personal lives, would first set about setting their hearts right. Those who wished to set their hearts right would first set about making their wills sincere. Those who wished to make their wills sincere would first set about achieving true knowledge. The achieving of true knowledge depended upon the investigation of things. When things are investigated, then true knowledge is achieved; when true knowledge is achieved, then the will becomes sincere; when the will is sincere, then the heart is set right (or then the mind sees right); when the heart is set right, then the personal life is cultivated; when the personal life is cultivated, then the family life is regulated; when the family life is regulated, then the national life is orderly; and when the national life is orderly, then there is peace in this world. From the emperor down to the common men, all must regard the cultivation of the personal life as the root or foundation. There is never an orderly upshoot or superstructure when the root or foundation is disorderly. There is never yet a tree whose trunk is slim and slender and whose top branches are thick and heavy. This is called "to know the root or foundation of things."

CONFUCIUS, *The Higher Education*

For the first two millennia of Western philosophy, the wise understanding of the human condition was the province of philosophers and poets. In the past three-quarters of a century, however, their intuitive insight has been supplemented, though not supplanted, by the systematic scientific investigations of countless theorists of human personality. Plato's brilliant recognition of the analogy between the health of the body and the health of the mind has been embodied in a branch of medicine called psychiatry, whose practitioners study the forms, causes, symptoms, and cures for what we now routinely call "mental illness." With psychiatrists, as with philosophers, there is a fundamental split between those who examine the individual psyche in separation from its social setting and those who study the connections between individual mental health or illness and the network of social and institutional relationships which surround the patient.

Sigmund Freud (1856–1939), the founder of modern psychoanalytic theory and practice, tended toward the first method of investigation. Although he wrote several provocative essays on the psychic roots of social phenomena, his primary interest was in the inner dynamics of the psyche itself. Among all those who have followed Freud's lead in developing a science of psychiatry, perhaps no figure comes closer to Plato both in spirit and in fineness of sensibility than the contemporary analyst, historian, author, and philosopher Erik H. Erikson. Erikson has sought to build on Freud's investigation of the infantile stages of personality development by analyzing the later stages through which each of us passes in coming either well or badly to maturity and old age. It was Erikson who actually coined the now familiar phrase "identity crisis" in an essay on the emotional upheaval that so many young men and women go through in late adolescence and early adulthood. But Erikson was also interested in the continuing development of personality later in life. He discovered from his clinical practice with patients of all ages that as an individual grew through infancy, childhood, adolescence, young adulthood, mature adulthood, and old age, he or she faced a series of turning points, or crises. At each stage, the individual might resolve the crisis successfully and grow into a stronger, more fulfilled person, or fail to handle the crisis well and bear ever after the scars of that failure. In old age, those who have lived the cycle of childhood, adulthood, and maturity well achieve thereby an inner harmony which Erikson calls "ego integrity." It is very much like what Plato calls wisdom and what Confucius calls true manhood. This ego integrity gives meaning to the life that has been lived, and permits the individual to face his own impending death with acceptance, dignity, and pride. Here is Erikson's description of this final stage of the life cycle. Erikson speaks of a "wise Indian, a true gentleman, and a mature peasant" recognizing in one another the property of ego integrity. I like to think that Socrates and Confucius, could they meet, would find the same spiritual kinship.

> Only in him who in some way has taken care of things and people and has adapted himself to the triumphs and disappointments adherent to

being the originator of others or the generator of products and ideas—
only in him may gradually ripen the fruit of these seven stages. I
know no better word for it than ego integrity. Lacking a clear definition, I shall point to a few constituents of this state of mind. It is the
ego's accrued assurance of its proclivity for order and meaning. It is a
post-narcissistic love of the human ego—not of the self—as an experience which conveys some world order and spiritual sense, no matter
how dearly paid for. It is the acceptance of one's one and only life
cycle as something that had to be and that, by necessity, permitted of
no substitutions: it thus means a new, a different love of one's parents.
It is a comradeship with the ordering ways of distant times and different pursuits, as expressed in the simple products and sayings of such
times and pursuits. Although aware of the relativity of all the various
life styles which have given meaning to human striving, the possessor
of integrity is ready to defend the dignity of his own life style against
all physical and economic threats. For he knows that an individual life
is the accidental coincidence of but one life cycle with but one seg-
ment of history; and that for him all human integrity stands or falls
with the one style of integrity of which he partakes. The style of integrity developed by his culture or civilization thus becomes the
"patrimony of his soul," the seal of his moral paternity of himself. . . .
In such final consolidation, death loses its sting.

The lack or loss of this accrued ego integration is signified by fear
of death: the one and only life cycle is not accepted as the ultimate
of life. Despair expresses the feeling that the time is now short, too
short for the attempt to start another life and to try out alternate roads
to integrity. Disgust hides despair, if often only in the form of "a
thousand little disgusts" which do not add up to one big remorse. . . .

Each individual, to become a mature adult, must to a sufficient
degree develop all the ego qualities mentioned, so that a wise Indian,
a true gentleman, and a mature peasant share and recognize in one
another the final stage of integrity. But each cultural entity, to develop the particular style of integrity suggested by its historical place,
utilizes a particular combination of these conflicts, along with specific
provocations and prohibitions of infantile sexuality. Infantile conflicts
become creative only if sustained by the firm support of cultural
institutions and of the special leader classes representing them. In
order to approach or experience integrity, the individual must know
how to be a follower of image bearers in religion and in politics, in
the economic order and in technology, in aristocratic living and in the
arts and sciences. Ego integrity, therefore, implies an emotional integration which permits participation by followership as well as acceptance of the responsibility of leadership.

Webster's Dictionary is kind enough to help us complete this outline in a circular fashion. Trust (the first of our ego values) is here
defined as "the assured reliance on another's integrity," the last of our

values. I suspect that Webster had business in mind rather than babies, credit rather than faith. But the formulation stands. And it seems possible to further paraphrase the relation of adult integrity and infantile trust by saying that healthy children will not fear life if their elders have integrity enough not to fear death.

ERIK H. ERICKSON, *Childhood and Society*

JOHN STUART MILL (1806–1873) was the most important English philosopher during the 125 years between the death of David Hume in 1776 and the turn of the twentieth century. Trained from his youth by his father, James Mill, to be a defender of the utilitarian doctrine of Bentham and the Philosophical Radicals, Mill devoted his early years to an unquestioning support of his father's principles. After a severe emotional crisis in his twenties, Mill gave up the narrow doctrine of Bentham, and became instead an eclectic synthesizer of the views of such diverse schools as the French utopian socialists and the German romantics.

Mill was active in the public life of England, first as an officer (and eventually head) of the great East India Company, a principal instrument of English economic expansion during the nineteenth century, and later as a member of parliament. In addition to the books on moral and political topics which have established him as one of the leading spokesmen of liberalism, Mill also wrote a number of highly influential works on logic and the theory of knowledge, including a *System of Logic* and *An Examination of Sir William Hamilton's Philosophy.*

As a young man, Mill befriended Mrs. Harriet Taylor, with whom he maintained a close relationship until, after her husband's death, they were married in 1851. Mill believed Mrs. Taylor to be an enormously gifted thinker, and he was convinced that she would have made her mark on English letters had it not been for the powerful prejudice against women that operated then, as it does now. His relationship with Mrs. Taylor made Mill sensitive to the discrimination against women, with the result that he became one of the few philosophers to speak out on the matter. His discussion of the problem appears in a late work, *The Subjection of Women*, published four years before his death.

Social Philosophy 3

Some, it is said, are born great; some achieve greatness; and some have greatness thrust upon them. To that saying we might add, and some are trained from birth for greatness. Of all the philosophers who have won for themselves a place in the ranks of the great, none was more carefully groomed, schooled, prodded, and pushed into greatness than the English empiricist and utilitarian thinker of the nineteenth century, John Stuart Mill. Never has a child been given less chance to "do his own thing," and never has a man defended with greater eloquence the right of every man and woman to be left free from the intrusions of well-meaning parents, friends, and governments. Though it would be wrong to reduce Mill's mature philosophical views to the level of mere psychological reflections on his childhood experiences, the temptation is irresistible to see in his adult career a reaction to the pressures of his youth.

Mill was born in 1806, at a time when a strong movement was developing to reform the political life of England. The intellectual leader of the movement was the same Jeremy Bentham whose utilitarian doctrines you encountered in Chapter Two. We took our first look at utilitarianism in its guise as a moral philosophy designed to lay down a principle for calculating what actions are right for an individual facing a decision. But as your

79

reading on the reform of the penal code makes clear, Bentham's primary interest was in social issues, not in private morality. He conceived the Principle of Utility as a weapon in the attack on the traditions, privileges, laws, and perquisites of the English upper classes. So long as courts and governments could hide behind precedent, or immemorial custom, it was extremely hard to force them to admit the injustices and irrationalities of the social system. But once those ancient customs were put to the test of the Principle of Utility, it was immediately clear how badly they failed to produce the greatest happiness for the greatest number.

JAMES MILL (1773–1836) was a close friend and colleague of Jeremy Bentham, the founder of the doctrine known as utilitarianism. Mill led a group of English political reformers who believed that social justice and wise government required a broadening of the franchise to include the industrial middle classes in England, and a thoroughgoing overhaul of the antiquated laws and governmental machinery which, in Mill's day, strongly favored the landed interests in England. Mill and the Philosophical Radicals, as his circle of supporters were called, succeeded in generating enough support to carry through a number of major reforms, culminating in the sweeping Reform Bill of 1832. Mill's son, the great John Stuart Mill, had this to say about his father's position in *The Autobiography of John Stuart Mill:*

> So complete was my father's reliance on the influence of reason over the minds of mankind, whenever it is allowed to reach them, that he felt as if all would be gained if the whole population were taught to read, if all sorts of opinions were allowed to be addressed to them by word and by writing, and if by means of the suffrage they could nominate a legislature to give effect to the opinions they adopted.

One of Bentham's close friends and associates in the reform movement was a philosopher named James Mill; Mill was a thinker of considerable distinction, although he has long since been eclipsed by his more famous son. His writings on economics and moral philosophy erected a system, on Benthamite foundations, which served as a fortress from which the "philosophical radicals," as they were called, sallied forth to do battle with the last remnants of the aristocratic hosts. Shortly after the birth of his son John Stuart, James Mill met Bentham and joined forces with him. Mill decided to train his son up as a soldier in the reform movement, and no medieval squire ever had a more rigorous preparation for combat. Little John Stuart began studying Greek at the age of three. His father surrounded him with Latin-speaking servants so that by the age of eight he could dig into that other ancient tongue. Logic was young John Stuart's fare at twelve, to be followed shortly by the study of the new science of political economy. Formal religion was deliberately omitted from the curriculum, but the poor lad may be forgiven for having somewhat formed the notion that he was being raised an orthodox utilitarian.

By the time he reached adulthood, John Stuart Mill was a brilliant, finely honed logical weapon in the armory of his father's political battles. He wrote attacks on the antiquated legal and political institutions of England, defending his points with straight utilitarian dogma.

Not surprisingly, Mill finally broke under the strain of this rigid doctrinaire discipline. At the age of twenty, he suffered an internal emotional crisis, and began what was to be a lifelong reevaluation of the Benthamism of his father and his father's allies. Though it is always a mistake to sum up a great philosopher's work in a single phrase, we can get some general overview of Mill's subsequent intellectual development by saying that he spent his life struggling to broaden, deepen, and complicate the extremely simple philosophical theory into which he was initiated as a boy.

The doctrine of the reformers was clear, coherent, and attractively free from the mystifications which clouded the writings of the conservative defenders of the old order. As Bentham had laid it down, the only good in this world is pleasure, the only evil pain. Human actions are goal-oriented, purposeful actions. Our desires determine what objects or experiences we choose as our goals, and reason aids us in discovering the most efficient path to those goals. The question, What ought I to do? is either a question of goals—What should I desire?—or else it is a question of means—How can I reach my goal most easily? But there is no point in disputing about desires. We either want something or we don't, and whatever pleasure we experience comes to us as the result of satisfying a desire. So the only questions worth debating are factual questions of means: is this the best way to satisfy my desire, or would that way be quicker, cheaper, easier?

If abstruse questions of natural rights and absolute goodness are to be disputed, then common men and women will be hard put to keep up with trained philosophers, lawyers, or theologians. But if Bentham is right, then the fundamental moral question is simply, Does it feel good? Is this experience pleasurable? Now each one of us is the best judge of whether he is feeling pleasure or pain, so utilitarianism has the effect of eliminating expertise and putting all men and women on an equal footing in moral debates. What is more, Bentham insisted, the only morally relevant distinction between pleasures and pains is a quantitative distinction of more and less. As Bentham put it, pushpin (a child's game) is as good as poetry, so long as it gives you an equal amount of pleasure. This doctrine too had the effect of leveling the social distinctions between the high- and low-born, for it had been easy for the cultivated upper classes to insist that they were privy to joys and sorrows too refined for the lower classes even to imagine. In these ways—by making each person the judge of his own happiness and by making quantity the only significant variable—utilitarianism provided a philosophical justification for a democratic, social program.

All persons are basically prudent, rationally self-interested actors. That is to say, each of us seeks to satisfy his desires in the most extensive and pleasurable way, and each of us uses the resources available to him— money, talent, power—in the most efficient manner possible. But there are two great obstacles to fully rational self-interested action. The first of these, the target of the eighteenth-century enlightenment, is superstition. So long as people falsely believe that they have no right to satisfy their desires; so long as religion, or ancient custom, or class distinctions inhibit common men and women from using the resources they have for the achievement of their own happiness; so long, in short, as the reasoning power of the mind is clouded by fear, awe, and false belief, then just so long will the injustices and inequalities of society continue. The second obstacle is the unavoidable ignorance, which even the enlightened man or woman must suffer, of the facts of science and public affairs, ignorance of the most efficient means for pursuing legitimate satisfactions.

Education was the weapon utilitarians aimed at these twin enemies, superstition and ignorance. Education was to perform two tasks: first, to liberate enslaved minds from the superstitious religious and political dogmas of the past; and second, to introduce the liberated minds to the facts of science and society. An educated population could then be counted on to support wise public policy, for such policy would aim at the greatest happiness of the greatest number, and that simply meant their own happiness as private citizens. Thus utilitarianism combined a psychological theory of individual motivation with a moral theory of the good and an educational theory of enlightenment to produce what we today call a political theory of liberal democracy.

It remains to mention one last element of the utilitarian system, an element which may well have been the most important of all, namely the laissez-faire economic theory created by Adam Smith and David Ricardo and deployed by James Mill and his son in the great debates over public policy. This is not an economics textbook, and philosophy is hard enough all by itself, but at least a few words must be said about the laissez-faire theory in order to fill out Mill's position and set the stage for the powerful attacks which Karl Marx launched against it a very few years later.

The major fact of the end of the eighteenth century and the beginning of the nineteenth was, of course, the growth of mercantile and industrial capitalism. The key to the new capitalism was the systematic investment of accumulated wealth, or "capital," for the purpose of producing goods which could be sold at a profit in the marketplace. The individual who set the economic activity in motion was called an "entrepreneur," which is French for "undertaker" and means someone who undertakes to do something, not someone who buries someone (although critics of capitalism might have argued that there was indeed a connection between the two meanings). The capitalist undertook to rent the land, hire the labor, buy the raw materials, and bring together these factors of production in a process which resulted in finished goods. The goods were put on sale in a market where no law fixed the prices that must be paid or the profits that could be made. Adam Smith, in his famous treatise *The Wealth of Nations*, argued that if everyone were permitted to do the best he could for himself—worker, capitalist, merchant, and consumer—then the net result would be the most efficient use of the resources of the nation for the production of goods designed to satisfy human desires. The consumers would spend their money in the marketplace in such a way as to get the greatest pleasure for value. If one sort of product rose too high in price, they would shift to another, for paying all your money for a single piece of meat would be foolish when the same money could buy you fish, eggs, shoes, and a coat. The capitalists would pull their capital out of areas where too much was being produced, because as supply exceeded demand, they would be forced to drop their prices in order to unload their inventory, and profits would tumble. In the same way, if

ADAM SMITH (1723–1790) was born in Scotland at a time when that small country was one of the liveliest intellectual centers in Europe. Like his countryman, David Hume, Smith wrote on a wide variety of problems in what we would now call the social sciences. His masterwork was a long, difficult, revolutionary study of the foundations of economic activity in a free market capitalist economy, entitled *Inquiry into the Nature and Causes of the Wealth of Nations*. With this book, Smith created the field of economics, and laid the theoretical basis for the doctrine of laissez faire which still has wide support two centuries later. *The Wealth of Nations* was published in 1776, just at the time when the American colonies were declaring their independence of the English crown, and it is fitting that history should have linked these two events, for the Founding Fathers were deeply imbued with the laissez-faire spirit of individual freedom, minimal government, and the pursuit of rational self-interest.

there were customers clamoring for a commodity that wasn't being produced, they would bid up the price in the market, drive up profits in that branch of business, and attract profit-seeking capitalists who would open new factories to "capitalize" on the unsatisfied demand.

Since happiness is pleasure, and pleasure results from the satisfaction of desire, and consumers buy goods to satisfy desires, it follows that the capitalists trying to make a profit are at the same time actually working to make the consumers happy. They aren't *trying* to make them happy, of course! The capitalists, like all men and women, are rationally *self-*interested pleasure-maximizers. But the genius of the new capitalist free market system was precisely that each person, seeking only his own good, automatically advanced the good of others. Thus selfishness could be counted on to do rationally and efficiently what altruism never quite managed—namely, to produce the greatest happiness possible for the greatest number of people. Here is how Adam Smith puts it in a passage that is much quoted and copied. Smith is actually in the midst of a discussion of restrictions on imports, but the thesis he enunciates has a quite general application:

> But the annual revenue of every society is always precisely equal to the exchangeable value of the whole annual produce of its industry, or rather is precisely the same thing with that exchangeable value. As every individual, therefore, endeavours as much as he can both to employ his capital in the support of domestic industry, and so to direct that industry that its produce may be of the greatest value; every individual necessarily labours to render the annual revenue of the society as great as he can. He generally, indeed, neither intends to promote the public interest, nor knows how much he is promoting it. By preferring the support of domestic to that of foreign industry, he intends only his own security; and by directing that industry in such a manner as its produce may be of the greatest value, he intends only his own gain, and he is in this, as in many other cases, led by an invisible hand to promote an end which was no part of his intention. Nor is it always the worse for the society that it was no part of it. By pursuing his own interest he frequently promotes that of the society more effectually than when he really intends to promote it. I have never known much good done by those who affected to trade for the public good. It is an affectation, indeed, not very common among merchants, and very few words need be employed in dissuading them from it.

ADAM SMITH, *The Wealth of Nations*

Mill read widely in authors whose views were far removed from those of Bentham and his father. He learned from the Romantic critics of the reform movement even as he sought to counter their arguments. He studied the writings of such acute conservative observers as Alexis de Tocqueville, and even absorbed the lessons of the French socialists, though he seems not to have read or appreciated the more powerful theoretical assault mounted by the great German socialist Karl Marx. The breadth of his learning and his personal dissatisfaction with the narrow dogma of his father led Mill to doubt or even to deny some of the central tenets of utilitarian philosophy and social policy. Nevertheless, to the end of his life, his mind remained trapped within the confines of the principles he had been taught as a youth.

In at least *three* important ways, Mill questioned the theses of the orthodox reform doctrine. First, he denied Bentham's egalitarian insistance that any pleasure, in and of itself, was as good as any other (which, as we have seen, was a roundabout way of saying that any man was as good as any other). As far back as Plato, philosophers had argued that some pleasures were simply finer, higher, morally better than other pleasures. Usually, as we might expect, they claimed that the pleasures of the mind were superior to the pleasures of the body. Bentham was prepared to admit that some pleasures were more intense, or more long-lasting, or had more pleasant after-effects than others. A quart of bad wine might give less pleasure than a sip of fine brandy. A night of drinking might be followed by such a horrendous morning after that the total experience would add up to a minus rather than a plus. Some pleasures, like some foods, might be acquired tastes, requiring knowledge and long practice before they could be properly appreciated. But after all this had been taken into account—and Bentham carefully did take it into account—utilitarianism still insisted that only quantity and not quality of pleasure mattered. Mill could not accept this teaching, fundamental though it was to the philosophy he had been trained to defend. He was stung by the critics of utilitarianism who made it out to be a brutish or degraded philosophy, a philosophy of the base appetites. In replying to their charge, he drew a distinction between higher and lower pleasures which fundamentally altered the significance and logical force of utilitarianism. Here is the passage, taken from an essay called "Utilitarianism" which Mill first published in a magazine and later as a short book:

> Now such a theory of life excites in many minds, and among them in some of the most estimable in feeling and purpose, inveterate dislike. To suppose that life has (as they express it) no higher end than pleasure—no better and nobler object of desire and pursuit—they designate as utterly mean and groveling, as a doctrine worthy only of swine, to whom the followers of Epicurus were, at a very early period, contemptuously likened; and modern holders of the doctrine are occa-

sionally made the subject of equally polite comparisons by its German, French, and English assailants.

When thus attacked, the Epicureans have always answered that it is not they, but their accusers, who represent human nature in a degrading light, since the accusation supposes human beings to be capable of no pleasures except those of which swine are capable. If this supposition were true, the charge could not be gainsaid, but would then be no longer an imputation; for if the sources of pleasure were precisely the same to human beings and to swine, the rule of life which is good enough for the one would be good enough for the other. The comparison of the Epicurean life to that of beasts is felt as degrading, precisely because a beast's pleasures do not satisfy a human being's conceptions of happiness. Human beings have faculties more elevated than the animal appetites and, when once made conscious of them, do not regard anything as happiness which does not include their gratification. . . .

. . . It is quite compatible with the principle of utility to recognize the fact that some kinds of pleasure are more desirable and more valuable than others. It would be absurd that, while in estimating all other things quality is considered as well as quantity, the estimation of pleasure should be supposed to depend on quantity alone.

If I am asked what I mean by difference of quality in pleasures, or what makes one pleasure more valuable than another, merely as a pleasure, except its being greater in amount, there is but one possible answer. Of two pleasures, if there be one to which all or almost all who have experience of both give a decided preference, irrespective of any feeling of moral obligation to prefer it, that is the more desirable pleasure. If one of the two is, by those who are competently acquainted with both, placed so far above the other that they prefer it, even though knowing it to be attended with a greater amount of discontent, and would not resign it for any quantity of the other pleasure which their nature is capable of, we are justified in ascribing to the preferred enjoyment a superiority in quality so far outweighing quantity as to render it, in comparison, of small account.

Now it is an unquestionable fact that those who are equally acquainted with and equally capable of appreciating and enjoying both do give a most marked preference to the manner of existence which employs their higher faculties. Few human creatures would consent to be changed into any of the lower animals for a promise of the fullest allowance of a beast's pleasures; no intelligent human being would consent to be a fool, no instructed person would be an ignoramus, no person of feeling and conscience would be selfish and base, even though they should be persuaded that the fool, the dunce, or the rascal is better satisfied with his lot than they are with theirs. They would not resign what they possess more than he for the most complete satisfaction of all the desires which they have in common with him. If they ever fancy they would, it is only in cases of unhappiness so extreme that to escape from it they would exchange their lot for almost any other, however undesirable in their own eyes. A being of higher faculties requires more to make him happy, is capable probably of more acute suffering, and certainly accessible to it at more points, than one of an inferior type; but in spite of these liabilities, he can never really wish to sink into what he feels to be a lower grade of existence.

There are a number of tricky logical problems with the position Mill defends here, the complete analysis of which would carry us into some rather dry and technical regions of the theory of utility. But one problem springs instantly from the page at us. If not all pleasures are equal in quality, if some persons of more refined sensibility are better able to judge of the quality of pleasures, then the basic democratic one-man-one-vote thrust of utilitarianism is lost. Instead of giving every person, however low his station or meagre his education, an equal voice in the choice of the ends of social policy, special weight shall have to be accorded to the opinions of that educated minority who have tasted the elevated pleasures of the mind—to those who claim, from the height of their culture, that Bach is better than rock, and cordon bleu better than cheeseburgers. The fact is that Mill does indeed exhibit just such an aristocratic bias in his political writings, both in regard to the privileged position of the upper classes within England and also in regard to England's privileged position in her colonies vis-a-vis the "subject races" not yet raised to her own level of culture. The cultural imperialism of Mill, as we may call it, is of course interesting as a fact about the man and his times. But it is also a first-rate example of the way in which an apparently trivial philosophical argument about a technical point can carry with it very large consequences for the most practical questions of politics.

Mill's second revision of his father's faith concerned the rationality and predictability of the laborers, capitalists, and consumers who interacted in the marketplace. The doctrine of laissez-faire, with its emphasis on limited government intervention in the market and a removal of all regulations on trade and commerce, depended upon two assumptions, as we have already seen. The first was that economic actors could be counted on to behave in a rationally self-interested manner, buying as cheaply as possible, taking the highest wages available, always looking for a profit; the second, which depended for its plausibility on the first, was that an economy run along laissez-faire lines and populated by rationally self-interested persons would maximize growth and production and thereby create the greatest happiness possible, within the limits of natural resources and technology, for the greatest number of people. In one of his major works, *The Principles of Political Economy,* Mill denied the first of these two assumptions, and thereby laid the theoretical groundwork for the rejection of the second.

First let us look at Mill's argument. Then we will consider its significance.

> Under the rule of individual property, the division of the produce is the result of two determining agencies: Competition, and Custom. It is important to ascertain the amount of influence which belongs to each of these causes, and in what manner the operation of one is modified by the other.
>
> Political economists generally, and English political economists above others, have been accustomed to lay almost exclusive stress upon the first of these agencies; to exaggerate the effect of competition, and to take into little account the other and conflicting principle. They are apt to express themselves as if they thought that competition actually does, in all cases, whatever it can be shown to be the tendency of competition to do. This is partly intelligible, if we consider that only through the principle of competition has political economy any pretension to the character of a science. So far as rents, profits, wages, prices, are determined by competition, laws may be assigned for them. Assume competition to be their exclusive regulator, and principles of broad generality and scientific precision may be laid down, according to which they will be regulated. The political economist justly deems this his proper business: and as an abstract or hypothetical science, political economy cannot be required to do, and indeed cannot do, anything more. But it would be a great misconception of the actual course of human affairs, to suppose that competition exercises in fact this unlimited sway. I am not speaking of monopolies, either natural or artificial, or of any interferences of authority with the liberty of production or exchange. Such disturbing causes have always been allowed for by political economists. I speak of cases in which there is nothing to restrain competition; no hindrance to it either in the nature of the case or in artificial obstacles; yet in which the result is not determined by competition, but by custom or usage; competition either not taking place at all, or producing its effect in quite a different manner from that which is ordinarily assumed to be natural to it.
>
> Since custom stands its ground against competition to so considerable an extent, even where, from the multitude of competitors and the general energy in the pursuit of gain, the spirit of competition is strongest, we may be sure that this is much more the case where people are content with smaller gains, and estimate their pecuniary interest at a lower rate when balanced against their ease or their pleasure. I believe it will often be found, in Continental Europe, that prices and charges, of some or of all sorts, are much higher in some places than in others not far distant, without its being possible to assign any other cause than that it has always been so: the customers are used to it,

and acquiesce in it. An enterprising competitor, with sufficient capital, might force down the charges, and make his fortune during the process; but there are no enterprising competitors; those who have capital prefer to leave it where it is, or to make less profit by it in a more quiet way.

Mill is saying that although the behavior of men and women in the market may be *predictable*, it is not *calculable*. The difference is fundamental, so perhaps we should take a moment to explain it more clearly. Suppose you are coming to visit me, and you have forgotten to tell me whether you will be taking the bus or the plane. I must meet you, and if I go to the airport, I cannot also go to the bus station. I say to myself, "He (or she) told me that he was short of money and intended to take the cheapest form of transportation. I know, and he knows too, that the bus is cheaper than the plane. Therefore, he will be on the bus, and I had better go to the station to meet him." I go, and sure enough there you are. What I do is to put myself in your place, assume your goals (to get to my town by the cheapest mode of travel), make a simple calculation (comparing the two costs), and thus figure out what you will do. This trivial and familiar sort of reasoning, which we all engage in every day, depends upon the assumption that you and I are both capable of making the same rational calculations of cost, and that you will act on the conclusion of your calculation. When you get to my house, I say, "Be careful of my dog. He snaps at strangers if they try to pet him." Now, how do I know that my dog will snap at a stranger who tries to pet him? Do I put myself in his place, assume his values, and carry out the same calculation he does? Of course not! Dogs are not rational agents, they are nonrational animals. But although they are not rational, their behavior is *regular*—it exhibits patterns which can be discovered by repeated observation. I know what my dog will do because I have seen him do it on many occasions in the past. I extrapolate from his past behavior, and make a prediction of what he will do in the future.

So long as economic actors in the marketplace act in a rationally self-interested way, I can predict their actions without any prior knowledge of their individual character, without elaborate collections of information about their past behavior. All I need know is (1) that they seek to maximize profits or enjoyments, and (2) that they will make use of the available information in a rational attempt to achieve that maximization. I can then carry out in my own head the same calculation they will carry out, and so I can predict their actions. But if they are influenced by what Mill calls *custom*, which is to say by *irrational* tastes, habits, and preferences that deviate from the strict rationality of profit maximization, then I cannot predict their behavior without vast quantities of systematically collected data about their past behavior. What is more, I cannot count on the "invisible hand" of the marketplace to direct their economic activities into the most productive areas. Capitalists may refrain, out of irrational habits or aversions, from shifting their capital into sectors of unfulfilled market demand. Consumers may go on shopping at a more expensive store when identical goods are offered more cheaply next door. Workers may fail to quit low-paying jobs and move to better-paying jobs in labor-short industries.

The result will be a breakdown of the automatic mechanisms of the market and a need for scientifically controlled management of the economy by a central authority possessing both the information and the power to implement its judgments. In short, the slight revision which Mill makes in the classical theory of laissez'faire leads directly, although not immediately, to the modern managed economy of welfare-state capitalism.

Mill's third alteration in the radical philosophy of James Mill follows directly from the first, and concerns the government's right to interfere with the private lives of its citizens. In his famous essay, *On Liberty*, Mill argues for an absolute ban on all State or social intervention in the inner life of thoughts and feelings. But in the last chapter of the *Principles*, he takes a somewhat different line. To be sure, he says, "*Laisser-faire* . . . should be the general practice: every departure from it, unless required by some great good, is a certain evil." But in considering permissible departures, Mill concedes a very great deal indeed. Listen to him in this suggestive passage:

> We have observed that, as a general rule, the business of life is better performed when those who have an immediate interest in it are left to take their own course, uncontrolled either by the mandate of the law or by the meddling of any public functionary. The persons, or some of the persons, who do the work, are likely to be better judges than the government, of the means of attaining the particular end at which they aim. Were we to suppose, what is not very probable, that the government has possessed itself of the best knowledge which had been acquired up to a given time by the persons most skilled in the occupation; even then, the individual agents have so much stronger and more direct an interest in the result, that the means are far more likely to be improved and perfected if left to their uncontrolled choice. But if the workman is generally the best selector of means, can it be affirmed with the same universality, that the consumer, or person served, is the most competent judge of the end? Is the buyer always qualified to judge of the commodity? If not, the presumption in favour of the competition of the market does not apply to the case; and if the commodity be one, in the quality of which society has much at stake, the balance of advantages may be in favour of some mode and degree of

intervention, by the authorized representatives of the collective interest of the state.

Now, the proposition that the consumer is a competent judge of the commodity, can be admitted only with numerous abatements and exceptions. He is generally the best judge (though even this is not true universally) of the material objects produced for his use. These are destined to supply some physical want, or gratify some taste or inclination, respecting which wants or inclinations there is no appeal from the person who feels them; or they are the means and appliances of some occupation, for the use of the persons engaged in it, who may be presumed to be judges of the things required in their own habitual employment. But there are other things of the worth of which the demand of the market is by no means a test; things of which the utility does not consist in ministering to inclinations, nor in serving the daily uses of life, and the want of which is least felt where the need is greatest. This is peculiarly true of those things which are chiefly useful as tending to raise the character of human beings. The uncultivated cannot be competent judges of cultivation.

JOHN STUART MILL, *Principles of Political Economy*

Despite all his qualifications and revisions in the utilitarian creed, Mill remained faithful to its spirit. But powerful intellectual attacks were mounted on laissez-faire liberalism and utilitarianism from both the right and the left. In the next two sections of this chapter, we shall listen to some of the voices of dissent. The attacks began as soon as industrial capitalism and its liberal defenders appeared. In the very first decades of the nineteenth century, Romantic conservative critics of industrialism and socialist critics of the capitalist organization of that industrialism appeared in England and on the Continent. But I do not want you to think that this is an ancient dispute, buried in dusty books written by men long dead. The very same argument continues today, and so we shall hear from a few of the contemporary philosophers who have questioned the foundations of both the theory and the practice of traditional liberal social philosophy.

II   Living as we do two centuries after industrial capitalism burst its bonds and rose to a position of domination in the economy and society of England, we tend to think of capitalists and capitalism as the Establishment, as the old order, entrenched in its position of superiority even though under attack from socialism and communism. But in its infancy, capitalism was a revolutionary social force which assaulted the bastions of landed wealth and power, toppled kings, and thrust a new class of men into the

Industrialism changed the lives and the work experiences of millions of men and women. The cultural gap between the fields and the factory can scarcely be imagined by those of us who have not known them both.

arena of politics. The philosophy that rationalized this emergence of a new ruling class was also a revolutionary philosophy, and its celebration of prudential rationality, its insistence upon the rights of the individual, its denial of immemorial custom, privilege, and inherited status grated on the philosophical sensibilities of the old order's defenders as much as the accents of the new industrial barons must have grated on their ears.

The conservative counterattack took many literary forms. It appeared in the speeches of Edmund Burke, in the poetry of Shelley, in the essays and history of Carlyle. Needless to say, there is no single "conservative" position, any more than there was or is a single "liberal" or "radical" position. But the critics from the right tended to concentrate their fire on two strong points of the liberal philosophy. These were the nature and role of *reason* in human affairs, and the legitimacy of *tradition* as a source of the bonds that united men and women in society. In each case, the conservatives argued that the liberals had got the matter badly wrong and had produced thereby a philosophy that was both false and socially harmful.

The prime target of conservative arguments was the utilitarian conception of human reason. By now you will have noted how often this matter of the nature of reason comes up in philosophical disputes. Cosmologists, epistemologists, moralists, and political theorists all argue about man's peculiar capacity of reason, about what role it should play in his personality, in his study of nature, and in his social arrangements. And as we shall see at the end of this chapter, when a philosopher wants to break as completely as possible with the entire tradition of Western thought, his most radical move is to deny completely the claims of reason itself. But to return to our discussion—Bentham, Mill, and company had made two claims about man's reason. First, they said that man was fundamentally a rational creature, despite the overlay of irrationality which might from time to time be produced by superstition, ignorance, or religious faith. By saying that man was rational, they meant that he had it within his power to deliberate, to weigh alternatives, and to make choices guided by knowledge and calculation. Second, they said that this power of reason had the function of selecting the efficient means for the achievement of those ends which had already been set by desire. So to the utilitarians, and to liberal philosophers in general, "rational man" essentially meant "prudent man."

The conservatives denied both of these theses about reason. First of all, they denied that reason should take the ruling place in man's soul. The poets insisted that the power of imagination was actually a higher faculty than reason. It had the capacity to put man in touch with eternal truths, with the ideal of beauty, with a deeper reality of man and nature that mere sensation and calculation could never reveal. They considered the utilitarians' prudent man to be a vulger, uninspired, diminished creature, capable only of adding up pleasures and pains, profits and losses. The mystery, awe, wonder, majesty, and sanctity of the human experience were reduced by a Bentham to the level of "pleasures", to be traded off against a good meal or a soft bed. One might as well use a Rembrandt masterpiece as a scratch pad or melt down a statue of the Blessed Virgin to make paperweights. Better by far to lift the masses, by even a little, through the exercise of the unquestioned authority of their cultivated betters, rather than reduce all art, all culture, all society to the lowest common denominator of popular taste.

I do not know of any philosopher who has attacked this celebration of reason more wittily, profoundly, and effectively than the modern English conservative Michael Oakeshott. In his essay, "Rationalism in Politics,"

Oakeshott takes on virtually the entire corpus of Western philosophers as he ridicules their conception of rationality. The principal target of Oakeshott's criticism is the familiar distinction between ends and means, a distinction which can be found in the writings of Aristotle, Hobbes, Bentham, Mill, Kant, and countless other philosophers of widely different theoretical persuasions. When a person acts, according to the most common view, first he identifies the state of affairs he wishes to bring about—his goal or *end*—and then he selects what seems to him, given his beliefs about the world, the best or most efficient way of bringing it about—his *means*. So when I mow my lawn, first I identify my end, which is to shorten the length of the grass on my lawn to a height that looks nice to me and also keeps the grass growing, and then I select the means available to me that seems likely to accomplish my end in the most efficient manner, according to my personal evaluation of the relative values or costs of the different means. In short, I tell my son to get out the lawnmower and mow the lawn. Or, if my son has gone off with his friends, I do it myself.

According to this analysis, my choice of ends is determined either by the mere, unanalyzable fact that I desire some thing (maybe I just *like* the look of short grass), or by some set of moral convictions (I may, for peculiar reasons, think that it is immoral to have long grass), or by the fact that I desire something else which this particular end is a means to getting (I may want to impress my neighbors, and past experience tells me that they are really impressed by a well-kept lawn). My choice of means is determined by my knowledge of the world taken together with what defense department planners call a "cost-benefit" calculation. I figure out the most efficient way to achieve my goal, and then decide whether the payoff is worth the price (if I have to mow the lawn myself, I may decide to pass up my neighbor's praise!).

The interesting thing about Oakeshott's position is that he thinks it is literally impossible for anyone to act in this ends-means way! He sometimes talks as though he thinks it is merely a foolish way to act, but his real claim is that we couldn't act that way even if we tried. What is more, though we always fail, the effort invariably makes things worse than they need be. Here is his argument.

> The general character and disposition of the Rationalist are, I think, not difficult to identify. At bottom he stands (he always *stands*) for independence of mind on all occasions, for thought free from obligation to any authority save the authority of 'reason'. His circumstances in the modern world have made him contentious: he is the *enemy* of authority, of prejudice, of the merely traditional, customary or habitual. His mental attitude is at once sceptical and optimistic: sceptical,

because there is no opinion, no habit, no belief, nothing so firmly rooted or so widely held that he hesitates to question it and to judge it by what he calls his 'reason'; optimistic, because the Rationalist never doubts the power of his 'reason' (when properly applied) to determine the worth of a thing, the truth of an opinion or the propriety of an action. . . .

He has no sense of the cumulation of experience, only of the readiness of experience when it has been converted into a formula: the past is significant to him only as an encumbrance. He has none of that *negative capability* (which Keats attributed to Shakespeare), the power of accepting the mysteries and uncertainties of experience without any irritable search for order and distinctness, only the capability of subjugating experience; he has no aptitude for that close and detailed appreciation of what actually presents itself which Lichtenberg called *negative enthusiasm*, but only the power of recognizing the large outline which a general theory imposes upon events . . . the mind of the Rationalist impresses us as, at best, a finely-tempered, neutral instrument, as a well-trained rather than as an educated mind. Intellectually, his ambition is not so much to share the experience of the race as to be demonstrably a self-made man. And this gives to his intellectual and practical activities an almost preternatural deliberateness and self-consciousness, depriving them of any element of passivity, removing from them all sense of rhythm and continuity and dissolving them into a succession of climacterics, each to be surmounted by a *tour de raison*. His mind has no atmosphere, no changes of season and temperature; his intellectual processes, so far as possible, are insulated from all external influence and go on in the void. And having cut himself off from the traditional knowledge of his society, and denied the value of any education more extensive than a training in a technique of analysis, he is apt to attribute to mankind a necessary inexperience in all the critical moments of life, and if he were more self-critical he might begin to wonder how the race had ever succeeded in surviving. With an almost poetic fancy, he strives to live each day as if it were his first, and he believes that to form a habit is to fail. And if, with as yet no thought of analysis, we glance below the surface, we may, perhaps, see in the temperament, if not in the character, of the Rationalist, a deep distrust of time, an impatient hunger for eternity and an irritable nervousness in the face of everything topical and transitory.

Every science, every art, every practical activity requiring skill of any sort, indeed every human activity whatsoever, involves knowledge. And, universally, this knowledge is of two sorts, both of which are always involved in any actual activity. It is not, I think, making too much of it to call them two sorts of knowledge, because (though in fact they do not exist separately) there are certain important differences between them. The first sort of knowledge I will call technical knowledge or knowledge of technique. In every art and science, and in every practical activity, a technique is involved. In many activities this technical knowledge is formulated into rules which are, or may be, deliberately learned, remembered, and, as we say, put into practice; but whether or not it is, or has been, precisely formulated, its chief characteristic is that it is susceptible of precise formulation, although special skill and insight may be required to give that formulation. The technique (or part of it) of driving a motor car on English roads is to be found in the Highway Code, the technique of cookery is contained in the cookery book, and the technique of discovery in natural science or in history is in their rules of research, of observation and verification. The second sort of knowledge I will call practical, because it exists only in use, is not reflective and (unlike technique) cannot be formulated in rules. This does not mean, however, that it is an esoteric sort of knowledge. It means only that the method by which it may be shared and becomes common knowledge is not the method of formulated doctrine. And if we consider it from this point of view, it would not, I think, be misleading to speak of it as traditional knowledge. In every activity this sort of knowledge is also involved; the mastery of any skill, the pursuit of any concrete activity is impossible without it. . . .

Now, as I understand it, Rationalism is the assertion that what I have called practical knowledge is not knowledge at all, the assertion that, properly speaking, there is no knowledge which is not technical knowledge. The Rationalist holds that the only element of *knowledge* involved in any human activity is technical knowledge, and that what I have called practical knowledge is really only a sort of nescience which would be negligible if it were not positively mischievous. The sovereignty of 'reason', for the Rationalist, means the sovereignty of technique.

MICHAEL OAKESHOTT, *Rationalism in Politics*

The second utilitarian thesis about reason got equally short shrift from the conservatives. Though they denied the primacy of reason, they insisted that reason could do more than merely select efficient means to any end desire might throw up before us. That, they thought, was a shopkeeper's conception of reason, a bookkeeper's notion of what it meant to be rational. "Two tickles on this side of the ledger, a twinge on that. Let us see how it balances out." Was this the highest peak to which man could aspire in the exercise of his rational powers? Hardly. Reason was far better employed in a reflection upon the truths of revealed religion, in a just appreciation of the wise ordering of statuses and classes in established society, in a contemplation of the eternal form of beauty.

Conservative critics were especially vigorous in their defense against the traditions which the utilitarians lumped together as "superstitions." A tradition is a way of acting, a style of personality, a form of human relationships, which has been enacted and reenacted over many generations, and has acquired through long usage an authority that exceeds any justification a calculating reason can produce. To a utilitarian, tradition is simply a polite name for thoughtless repetition, for the doing once more of something that could not be justified the first time. This harsh view of tradition assumes that men can know enough about their social affairs to make reliable calculations of the best institutions and policies. But if man's capacity to discover the underlying nature of society is limited at best; if the power of reason within each man is only a feeble check against powerful, destructive passions lurking beneath the surface of civilization; if the experiences of past generations are a fund of unspoken wisdom on which the present can draw through the reenactment of the old ways; if all of this be the case, then tradition will be our best guide rather than our worst. It will preserve for us what is soundest in the history of the human race, while also containing, through its authority, those antisocial passions which mere calculative reason cannot adequately suppress.

One way to bring the dispute between the liberals and the conservatives into focus is to embody their abstract philosophies in concrete human form, to try to imagine what the ideal utilitarian liberal would be like and what the ideal conservative would be like. This is a risky business, and I will probably end up by offending both liberals and conservatives, but let me have a go at it anyway. I think it will help you to see what is at stake. The ideal utilitarian liberal can be imagined as a solid, cautious, open-minded, prudent businessman. He is self-made, having earned his present position by hard work, self-denial, and a shrewd calculation of advantage. He is not public-spirited, if by that is meant a desire to help others at the expense of himself. But since his own interests are best advanced in the marketplace by satisfying the desires of his customers, he manages to do good for others in the process of doing well by himself.

The ideal conservative is an aristocrat, born into a family with wealth, tradition, and a name to uphold. He is quirky, individualistic, disdainful of the opinions of anyone not in his own social class, but fiercely proud of his honor and determined to uphold it at all costs. He scorns calculation, and considers a good head for business to be a somewhat degrading trait. He has a cultivated mind, and is at ease with great art and great literature, though he does not work at it like a dry professor. His morals are sometimes a trifle loose, but his word is his bond, and in a war he can be counted on to stand his position until the death. His life has style, a certain flamboyance, and it is his own style, not purchased at a clothing store or copied from the pages of a magazine.

Each one—the businessman and the aristocrat—has his strengths, and each has his weaknesses. The businessman is practical, open to experiment, willing to try new ways to solve intractable problems. He is flexible, capable of compromise, able to deal with men and women of all classes and backgrounds. He is respectful of the manners and mores of others (for he never knows when they will be his customers). If you need a railroad constructed, a new technology exploited, or a dispute settled between labor and management, he is your man.

But the same instrumental calculation that stands the businessman in such good stead when he is faced with a problem of resource management can be his downfall when hard choices of honor and morality come his way. The utilitarian mentality tends to lead to the subversion of principle in the interest of some "larger" end. Benjamin Franklin said in his autobiography that the *appearance* of honesty was more important in business than honesty itself, and such an attitude easily degenerates into an obsessive concern with public relations, with the salability of a policy or a product rather than its soundness. Liberals are long on practical proposals for benevolent social management, but short on backbone when it comes to defending basic principles against attack.

The conservative's strengths and weaknesses are the mirror opposites of the businessman's. The conservative is set in his ways, unwilling to experiment with new industrial or social programs, uninterested in compromise, unable to accommodate himself to the manners of those from different social backgrounds. But he has the capacity to take offense, to feel that his honor has been insulted, and when that happens he will stand and fight, not out of a rational calculation of future advantage but simply from an irrational conviction that certain things are "not done."

In the 1950s, a Wisconsin senator named Joseph McCarthy raised an enormous stir in America by making a series of wild charges about the presence of "communists" in the State Department and other branches of the federal government. He used his position as chairman of an investigative subcommittee of the Congress to hold hearings in which citizens were accused of treason, professors were charged with teaching "un-American" doctrines, and the president himself (Dwight David Eisenhower) was tainted as a "coddler" of the dreaded communists. In retrospect, it is hard to understand why McCarthy had such success with his charges. He had virtually no evidence to support them, and the people he accused were for the most part solidly respectable members of their communities and professions. But the country was turned inside out by the witch hunt he carried on. I was a student during what is now referred to as "the McCarthy era" at an Eastern university that was accused of harboring "Commies" on its faculty. McCarthy brought his traveling committee hearings to town and started listening to accusations by witnesses. A prime target of his attack was a physics professor whose course in elementary physics I had actually taken the previous semester. This man, on the strength of having donated money to certain committees and causes, was charged with being an agent of the Soviet Union and a traitor unfit to educate the young. I knew that he hadn't tried to indoctrinate us with "subversive" propaganda. Indeed, he hadn't had much success indoctrinating us with the elements of physics! But senior though he was, tenured though he was, a cry went up to dismiss him from the faculty. The "liberals" during that era made a rather sorry record, by and large. They trimmed, they calculated, and save for some honorable exceptions, they did not simply stand up and say, "This maniac has gone too far!" Instead, it was left to a collection of conservative, aristocratic trustees of the university to rebuff the terrible Senator McCarthy. These trustees were all members of old, proud families; as it happens, they were all upper-class Protestants, and McCarthy was an Irish Catholic. They met in private, weighed the Senator's charges and demands, and then simply dismissed them out of hand. The professor was not removed, and McCarthy was forced to take his road show elsewhere. I cannot be sure, of course, for I was not privy to their deliberations; but I always suspected that in the end, what decided the trustees against McCarthy was a simple sense of their own honor. This was just not the sort of man they were accustomed to paying attention to, and it would have been beneath their dignity to permit the conduct of their affairs to be influenced by his accusations.

ALEXIS DE TOCQUEVILLE (1850–1859) was a French writer, politician, and commentator on public affairs. After a visit to the United States in 1831, he wrote a two-volume study of American politics and national character, *Democracy in America*, which remains to this day the most penetrating analysis of the distinctive American contribution to democratic culture. Tocqueville was one of a number of mid-nineteenth century writers who believed that complete social and economic equality could be a threat to individual liberty.

Much these same sentiments were expressed with considerably greater elegance a century and a half ago by the brilliant French historian and observer of social affairs, Alexis de Tocqueville. In his elegant book, *The Old Régime and the French Revolution*, de Tocqueville analyzed the paradoxical connection between the presence of an aristocracy in the old regime and the preservation of true—though not in the liberal sense *rational*—freedom. These selections should provide us with some second thoughts about our own tendency to identify class inequality with a loss of freedom.

Many of the prejudices, false ideas, and privileges which were the most serious obstacles to the establishment of a healthy, well-ordered freedom had the effect of maintaining in the minds of Frenchmen a spirit of independence and encouraging them to make a stand against abuses of authority. The nobility had the utmost contempt for the administration properly so called, though now and again they addressed petitions to it. Even after the surrender of their former power

they kept something of their ancestral pride, their traditional antip-
athy to servitude and subordination to the common law. True, they
gave little thought to the freedom of the populace at large and were
quite ready to let the authorities rule those around them with a heavy
hand. But they refused to let that hand weigh on themselves and were
prepared to run the greatest risks in the defense of their liberties if and
when the need arose. When the Revolution broke out, the nobility,
destined as they were to be swept away with the throne, still maintained in their dealings with the King an attitude vastly more arrogant
and a freedom of speech far greater than those of the Third Estate,
who were soon to overthrow the monarchy. Almost all the safeguards
against the abuse of power which the French nation had possessed
during its thirty-seven years of representative government were vigorously demanded by the nobles. When we read the *cahiers* they presented to the Estates-General, we cannot but appreciate the spirit and
some of the high qualities of our aristocracy, despite its prejudices and
failings. It is indeed deplorable that instead of being forced to bow to
the rule of law, the French nobility was uprooted and laid low, since
thereby the nation was deprived of a vital part of its substance, and a
wound that time will never heal was inflicted on our national freedom.
When a class has taken the lead in public affairs for centuries, it develops as a result of this long, unchallenged habit of pre-eminence a
certain proper pride and confidence in its strength, leading it to be the
point of maximum resistance in the social organism. And it not only
has itself the manly virtues; by dint of its example it quickens them in
other classes. When such an element of the body politic is forcibly
excised, even those most hostile to it suffer a diminution of strength.
Nothing can ever replace it completely, it can never come to life
again; a deposed ruling class may recover its titles and possessions but
nevermore the spirit of its forebears. . . .

. . . We must be chary of regarding submission to authority as *per se*
a sign of moral abjection—that would be using a wrong criterion.
However subservient was the Frenchman of the old régime to the
King's authority there was one kind of subservience to which he never
demeaned himself. He did not know what it was to bend the knee to
an illegitimate or dubious authority, a government little honored and
sometimes heartily despised, which it is well to truckle to because it has
power to help or harm. This degrading form of servitude was something quite unknown to our forefathers. Their feeling for the King was
unlike that of any other modern nation for its monarch, even the most
absolute; indeed, that ancient loyalty which was so thoroughly eradicated
by the Revolution has become almost incomprehensible to the modern
mind. The King's subjects felt towards him both the natural love of
children for their father and the awe properly due to God alone. Their
compliance with his orders, even the most arbitrary, was a matter far
less of compulsion than of affection, so that even when the royal yoke

pressed on them most heavily, they felt they still could call their souls their own. To their thinking, constraint was the most evil factor of obedience; to ours, it is the least. Yet is not that type of obedience which comes of a servile mind the worst of all? Indeed, we should be ill advised to belittle our ancestors; and would do better to regain, even if it meant inheriting their prejudices and failings, something of their nobility of mind.

Incidentally, Mill read Tocqueville and sought to incorporate his insights into the utilitarian position. Whether he succeeded is a question that I can leave to you for a decision.

III   The conservative reaction to industrialism and liberalism was powerful, and it gave rise in the social sciences to an enormous body of impressive theory and research. But more powerful still was the attack from the left. The misery of the workers in the early factories, the squalor of the slums in which they and their families suffered, the gross contrast between their poverty and the wealth of the entrepreneurs provoked a flood of scathing condemnations of the new industrial order. Some of the criticisms were merely cries from the heart, but especially in France, a number of philosophers and economists made an effort to discover the underlying causes of the suffering created by capitalism. It was the German Karl Marx, however, who mounted the most sustained, thoroughgoing, and intellectually impressive critique of the institutions, economic theories, and philosophical rationalizations of industrial capitalism.

The genius of Marx's critique was that it met the liberal philosophy head on at its strongest point, and turned its own arguments against itself. Liberalism and laissez faire claimed to be rational doctrines, stripped of all superstitious mystification. The conservatives had denied the primacy of reason, and attempted instead to elevate imagination or tradition to the first place. But Marx accepted the challenge of liberalism. Industrial capitalism, he insisted, was not rational. Instead, it was profoundly irrational, and its claims to rationality, expressed in its economic theory and in its philosophy, were no more than an ideological rationalization designed to conceal the inner illogic of capitalism and thereby preserve a system which favored the interests of a few at the expense of the lives of the many.

Marx argued that industrial capitalism was irrational in two different ways. First of all, it was instrumentally irrational. That is to say, it systematically chose inefficient means to attain the ends it claimed to set for itself. The triumphant claim of Smith and the other capitalist apologists

Karl Marx

KARL MARX (1818–1883) is the founder of modern socialism. Born in Prussia, he studied philosophy, and in his twenties joined a circle of young radical social critics and philosophers known as the Young Hegelians. After a number of years as a pamphleteer and intellectual agitator in Germany and France, Marx moved to London to escape political persecution. Once in England, he settled into a rather quiet life of scholarship, reflection, writing, and political organization. Throughout a lifetime of collaboration with Friedrich Engels, Marx systematically elaborated a full-scale economic, political, philosophical, historical, and moral critique of the industrial capitalist system which had developed first in England and then throughout the rest of Europe.

As a young man, Marx was inflamed with the revolutionary conviction that the capitalist order was on the brink of total collapse. After the failure of the workers' uprisings in 1848, and the reactionary turn of most continental governments, Marx developed a deeper and more long-term analysis of the internal weaknesses of capitalism. Though his writings fill many volumes, there can be no doubt that the masterpiece of his life was the book called, simply, *Capital.*

Unlike many of his followers, Marx was always ready to alter his theories in the face of new evidence. Although he was certain in his youth that socialism could only come by way of a violent revolutionary overthrow of capitalist society and government, later in his life he concluded that in such countries as England and America socialism might come through the relatively peaceful avenue of political agitation and election.

had been that a free market profit system would make maximally efficient use of the resources and technology available to a society at any moment, and generate new economic production more expeditiously than any system of government management or tradition. Marx agreed that capitalism was unequaled at the task of production, but the very same capitalism was unable to solve the even more important problem of distributing what its factories had produced. In a capitalist system, production is for profit, not for use. If the capitalist cannot make a good return on his investment, he is forced to close up shop, even though there may be men and women in the society crying for the goods he produces. By the same token, as long as he is making a good profit, he goes on churning out goods regardless of whether they are high on society's list of genuine needs. The market is the distribution mechanism, which means that only consumers with cash in hand can buy what the capitalists have produced. But in order for the capitalist to make a high profit, he must keep his wages down, for—Marx argues—profits come out of the difference between the value of what the workers produce and the wages they are paid by their employers. So the same capitalist who cuts his workers' wages to the bone finds no one in the market with money to buy his products.

Competition with other capitalists pushes each producer to cut prices and increase volume, in an attempt to seize a larger share of the market. The result is a cycle of overproduction, leading to layoffs, recession, depression, general misery, and then an upswing into new overproduction. Now, since man has been on this earth, natural disasters have afflicted him, blighting his crops, flooding his home, striking him down with disease. But the depressions produced periodically in the nineteenth and twentieth centuries by capitalism were not natural disasters; they were man-made disasters, arising out of the inner irrationality of the capitalist system. Hunger resulted not from crop failures, but from the inability of the market system to distribute what had been produced. There was famine in the midst of plenty, until in America in the great Depression of the 1930s, farmers were literally forced to plow piglets under with their tractors while millions hovered on the brink of malnutrition and actual starvation. These "inner contradictions" of capitalism, as Marx called them, were living evidence of the irrationality of that social system which the utilitarians had proclaimed the reign of reason.

Even this terrible instrumental irrationality of capitalism, however, was merely a means, as it were, to the substantive irrationality, the debasing inhumanity of capitalism as it was actually lived by industrial workers. You have all heard the term "alienation." These days it has become a catchword, and is used to apply to everything from psychic disorder to mere boredom. The term was invented by the German philosopher Georg F. W. Hegel, and was taken over by Marx to describe what happens to men and women who labor under capitalism. Marx held that man is by nature a productive animal who lives in this world by intelligently, purposefully transforming nature, in cooperation with his fellow men, into commodities that can satisfy his needs and desires. In the process of production, men and women "externalize" themselves; that is, they make what was first a mere idea in their minds external to themselves in the form of an object or state of affairs which they create by their labor. The most important act of such self-externalizing creation is birth itself, but the same structure of creativity can be seen in the farmer's planning, planting, tending, and harvesting of a field of grain, in the carpenter's conceiving, cutting, fashioning, and finishing of a piece of furniture, and also in an artist's sculpting of a statue or a poet's forming of a sonnet.

Men and women need productive, creative, fulfilling labor in order to be truly happy, Marx thought. He rejected the utilitarian notion that happiness consisted simply in the satisfaction of desire. On that view, a life of passive inactivity, filled with food and drink and amusement pro-

The Book of Genesis tells us that work
is a curse laid upon man for his sins.
Marx insists that unalienated work
is the fulfillment of human existence.
Would you prefer a world with no work,
or with demanding, satisfying work?

duced by the gods or by slaves, would be true happiness. Rather, Marx argued that genuine human happiness, if it could ever be brought about, would consist in unalienated labor, labor that was self-determined (or autonomous, as Kant might have said), designed to satisfy human wants rather than to make a profit, truly cooperative rather than competitive.

Perhaps it is worth pointing out that Marx's conception of the good life directly contradicts the ancient view, first expressed in the opening chapters of the Book of Genesis of the Old Testament, according to which productive work is a curse laid upon man for his sins. According to the Bible, the Garden of Eden was a place where the food fell from the trees and man had no need to get his bread by the sweat of his brow. But Adam and Eve transgressed, and so God cursed them with labor. Man's labor was to till the fields and tend flocks; woman's labor was to bear children in pain and suffering. Heaven, we may suppose, would be a return to the endless holiday of Eden.

Capitalism systematically frustrated man's need for satisfying labor in every possible way, according to Marx. There was plenty of labor, to be sure. But it was not autonomous labor, it was not labor directed at satisfying genuine human needs, it was not healthful, fulfilling labor; it was competitive labor that set worker against worker, worker against capitalist, and capitalist against capitalist. The very productivity of capitalism made it a hell on earth, for at the moment in history when man first achieved the technology to raise himself above famine, sickness, and misery, the inner contradictions of his system of property plunged him into depths of suffering worse than anything that had been known in the Middle Ages.

Here is just a short selection from Marx's essay on alienated labor from the unpublished and unfinished papers which are known today as the *Economic-Philosophic Manuscripts* of 1844.

What constitutes the alienation of labour? First, that the work is *external* to the worker, that it is not part of his nature; and that, consequently, he does not fulfil himself in his work but denies himself, has a feeling of misery rather than well-being, does not develop freely his mental and physical energies but is physically exhausted and mentally debased. The worker, therefore, feels himself at home only during his leisure time, whereas at work he feels homeless. His work is not voluntary but imposed, *forced labour*. It is not the satisfaction of a need, but only a *means* for satisfying other needs. Its alien character is clearly shown by the fact that as soon as there is no physical or other compulsion it is avoided like the plague. External labour, labour in which man alienates himself, is a labour of self-sacrifice, of mortification. Finally, the external character of work for the worker is shown by the fact that it is not his own work but work for someone else, that in work he does not belong to himself but to another person.

What could be done about the irrationality and dehumanization of capitalism? Marx's answer, as you all know, was a revolution, a socialist revolution made by the workers against the capitalists. The revolution, Marx believed, would accomplish several things. First of all, it would overthrow the system of ownership of the means of production which, under capitalism, placed in the hands of a few the accumulated technology, factories, raw materials, and machinery that had been produced collectively by the labor of generations of working men and women. Second, it would replace the system of production for profit in the marketplace by a system of production for the satisfaction of human needs. Men and women would collectively determine what they needed, and put their talents to work to produce it. The mere accident of profitability would no longer be permitted to govern decisions about capital investment and economic growth. It might be, for example, that a large profit could be made in the United States by building luxury housing for which there was no burning need, but that little or no profit could be made from the production of well-made, gracefully designed, low-cost housing. No matter. If the low-cost housing was needed, it would get first call on the available building materials and construction work force. Finally, the capitalist system of distribution through the market would be replaced by a rational and humane system of distribution for human need. Under capitalism, the ruling slogan might be "From each as much as you can get out of him; to each as little as you can get away with giving him." Under socialism, however, the ruling slogan would be "From each according to his ability; to each according to his work." When the final stage of communism was reached, Marx said, the slogan on society's banner would be "From each according to his ability; to each according to his needs."

Collective ownership of the means of production, production for use rather than for profit, distribution for need rather than for ability to pay. With these changes, socialism would overcome the instrumental and substantive irrationality of capitalism, and eliminate the alienation of man from his product, his labor, his own human nature, and his fellow workers.

But Marx wrote in the middle of the nineteenth century, and it is now more than one hundred years later. The last great Depression was almost half-century ago. In the major industrial nations, despite continuing inequalities of wealth, the workers enjoy a standard of living beyond Marx's wildest dreams. Governments have stepped in with active policies of budget management and monetary control to dampen the boom to bust swings which Marx saw as proof of the unstable inner nature of capitalism. Despite the fact that half the world calls itself Marxist, despite the existence of something purporting to be communism in the Soviet Union, in the People's Republic of China, and in a dozen smaller nations, hasn't Marx simply been proved wrong by the passage of time and the flow of events? Is his critique of capitalism relevant today?

No question generates more heated dispute in economics, in political science, or in philosophy. One of the social critics who has defended a modern version of Marx's argument is the German-born philosopher, Herbert Marcuse. Marcuse (1898–) was educated at Berlin and Freiburg, and then joined the Institute for Social Research at Frankfurt. He came to the United States in 1934 to escape the Nazi persecution of Jews and intellectuals. He taught at Brandeis University for many years, and then at the University of California at San Diego. Marcuse belongs to a group of twentieth-century social thinkers who have sought to fuse the social insights of Marx with the psychological insights of Freud, in an attempt to arrive at an integrated critical social theory. In *One-Dimensional Man*, which is perhaps his most influential book, Marcuse insists that the managed economy and increased material well-being of workers under modern capitalism do not in the slightest diminish the fundamental substantive and instrumental irrationality that Marx perceived more than a century ago. He argues that the satisfaction of the needs of workers under advanced capitalism is apparent rather than real. Through the manipulation of desire in advertising, in popular culture, in television, and in education, workers are conditioned to like what they get, rather than to insist on getting what they would truly like. To avoid inflation and recession, capitalism pours wasteful trillions into needless defense spending while inner cities rot and human potential goes unfulfilled. The very smoothness of the surface of modern capitalist society is only an added measure of irrationality, for whereas nineteenth-century capitalism was visibly inhuman, and thereby at least made manifest its own inadequacy, modern capitalism has successfully concealed its inhumanity from the very persons it dehumanizes. To call that progress is to suppose that a slave has been made free when he finally is forced to love his chains. This selection comes from the introduction to Marcuse's book. It sets the stage for his critique of capitalist society, philosophy, and ideology.

> Does not the threat of an atomic catastrophe which could wipe out the human race also serve to protect the very forces which perpetuate this danger? The efforts to prevent such a catastrophe overshadow the search for its potential causes in contemporary industrial society. These causes remain unidentified, unexposed, unattacked by the public because they recede before the all too obvious threat from without—to the West from the East, to the East from the West. Equally obvious is the need for being prepared, for living on the brink, for facing the challenge. We submit to the peaceful production of the means of destruction, to the perfection of waste, to being educated for a defense which deforms the defenders and that which they defend.
> If we attempt to relate the causes of the danger to the way in which society is organized and organizes its members, we are immediately confronted with the fact that advanced industrial society becomes

richer, bigger, and better as it perpetuates the danger. The defense structure makes life easier for a greater number of people and extends man's mastery of nature. Under these circumstances, our mass media have little difficulty in selling particular interests as those of all sensible men. The political needs of society become individual needs and aspirations, their satisfaction promotes business and the commonweal, and the whole appears to be the very embodiment of Reason.

And yet this society is irrational as a whole. Its productivity is destructive of the free development of human needs and faculties, its peace maintained by the constant threat of war, its growth dependent on the repression of the real possibilities for pacifying the struggle for existence—individual, national, and international. This repression, so different from that which characterized the preceding, less developed stages of our society, operates today not from a position of natural and technical immaturity but rather from a position of strength. The capabilities (intellectual and material) of contemporary society are immeasurably greater than ever before—which means that the scope of society's domination over the individual is immeasurably greater than ever before. Our society distinguishes itself by conquering the centrifugal social forces with Technology rather than Terror, on the dual basis of an overwhelming efficiency and an increasing standard of living.

The fact that the vast majority of the population accepts, and is made to accept, this society does not render it less irrational and less reprehensible. The distinction between true and false consciousness, real and immediate interest still is meaningful. But this distinction itself must be validated. Men must come to see it and to find their way from false to true consciousness, from their immediate to their real interest. They can do so only if they live in need of changing their way of life, of denying the positive, of refusing. It is precisely this need which the established society manages to repress to the degree to which it is capable of "delivering the goods" on an increasingly large scale, and using the scientific conquest of nature for the scientific conquest of man.

HERBERT MARCUSE, *One-Dimensional Man*

Marcuse's critique of American society raises political and moral questions, of course, but it also raises very deep metaphysical issues which have been the subject of philosophical debate ever since the time of Plato. Marcuse knows that Americans are, at least legally speaking, free to accept or reject the economic and social arrangements which he condemns as "one-dimensional." He is even willing to concede that most Americans, if asked by a pollster, would say that they like the consumer goods they buy with their money and the amusements with which they fill up their leisure hours. But Marcuse insists that despite their legal freedom and their apparent contentment with the politics and culture of American society, Americans are really fundamentally *unfree*, because their reasoning has been corrupted and their very desires twisted by the repressive institutions of capitalist society.

Does it make any sense to say that a person is unfree when he thinks he is free? Can a person really *not* desire something although consciously he believes that he does desire it? Bentham and the utilitarians say not. Desire is a conscious state of mind which I am immediately and unmistakably aware of. I may be wrong to believe that the thing I desire is going to give me pleasure, but I cannot be wrong about whether I really do desire it. What is more, the utilitarians go on, happiness or pleasure is also a conscious state of mind, and I can simply not be mistaken about whether I am happy. Other people may be wrong about how I feel—I may have the peculiar habit of frowning when I feel good—but I myself can never be wrong about my own happiness.

Plato doesn't agree, and neither does Marcuse. Both of them, and many other philosophers as well, hold that a man or woman can actually be unhappy without knowing it. People deceive themselves, they lie to themselves, they sometimes refuse to recognize the misery they are experiencing, because it is too hard to face the fact of that misery. And deceiving themselves about their own happiness, men and women can be slaves to passion, to ideology, to habit, or to fantasy, while all the time imagining that they are free.

This is a powerful argument, but a dangerous one. As we have already seen, the simple psychology of Bentham serves as a foundation for the democratic political philosophy of the liberal movement. Once we start arguing that ordinary men and women cannot judge whether they are truly happy, it is only a short step to the conclusion that some wise and powerful dictator had better make their decisions for them. That way lies tyranny and the totalitarianism of the twentieth-century state. But if we reject the notion of false pleasures and self-deception, then we lose all critical purchase on our society. We are forced to accept the superficial notion that whatever *seems* pleasant to people really is truly enjoyable. We rule out the possibility that men and women grow in self-knowledge.

My own judgment is that Plato, Marx, Marcuse, and the rest are correct in their fundamental claim that people can be unhappy and yet not "know" it—not admit it even to themselves. But like all powerful critical arguments, this one is dangerous and must be used carefully. Solid empirical evidence is needed (such as the evidence used by a psychiatrist in diagnosing mental illness) before we are justified in claiming that someone is deceiving himself about his own state of happiness. And even after we have made a solidly based judgment, we may still have no right to *force* someone to do what will really make him happy.

IV We began this chapter with John Stuart Mill's confident hope for a rational, empirically grounded social philosophy that could be used by public men and women to manage society scientifically. We end with a violent attack on the methods, the ideals, the very concepts of science itself.

For four centuries now, science has been in the ascendancy. It has conquered its most powerful competitor, religion, and has emerged as the world-view, the method, the conceptual framework, of every political and intellectual establishment in the world today. Art, philosophy, even the study of society, have been forced to submit to the political dogma of this or that ruling clique. But science stands inviolate. Adolph Hitler, Joseph Stalin, and Franklin Roosevelt all gave the physicists of their countries free rein to develop whatever new and terrible weapons of war the wonders of science could devise. Novelists may be expelled from Russia for dissenting from the official party line, but mathematicians are left to construct their theorems. Who can possibly stand against the power, the success, of science?

Nevertheless, there are voices of dissent. The scientific world-view is soulless, they say. It claims to be objective, impartial, devoid of moral significance of any sort. But its very "objectivity" is a value-laden denial of much of the human experience. What cannot be observed, measured, reduced to operational equivalents, and reproduced in controlled experiments is denied objective reality, and consigned to the rubbish heap of hallucinations and dreams. The human race has lived on this planet for one million years, and yet science, which has made its appearance in the very latest moments of that enormous span, arrogantly rejects the spiritual teachings, the nonrational experiences which have sustained and given meaning to men's lives over countless generations.

In the past ten or fifteen years, we have begun to see a reaction to the domination of science. Astrology, black magic, drug-induced inner explorations, bits and fragments of Eastern religions, all have been taken up by young Americans dissatisfied with the world that science has made and the picture science has constructed of that world. The searching is disorderly and at times even comical, though much the same could be said for the beginnings of modern science. It is too early to tell whether we are witnessing a genuine revulsion against four centuries of domination by the scientific way of thought, or whether these movements add up to nothing more than media-inspired fads. Nevertheless, intelligent social philosophers have begun to pay serious attention to this counterscientific movement, and even to give it their approval. One of the most striking documents in this new branch of social thought is a book entitled *The Making of a Counter Culture*, by Theodore Roszak. Much of Roszak's book is devoted to a survey of the other thinkers who have criticized what

110

Not everyone these days believes that
reason is our salvation. Mysticism has
enjoyed enormous popularity in America
in recent years.

we might call the *scientistic* way of thinking. In his last chapter, however,
he stakes out his own position. Here is an excerpt that will give you the
substance and some of the flavor of his writing.

> Yet, if there is to be an alternative to the technocracy, there *must* be
> an appeal from this reductive rationality which objective conscious-
> ness dictates. This, so I have argued, is the primary project of our
> counter culture: to proclaim a new heaven and a new earth so vast, so
> marvelous that the inordinate claims of technical expertise must of
> necessity withdraw in the presence of such splendor to a subordinate
> and marginal status in the lives of men. To create and broadcast such
> a consciousness of life entails nothing less than the willingness to open
> ourselves to the visionary imagination on its own demanding terms.
> We must be prepared to entertain the astonishing claim men like
> Blake lay before us: that here are eyes which see the world not as

111

commonplace sight or scientific scrutiny sees it, but see it transformed, made lustrous beyond measure, and in seeing the world so, see it as it really is. Instead of rushing to downgrade the rhapsodic reports of our enchanted seers, to interpret them at the lowest and most conventional level, we must be prepared to consider the scandalous possibility that wherever the visionary imagination grows bright, magic, that old antagonist of science, renews itself, transmuting our workaday reality into something bigger, perhaps more frightening, certainly more adventurous than the lesser rationality of objective consciousness can ever countenance. . . .

Shamans were "witch doctors," men whose visionary experiences were believed to put them in touch with a world of spirits beyond the world of the five senses. Shamans were thought to have the power to heal the sick as well as to communicate with spirits. In some primitive cultures, much of the medical, religious and scientific knowledge of the society was preserved and transmitted by the shamans. The word "shaman" actually comes from a Manchurian word, "saman," which means "he who knows." Theodore Roszak uses the term more broadly to apply to "medicine men" and priests of primitive societies.

When we look more closely at the shaman, we discover that the contribution this exotic character has made to human culture is nearly inestimable. Indeed, the shaman might properly lay claim to being the culture hero *par excellence*, for through him creative forces that approach the superhuman seem to have been called into play. In the shaman, the first figure to have established himself in human society as an individual personality, several great talents were inextricably combined that have since become specialized professions. It is likely that men's first efforts at pictorial art—and brilliant efforts they were as they survive in the form of the great paleolithic cave paintings— were the work of shamans practising a strange, graphic magic. In the shaman's rhapsodic babbling we might once have heard the first rhythms and euphonics of poetic utterance. In his inspired taletelling we might find the beginnings of mythology, and so of literature; in his masked and painted impersonations, the origin of the drama; in his entranced gyrations, the first gestures of the dance. He was—besides being artist, poet, dramatist, dancer—his people's healer, moral counsellor, diviner, and cosmologer. Among his many skills, nearly the whole repertory of the modern circus entertainer could be found in its primordial form: ventriloquism, acrobatics, contortionism, juggling, fire eating, sword swallowing, sleight of hand. Still today, we find, among surviving primitives, shamans who are proficient in most of these talents, combining in their ancient craft things we consider high art and religion with things we consider profane diversions. . . .

In harking back to the shamanistic world view, a cultural stage buried in the primitive past of our society, I may seem to have strayed a long way from the problems of our contemporary dissenting youth. But that is hardly the case. The young radicalism of our day gropes toward a critique that embraces ambitious historical and comparative cultural perspectives. The New Left that rebels against technocratic manipulation in the name of participative democracy draws, often without realizing it, upon an anarchist tradition which has always championed the virtues of the primitive band, the tribe, the village. The spirit of Prince Kropotkin, who learned the anti-statist values of mutual aid from villagers and nomads little removed from the neolithic or even paleolithic level, breathes through all the young say about community. Our beatniks and hippies press the critique even further. Their instinctive fascination with magic and ritual, tribal lore, and psychedelic experience attempts to resuscitate the defunct shamanism of the distant past. In doing so, they wisely recognize that participative democracy cannot settle for being a matter of political-economic decentralism—only that and nothing more. As long as the spell of the objective consciousness grips our society, the regime of experts can never be far off; the community is bound to remain beholden to the high priests of the citadel who control access to reality. It is, at last, reality itself that must be participated in, must be seen, touched, breathed with the conviction that *here* is the ultimate ground of our existence, available to all, capable of ennobling by its majesty the life of every man who opens himself. It is participation of this order—experiential and not merely political—that alone can guarantee the dignity and autonomy of the individual citizen. The strange youngsters who don cowbells and primitive talismans and who take to the public parks or wilderness to improvise outlandish communal ceremonies are in reality seeking to ground democracy safely beyond the culture of expertise. They give us back the image of the paleolithic band, where the community during its rituals stood in the presence of the sacred in a rude equality that predated class, state, status. It is a strange brand of radicalism we have here that turns to prehistoric precedent for its inspiration.

THEODORE ROSZAK, *The Making of a Counter Culture*

JEAN-JACQUES ROUSSEAU (1712–1778) is one of the most paradoxical figures in modern European letters. Born in Geneva, Switzerland, his early years were spent in a succession of homes (his mother having died only a few days after his birth). At the age of sixteen he converted to Catholicism, though he seems not to have been devout in any orthodox manner. After trying his hand at such tasks as music teacher and tutor, Rousseau finally found his true calling, which was to be a writer, a man of letters.

Rousseau's writings fall into two groups which seem entirely to contradict each other in their teachings. His autobiographical *Confessions*, his novels *Emile and La Nouvelle Heloise*, and his *Discourse on the Sciences and the Arts*, all set forth in the most moving and powerful way the sentimental doctrine that man's nature is inherently good, that civilization is the great corrupter, that feeling rather than reason is the proper guide to life, and that men (and women) will be naturally moral if only the impediments of cultivated life can be cleared away. But in his greatest work, *Of the Social Contract*, Rousseau argues in a spare and rigorously logical way for the proposition that the just state and morality itself arise from the exercise of man's rational powers. Rousseau is thus an apostle both of sentiment—of feeling, of tears and sympathy—and also of reason.

Rousseau was a highly sensitive man; as his novels and his autobiography make clear, he was also a deeply troubled man, and in the last two years of his life, he appears to have suffered progressively more serious mental disorder, culminating in genuine insanity. In the world of fiction, he is the first and perhaps the greatest of the sentimentalists; countless eighteenth and nineteenth century novels echo his celebration of the feeling heart and the natural goodness of human nature. In political philosophy, he is a classic articulator of the doctrine of the social contract, on which modern democratic theory is built.

Political Philosophy 4

~~~~~~~~

❚ The literary world loves to gossip, and in Jean-Jacques Rousseau, the *enfant terrible* of eighteenth-century letters, it found a subject of endless speculation and titillation. Not since the great medieval logician Abelard married his young ward, Heloise, and got himself castrated for his trouble, has there been a philosopher whose personal turmoil contrasted so perfectly with the clarity and rigor of his thought. Rousseau's life and writings offer us an endless series of paradoxes and contradictions. He is the greatest apostle of what the eighteenth century called "sentiment," the feeling heart, the weeping eye, the rhapsodical outpouring of unstructured emotion. And yet his works deeply influenced that stern champion of pure reason, Immanuel Kant. Rousseau celebrated nature, the pastoral countryside; he condemned civilization and city life as a corrupter and destroyer of man's innate goodness. And yet he was born in Geneva, one of the great city-states of the eighteenth century, and spent some of his most productive years in the capital of all Europe, Paris. His political philosophy, his novels, even his famous autobiography, at once so revealing and so misleading, all conspire to create for us the image of the eternal adolescent, in rebellion against the grown-up world, chafing against the restrictions of discipline and responsibility. Yet surprisingly, Rousseau did not begin to make his mark in the world of European letters until close to his

*"First of all, I would like to express my gratefulness to all those wonderful ancestors of mine who helped to make this glorious day possible."**

fortieth year, and the most fruitful decade of his life, his forties, is the time when most philosophers and authors put behind them their youthful fantasies and accept the compromises of adult maturity.

Rousseau was born in 1712 in the extremely Calvinist city of Geneva. His youth and young adulthood were chaotic. His mother died almost immediately after his birth, his rather irresponsible father looked after him only fitfully until his tenth birthday, and not at all thereafter. He had little formal education, even by the standards of his day, and throughout his twenties and thirties he drifted about, trying to make his mark as a music theoretician among other things. Finally, at the age of thirty-eight, he entered a contest held by the Academy of the French city of Dijon. The topic was a popular one in enlightenment circles at that time— namely whether the revival of the sciences and arts after their decline during the Middle Ages had helped to corrupt or to purify morals. Rousseau defended the unpopular position that the revival of ancient culture had corrupted morals! He won first prize, and his name was made; So too was his reputation as an iconoclast, a destroyer of received opinions and accepted doctrines.

Rousseau nursed a veritable storehouse of resentments throughout his lifetime, and as he grew older and more famous, he also grew more paranoid. The high point of his madness generated one of the great teapot tempests of the cultivated world, and demonstrated, if indeed any demon-

*Drawing by W. Miller; © 1969 The New Yorker Magazine, Inc.

stration was needed, that even philosophers are not immune from childish bickering. The story, in brief, is this. Rousseau's writings in the late 1750s and early 1760s had brought him into considerable disfavor with the governments of Switzerland and France, both because of his attacks on organized orthodox religion and because of his dangerous republican political sympathies. At that time there was close contact and communication between the literary worlds of England and France. David Hume, the great Scottish philosopher, had many friends in the circle of French "*philosophes,*" as they were called and he offered to arrange a deal to help Rousseau. It was the practice for kings to give pensions to prominent literary and artistic figures, and Hume wanted to work out such a pension for Rousseau from the English King George III. Rousseau came to England, but he was convinced that Hume was actually secretly plotting against him to destroy his reputation. So he began to make scurrilous attacks on

The United States was the first state actually to be brought into existence by a social contract. We call it our Constitution.

Hume's name and writings in letters to a number of the prominent people of literary London. Now David Hume was one of the sweetest, gentlest, most decent human beings imaginable except where one subject was concerned—his own literary reputation. You could attack his morals, ridicule his fat, bear-shaped body, tease him at a dinner party or laugh at him in a salon, and he would merely respond with a smile or a gentle witticism. But criticize the quality and originality of his writings, and you aroused him to fury! So Hume struck back with a series of letters of his own, defending himself and attacking Rousseau. Jean-Jacques, now convinced that his life was in danger, leaped into a carriage, fled from the country house where Hume had arranged for him to stay, and fled toward the English Channel to catch a boat back to France before Hume and his supposed fellow conspirators could finish him off. Meanwhile, all literary Europe roared with laughter, and wrote Rousseau off as a madman.

Could such a creature actually write philosophy? Could he indeed! Judgments differ among philosophers, as much as they do among the compilers of all-time baseball or football teams, but in my personal judgment, Jean-Jacques Rousseau is the greatest political philosopher who has ever lived. His claim to immortality rests upon one short book, *Of the Social Contract*, an essay scarcely more than a hundred pages long. In that brief, brilliant work, Rousseau formulates the fundamental question of the philosophy of the state, and makes a valiant, although ultimately unsuccessful effort to solve it. Why such fame, you might ask, if he failed to solve the problem? In philosophy, as in the sciences, the most important step frequently is to ask the right question, and although philosophers had been analyzing the nature of the state for more than 2000 years before Rousseau, he was the first to see exactly what the problem was and to recognize how difficult it would be to solve.

Political philosophy is, before all else, the philosophical study of the *state*, so before we go any further, we had best determine what we mean by a *state*, and what philosophical problems are raised by states. Everywhere we look, across historical time and around the globe, men and women are organized into social groupings within defined territorial limits or borders. Within each one of these geographical units, there is some smaller group of people who rule, who give orders, run things, use force to get others to obey—some group who make and enforce laws. This smaller group is what we call *the state*. Sometimes the group that rules consists of a single person and his or her personal followers: a king or queen, a general or dictator, a priest or pope, plus a group of loyal underlings. Sometimes the group consists of a hereditary class, such as a military aristocracy. The group may be a political clique or party which has led a successful revolution against the previous rulers. It may even, as in our own country, be a large group of men and women who have been chosen in an election by a much larger group of citizens. But whoever makes the laws, gives the commands, and enforces them on everyone living within that territory *is* the state.

States may exist for any number of purposes: they may exist to carry out the tenets of a religious faith, to maintain general peace and security, to see to the well-being of some or all of the people within the territory, or to ensure justice and tranquility. The state may even exist merely for the purpose of lining the pockets and satisfying the desires of itself, regardless of what the rest of the population wants or needs. There are so many different purposes for which states have existed that it is not much use to look for some basic or underlying function which all states perform insofar as they are states. Philosophers express this fact by saying that the state cannot be defined *teleologically*. That simply means that we cannot explain what a state is in terms of the goals (*telos* is Greek for end or goal) at which it aims. But all states, regardless of who comprises them and no matter what purposes they pursue, have *two* characteristics in common. Once you understand these two characteristics, you will know what a state *is*, and also what the fundamental problem is of political philosophy.

First of all, states everywhere and always use force to obtain obedience to their commands. Sometimes force takes the form of armed troops, policemen, jails, and death rows. Sometimes merely the threat of force is enough to bring recalcitrant citizens into line. Economic threats can be used as effectively as the whip or the club. But beneath the judge's robes always hangs the sword of justice, and that sword is not there for decoration only.

But force alone does not make a group of people into a state, for a band of robbers, an invading army, even a lone gunman holding you up on a dark street, all use force to make you obey, and no one would call robbers, an army, or a mugger "the state." The second, and more important mark of the state is that as it issues its commands and shows its sword, it also claims to have the *right* to command and the *right* to be obeyed. Now a mugger does not claim the *right* to rob you. He says, "Your money or your life!"; he does not say, "Your money, for I have a right to it." But when the state sends you a bill for taxes, or commands you to report for induction into the armed forces, or orders you to stop at red lights and drive only with a valid license, it claims to have a right to your obedience. In the language of political philosophy, the state claims to be *legitimate*.

There is a wonderful scene in one of Shakespeare's plays (*Henry IV, Part I*) in which a group of conspirators are planning their attack on the forces of the king. One of the group is a flamboyant Welsh chieftain named Glendower, who claims to have some magical powers in addition to some usable troops. At one point, in an effort to impress his fellow conspirators with the wonderfulness of his powers, he brags, "I can call spirits from the vasty deep." The leader of the conspiracy, Hotspur, is not very impressed, and he answers, "Why so can I, and so can any man / but will they come when you do call them?" The point, of course, is that it is one thing to make a claim, and quite another to get anybody to believe it.

Now the really remarkable thing about human beings is that they are so prone to accept the claims of legitimacy made by the states that rule the territories in which they live. From time to time, people rebel against the state, and as we shall see later in this chapter, a few philosophers called *anarchists* have denied the state's claim to have a right to rule. But by and large, when states make laws and claim the right to enforce them, people believe their claim and obey *even when they aren't actually being forced to do so.* Those last few words are crucial, of course, for most of us "obey" a gunman who holds us up or an army that invades our city and points its guns at us. We "obey" because we don't want to get shot. Cynics might say that that is really the only reason anyone ever obeys the law, but all the historical and sociological evidence points in the opposite direction. Save in the most unusual circumstances, men and women obey the law far more faithfully than the threat of punishment requires. They obey from habit, to be sure, but they also obey because they genuinely believe that the state has the right to command them. After all, they think, it is *the law*. How often has each of us done something or refrained from doing something merely because the law says that we must or mustn't? How, save by playing on this belief in the legitimacy of the law, could a single official or policeman control the behavior of a large crowd? How could several thousand overworked employees of the Internal Revenue Service collect taxes from two hundred million Americans? How could a lieutenant lead a platoon of frightened soldiers into withering enemy fire? How, indeed, could an old and feeble king bend young, vigorous, ambitious dukes, princes, and generals to his will?

The belief in the legitimacy of the authority of the state is the glue that holds a political society together. It is, more even than armies or police or jails, the means by which the state gets its laws obeyed. So we may sum up the two universal characteristics of states by saying that the state is *a group of people who claim the right to enforce obedience to their commands within a territory, and succeed in getting most of the people in the territory to accept that claim.* A group of people who make a claim of this sort are said to be claiming *political authority.* So a state is a group of people who claim political authority, and have their claim accepted by most of those against whom the claim is made.

Well, states claim political authority, and they get their claims accepted. But it is one thing to get other people to accept something you say; it is quite another to be right. I may claim to be a doctor, and if enough people believe me, I can open an office and start prescribing medicine. But that doesn't make me a doctor. My "patients" may fail to notice that I am not curing them, but even that does not make me a doctor. So too, a group may claim the right to rule, and the people may accept their claim, but that does not make their claim *true*.

The fundamental question of all political philosophy is obviously: When does a group calling itself the state really have a *right* to command? Or, since that way of putting the question seems to assume that states sometimes have such a right, we can ask: Does any group of persons ever have the right to command?

The same question can be turned around to focus our attention on the people doing the obeying rather than the people doing the commanding. From the point of view of the citizen, a state is a group of people who command him. If he believes that he has an obligation to obey their commands, then he considers them as constituting a legitimate state. Otherwise, he considers them tyrants. To the citizen, the fundamental question of political philosophy is: Do I ever have an obligation to obey the commands issued by some group calling itself the state?

In ancient and medieval times, the citizen's obligation to the ruler was considered to be limited and conditioned upon the ruler's just performance of his sovereign duties. But in the sixteenth and seventeenth centuries, in response to fundamental shifts in the relative power of the aristocracy, the monarchy, and the new middle class, the theory began to be put forward that the authority of the ruler was absolute. The king, it was said, was the sole possessor of the ultimate political authority—"sovereignty," as it was called. All others in the society were unconditionally obligated to obey his commands. Usually, a religious justification was advanced for this claim—the king was considered God's representative on earth—but sometimes the theory of an original agreement or contract was also appealed to.

The unqualified claim of absolute kingly authority was unacceptable to the philosophers of the Enlightenment. A man who bows his head to God or his knee to the king merely makes himself the slave of another. In the words of Immanuel Kant, who was, as we have seen, deeply influenced by Rousseau, submission to the commands of another means a loss of autonomy, a denial of one's own reason.

So for the political philosophers of the seventeenth and eighteenth centuries, the question of obligation to the state became a new and more complicated question: Is there any way in which I can submit to the commands of a legitimate state without giving up my freedom and autonomy? It was the special genius of Rousseau that he saw this question more clearly than anyone before him, and expressed it with greater precision and force. Here are the words in which he framed the problem, taken from the sixth chapter of *The Social Contract:*

Where shall we find a form of association which will defend and protect with the whole common force the person and the property of each associate, and by which every person, while uniting himself with all, shall obey only himself and remain as free as before?

For the philosophers of the state who struggled with the question of legitimate authority in the seventeenth and eighteenth centuries, the standard solution to the problem was the device which they called the "social contract." The authority of the state, it was argued, could only be founded upon an agreement among all the persons who were to be ruled by the state. The idea of a contract, of course, was taken from the law, where it applied to an agreement between two parties for their mutual advantage. A buyer and a seller in the marketplace made a contract with one another, according to which the seller would supply goods in such and such a quantity, and of so and so quality, and the buyer would pay so much money for them at a particular time. The heart and soul of a contract is what the lawyers called a *quid pro quo* or a "this for that"; each side must stand to benefit from the deal in order to make the contract binding. The right of either party to have the contract enforced on the other derives from *two* things: first of all, each party has freely promised to abide by the contract, and so is bound by his word; second, each party benefits from the contract, and so has an obligation to return the benefit to the other according to the agreed terms.

The social contract theorists, as they have become known, conceived the idea of tracing the citizen's political obligation back to a contract or social agreement between himself and all the other members of the society. If each citizen could be imagined to have actually made such an agreement, then the riddle of legitimate state authority would be solved. First, it would then be possible to explain why, and under what conditions, the citizen had a duty to obey the law. Very simply, he would have a duty to obey laws made by a state which he had freely contracted or agreed to bring into existence. If he said to the judge, "Who are you to command me? Who are you to threaten me with punishment if I fail to obey?" the judge would answer, "I am a representative of that state which you yourself promised to obey, when you signed the social contract." And if the citizen, still resistant, went on to ask, "What have I received from my fellow citizens that I should keep the agreement I made with them?" the judge could answer, "You have received peace, social order, even-handed justice, and the benefits of a civilized society."

But even more important, if the citizen asked, "How can I obey this state I have brought into existence without forfeiting my autonomy and giving up my freedom?" the judge could answer, "In this state, and only in this state, those who obey remain free. For the state that makes the laws consists not of *some* of the people who live in this nation, but of all the people. The commands you obey are the very commands which you, as a citizen, have issued in your role as a law-maker. In this state, the law-obeyers and the law-makers are one! Through the device of a social contract, the people become the rulers." Indeed, since the traditional word for ruler is "sovereign," the social contract theory is a doctrine of people's sovereignty, or, as it is usually known, "popular sovereignty." (That doesn't mean that people like it! It means that the people are sovereign. This is what Lincoln meant when he said that we live under a government that is by the people, as well as of and for the people.)

Here is how Rousseau describes the social contract. This passage directly follows the question quoted earlier:

The articles of this contract are so unalterably fixed by the nature of the act that the least modification renders them vain and of no effect; so that they are the same everywhere, and are everywhere tacitly understood and admitted, even though they may never have been formally announced; until, the social compact being violated, each individual is restored to his original rights, and resumes his native liberty, while losing the conventional liberty for which he renounced it.

The articles of the social contract will, when clearly understood, be found reducible to this single point: the total alienation of each associate, and all his rights, to the whole community; for, in the first place, as every individual gives himself up entirely, the condition of every person is alike; and being so, it would not be to the interest of any one to render that condition offensive to others.

Nay, more than this, the alienation being made without any reserve, the union is as complete as it can be, and no associate has any further claim to anything: for if any individual retained rights not enjoyed in general by all, as there would be no common superior to decide between him and the public, each person being in some points his own judge, would soon pretend to be so in everything; and thus would the state of nature be continued and the association necessarily become tyrannical or be annihilated.

Finally, each person gives himself to all, and so not to any one individual; and as there is no one associate over whom the same right is not acquired which is ceded to him by others, each gains an equivalent for what he loses, and finds his force increased for preserving that which he possesses.

If, therefore, we exclude from the social contract all that is not essential, we shall find it reduced to the following terms:

Each of us places in common his person and all his power under the supreme direction of the general will; and as one body we all receive each member as an indivisible part of the whole.

From that moment, instead of as many separate persons as there are contracting parties, this act of association produces a moral and collective body, composed of as many members as there are votes in the assembly, which from this act receives its unity, its common self, its life, and its will. This public person, which is thus formed by the union of all other persons, took formerly the name of "city," and now takes that of "republic" or "body politic." It is called by its members "State" when it is passive, "Sovereign" when in activity, and whenever it is compared with other bodies of a similar kind, it is denominated "power." The associates take collectively the name of "people," and separately, that of "citizens," as participating in the sovereign authority, and of "subjects," because they are subjected to the laws of the State. But these terms are frequently confounded and used one for the other; and it is enough that a man understands how to distinguish them when they are employed in all their precision.

JEAN-JACQUES ROUSSEAU, *The Social Contract*

Two problems arise immediately. First, it is going to be difficult to get everyone together when laws need to be made. How can the people obey only themselves if they don't personally make the laws? The usual solution both in political theory and in political practice is to institute a system of elected representatives. But Rousseau will have none of that. If the state is not kept small enough for everyone to participate in the law-making, then so far as he is concerned, tyranny replaces liberty. Of course, that means that all citizens, and not just a few professionals, are going to have to pay attention to public affairs. But that is the price of freedom, Rousseau insists. As he says later on in the *Social Contract*:

As soon as men cease to consider public service as the principal duty of citizens, and rather choose to serve with their purse than with their persons, we may pronounce the State to be on the very verge of ruin. Are the citizens called upon to march out to war? They pay soldiers for the purpose, and remain at home. Are they summoned to council? They nominate deputies, and stay at home. And thus, in consequence of idleness and money, they have soldiers to enslave their country, and representatives to sell it.

It is the hurry of commerce and of the arts, it is the greedy thirst of gain, and the effeminate softness and love of comfort, that occasion this commutation of money for personal service. Men give up a part of the profits they acquire in order to purchase leisure to augment them. Give money, and you will soon have chains. The word "finance" is a term of slavery; it is unknown in the true city. In a State truly free, the citizens do all with their own arms and nothing with their money; and, instead of purchasing exemption from their duty, they would even pay for fulfilling it themselves. My ideas on this subject are indeed very different from those commonly received; I even think the *corvées* are less an infringement upon liberty than taxes.

The better a State is constituted, the more do public affairs intrude upon private affairs in the minds of the citizens. Private concerns even become considerably fewer, because each individual shares so largely in the common happiness that he has not so much occasion to seek for it in private resources. In a well-conducted city, each member flies with joy to the assemblies; under a bad government, no one is disposed to bend his way thither, because no one is interested in proceedings where he foresees that the general will will not prevail, and in the end every man turns his attention to his own domestic affairs. Good laws lead on to better, and bad ones seldom fail to generate still worse. When once you hear some one say, when speaking of the affairs of the State, "What is it to me?" you may give over the State for lost.

It was the decline of patriotism, the activity of private interest, the immense extent of States, the increase of conquests, and the abuses of government, that suggested the expedient of having deputies or representatives of the people in the assemblies of the nation. These representatives are the body to which, in certain countries, they have dared to give the name of the "Third Estate," as if the private interest of the two other orders deserved the first and second rank, and the public interest should be considered only in the third place.

Sovereignty cannot be represented for the same reason that it cannot be alienated; its essence is the general will, and that will must speak for itself, or it does not exist: it is either itself or not itself: there is no intermediate possibility. The deputies of the people, therefore, are not and cannot be their representatives; they can only be their commissioners, and as such are not qualified to conclude anything definitively. No act of theirs can be a law, unless it has been ratified by the people in person; and without that ratification nothing is a law. The people of England deceive themselves when they fancy they are free; they are so, in fact, only during the election of members of parliament: for, as soon as a new one is elected, they are again in chains, and are nothing. And thus, by the use they make of their brief moments of liberty, they deserve to lose it.

The second problem is how to make decisions when there is disagreement. The natural solution that springs to our minds is to take a vote and let the majority rule. We have become so accustomed to deciding questions by majority vote that it sometimes seems as though little children learn to vote in school before they learn how to count the votes. But Rousseau had the clarity of mind to see that majority rule presented a very serious obstacle to freedom. I might promise, in the original unanimous contract, to abide by the vote of the majority. But in so doing, I seem simply to be agreeing to a sort of voluntary slavery. If I have voted against a proposed law, believing that it is a bad law, contrary to the national interest, then how can I be said to "obey only myself, and remain as free as before," when I am forced to submit to it? Rousseau has an extremely subtle answer to this question. First read what he has to say, and then we can talk about it a bit.

There is one law only which, by its nature, requires unanimous consent; I mean the social compact: for civil association is the most voluntary of all acts; every man being born free and master of himself, no person can under any pretense whatever subject him without his consent. To affirm that the son of a slave is born a slave is to pronounce that he is not born a man.

Should there be any men who oppose the social compact, their opposition will not invalidate it, but only hinder their being included: they are foreigners among citizens. When the State is instituted, residence constitutes consent; to inhabit a territory is to submit to the sovereignty.

Except in this original contract, a majority of votes is sufficient to bind all the others. This is a consequence of the contract itself. But it may be asked how a man can be free and yet forced to conform to the will of others. How are the opposers free when they are in submission to laws to which they have never consented?

I answer that the question is not fairly stated. The citizen consents to all the laws, to those which are passed in spite of his opposition, and even to those which sentence him to punishment if he violates any one of them. The constant will of all the members of the State is the general will; it is by that they are citizens and free. When any law is proposed in the assembly of the people, the question is not precisely to enquire whether they approve the proposition or reject it, but if it is conformable or not to the general will, which is their will. Each citizen, in giving his suffrage, states his mind on that question; and the general will is found by counting the votes. When, therefore, the motion which I opposed carries, it only proves to me that I was mistaken, and that what I believed to be the general will was not so. If my particular opinion had prevailed, I should have done what I was not willing to do, and, consequently, I should not have been in a state of freedom.

Something very tricky is going on in this passage. How can a man be free when he doesn't get what he voted for? Earlier in the *Social Contract*, Rousseau put his point even more dramatically. A citizen who refuses to obey the general will, he said, must be compelled to do so. "This in fact only forces him to be free." What on earth can Rousseau have meant?

The full answer would take a book by itself, but we can say a few things to clear away some of the mystery. Rousseau believed that the people had a right to make laws only as long as they were all genuinely attempting to legislate in the public interest rather than in their own individual and private interests. Now, if the majority could be counted on always to be right about the general good, then no one in the minority would want his view to become law. For if I want what is for the general good, and if the majority is always right about the general good, and if I am in the minority, then what I mistakenly wanted is *not* for the general good, and hence not what I really want. And if freedom is getting what you really want, then only by being forced to abide by the majority can I really be free!

There is a flaw in the argument, of course. The majority may always aim at the general good, but it does not always aim accurately. More often than not, even when every citizen is public-spiritedly seeking what is best for all, the truth will be seen only by one citizen or a few. Rousseau confused aiming at and hitting the target.

Americans have a vested interest in the theory of the social contract, with all its flaws, because we are the first nation ever actually to bring itself into existence as a state by means of a real, historical, explicit contract. We call it our Constitution, but what the Founding Fathers actually wrote was the first operative social contract. When it was ratified in 1788, there came into being for the first time in Western history a state truly founded upon a contract.

Although the theory of the social contract has dominated liberal political theory since the seventeenth century, it has been subjected to a number of powerful criticisms. The most obvious objection is that, save for the special case of the United States, no actual state has ever been brought into existence by such an explicit contractual agreement among the citizens-to-be. Hence, the theory just does not provide any justification at all for the claims of even the most "democratic" governments. David Hume was one of the earliest anti–contract writers to make this point. In an essay entitled "Of The Original Contract," he presents the following critique:

> Philosophers ... assert, not only that government in its earliest infancy arose from consent or rather the voluntary acquiescence of the people; but also, that, even at present, when it has attained its full maturity, it rests on no other foundation. They affirm, that all men are still born equal, and owe allegiance to no prince or government, unless bound by the obligation and sanction of a promise. And as no man, without some equivalent, would forego the advantages of his native liberty, and subject himself to the will of another; this promise is always understood to be conditional, and imposes on him no obliga-

tion, unless he meet with justice and protection from his sovereign. These advantages the sovereign promises him in return; and if he fail in the execution, he has broken, on his part, the articles of engagement, and has thereby freed his subject from all obligations to allegiance. Such, according to these philosophers, is the foundation of authority in every government, and such the right of resistance, possessed by every subject.

But would these reasoners look abroad into the world, they would meet with nothing that, in the least, corresponds to their ideas, or can warrant so refined and philosophical a system. On the contrary, we find, every where, princes, who claim their subjects as their property, and assert their independent right of sovereignty from conquest or succession. We find also, every where, subjects who acknowledge this right in their prince, and suppose themselves born under obligations of obedience to a certain sovereign, as much as under the ties of reverence and duty to certain parents. These connections are always conceived to be equally independent of our consent, in Persia and China; in France and Spain; and even in Holland and England, wherever the doctrines above-mentioned have not been carefully inculcated. Obedience or subjection becomes so familiar, that most men never make any enquiry about the principle of gravity, resistance, or the most universal laws of nature. Or if curiosity ever move them; as soon as they learn, that they themselves and their ancestors have, for several ages, or from time immemorial, been subject to such a form of government or such a family; they immediately acquiesce, and acknowledge their obligation to allegiance. Were you to preach, in most parts of the world, that political connections are founded altogether on voluntary consent or a mutual promise, the magistrates would soon imprison you, as seditious, for loosening the ties of obedience; if your friends did not before shut you up as delirious for advancing such absurdities. It is strange, that an act of the mind, which every individual is supposed to have formed, and after he came to the use of reason too, otherwise it could have no authority; that this act, I say, should be so much unknown to all of them, that, over the face of the whole earth, there scarcely remain any traces or memory of it.

But the contract, on which government is founded, is said to be the *original contract*; and consequently may be supposed too old to fall under the knowledge of the present generation. If the agreement, by which savage men first associated and conjoined their force, be here meant, this is acknowledged to be real; but being so ancient, and being obliterated by a thousand changes of government and princes, it cannot now be supposed to remain any authority. If we would say any thing to the purpose, we must assert, that every particular government, which is lawful, and which imposes any duty of allegiance on the subject, was, at first, founded on consent and a voluntary compact. But besides that this supposes the consent of the fathers to bind the children even to the most remote generations, (which republican writers will never allow) besides this, I say, it is not justified by history or experience, in any age or country of the world.

Almost all the governments, which exist at present, or of which there remains any record in story, have been founded originally, either on usurpation or conquest, or both, without any pretence of a fair consent, or voluntary subjection of the people. When an artful and bold man is placed at the head of an army of faction, it is often easy for him, by employing, sometimes violence, sometimes false pretences, to establish his dominion over a people a hundred times more numerous than his partizans. He allows no such open communication, that his enemies can know, with certainty, their number or force. He gives them no leisure to assemble together in a body to oppose him. Even all those, who are the instruments of his usurpation, may wish his fall; but their ignorance of each other's intention keeps them in awe, and is the sole cause of his security. By such arts as these, many governments have been established; and this is all the *original contract*, which they have to boast of.

But the mere historical absence of a contract is not the worst of the problems confronting social contract theories. Even if a group of men and women had indeed contracted together, some time in the dim past, to submit themselves to the collective will of all, that would still leave those of us in the present generation without any reason for obeying the commands of the state. After all, I am not bound by the marriage contracts or the business contracts made by my ancient ancestors; why should I be bound by whatever political contracts they may have made?

To this, the social contract theorists answer that each of us, upon reaching the legal age of adulthood, *implicity* signs his name to that original contract by remaining in the country, living under its laws, and entering actively into its legal arrangements. John Locke, the spiritual father of our Constitution, especially emphasizes the owning of property in this selection from his most famous political work, the *Second Treatise of Civil Government*.

Every man being, as has been shown, naturally free, and nothing being able to put him into subjection to any earthly power but only his own consent, it is to be considered what shall be understood to be sufficient declaration of a man's consent to make him subject to the laws of any government. There is a common distinction of an express and a tacit consent, which will concern our present case. Nobody doubts but an express consent of any man entering into any society makes him a perfect member of that society, a subject of that government. The difficulty is, what ought to be looked upon as a tacit consent, and how far it binds, *i.e.*, how far any one shall be looked on to have consented,

JOHN LOCKE (1632–1704) had a philosophical career which was, in a sense, the reverse of David Hume's. Locke's great works were not published until close to his sixtieth year, and they were received almost immediately with great acclaim. During the troubled times in England which followed the restoration of the Catholic monarchy (in 1660) after the English Civil War, Locke sided with the moderate faction which sought to limit the power of the King and bring the throne under some control by Parliament. In 1689, one year after the so-called Glorious Revolution which established a limited monarchy in England, Locke published a pair of long essays on the subject of the foundations of the authority of the state. The second of these essays, known now as the *Second Treatise of Civil Government*, is the most important single document in the literature of constitutional democracy. Appearing when it did, the *Second Treatise* naturally was interpreted as a justification for the new regime of William and Mary, for it defended the sort of limited monarchy, hedged round with parliamentary restraints, which the English people adopted as their form of government in 1688. Actually, we now know that the two *Treatises* were written in the early 1680s, some years before the change in government took place.

The next year, 1690, Locke published a massive work on the foundations of human knowledge, the *Essay Concerning the Human Understanding.* (See Chapter 7). The *Essay* is the foundation-stone of the school of philosophy known as empiricism. Locke's arguments profoundly affected Berkeley, Hume, and the other British philosophers who followed him. It was very soon translated into French, and had a major influence as well on continental thought. A century later, Immanuel Kant was to acknowledge it as one of the most important influences on his own thinking.

and thereby submitted to any government, where he has made no expressions of it at all. And to this I say that every man that hath any possession or enjoyment of any part of the dominions of any government doth thereby give his tacit consent, and is as far forth obliged to obedience to the laws of that government during such enjoyment as any one under it; whether this his possession be of land to him and his heirs for ever, or a lodging only for a week; or whether it be barely travelling freely on the highway; and in effect it reaches as far as the very being of any one within the territories of that government.

To understand this the better, it is fit to consider that every man when he at first incorporates himself into any commonwealth, he, by his uniting himself thereunto, annexes also, and submits to the community those possessions which he has or shall acquire that do not already belong to any other government; for it would be a direct contradiction for any one to enter into society with others for the securing and regulating of property, and yet to suppose his land, whose property is to be regulated by the laws of the society, should be exempt from the jurisdiction of that government to which he himself, and the property of the land, is a subject. By the same act, therefore, whereby any one unites his person, which was before free, to any commonwealth, by the same he unites his possessions, which was before free, to it also; and they become, both of them, person and possession, subject to the government and dominion of that commonwealth as long as it hath a being. Whoever therefore from thenceforth by inheritance, purchases, permission, or otherwise, enjoys any part of the land so annexed to, and under the government of that commonwealth, must take it with the condition it is under, that is, of submitting to the government of the commonwealth under whose jurisdiction it is as far forth as any subject of it.

But since the government has a direct jurisdiction only over the land, and reaches the possessor of it (before he has actually incorporated himself in the society), only as he dwells upon, and enjoys that: the obligation any one is under, by virtue of such enjoyment, to submit to the government, begins and ends with the enjoyment; so that whenever the owner, who has given nothing but such a tacit consent to the government, will by donation, sale, or otherwise, quit the said possession, he is at liberty to go and incorporate himself into any other commonwealth, or to agree with others to begin a new one (*in vacuis locis*) in any part of the world they can find free and unpossessed. Whereas he that has once by actual agreement and any express declaration given his consent to be of any commonweal is perpetually and indispensably obliged to be and remain unalterably a subject to it, and can never be again in the liberty of the state of nature; unless, by any calamity, the government he was under comes to be dissolved, or else by some public acts cuts him off from being any longer a member of it.

You may wonder how a person can enter into a contract by "tacit consent." Don't I have to actually *say* that I am making a contract in order to do so? Locke here is relying on the ancient legal principle that when a person, over a period of time, acts in such a way as to give other persons a reasonable expectation that he will continue so to act, and if he benefits from that unspoken understanding, then he has made a "quasi-contract," which the law will enforce just as it will an explicit, spoken contract.

But Locke's argument depends on the assumption that a citizen can pick up and leave if he is dissatisfied with the laws of the state under which he lives. In Locke's day (the late 1600s) that was still possible. The pilgrims who came to America, and many millions who followed them, were exercising precisely that option. Today, unfortunately, there is no more unsettled territory to which dissenters can emigrate. Every square foot of inhabitable earth is claimed by some state or other, so that the most anyone can do is to go from the rule of one state to the rule of another. Under this condition, it is harder and harder to see what truth there is in the theory of the implicit, or tacit, contract.

II The liberal theory of the state dominates early modern political theory, but the nineteenth and twentieth centuries have seen the rise to intellectual prominence and political importance of significant alternatives on both the right and the left of the political spectrum. (In Chapter Three, you encountered this same phenomenon of the central liberal philosophy flanked by right-wing and left-wing countertheories. That is really the basic story of social and political thought in the West for the last two hundred years.) In this section, we will look at the historically most important right-wing attack on liberal philosophy—fascism. In order to prepare the way, we must go all the way back to the late eighteenth century and consider a criticism of the liberal conception of society and the state articulated by the English philosopher Edmund Burke. Burke argued that the notion of a contract, and with it the notion of a society of rationally self-interested pleasure-maximizers, could not do justice to the true nature of the human experience. A business partnership might be founded upon a contract, entered into by a pair of self-interested entrepreneurs who estimated that they would profit from the deal. But it was monstrous and inhuman, Burke insisted, to suppose that the association of men and women in the ongoing social intercourse of life rested upon a similar calculation. It was equally absurd, he said, to reduce men's submission to the majesty of the state to such a contract. Loyalty, honor, love of one's nation, all disappear in the double-entry bookkeeping of the social contract theories. Here, in a passage from his essay attacking the French Revolution, is Burke's most famous statement of the anti-contract conception of society and the state.

EDMUND BURKE (1729–1797) is the father of modern conservative political thought, and its most eloquent spokesman. During his long political career in England, he defended a moderate position on political liberties and the rights of the American colonies, but turned violently against the French revolution, which he saw as a subversion of the just and natural order of human society. In a moving message to his constituency, Burke defended the duty of a representative to vote his conscience, even against the wishes of the electorate which had put him in office.

Society is indeed a contract. Subordinate contracts for objects of mere occasional interest may be dissolved at pleasure—but the state ought not to be considered as nothing better than a partnership agreement in a trade of pepper and coffee, callico or tobacco, or some other such low concern, to be taken up for a little temporary interest, and to be dissolved by the fancy of the parties. It is to be looked on with other reverence; because it is not a partnership in things subservient only to the gross animal existence of a temporary and perishable nature. It is a partnership in all science; a partnership in all art; a partnership in every virtue, and in all perfection. As the ends of such a partnership cannot be obtained in many generations, it becomes a partnership not only between those who are living, but between those who are living, those who are dead, and those who are to be born. Each contract of each particular state is but a clause in the great primeval contract of eternal society, linking the lower with the higher natures, connecting the visible and invisible world, according to a fixed compact sanctioned by the inviolable oath which holds all physical and all moral natures, each in their appointed place. This law is not subject to the will of those, who by an obligation above them, and infinitely superiour, are bound to submit their will to that law. The municipal corporations of that universal kingdom are not morally at liberty at their pleasure, and on their speculations of a contingent improvement, wholly to separate and tear asunder the bands of their subordinate community, and to dissolve it into an unsocial, uncivil, unconnected chaos of elementary principles. It is the first and supreme necessity only, a necessity that is not chosen but chooses, a necessity paramount to deliberation, that admits no discussion, and demands no evidence, which alone can justify a resort to anarchy. This necessity is no exception to the rule; because this necessity itself is a part too of that moral and physical disposition of things to which man must be obedient by consent or force; but if that which is only submission to necessity should be made the object of choice, the law is broken, nature is disobeyed, and the rebellious are outlawed, cast forth, and exiled, from this world of reason, and order, and peace, and virtue, and fruitful penitence, into the antagonist world of madness, discord, vice, confusion, and unavailing sorrow.

EDMUND BURKE, *Reflections on the French Revolution*

This passage is an early expression of what later came to be known as the "organic" theory of the state. A business partnership or contractual association is a coming together of independent individuals, each of whom has his own interests, desires, plans, and standards of judgment. The association combines their efforts but it does not merge them into a single entity. Even a marriage, which in the eyes of the law is a contract, cannot obliterate the distinction between the husband and wife, though the usual talk of "making two one" sounds as though it does.

According to another philosophical tradition, however, society is more accurately compared to a living organism than to a business partnership. In an organism, the "parts" are merged into, and exist for, the whole. The feet, heart, hands, brain, and liver do not have separate interests, plans, or purposes. Indeed, when one organ of the body starts aggrandizing itself at the expense of the others, doctors suspect that the body is sick. An organism is an interconnected system of parts, all of which subserve the interests of the total living thing. There is proper subordination, not equality, among the parts. The brain gives orders which the nerves transmit to the muscles. If the survival of the organism requires it, a part may be amputated or removed, for each part exists only for the whole, not for itself.

Ever since Plato drew a double analogy between body and soul, and soul and state, some philosophers have said that a society is really like an organism. Men and women take their existence and their purpose from their role in the totality; the ruler, like the brain, gives the orders which the subordinate members of the whole must obey. Sacrifice for the good of the state, not self-interested calculation of personal advantage, is the fundamental principle of the organic state. Just as a healthy individual has a coherent personality that gives form and style to his life, so a healthy state has a culture that unites its people and gives their social life a distinctive style. Societies may enter into alliances with one another, just as individuals may enter into contracts with one another. But no alliance between disparate social organisms can overcome the organic wholeness of each.

In the early expressions of this theory, by de Tocqueville, Burke, and others, great emphasis is placed upon the traditions of the society, on its religious faith, and on its hierarchical political and social structure. As Oakeshott makes clear (though he is writing in our own century), the entry of new men onto the political scene is a violation of those traditions, a potentially destructive intrusion into the settled style of the politics of the society. But in the nineteenth century, great social and economic changes destroyed the old pre-industrial patterns of life and politics. First the rising capitalist class, then the new working class formed by industrialism, thrust into the political life of nation after nation.

At the same time, the political rearrangements produced by Napoleon's wars released cultural forces which had been pent up by the old imperial order. Nationalities—that is to say, peoples with a common language, culture, and history—began to insist upon political independence. Czechs, Poles, Slovaks, Hungarians, Serbians, Rumanians, Estonians, Lithuanians, Croations—each group with its special style of culture and society—demanded the chance to determine their own destiny. In the nineteenth century, there was a great surging up of interest in the music and literature of the people, and with it a rejection of the tradition of high Latin culture going back to the time of the Roman empire. The Grimms' fairy tales, the études of Chopin, the rediscovery of Aryan or Teutonic culture, all were manifestations of this same search for the indigenous culture of the peoples of Central Europe.

In the early years of this movement, the doctrine of the folk or people was a progressive and liberating influence in Europe. But the turning point was the unimaginable upheaval of the World War I. In the aftermath of that "war to end all wars," the political unity of Europe was permanently shattered and its economic health gravely damaged. The search for cultural unity took on the darker color of political absolutism. Economic depression and social disintegration fostered a powerful desire for unity, together with a hatred of foreigners and a rejection of the individualistic doctrines of liberalism. The most famous form of this new organicism, of course, was the National Socialism of Adolf Hitler in Germany. But a full decade before Hitler's rise to power, Benito Mussolini gave the doctrine a name, fascism, and a home, Italy. Mussolini cannot really be called a political philosopher, but he stated the fundamental teachings of fascism as clearly and unambiguously as any political leader ever has. In this lengthy section from Mussolini's *The Doctrine of Fascism*, we find all the key elements of fascism: the exaltation of the state, the antilib-

BENITO MUSSOLINI (1883–1945) was the founder and leader of the Italian fascist movement. He ruled Italy, first as premier, later as dictator, from 1922 until his overthrow in 1943. Two years later he was captured by Italian underground fighters and assassinated. Mussolini was the first fascist leader in Europe, though he took a back seat to Adolf Hitler in the German–Italian alliance which started and waged the European portion of World War II.

Like Hitler, Mussolini was an enemy of the liberal politics, life style, and economic policies which flourished in much of Europe and America after World War I. Italy was a devoutly religious country, and Mussolini concluded an agreement with the papacy which gained him the support, or at least the acquiescence, of that major force in Italian life.

eralism, the totalitarianism, and the celebration of war rather than peace, struggle rather than accommodation.

Fascism is a religious conception in which man is seen in his immanent relationship with a superior law and with an objective Will that transcends the particular individual and raises him to conscious membership of a spiritual society. Whoever has seen in the religious politics of the Fascist regime nothing but mere opportunism has not understood that Fascism besides being a system of government is also, and above all, a system of thought.

Fascism is a historical conception, in which man is what he is only in so far as he works with the spiritual process in which he finds himself, in the family or social group, in the nation and in the history in which all nations collaborate. From this follows the great value of tradition, in memories, in language, in customs, in the standards of social life. Outside history man is nothing. Consequently Fascism is opposed to all the individualistic abstractions of a materialistic nature like those of the eighteenth century; and it is opposed to all Jacobin utopias and innovations. It does not consider that "happiness" is possible upon earth, as it appeared to be in the desire of the economic literature of the eighteenth century, and hence it rejects all teleological theories according to which mankind would reach a definitive stabilized condition at a certain period in history. This implies putting oneself outside history and life, which is a continual change and coming to be. Politically, Fascism wishes to be a realistic doctrine; practically, it aspires to solve only the problems which arise historically of themselves and that of themselves find or suggest their own solution. To act among men, as to act in the natural world, it is necessary to enter into the process of reality and to master the already operating forces.

Against individualism, the Fascist conception is for the State; and it is for the individual in so far as he coincides with the State, which is the conscience and universal will of man in his historical existence. It is opposed to classical Liberalism, which arose from the necessity of reacting against absolutism, and which brought its historical purpose to an end when the State was transformed into the conscience and will of the people. Liberalism denied the State in the interests of the particular individual; Fascism reaffirms the State as the true reality of the individual. And if liberty is to be the attribute of the real man, and not of that abstract puppet envisaged by individualistic Liberalism, Fascism is for liberty. And for the only liberty which can be a real thing, the liberty of the State and of the individual within the State. Therefore, for the Fascist, everything is in the State, and nothing human or spiritual exists, much less has value, outside the State. In this sense Fascism is totalitarian, and the Fascist State, the synthesis and unity of all values, interprets, develops and gives strength to the whole life of the people.

Outside the State there can be neither individuals nor groups (political parties, associations, syndicates, classes). Therefore Fascism is opposed to Socialism, which confines the movement of history within the class struggle and ignores the unity of classes established in one economic and moral reality in the State; and analogously it is opposed to class syndicalism. Fascism recognizes the real exigencies for which the socialist and syndicalist movement arose, but while recognizing them wishes to bring them under the control of the State and give them a purpose within the corporative system of interests reconciled within the unity of the State.

Individuals form classes according to the similarity of their interests, they form syndicates according to differentiated economic activities within these interests; but they form first, and above all, the State, which is not to be thought of numerically as the sum-total of individuals forming the majority of a nation. And consequently Fascism is opposed to Democracy, which equates the nation to the majority, lowering it to the level of that majority; nevertheless it is the purest form of democracy if the nation is conceived, as it should be, qualitatively and not quantitatively, as the most powerful idea (most powerful because most moral, most coherent, most true) which acts within the nation as the conscience and the will of a few, even of One, which ideal tends to become active within the conscience and the will of all—that is to say, of all those who rightly constitute a nation by reason of nature, history or race, and have set out upon the same line of development and spiritual formation as one conscience and one sole will. Not a race, nor a geographically determined region, but as a community historically perpetuating itself, a multitude unified by a single idea, which is the will to existence and to power: consciousness of itself, personality.

This higher personality is truly the nation in so far as it is the State. It is not the nation that generates the State, as according to the old naturalistic concept which served as the basis of the political theories of the national States of the nineteenth century. Rather the nation is created by the State, which gives to the people, conscious of its own moral unity, a will and therefore an effective existence. The right of a nation to independence derives not from a literary and ideal consciousness of its own being, still less from a more or less unconscious and inert acceptance of a *de facto* situation, but from an active consciousness, from a political will in action and ready to demonstrate its own rights: that is to say, from a state already coming into being. The State, in fact, as the universal ethical will, is the creator of right.

The nation as the State is an ethical reality which exists and lives in so far as it develops. To arrest its development is to kill it. Therefore the State is not only the authority which governs and gives the form of laws and the value of spiritual life to the wills of individuals, but it is also a power that makes its will felt abroad, making it known and respected, in other words, demonstrating the fact of its universality in all the necessary directions of its development. It is consequently organization and expansion, at least virtually. Thus it can be likened to the human will which knows no limits to its development and realizes itself in testing its own limitlessness.

The Fascist State, the highest and most powerful form of personality, is a force, but a spiritual force, which takes over all the forms of the moral and intellectual life of man. It cannot therefore confine itself simply to the functions of order and supervision as Liberalism desired. It is not simply a mechanism which limits the sphere of the supposed liberties of the individual. It is the form, the inner standard and the discipline of the whole person; it saturates the will as well as the intelligence. Its principle, the central inspiration of the human personality living in the civil community, pierces into the depths and makes its home in the heart of the man of action as well as of the thinker, of the artist as well as of the scientist: it is the soul of the soul.

Fascism, in short, is not only the giver of laws and the founder of institutions, but the educator and promoter of spiritual life. It wants to remake, not the forms of human life, but its content, man, character, faith. And to this end it requires discipline and authority that can enter into the spirits of men and there govern unopposed. Its sign, therefore, is the Lictors' rods, the symbol of unity, of strength and justice.

III   To Karl Marx and his lifelong collaborator Friedrich Engels, the liberal social contract theory of the state was merely a convenient fiction designed to justify the rise to power of the new capitalist class. In order to understand the Marxist conception of the state, we must get at least a preliminary picture of Marx's doctrine of *historical materialism*.

As we saw in Chapter Three, Marx began with the fact of the sheer misery of the working class in England during the first part of the nineteenth century, and added to this the instability of industrial capitalism as he observed it. Out of these elements, and the philosophical theories he had studied in his youth, Marx constructed a full-scale theory about man, society, and history. The theory explained past history, analyzed the situation of industrial capitalism in the mid-nineteenth century, and predicted the future course of economic, social, and political developments. Simplifying somewhat, we can see Marx's theory as consisting of three parts: a theory of human nature; a theory of social organization; and a theory of social change, historical development, and revolution.

You have already studied Marx's theory of human nature in Chapter Three. The keynote is the concept of *alienation*. Man is considered by Marx to be a socially productive creature who finds fulfillment and happiness through the free, productive, healthful exercise of his natural powers in cooperative labor with his fellow men and women. Capitalism thwarts that exercise, causing an alienation of man from the product of his labor, from the labor itself, from his own human nature, and from his fellow workers. The result is misery in the midst of plenty, unreason in the midst of technical rationality.

The second element of Marx's theory is his conception or model of social and economic organization. At first inspection, society at any one time seems an unorganized beehive of multifarious activities, without any system, pattern, or rationale. Agriculture, the arts, science, industry, government, religion, entertainment, marketing, war, charity, crime—the things men and women do are endless in number and variety. Merely to list all the categories of jobs being performed by someone or other is to lose oneself in a confusion of diversity. But Marx saw order in the chaos. He argued that in order to make sense of social life, we must distinguish a certain group of activities which are basic to the survival and reproduction of the human race. Each day, men and women work to transform nature into the food, clothing, and shelter they need to live. These economic activities form the base, or foundation, on which all else in the society rests. In order to distinguish the productive economic activities from the philosophical theorizing which his German idealist predecessors had made so much of, Marx called the productive elements of the society its *material base*. In calling the base "material" he did not mean to suggest that it consisted of physical bodies rather than human thoughts, purposes, and plans, for even man's productive activities are intelligent, purposeful activities involving "ideas." Rather, Marx wanted to emphasize the fundamental role of economic production as opposed to philosophy, religion, or art.

The material base of a society consists of three subelements. The first is the *means* of production—the raw materials, land, and energy resources with which men and women work. The second is the *forces* of production, which includes the factories, machinery, technology, industrial knowledge, and accumulated skills of those who transform the means of production by their labor. The third, and by far the most important subelement of the material base is what Marx called the *social relationships of production*. Since everything in Marx's theory depends on this last element, we must take a few paragraphs to explain it in some detail.

Man is a productive creature, to be sure. But according to Marx, he is a *socially* productive creature. Men divide the labor among themselves, differentiating the process of production into a series of sub-jobs or specialties and then parceling these pieces of the total productive process out among different workers. Some men raise grain, others dig iron ore out of the ground. Others bake the grain into bread, and still others work the ore into tools and weapons. This *division of labor* requires also a system

Marx's theory of the structure of society.

of exchange, for no man can live on the products of his own labor alone. The farmer needs the products of the carpenter, the carpenter needs the products of the metal worker, and the metal worker needs the grain grown by the farmer. The market is the system by which a never-ending chain of trades, or purchases and sales, distributes the products of labor among the members of the society.

Although man's productive activity is cooperative, in the sense that there is a division of function and an exchange of products, it is by no means harmonious, equitable, or universally beneficent. Very early in hu-

140

man history, according to Marx, some men by force of arms succeed in seizing control over the vital means of production. They take the land, the streams, the mines, and the forests, and they prevent other men from using them. Once these men have successfully asserted ownership of the means of production, they are in a position to extract a ransom from the rest of the men and women in the society. Pay me half of all you grow, the landholder says to the farmer, or I will not allow you to farm the land. The farmer has no choice, for if he does not farm, he starves. So two classes of people crystallize out of the social situation: the ruling class, which controls the means of production, and the underclass, which is forced to give up a part of the product of its labor in order to survive.

At first, of course, the naked force which holds the underclass down is obvious to all. But as time passes and generations succeed one another, sheer custom and familiarity confer legitimacy on what was originally mere might. The rulers pass on the control of the means of production to their sons and daughters, who grow up believing that it is theirs by right. The free time which the rulers have—because they eat and drink and wear what they do not have to produce—permits them to develop a culture and style of life quite different from that of the laboring majority. Small wonder that even those in the underclass soon come to believe that the rulers are "different." They may not have been originally, but their descendants have certainly become so! As regular patterns of work, exchange, land ownership, and personal subordination develop, the rulers hold periodic courts to settle disputes that may have arisen in the enactment of those patterns. The decisions of these courts become the law of the land. Needless to say, the decisions rarely threaten the interests of the rulers, for it is they who convene the courts, they who sit on the bench, and they who enforce the orders of the courts with their soldiers. Nor is it surprising that the religious men and women of the society bless the rulers and their dominance. Churches are economically unproductive institutions, and they can survive only by sharing in that portion of the product which the rulers have taken from the laborers.

The system of relationships connecting those who control the means of production and those who do not is called the *social relationships of production*. It is the basic fact about a society, and from it grow such other, secondary facts as the structure of the law, the dogmas of the dominant religion, the underlying themes of the art and literature, *and also the form and organization of the state*. Marx calls these subordinate or secondary features of a society its *superstructure*, conveying by this metaphor the notion that a society rests on, or is built on, that portion of it which is the "base." A more modern way of putting the same idea would be to say that the means, forces, and social relationships of production are the independent variables in a society; and the law, politics, art, religion and philosophy are the dependent variables.

In the superstructure, the state occupies a central place, for it is the instrument the ruling class uses to maintain its domination of the rest of the society. As the character of the social relationships of production changes, so does the character of the state. Under feudalism, which is a system of production based on ownership of land, the state is controlled by the landed aristocracy, which employs it to maintain control of the agricultural workers (or "serfs") and to regulate the relationships between the great land holders (or "lords") and their subordinate tenants (or "vassals"). This same system of landholding also forms the basis for the military organization of the society, thereby combining the control of the means of production with the supply of the force to maintain that control. In an industrial system of production, where capital rather than land is central to the productive process, the class that owns the capital (the "capitalists") also controls the state. As Marx and Engels say in their most famous work, *The Communist Manifesto*, "The executive of the modern state is but a committee for managing the common affairs of the whole bourgeoisie."

Political philosophers claim that they are disinterestedly pursuing eternal truth when they write their treatises, essays, and dialogues, but Marx pointed to the curious fact that in each era, quite intelligent and reasonable philosophers just happened to argue for precisely that system of politics and law which best served the interests of the ruling class. Aristotle enunciated the dictum that man is a rational animal, and then proceeded to conclude that because some men are more rational than others, nature has obviously created "natural slaves" and "natural masters." That Greek society was at that time built on slave labor was, presumably, irrelevant. St. Thomas Aquinas contemplated the infinite, and came to the conclusion that God had intended a hierarchical organization of the universe remarkably similar to the feudal system then flourishing in Aquinas' Europe. John Locke examined the law of nature, and deduced from it a justification for the contractual freedom and legal equality necessary to the growth of the rising capitalist class of England. In an early essay intended as a review of a book by Bruno Bauer, Marx took the declaration of the rights of man and the citizen which had been proclaimed by the French Revolution, and showed in a clause-by-clause analysis that it was nothing more than a rationalization for bourgeois capitalism.

The same analysis could be given for Marx's own philosophy, as he himself realized. His theory of historical materialism was a justification for the working-class revolution which he hoped for, predicted, and confidently expected. The intellectual superstructure, as a reflection of the economic or material base, could not be expected to achieve a transhistorical truth. At best, it could give expression to the real social relationships of production and distribution through which men and women, day by day, labored to transform nature into the means for human life.

The third part of Marx's theory was his account of the way in which societies change over time. At any given moment, we may speak of the ruling class and the underclass. But as new technology develops, as the division of labor is carried further and further, slow shifts take place in the material base. Within the feudal order, capitalism begins to grow. New ways of production and exchange give rise to new systems of relationships. At first, the changes seem minute by comparison with the overwhelming preponderance of economic activity. But little by little, more men and women are drawn into the new patterns of economic activity. The economically progressive group, or class, is at first disadvantaged, for the rules have all been made to favor the dominant class. But as the real economic power of the progressive class grows, it begins to demand a place in the ruling circles of the society. It wants laws changed to help rather than hinder its economic interests. It wants a share of the power that comes from controlling the means of production.

Now Marx was an optimist, if by that we mean that he thought the human race was heading toward better times. But he was not a fool. It was perfectly obvious to him that whenever a growing class challenged the dominance of a ruling class, there was going to be violence. There was no way that capitalists could compromise their interests with the landed aristocrats of the old order; one of them was going to have to go. According to Marx and Engels, the two centuries of civil war and social upheaval beginning with the English Civil War, continuing on through the French and American Revolutions, and ending with the American Civil War, was simply the protracted struggle between the landed aristocracy of the precapitalist order and the capitalist class which controlled the new industrial means of production.

In exactly the same way, he predicted that the new rising class of industrial workers, the proletariat, would one day do battle with the ruling class, the capitalists. Out of that revolutionary struggle would emerge a post-capitalist society in which a new system of social relationships of production would replace the old. No longer would there be a small group that controlled the means of production and a large group forced to work for it in an unjust, exploitative, alienated manner. Instead, the entire society would collectively take control of the means of production, and the division of labor would serve the interests of all, not merely the interests of the few. Under this new system of society, called socialism, there would be no domination of one man by another. Hence, there would be no need for a *state*, for the function of the state in every previous society had been to enforce the domination of the ruling class. There would, of course, be some sort of central direction of economic activity, for in a highly complex industrial economy, a sophisticated coordination of millions of workers would be indispensable. But this would merely be an "administration of things," not the "domination of men."

What then would become of the state? The answer, Engels stated, was that it would cease to exist as any unnecessary organ ceases to exist. It would "wither away." Here is Engels' analysis of the future of the state after the proletarian revolution.

> The proletariat takes control of the State authority and, first of all, converts the means of production into State property. But by this very act it destroys itself, as a proletariat, destroying at the same time all class differences and class antagonisms, and with this, also, the State. Past and present Society, which moved amidst class antagonisms, had to have the State, that is, an organization of the exploiting class for the support of its external conditions of production, therefore, in particular, for the forcible retention of the exploited class in such conditions of oppression (such as slavery, serfdom, wage-labor), as are determined by the given methods of production. The State was the official representative of the whole of Society, its embodiment in a visible corporation; but it was only in so far as it was the State of that class which, in the given epoch, alone represented the whole of society. In ancient times it was the State of the slave owners—the only citizens of the State; in the middle ages it was the State of the feudal nobility: in our own times it is the State of the capitalists. When ultimately, the State really becomes the representative of the whole of society, it will make itself superfluous. From the time when, together with class domination and the struggle for individual existence, resulting from the present anarchy in production, those conflicts and excesses which arise from this struggle will all disappear—from that time there will, therefore, be no need for the State. The first act of the State, in which it really acts as the representative of the whole of Society, namely, the assumption of control over the means of production on behalf of society, is also its last independent act as a State. The interference of the authority of the State with social relations will then become superfluous in one field after another, and finally will cease of itself. The authority of the Government over persons will be replaced by the administration of things and the direction of the processes of production. The State will not be 'abolished'; it will wither away. It is from this point of view that we must appraise the phrase, "a free popular State"

—a phrase which, for a time, had a right to be employed as a purely propaganda slogan, but which in the long run is scientifically untenable. It is also from this point of view that we must appraise the demand of the so-called anarchists that the State "should be abolished overnight."

FRIEDRICH ENGELS, *Herr Eugen Dühring's Revolution in Science*

Engels wrote these words just about a century ago (in 1878). Since then, something calling itself a "proletarian revolution" has taken place in a dozen countries, including two of the largest in the world. Were Marx and Engels correct? Has the state withered away?

The question is a tricky one, because neither Russia nor China was an advanced bourgeois capitalist industrial society at the time of its communist revolution. Nevertheless, a number of modern political philosophers, sympathetic with Marx but skeptical of much of his theory, have argued that even in a truly socialist society, the state will not disappear. Marx and Engels based their prediction on the expectation that after the revolution, there would be no further class divisions within society. But the evidence of Russia (and to some extent, of China) suggests that even when the means of production are, technically speaking, owned by everyone collectively, there still springs up a distinction between those who labor and those who manage, those who are on the receiving end of decisions and those who issue the orders. In the Soviet Union, this distinction has given rise to systematic inequalities in the distribution of wealth, educational opportunities, status, and power.

Mao Tse-Tung, the political and philosophical leader of the Chinese revolution, has throughout his long career been especially concerned about this tendency for class distinctions to reappear after the official elimination of private ownership of the means of production. The People's Republic of China has tried a number of tactics to overcome the tendency, including the quite unusual practice of requiring technical experts and industrial managers to spend time in the fields or on the production line doing ordinary labor. It remains to be seen whether Marx's dream of a classless society can be achieved. And even if it can be, we shall still have to wait to see whether in such a society, the state will wither away.

IV   So far in this chapter we have been dealing with the dominant political theories of the past three centuries: liberalism, fascism, and communism. But over the years, a small, persistent group of political philosophers has taken an entirely different point of view toward the state. They have argued that the state, whenever and wherever it appears, infringes unjustly on the liberty of the individual, and that society would be better off with no state at all. Taking up Rousseau's question, How shall we form a state that shall both protect us and leave us free? they answer, There is no way! What men need is not rule by priests, or rule by kings, or rule by parliaments, or rule by revolutionary parties, but no rule at all. These philosophers call themselves *anarchists* (from the Greek, meaning "no leader"), and their philosophy has been a sort of underground counterdoctrine to the major political philosophies of recent times.

Anarchism has taken many forms during its history. At times, it has been used as justification for acts of terror and violence, at others as a justification for a pacifist refusal to participate in violence. Despite some very important philosophical differences among its defenders, we can, I think, find a common set of theses which unite philosophical anarchists.

First of all, anarchists are believers in the innate goodness of the human spirit. Like Rousseau, they believe that man is by nature creative rather than destructive, cooperative rather than aggressive. Hence, they do not assume, as Hobbes or Burke or even Plato would, that a coercive state is needed to hold in check man's hostile and divisive tendencies.

Second, anarchists hold that the state is positively harmful to human beings. Domination thwarts the natural growth of human potential, corrupts those who exercise power, and diminishes those against whom it is exercised. Some anarchists claim that in the absence of a coercive state, the untrammeled workings of the free market system will suffice to coordinate and regulate human behavior. These individualistic anarchists take what is in effect an extreme version of the classical liberal position. A different tradition of anarchist thought holds that in the absence of the state, collective or communal social decision-making will serve to coordinate human behavior and direct the cooperative activities of the society. During the nineteenth century, a number of utopian anarchist communities were founded in America and elsewhere to put this communitarian doctrine into practice. The agricultural communes known as kibbutzim in modern-day Israel are, in a sense, the ideological descendants of this older utopian movement.

Finally, anarchists all agree that the classical social contract theory of the origin of the state simply does not justify state authority. Even majoritarian democracy is unacceptable to the anarchists, for exactly the reason that Rousseau so shrewdly foresaw. Under the rule of a majority, the minority are forced to do what they have not chosen to do, and anarchists insist that all of Rousseau's tricky arguments will not serve to turn that coercion into freedom.

Thus far, I have tried to choose selections from the most famous philosophers of the Western tradition, on the theory that if you are going to read some philosophy, you might as well read some of the best. But for our anarchist reading, I have selected a passage from an author so obscure that he was virtually forgotten until a few years ago. Lysander Spooner is an American original, a lawyer and abolitionist who was driven by the experience of the Civil War to the realization that he was an anarchist rather than a constitutionalist. In his pamphlet, *No Treason*, he sets forth his reasons for believing that the legitimacy of the American government can not be founded upon a theory of consent of the governed.

> . . . Majorities, *as such*, afford no guarantees for justice. They are men of the same nature as minorities. They have the same passions for fame, power, and money, as minorities; and are liable and likely to be equally—perhaps more than equally, because more boldly—rapacious, tyrannical and unprincipled, if intrusted with power. There is no more reason, then, why a man should either sustain, or submit to, the rule of a majority, than of a minority. Majorities and minorities cannot rightfully be taken at all into account in deciding questions of justice. And all talk about them, in matters of government, is mere absurdity. Men are dunces for uniting to sustain any government, or any laws, *except those in which they are all agreed*. And nothing but force and fraud compel men to sustain any other. To say that majorities, as such, have a right to rule minorities, is equivalent to saying that minorities have, and ought to have, no rights, except such as majorities please to allow them.
>
> . . . It is not improbable that many or most of the worst of governments—although established by force, and by a few, in the first place —come, in time, to be supported by a majority. But if they do, this majority is composed, in large part, of the most ignorant, superstitious, timid, dependent, servile, and corrupt portions of the people; of those who have been over-awed by the power, intelligence, wealth, and arrogance; of those who have been deceived by the frauds; and of those who have been corrupted by the inducements, of the few who really constitute the government. Such majorities very likely, could be found in half, perhaps in nine-tenths, of all the countries on the globe. What do they prove? Nothing but the tyranny and corruption of the very governments that have reduced so large portions of the people to their present ignorance, servility, degradation, and corruption; an ignorance, servility, degradation, and corruption that are best illustrated in the simple fact that they *do* sustain the governments that have so oppressed, degraded, and corrupted them. They do nothing towards proving that the governments themselves are legitimate; or that they

ought to be sustained, or even endured, by those who understand their true character. The mere fact, therefore, that a government chances to be sustained by a majority, of itself proves nothing that is necessary to be proved, in order to know whether such government should be sustained, or not. . . .

But to say that the consent of either the strongest party, or the most numerous party, *in a nation*, is a sufficient justification for the establishment or maintenance of a government that shall control the whole nation, does not obviate the difficulty. The question still remains, how comes such a thing as "a nation" to exist? How do many millions of men, scattered over an extensive territory—each gifted by nature with individual freedom; required by the law of nature to call no man, or body of men, his masters; authorized by that law to seek his own happiness in his own way, to do what he will with himself and his property, so long as he does not trespass upon the equal liberty of others; authorized also, by that law, to defend his own rights, and redress his own wrongs; and to go to the assistance and defence of any of his fellow men who may be suffering any kind of injustice— how do many millions of such men *come to be a nation*, in the first place? How is it that each of them comes to be stripped of all his natural, God-given rights, and to be incorporated, compressed, compacted, and consolidated into a mass with other men, whom he never saw; with whom he has no contract; and towards many of whom he has no sentiments but fear, hatred, or contempt? How does he become subjected to the control of men like himself, who, by nature, had no authority over him; but who command him to do this, and forbid him to do that, as if they were his sovereigns, and he their subject; and as if their wills and their interests were the only standards of his duties and his rights; and who compel him to submission under peril of confiscation, imprisonment, and death?

Clearly all this is the work of force, or fraud or both. . . .

One essential of a free government is that it rest wholly on voluntary support. And one certain proof that a government is not free, is that it coerces more or less persons to support it, against their will. All governments, the worst on earth, and the most tyrannical on earth, are free governments to that portion of the people who voluntarily support them. And all governments—though the best on earth in other respects—are nevertheless tyrannies to that portion of the people— whether few or many—who are compelled to support them against their will. A government is like a church, or any other institution, in these respects. There is no other criterion whatever, by which to determine whether a government is a free one, or not, than the single one of its depending, or not depending, solely on voluntary support.

No middle ground is possible on this subject. Either "taxation without consent is robbery," or it is not. If it is *not*, then any number of men, who choose, may at any time associate; call themselves a government; assume absolute authority over all weaker than themselves; plunder them at will; and kill them if they resist. If, on the other hand, "taxation without consent *is* robbery," it necessarily follows that every man who has not consented to be taxed, has the same natural right to defend his property against a tax-gatherer, that he has to defend it against a highwayman.

PLATO (427?–347 B.C.) is one of the immortal geniuses of philosophy. Born in Athens to a wealthy and politically influential, aristocratic family, he was closely associated as a young man with Socrates, who died when Plato was in his late twenties. When the democracy was restored, Plato's family fell out of favor, and his hostility to democratic government is reflected in a number of his works. At some time after Socrates' death, perhaps as much as fifteen years or more, Plato started to write Dialogues in which moral, political, religious, cosmological, logical and other subjects were explored. In the early dialogues, Socrates is always the principal speaker, and there is some reason to suppose that Plato's picture of Socrates' personality and doctrines bears a close resemblance to the actual historical man who was his teacher. Later on, however, the dialogues clearly come more and more to reflect Plato's own philosophical investigations, and in the works composed last, Socrates disappears altogether as a character.

Retreating from public life, Plato founded a school at his home in Athens. The home was called the "Academy," and the word has since then meant a school or university. Many of the most gifted philosophers of the day worked or studied at the Academy, including the other great genius of ancient thought, Aristotle. Eventually, the Academy became an independent institution, and it continued for almost 900 years before it was finally closed by the Roman emperor Justinian in 529 A.D.

Plato's greatest work was the *Republic*, a dialogue on the nature of justice, but much of his work in later life was devoted to mathematics and cosmology, and members of the Academy made significant contributions to formal logic and to such mathematical fields as solid geometry.

Philosophy of Art 5

I   Here is a short parable: There was a singer with a clear, strong, beautiful voice, whose songs were so lovely that people would come from miles round to hear him sing. The singer was a thoughtful, compassionate man whose heart was troubled by the poverty and misery of the people for whom he sang. After much reflection, he concluded that the people should rise up and change their condition. And he realized that his songs, because of their loveliness, were a distraction to the people, making them forget for the moment the real causes of their misery. He decided to tell the people what he had discovered, but alas, they would only listen to him when he sang. So he wrote a song about the misery of the people and the dangerousness of lovely songs. But because he was a great singer, his song was a lovely song, and the people, listening to it, were soothed and distracted from their misery, and so did nothing.

Plato was just such a singer of philosophical songs, and nothing is more poignant or paradoxical than his attitude toward the great works of art which he himself created. You have several times met Socrates in these pages, always in his role as the principal character in Plato's Dialogues (his "philosophical songs"). But Plato, the artist himself, is not to be confused with the dramatic character who sometimes speaks for him in his dialogues, any more than the real historical Socrates should be con-

151

*"The edges are nice and hard, but your colors aren't icky enough."** *

Sometimes meaning, as well as beauty,
is in the eye of the beholder!

fused with that character. Socrates wrote nothing himself, as Plato's own portrait of him tells us; but Plato wrote a great deal, and so he was forced to ask himself, as every artist must, whether artistic creation is good or evil, whether a life spent in the forming of artworks is a life well-spent, what indeed the function of art is in human life and society, and whether there is a place for art in the good society.

Since Plato's Dialogues, at least as we encounter them today, are classified as philosophical works rather than as works of art, it might be worth saying a few words about what sets them off from all the other philosophical works which no one would dream of calling "artistic." A philosophical dialogue is easy enough to write, if all you care about is getting the arguments down on paper. Just put your own theories in the mouth of one character—call him Mr. Wiseman—and whatever objections you can think of in the mouth of a second character—"The Fool," perhaps—and then write the whole thing down as though it were a play. The result will not exactly be beautiful, but as long as it has two characters in it, you can call it a dialogue. A number of great and not-so-great philosophers have actually written some of their philosophy in roughly this way, including the seventeenth-century Dutch metaphysician Baruch Spinoza, who was no artist at all, and the eighteenth-century Irish cleric George Berkeley, who wasn't either.

But Plato's Dialogues are quite another thing altogether. Their artistic

*Drawing by W. Miller; © 1968 The New Yorker Magazine, Inc.

brilliance results from Plato's ability to do three things at the same time, and to do them all superbly. First, his dialogues are not shadowboxing, or put-up jobs. Plato constructs real arguments, in which Socrates' opponents score points and make philosophical moves that are genuinely persuasive. We have already seen how Plato puts into the mouth of Callicles an argument against the practice of philosophy which many readers have considered overpowering. Second, the characters in the dialogues are not cardboard figures, two-dimensional pop-ups with name tags attached. They are fully realized human beings, with feelings, passions, characteristic ways of speaking. Some of them run on in great long speeches; others are mulish, grudging, giving nothing in an argument and resisting even the most obvious implications of their own statements. Some are dignified old men, full of years and self-confident in an awareness that they are nearing the end of life with their honor unsullied; others are eager, ambitious young men, out to score a quick knockout over Socrates and make their reputations. Most of the characters in the dialogues were apparently modeled after real people, and the original readers presumably could judge how skilfully Plato had caught their characters in his portraits. But for those of us who read the dialogues two millennia later, it matters only that they are completely successful artistic creations.

Finally, Plato accomplishes the most difficult creative feat of all—he makes the personalities and speech of his characters actually exemplify, and thereby provide evidence for, the philosophical theories he is trying to expound. His characters are not merely believable; they are just what they ought to be, given the philosophy they are expressing, if Plato's own theories are true. This fit between character and belief is designed by Plato as an expression of the central thesis of his philosophy: the doctrine that the metaphysical order of the universe is mirrored in the inner psychic order of the soul. Plato bases his philosophy upon a distinction between *appearance* and *reality*, a distinction that turns up over and over in many different guises throughout his works (indeed, we can quite accurately say that although the distinction *appears* in many different forms, it is *really* always the same distinction, and that is just one more example, Plato would say, of the distinction between appearance and reality). For example, a straight stick looks bent when half of it is put in water (because of the refraction of light). Sugar may seem good to a diabetic even though it would really make him sick. A tricky argument may look correct, but really be invalid. A devil may appear to be an angel of the Lord, but really be a messenger from Satan. It may seem smart to cheat on an exam, even though it is really wrong. Popular opinion may sound wise, but really be foolish.

In all these cases, and countless others besides, there is an image, a belief, an action, a feeling, which seems to be right, true, good, accurate, veridical, or healthy but is really wrong, false, evil, misleading, fallacious, or harmful. The ability to tell the difference between the two is always, according to Plato, a matter of some sort of knowledge, and the power or part of the soul whose job it is to make that distinction is *reason*. Reason tells us that the stick is really straight, even though it looks bent; reason tells the diabetic not to eat the apparently good sugar; reason finds the flaw in the valid-looking argument; and reason shows us when the easy way—cheating, or going along with popular opinion—is in the end the harmful, destructive way.

As these examples suggest, knowledge of reality, and the ability to distinguish it from misleading appearance, is more than just "book learning." You can study the principles of optics in the classroom, but you need some common sense and the power of observation to tell when to apply the formulae to a real stick in some real water. The diabetic patient can carefully write down his doctor's instructions not to eat candy, but he needs a quite different kind of knowledge and a much stronger power of reason to apply those instructions when temptation appears in the guise of a rich, tasty dessert. Socrates needed more than just a "philosophical" understanding of justice to resist the chance to escape from his punishment by the Athenians and instead remain, calm and resigned, to drink the hemlock.

According to Plato, a man who has some true opinions but does not really understand what makes them true will *look* wise as long as he doesn't get into morally difficult or complicated situations, but he will not *really be* wise. We are liable to confuse his good habits and his true opinions with real knowledge until we see him come unstuck in a crunch. Then we will realize that we were deceived, and that what we took for real wisdom was only its appearance. So too, a man who mouths current arguments without really having thought them through for himself will sound very knowledgeable until we press him with some hard questions. Then we will discover that his knowledge is only appearance. Worst of all, according to Plato, a person who has no systematic grasp of the true good for man will not be able to tell what is going to make him truly happy, and so he will do what looks pleasant but is ultimately harmful. He will allow himself to be flattered into betraying a trust, or beguiled away from the hard work that brings real satisfaction, or frightened by imagined evils into shameful or dishonorable deeds.

Plato weaves his philosophical theory about appearance and reality together with his psychological insights into human character to produce a series of persuasive and fundamentally true portraits in his Dialogues. (Needless to say, he deliberately intends the dramatic persuasiveness of his characters—their appearance—to reveal, rather than conceal, the truth about their souls—their reality.)

One example may make all this a bit clearer. In the dialogue entitled *Gorgias*, you will remember, there are three characters who argue with Socrates. The first is the title role, a traveling public speaker and teacher named Gorgias; the second is a young disciple named Polus; and the third is the hot-headed, brilliant Callicles. Now Plato sees Gorgias as one of those decent human beings who personally would not do anything shameful or wicked, but who does not really have rational knowledge of the right moral principles. In fact, although in his own life he is an upright person, the philosophy he expounds is totally false. Plato thinks that Gorgias is dangerous, because his pupils tend to do as he says, not as he does. Instead of imitating the decency and honorableness of Gorgias' private life, his pupils listen to his relativistic moral arguments and act on them in the law courts and public life of Athens. Plato presents Gorgias as a man who is stuffily self-confident, easily trapped into logical contradictions, but personally horrified at the thought that anyone would take his philosophy as an excuse for dishonorable behavior. Plato lets him off rather easily in the dialogue, because he respects Gorgias' personal decency as a human being, while nevertheless condemning the confusion of his thought. When Polus, the young disciple, enters the argument in Gorgias' place, the tone changes immediately. Polus is one of those impressionable young men who has been misled by Gorgias' statements and insufficiently impressed by Gorgias' actual character. Polus argues better than Gorgias, because he is not restrained—as Gorgias is—by a well-developed sense of what it is fitting and proper to maintain in a moral argument. Gorgias cannot bring himself to say something he knows to be wrong merely to make a point in a debate, but Polus is not so hesitant. Nevertheless, since he is merely repeating things he has heard in current conversation, without any deep thought, he is easily refuted by Socrates. But Plato permits Socrates to make fun of Polus, thereby expressing his moral evaluation of Polus as compared with Gorgias. When Callicles jumps into the debate to replace Polus, a real tension develops between him and Socrates. Callicles really believes, as he says, that might makes right, that there are no universal rational principles binding the weak and the strong, the ordinary and the extraordinary, to a single standard of conduct. This total confusion (as Plato sees it) is mirrored in the disorder of Callicles' soul. He rants, he shouts, he grows abusive, he loses whatever dignity he may have possessed. In short, his personality exhibits precisely that breakdown of true reason which his philosophy also reveals. The dialogue becomes, at one and the same time, an argument between two philosophies and a contrast between two personalities. The truth of Socrates' position is shown as much by his composure, his ironic self-deprecation, his inner peace, as it is by the forcefulness of his arguments.

Now let me connect up the parable at the beginning of the chapter with Plato's theory of appearance and reality and this long example from the *Gorgias* of Plato's artistic skill. Strange and paradoxical as it may seem, Plato actually believed, on the basis of his theoretical distinction between appearance and reality, that artistic creations were forms of *appearance*, and that as such they led us away from knowledge and away from a proper inner harmony of the soul. And like the singer in the parable, Plato expressed this conviction in a series of artistic works of such beauty that the attention of his audience is turned away from the message rather than toward it!

Our first selection in this chapter is, once again, from the *Republic*. It contains Plato's reasons for believing that art is misleading, harmful, and therefore that it ought not to be permitted a place in the ideal society he is sketching. In much of this selection, Plato seems to be talking about what philosophers call *metaphysics*, or the study of the forms and nature of being, as much as about art. This interconnection of the different branches of philosophy is typical of the work of the great philosophers, and you should not be misled by the organization of this book into supposing that philosophy consists of a number of separate subfields locked away in watertight compartments. Indeed, the distinction between appearance and reality also bears directly on John Stuart Mill's claim, in the last chapter, that some pleasures are higher or truer or better than others. Plato held the same view, and he defended it precisely by saying that some pleasures are *more real* than others.

Plato's objections to art focus on two distinct but related questions: First, does art give us knowledge, or does it mislead us about the nature of reality? and second, does art help us to achieve a proper, harmonious inner psychic order, or does it stir up our emotions and destroy the rule of reason within the personality. Plato convicts art on both counts. Art leads us away from reality rather than toward it, he claims, and it destroys our psychic harmony rather than reinforcing it. These twin issues, of the truthfulness of art and the psychological effect of art on the audience, run through all the philosophies of art that we shall be examining in this chapter.

Can you tell me what is meant by representation in general?

. . . shall we proceed as usual and begin by assuming the existence of a single essential nature or Form for every set of things which we call by the same name? . . .

Then let us take any set of things you choose. For instance there are any number of beds or of tables, but only two Forms, one of Bed and one of Table. . . .

And we are in the habit of saying that the craftsman, when he makes the beds or tables we use or whatever it may be, has before his mind the Form of one or other of these pieces of furniture. The Form itself is, of course, not the work of any craftsman. . . .

Now what name would you give to a craftsman who can produce all the things made by every sort of workman?

He would need to have very remarkable powers!

Wait a moment, and you will have even better reason to say so. For, besides producing any kind of artificial thing, this same craftsman can create all plants and animals, himself included, and earth and sky and gods and the heavenly bodies and all the things under the earth in Hades.

That sounds like a miraculous feat of virtuosity.

Are you incredulous? Tell me, do you think there could be no such craftsman at all, or that there might be someone who could create all these things in one sense, though not in another? Do you not see that you could do it yourself, in a way?

In what way, I should like to know.

There is no difficulty; in fact there are several ways in which the thing can be done quite quickly. The quickest perhaps would be to take a mirror and turn it round in all directions. In a very short time you could produce sun and stars and earth and yourself and all the other animals and plants and lifeless objects which we mentioned just now.

Yes, in appearance, but not the actual things.

Quite so; you are helping out my argument. My notion is that a painter is a craftsman of that kind. You may say that the things he produces are not real; but there is a sense in which he too does produce a bed.

Yes, the appearance of one.

And what of the carpenter? Were you not saying just now that he only makes a particular bed, not what we call the Form or essential nature of Bed?

Yes, I was.

If so, what he makes is not the reality, but only something that resembles it. It would not be right to call the work of a carpenter or of any other handicraftsman a perfectly real thing. . . .

We must not be surprised, then, if even an actual bed is a somewhat shadowy thing as compared with reality.

True.

Now shall we make use of this example to throw light on our question as to the true nature of this artist who represents things? We have here three sorts of bed: one which exists in the nature of things and which, I imagine, we could only describe as a product of divine workmanship; another made by the carpenter; and a third by the painter. So the three kinds of bed belong respectively to the domains of these three: painter, carpenter, and god.

Yes.

Each physical bed is a copy of the eternal Idea of Bed.
The artist's painting is a copy of one
of those physical beds. Thus, the painting is,
according to Plato, merely a copy of a copy.
It is twice removed from true Reality.

Now the god made only one ideal or essential Bed, whether by choice or because he was under some necessity not to make more than one; at any rate two or more were not created, nor could they possibly come into being.

Why not?

Because, if he made even so many as two, then once more a single ideal Bed would make its appearance, whose character those two would share; and that one, not the two, would be the essential Bed. Knowing this, the god, wishing to be the real maker of a real Bed, not a particular manufacturer of one particular bed, created one which is essentially unique.

So it appears.

Shall we call him, then, the author of the true nature of Bed, or something of that sort?

Certainly he deserves the name, since all his works constitute the real nature of things.

And we may call the carpenter the manufacturer of a bed?

Yes.

Can we say the same of the painter?

Certainly not.

Then what is he, with reference to a bed?

I think it would be fairest to describe him as the artist who represents the things which the other two make.

Very well, said I; so the work of the artist is at the third remove from the essential nature of the thing?

Exactly.

The tragic poet, too, is an artist who represents things; so this will apply to him: he and all other artists are, as it were, third in succession from the throne of truth.

Just so.

We are in agreement, then, about the artist. But now tell me about our painter: which do you think he is trying to represent—the reality that exists in the nature of things, or the products of the craftsman?

The products of the craftsman.

As they are, or as they appear? You have still to draw that distinction.

How do you mean?

I mean: you may look at a bed or any other object from straight in front or slantwise or at any angle. Is there then any difference in the bed itself, or does it merely look different?

It only looks different.

Well, that is the point. Does painting aim at reproducing any actual object as it is, or the appearance of it as it looks? In other words, is it a representation of the truth or of a semblance?

Of a semblance.

The art of representation, then, is a long way from reality; and apparently the reason why there is nothing it cannot reproduce is that it grasps only a small part of any object, and that only an image. Your painter, for example, will paint us a shoemaker, a carpenter, or other workman without understanding any one of their crafts; and yet, if he were a good painter, he might deceive a child or a simple-minded person into thinking his picture was a real carpenter, if he showed it them at some distance.

. . . the content of this poetical representation is something at the third remove from reality, is it not?

Yes.

On what part of our human nature, then, does it produce its effect?

What sort of part do you mean?

Let me explain by an analogy. An object seen at a distance does not, of course, look the same size as when it is close at hand; a straight stick looks bent when part of it is under water; and the same thing appears concave or convex to an eye misled by colours. Every sort of confusion like these is to be found in our minds; and it is this weakness in our nature that is exploited, with a quite magical effect, by many tricks of illusion, like scene-painting and conjuring.

. . . Instead of trusting merely to the analogy from painting, let us directly consider that part of the mind to which the dramatic element in poetry appeals, and see how much claim it has to serious worth. We can put the question in this way. Drama, we say, represents the acts and fortunes of human beings. It is wholly concerned with what they do, voluntarily or against their will, and how they fare, with the consequences which they regard as happy or otherwise, and with their feelings of joy and sorrow in all these experiences. That is all, is it not?

Yes.

And in all these experiences has a man an undivided mind? Is there not an internal conflict which sets him at odds with himself in his conduct, much as we were saying that the conflict of visual impressions leads him to make contradictory judgments? However, I need not ask that question; for, now I come to think of it, we have already agreed that innumerable conflicts of this sort are constantly occurring in the mind. But there is a further point to be considered now. We have said that a man of high character will bear any stroke of fortune, such as the loss of a son or of anything else he holds dear, with more equanimity than most people. We may now ask: will he feel no pain, or is that impossible? Will he not rather observe due measure in his grief?

Yes, that is nearer the truth.

Now tell me: will he be more likely to struggle with his grief and resist it when he is under the eyes of his fellows or when he is alone?

He will be far more restrained in the presence of others.

Yes; when he is by himself he will not be ashamed to do and say much that he would not like anyone to see or hear.

Quite so.

What encourages him to resist his grief is the lawful authority of reason, while the impulse to give way comes from the feeling itself; and, as we said, the presence of contradictory impulses proves that two distinct elements in his nature must be involved. One of them is law-abiding, prepared to listen to the authority which declares that it is best to bear misfortune as quietly as possible without resentment, for several reasons: it is never certain that misfortune may not be a blessing; nothing is gained by chafing at it; nothing human is matter for great concern; and, finally, grief hinders us from calling in the help we most urgently need. By this I mean reflection on what has happened, letting reason decide on the best move in the game of life that the fall of the dice permits. Instead of behaving like a child who goes on shrieking after a fall and hugging the wounded part, we should accustom the mind to set itself at once to raise up the fallen and cure the hurt, banishing lamentation with a healing touch.

Certainly that is the right way to deal with misfortune.

And if, as we think, the part of us which is ready to act upon these reflections is the highest, that other part which impels us to dwell upon our sufferings and can never have enough of grieving over them is unreasonable, craven, and faint-hearted.

Yes.

Now this fretful temper gives scope for a great diversity of dramatic representation; whereas the calm and wise character in its unvarying constancy is not easy to represent, nor when represented is it readily understood, especially by a promiscuous gathering in a theatre, since it is foreign to their own habit of mind. Obviously, then, this steadfast disposition does not naturally attract the dramatic poet, and his skill is not designed to find favour with it. If he is to have a popular success, he must address himself to the fretful type with its rich variety of material for representation.

Obviously.

We have, then, a fair case against the poet and we may set him down as the counterpart of the painter, whom he resembles in two ways: his creations are poor things by the standard of truth and reality, and his appeal is not to the highest part of the soul, but to one which is equally inferior. So we shall be justified in not admitting him into a well-ordered commonwealth, because he stimulates and strengthens an element which threatens to undermine the reason. As a country may be given over into the power of its worst citizens while the better sort are ruined, so, we shall say, the dramatic poet sets up a vicious form of government in the individual soul: he gratifies that senseless part which cannot distinguish great and small, but regards the same things as now one, now the other; and he is an image-maker whose images are phantoms far removed from reality.

Quite true.

PLATO, *Republic*

One final word on the paradox of the parable before we move on to the views of other philosophers. Plato feared that art would lead us away from reality, rather than toward it. Considering how famous Plato has become, how widely his works have been read and studied in both the West and the East, it is tempting to dismiss his fears as foolish. But the fact is that in a peculiar way, Plato's own success is evidence that he was right. Through the dramatic power of Plato's art, Socrates has become an immortal figure of Western thought. When we read the Dialogues today, all of us—students and trained philosophers alike—instinctively cast Socrates as the hero and his opponents as the villains of the drama. This encourages us to accept Socrates' (and Plato's) doctrines without properly criticizing them or evaluating them. In other words, we treat Socrates in exactly the way that the ancient Athenians treated Gorgias and the other popular speakers. We are swayed by Plato's art, rather than persuaded by his arguments. Now, Socrates took what we today would call a conservative political position, and his opponents—at least according to some scholars—were the "liberals" of their society. Strange as it may seem, many modern philosophers whose own political opinions are liberal still treat Socrates as the good guy and Gorgias or Protagoras or Thrasymachus or Callicles as the bad guys. In short, they are so beguiled by the beauty of Plato's song that they do not reflect, calmly and rationally, on its words. That is just the danger Plato saw and warned of when he banned the artists from his ideal Republic.

II   Plato was not yet thirty when Socrates died. Later in life, he founded a school or center for mathematical, cosmological, and philosophical investigation called the Academy. Far and away the most distinguished "student" at the Academy, if we can speak of students at all, was a man named Aristotle. There are many students of philosophy who consider Aristotle the greatest philosopher of all. St. Thomas Aquinas, the medieval theologian who figures so prominently in the development of Catholic doctrine, had so high an opinion of Aristotle that he referred to him simply as "the philosopher," as if there were no other. When you think about it, the odds must be simply astronomical against such a sequence of teachers and students as Socrates, Plato, and Aristotle.

Aristotle was not at all gifted artistically as Plato was, though in his youth he tried his hand at writing some dialogues. His temperament was rather that of a scientist, and the writings which we have today by him are actually treatises or lecture notes for the teaching he did at the Academy. Because they were written for a specialized audience rather than for the general public, they are very condensed, rather dry, and sometimes hard to follow if you aren't already pretty well up on what Aristotle is talking about. The range of Aristotle's investigations was simply staggering. In addition to his great work in logic, he wrote on systematic comparative political science, moral philosophy, cosmology, psychology, biology, astronomy, physics, and he even developed several proofs for the existence of a "prime mover," or God. In Athens at that time, the public theater was an important part of the religious and civic as well as cultural life of the people, and the annual performances of the tragedies written by the great Greek playwrights were a focus of public interest. Aristotle wrote a short treatise on the subject of tragedy, which was considered to be a kind of poetry. We know that little work today as *The Poetics,* and despite its brevity, it is much read and quoted, for it has had a wide and deep influence throughout the ages on philosophical theories about art.

For our purposes, Aristotle's treatise is interesting because of its defense of art against the twofold attack of his teacher, Plato. Recall the

ARISTOTLE (384–322 B.C.) is the most influential figure in the history of Western philosophy. Born in Stagira, a Greek colony on the Aegean Sea, he came to Athens as a very young man to study with Plato in the school known as the Academy. He remained a student and member of the Academy for twenty years, leaving only in 347 B.C. on Plato's death. Eventually, he founded his own school, where he lectured on a range of subjects so broad that he must have been virtually a one-man faculty. In addition to his major philosophical discoveries in the fields of logic, metaphysics, and the theory of knowledge, Aristotle did an enormous amount of empirical work on problems of astronomy, biology, comparative politics, and anatomy.

Aristotle is remembered today for his philosophy, but during his middle life, after leaving Plato's Academy and before founding his own school, he spent seven years as a tutor to the young prince who was to become Alexander the Great. Alexander, heir to the throne of Macedonia, eventually conquered the entire Greek world, and pushed his military compaigns as far east as India. Aristotle persuaded Alexander to send back biological specimens and other data from his explorations.

Although much of Aristotle's work has been surpassed by later investigators in the 2000 years and more since his death, some of his writings, particularly in psychology and in the theory of art, remain as suggestive and useful as they were in ancient times.

charge that Plato had leveled against poetry: it leads us away from truth, and it disorders the soul. Aristotle does not say a great deal about these two criticisms, but he indicates rebuttals to both. First of all, consider the claim that art misleads us by offering nothing more than imperfect copies of the world of the senses, which is itself no better than an imperfect copy or realization of the ideal standards of beauty, goodness, and justice which Plato calls the Forms or Ideas. If I want to know the true nature of a circle, I had better turn my eyes away from physical objects and reflect instead upon the pure definitions of mathematical forms. It is bad enough that my inadequate intelligence sometimes needs the aid of wheels, coins, and other imperfectly round objects which I encounter in life. I will simply stray farther from the truth if I fix my eyes on a picture of a wheel! The same is true for the knowledge of the human soul. True or ideal justice has never been achieved by a living man or woman, so I can learn very little about the eternal standard of justice through an examination of the lives of even the noblest men and women. What can a tragedian do, save conjure up for me on the stage an admittedly imperfect imitation of an admittedly imperfect character! I might as well try to get a feel for fine cowhide by looking at a photograph of imitation leather!

Not so, Aristotle replies. Plato is right in insisting that we should seek a knowledge of the unchanging, universal forms of justice, beauty, and goodness, but he is wrong in supposing that art merely provides us with imperfect copies of particular instances of those universal forms. The great artist has the ability, through his art, to grasp the universal that lies within the particular, and to present it to us in such a way that we achieve a greater knowledge than we would otherwise have. When Shakespeare creates for us the character of Hamlet (needless to say, this is my example, not Aristotle's), he shows us, through the particularities of the vacillations and inner conflicts of one young prince, some universal truths about fathers and sons, sons and mothers, intellect and will, thought and action. Plato to the contrary notwithstanding, we are wiser for seeing a performance of *Hamlet* than we would be were we to travel back in time and meet the real man on whom the play is based.

The dispute between Plato and Aristotle is partly a disagreement about art, of course, but it is, at a deeper level, a disagreement about metaphysics. Plato seems to have held that the universal, eternal, unchanging Forms actually exist independently of the particular, time-bound, changing objects and events which fitfully and inadequately embody them. (I say, "seems to have held," because this is a subject on which scholars differ among themselves.) In other words, Plato believed that there is a reality which transcends the appearances of the senses and the world of space, time, and physical things. True knowledge was for him, therefore, a rational understanding of that transcendent realm of universal Forms. Aristotle, on the other hand, held that the universal Forms were completely embodied in the particular things of the world of space and time. True knowledge did indeed consist of a grasp of those forms, and Plato was certainly right that we must penetrate the changing particularity of this and that moment or event in order to get at the universal truths. But because the universals were embodied in the particulars—because true circularity was to be found within actual circular things, true rationality within actual rational creatures, true beauty within actual works of art, our attention should be focused even more intently on those particular instances, rather than directed entirely away from them toward an independent realm of eternal Forms.

Aristotle's answer to Plato's second charge rests on a point of psychology rather than metaphysics. Plato was afraid that tragedy would arouse uncontrollable passions in the audience and thereby disarrange the proper harmony of the soul. It would weaken the ascendency of the rational forces within the personality and release erotic and aggressive elements that were destructive and deluding. Aristotle argued that just the opposite was the case. Since those harmful passions are present anyway, far better to release them in the controlled setting of the drama than to bottle them up entirely. In art, we experience those terrible feelings vicariously, through our identification with the characters in the play. When they suffer, triumph, love, hate, rage, and mourn, we in the audience do also. When the play ends, we are purged of the pent-up passions without having expressed them in the terrible deeds that the playwright has depicted on the stage. We leave the theater calmed, not aroused.

All this seems thin, bloodless, "academic" until we realize that exactly the same debate now rages in America about violence and sex in our movies and television shows. Does the portrayal of violence make our children more prone to act violently in their real lives, or does it drain away the violence that lies within all of us, giving it a safe, harmless outlet? Does sado-masochistic pornography stimulate its viewers to commit sex crimes, or does it divert passions which otherwise would lead to rape or mutilation?

The following brief selections from Aristotle's *Poetics* will give you some sense of his approach to the analysis and justification of art, but they will hardly settle such a host of difficult and controversial questions. In the remainder of this chapter, we shall take a look at a number of other conceptions of the nature and rationale of art. Perhaps somewhere in this debate you will find your own answer to Plato's question: Does art have a legitimate place in the good society?

> From what we have said it will be seen that the poet's function is to describe, not the thing that has happened, but a kind of thing that might happen, i.e. what is possible as being probable or necessary. The distinction between historian and poet is not in the one writing prose and the other verse—you might put the work of Herodotus into verse, and it would still be a species of history; it consists really in this, that the one describes the thing that has been, and the other a kind of thing that might be. Hence poetry is something more philosophic and of graver import than history, since its statements are of the nature rather of universals, whereas those of history are singulars. . . .
>
> . . . A tragedy, then, is the imitation of an action that is serious and also, as having magnitude, complete in itself; in language with pleasurable accessories, each kind brought in separately in the parts of the work; in a *dramatic*, not in a narrative *form*; with incidents arousing pity and fear, wherewith to accomplish its catharsis of such emotions. . . .
>
> We assume that, for the finest form of Tragedy, the Plot must be

not simple but complex; and further, that it must imitate actions arousing fear and pity, since that is the distinctive function of this kind of imitation. It follows, therefore, that there are three forms of Plot to be avoided. (1) A good man must not be seen passing from happiness to misery, or (2) a bad man from misery to happiness. The first situation is not fear-inspiring or piteous, but simply odious to us. The second is the most untragic that can be; it has no one of the requisites of Tragedy; it does not appeal either to the human feeling in us, or to our pity, or to our fears. Nor, on the other hand, should (3) an extremely bad man be seen falling from happiness into misery. Such a story may arouse the human feeling in us, but it will not move us to either pity or fear; pity is occasioned by undeserved misfortune, and fear by that of one like ourselves; so that there will be nothing either piteous or fear-inspiring in the situation. There remains, then, the intermediate kind of personage, a man not pre-eminently virtuous and just, whose misfortune, however, is brought upon him not by vice and depravity but by some error of judgement, of the number of those in the enjoyment of great reputation and prosperity; e.g. Oedipus, Thyestes, and the men of note of similar families. The perfect Plot, accordingly, must have a single, and not (as some tell us) a double issue; the change in the hero's fortunes must be not from misery to happiness, but on the contrary from happiness to misery; and the cause of it must lie not in any depravity, but in some great error on his part; the man himself being either such as we have described, or better, not worse, than that . . .

The tragic fear and pity may be aroused by the Spectacle; but they may also be aroused by the very structure and incidents of the play—which is the better way and shows the better poet. The Plot in fact should be so framed that, even without seeing the things take place, he who simply hears the account of them shall be filled with horror and pity at the incidents; which is just the effect that the mere recital of the story in *Oedipus* would have on one. To produce this same effect by means of the Spectacle is less artistic, and requires extraneous aid. Those, however, who make use of the Spectacle to put before us that which is merely monstrous and not productive of fear, are wholly out of touch with Tragedy; not every kind of pleasure should be required of a tragedy, but only its own proper pleasure.

The tragic pleasure is that of pity and fear, and the poet has to produce it by a work of imitation; it is clear, therefore, that the causes should be included in the incidents of his story. Let us see, then, what kinds of incident strike one as horrible, or rather as piteous. In a deed of this description the parties must necessarily be either friends, or enemies, or indifferent to one another. Now when enemy does it on enemy, there is nothing to move us to pity either in his doing or in his meditating the deed, except so far as the actual pain of the sufferer is concerned; and the same is true when the parties are indifferent to one

another. Whenever the tragic deed, however, is done within the family
—when murder or the like is done or meditated by brother on brother,
by son on father, by mother on son, or son on mother—these are the
situations the poet should seek after.

ARISTOTLE, *Poetics*

III   Plato claims that art is harmful, both intellectually and emotionally. Aristotle replies that art teaches and purges, that it aids us in acquiring knowledge of universal truths and in maintaining the proper internal order of
our psyches. Though they seem to disagree fundamentally, nevertheless
they are united in believing that art should be judged according to the
positive or negative value of its effects on us. Most philosophers who have
reflected on the value of art have judged it in this way, as useful or harmful for some purpose. But one group of defenders of art, repelled by the
merely instrumental conception of art, developed the view that art needs
no justification outside itself, that art should be encouraged, valued,
cherished for itself alone. The slogan of this group, who lived and wrote
in the nineteenth century, was "art for art's sake," and before going on
to several of the more prominent philosophical defenses of art, it might
be interesting to spend a few moments looking at the "art for art's sake"
doctrine.

The central notion that we need here is a distinction, long current in
philosophy, between what is sometimes called *instrumental value* and *intrinsic value*. Human beings are purposive creatures. They have goals or
ends or purposes which they pursue by choosing what seem to them to be
appropriate means. (As you know, Michael Oakeshott dissents from this
view of human action. There probably isn't any statement ever made,
and certainly not an interesting or important statement, which every
philosopher would agree to—not even the statement that philosophy is a
worthwhile enterprise!) Very often, when we describe something as valuable, or useful, or good, we simply mean that it is especially helpful to us in
achieving some purpose or getting to some goal that we have. If I call a
car a good car, I probably mean that it runs smoothly, or rarely breaks
down, or uses relatively little gas. In short, I mean that it is a useful means or *instrument* for doing what I want to do, which may be to
get somewhere fast, or safely, or cheaply, or reliably. If I say that a good
education is the most valuable gift that parents can give their child, I probably mean that in the modern world, a good education will be more useful
to that child in achieving his or her goals than anything else. Someone
who replies that strong character is even more valuable than a good educa-

tion will probably mean that certain strengths of personality turn out to make more difference in the adult world than formal book learning or credits and degrees.

A good car is good *for* doing something; an education is valuable as a means *to* something; character will be a source of strength *for* some end. All these, and countless other things besides, are valuable as means or instruments, which is to say that they have *instrumental value*. Now, if you stop and think about it for a moment, it should be obvious that you will never consider something valuable *as a means* unless there is something else that you consider just plain valuable in itself. If there is nothing you want *for itself*, nothing you like or desire or consider worthy *in and of itself*, then it would make no sense to value other things simply as "useful." Suppose for example that you are quite happy right where you are, and have no desire whatsoever to go anywhere else. A friend comes along and says, "Now that road there is a really great road. You ought to take a ride down it." You say, "Why should I take a ride down it? I don't want to go where it leads." And he answers, "It doesn't matter! It is such a great road, you ought to take it anyway." Well, your friend is either joking, or he is crazy. As the old saying goes, a bargain isn't a bargain unless it is a bargain for you. And a road isn't a good road for you unless it is a good road to somewhere you want to go.

Or you might go into a hardware store to buy a hammer so that you can hang some pictures. But even if the store has nothing better than a mediocre hammer and a really great sale on saws, the sensible thing to do is to buy the hammer. You don't want "a good tool." You want a tool that is *good for* whatever you want to do, which in this case is to hang some pictures.

By contrast things which are good in themselves, rather than being good for something else, are said to have *intrinsic value*. That simply means that their merit, value, goodness, or whatever is possessed by them independently of anything else in the world. One way to make this point about something that has intrinsic value is to say that it would be valuable even if nothing else in the world existed. A road has only instrumental value, for if there were nothing in the world but that road—and in particular, if there were noplace at the other end of it—who would value it as a road? Similarly, if there were no nails, no pictures to hang, nothing to hit, who would value a hammer? But when something has intrinsic value, it retains that value even in the absence of other objects, places, events, or states of affairs with regard to which it might be useful.

Is there anything at all that has intrinsic value? Well, we might argue that unless *something* has intrinsic value, then nothing has instrumental value. If one thing is useful for getting another, and that other is not valuable in itself, but simply useful for getting a third thing, and so on and on, we get into what is sometimes called "an infinite regress." It is like the ancient Hindu theory that the world rests on the back of an elephant, which stands on the back of a giant sea turtle, which swims in an enormous ocean. The obvious question is, what is the ocean in? So something must have intrinsic value, if anything is to have any sort of value at all.

We have already encountered two philosophical candidates for the title of intrinsic value, although we didn't use that language when we met them. Immanuel Kant said that humanity is an end in itself, and that is another way of claiming that *humanity* has intrinsic value. And Jeremy Bentham said that the only good thing is *pleasure,* by which he obviously meant that pleasure was the only thing that is intrinsically valuable. In the nineteenth century, Walter Pater, Clive Bell, and Oscar Wilde, all of them British, argued that art has intrinsic value that it is valuable in and of itself. Wilde carried this view to such lengths that he ended by reversing the usual order of priority between life and art. Instead of saying, as most philosophers have, that art is valuable insofar as it contributes to life, Wilde argued that life acquired value by contributing to art! In this selection from his book, *Intentions,* Wilde summarizes his doctrine. Incidentally, Wilde was a gifted and successful playwright, as well as a thoughtful philosopher of art. You probably know the old joke that those who can, do, and those who can't, teach. Sometimes a third line is added: and those who cannot even teach, philosophize. But in this chapter, most of the philosophers we read are also able practitioners of some form of artistic creation.

OSCAR WILDE (1854–1900) was a brilliant Irish playwright and novelist whose super-aesthetic mannerisms typified the movement known as "art-for-art's sake." He wrote *The Picture of Dorian Gray*, which was made many years later into a truly scary horror film, and the much-revived play *The Importance of Being Earnest*. In Gilbert and Sullivan's delightful light opera, *Patience*, the character of Bunthorne is a take-off on Wilde.

CYRIL . . . But in order to avoid making any error I want you to tell me briefly the doctrines of the new aesthetics.
VIVIAN.   Briefly, then, they are these. Art never expresses anything but itself. It has an independent life, just as Thought has, and develops purely on its own lines. It is not necessarily realistic in an age of realism, nor spiritual in an age of faith. So far from being the

creation of its time, it is usually in direct opposition to it, and the only history that it preserves for us is the history of its own progress. Sometimes it returns upon its footsteps, and revives some antique form, as happened in the archaistic movement of late Greek Art, and in the pre-Raphaelite movement of our own day. At other times it entirely anticipates its age, and produces in one century work that it takes another century to understand, to appreciate and to enjoy. In no case does it reproduce its age. To pass from the art of a time to the time itself is the great mistake that all historians commit.

The second doctrine is this. All bad art comes from returning to Life and Nature, and elevating them into ideals. Life and Nature may sometimes be used as part of Art's rough material, but before they are of any real service to art they must be translated into artistic conventions. The moment Art surrenders its imaginative medium it surrenders everything. As a method Realism is a complete failure, and the two things that every artist should avoid are modernity of form and modernity of subject-matter. To us, who live in the nineteenth century, any century is a suitable subject for art except our own. The only beautiful things are the things that do not concern us. It is, to have the pleasure of quoting myself, exactly because Hecuba is nothing to us that her sorrows are so suitable a motive for a tragedy. Besides, it is only the modern that ever becomes old-fashioned. M. Zola sits down to give us a picture of the Second Empire. Who cares for the Second Empire now? It is out of date. Life goes faster than Realism, but Romanticism is always in front of Life.

The third doctrine is that Life imitates Art far more than Art imitates Life. This results not merely from Life's imitative instinct, but from the fact that the self-conscious aim of Life is to find expression, and that Art offers it certain beautiful forms through which it may realise that energy. It is a theory that has never been put forward before, but it is extremely fruitful, and throws an entirely new light upon the history of Art.

It follows, as a corollary from this, that external Nature also imitates Art. The only effects that she can show us are effects that we have already seen through poetry, or in paintings. This is the secret of Nature's charm, as well as the explanation of Nature's weakness.

The final revelation is that Lying, the telling of beautiful untrue things, is the proper aim of Art. But of this I think I have spoken at sufficient length. And now let us go out on the terrace, where "droops the milk-white peacock like a ghost," while the evening star "washes the dusk with silver." At twilight nature becomes a wonderfully suggestive effect, and is not without loveliness, though perhaps its chief use is to illustrate quotations from the poets. Come! We have talked long enough.   OSCAR WILDE, *Intentions*

Nicolo Paganini, violinist and composer
of the Romantic era, painted in the
Romantic style by Eugene Delacroix.

IV The most powerful and influential aesthetic movement of the past several centuries, both in England and on the continent of Europe, is undoubtedly romanticism. In the late eighteenth century, poets, painters, and philosophers of art rebelled against the style and tenets of the neo-classicism which had until then dominated the theory and practice of art. Neo-classicism exalted order, proportion, reason, and the subordination of the creative artist to objective principles of aesthetic taste. In England especially, neo-classicism looked back to the calm gravity of the art and language of the great period of Roman culture known—after the emperor Caesar Augustus—as the Augustan Age. The English romantic poets overturned all of the entrenched tenets of neo-classical art, and in doing so carried out a revolution whose effects are still being felt today even beyond the confines of the world of art and literature.

The key to the romantic rebellion was two reversals or denials of the

171

traditional doctrine. First, the romantics denied the supremacy of *reason* in art and life. Instead, they insisted that the power of creative *imagination* was the highest human faculty. From Plato on, philosophers and students of art had insisted that reason is man's primary organ of knowledge, his source for whatever truth he could attain. The romantics granted the power of reason to accumulate knowledge of the ordinary, or work-a-day sort. But for deep insight into the inner being of man and nature, for a grasp of that eternal, unchanging realm beyond the world of the senses, artistic imagination was necessary.

The second reversal was the substitution of the subjective for the objective as the test and source of true knowledge. Philosophers traditionally had dismissed the subjective, the particular, the individual, as lacking in value or cognitive significance. What mathematics or philosophy or science could validate as universally and objectively true, independently of the momentary subjective state of the individual investigator, could be accepted as established. But the intense fleeting feeling of the lone artist could not possibly serve as a conduit of important truth. The romantics turned this traditional view on its head. They insisted that the most intense and momentary emotional states of the most extraordinary individuals were man's glimpse of the infinite, his window on eternity.

Plato was suspicious of poets and the poetic impulse, because he believed that the act of artistic creation had more than a touch of madness about it. Poets were, in popular Greek opinion, possessed by the gods, and certainly their moments of inspiration bore little resemblance to the quiet rational progress of dialectical philosophical argument. Art, Plato

WILLIAM WORDSWORTH (1770–1850) was one of the leading poets of the English romantic movement. In his youth, he traveled in France, and became an enthusiastic supporter of the revolution. After fathering an illegitimate child by a French woman, Marie Anne Vallen, he returned to England and eventually settled in Somerset, near Samuel Coleridge. During the last years of the old century and the first years of the new, Coleridge and Wordsworth wrote a series of poems, entitled *Lyrical Ballads*, which remain among the classic works of romanticism.

In middle life, Wordsworth turned against the liberal views of his youth, and became increasingly conservative. He continued to write poetry throughout his lifetime, but never achieved the heights of his early work. In 1843, he was named Poet Laureate of England, succeeding Robert Southey.

said, could not put us in touch with the eternal because it was irrational. The romantics turned Plato completely around, and asserted that art *could* put us in touch with the eternal precisely *because* it was ecstatic, subjective, emotionally intense, and in that sense irrational. The great irony of the romanticists is that they considered themselves Neo-Platonists!

One of the finest statements of the romantic philosophy is, as you might expect, a poem, namely the ode by William Wordsworth entitled "Intimations of Immortality from Recollections of Early Childhood." I would like to use it as our selection, but as this is a philosophy text, I have instead selected a portion of the preface which Wordsworth wrote for a book of verse entitled *Lyrical Ballads*. Ask your English teachers to read Wordsworth's ode with you.

> . . . All good poetry is the spontaneous overflow of powerful feelings: and though this be true, Poems to which any value can be attached were never produced on any variety of subjects but by a man who, being possessed of more than usual organic sensibility, had also thought long and deeply. For our continued influxes of feelings are modified and directed by our thoughts, which are indeed the representatives of all our past feelings; and, as by contemplating the relation of these general representatives to each other, we discover what is really important to men, so, by the repetition and continuance of this act, our feelings will be connected with important subjects, till at length, if we be originally possessed of much sensibility, such habits of mind will be produced, that, by obeying blindly and mechanically the impulses of those habits, we shall describe objects, and utter sentiments, of such a nature, and in such connexion with each other, that the understanding of the Reader must necessarily be in some degree enlightened, and his affections strengthened and purified. . . .
>
> However exalted a notion we would wish to cherish of the character of a Poet, it is obvious, that while he describes and imitates passions, his employment is in some degree mechanical, compared with the freedom and power of real and substantial action and suffering. So that it will be the wish of the Poet to bring his feelings near to those of the persons whose feelings he describes, nay, for short spaces of time, perhaps, to let himself slip into an entire delusion, and even confound and identify his own feelings with theirs; modifying only the language which is thus suggested to him by a consideration that he describes for a particular purpose, that of giving pleasure. Here, then, he will apply the principle of selection which has been already insisted upon. He will depend upon this for removing what would otherwise be painful or disgusting in the passion; he will feel that there is no necessity to trick out or to elevate nature: and, the more industriously he applies this principle, the deeper will be his faith that no words, which *his*

fancy or imagination can suggest, will be to be compared with those which are the emanations of reality and truth.

But it may be said by those who do not object to the general spirit of these remarks, that, as it is impossible for the Poet to produce upon all occasions language as exquisitely fitted for the passion as that which the real passion itself suggests, it is proper that he should consider himself as in the situation of a translator, who does not scruple to substitute excellencies of another kind for those which are unattainable by him; and endeavours occasionally to surpass his original, in order to make some amends for the general inferiority to which he feels that he must submit. But this would be to encourage idleness and unmanly despair. Further, it is the language of men who speak of what they do not understand; who talk of Poetry as of a matter of amusement and idle pleasure; who will converse with us as gravely about a *taste* for Poetry, as they express it, as if it were a thing as indifferent as a taste for rope-dancing, or Frontiniac or Sherry. Aristotle, I have been told, has said, that Poetry is the most philosophic of all writing: it is so: its object is truth, not individual and local, but general, and operative; not standing upon external testimony, but carried alive into the heart by passion; truth which is its own testimony, which gives competence and confidence to the tribunal to which it appeals, and receives them from the same tribunal. Poetry is the image of man and nature. The obstacles which stand in the way of the fidelity of the Biographer and Historian, and of their consequent utility, are incalculably greater than those which are to be encountered by the Poet who comprehends the dignity of his art. The Poet writes under one restriction only, namely, the necessity of giving immediate pleasure to a human Being possessed of that information which may be expected from him, not as a lawyer, a physician, a mariner, an astronomer, or a natural philosopher, but as a Man. Except this one restriction, there is no object standing between the Poet and the image of things; between this, and the Biographer and Historian, there are a thousand.

V The romantics follow Plato, Aristotle, and most other philosphers of art in assigning instrumental value to art, but their conception of its instrumentality leads them to emphasize the unusual rather than the ordinary, the outstanding rather than the commonplace. The characteristic romantic image of the artist is the gifted, tortured genius, alone in his garret, unappreciated by the multitudes but nevertheless tearing great works of art quivering from his breast.

Just about the most completely opposite conception of art and the artist was put forward by another great literary figure, the Russian nov-

COUNT LEO TOLSTOY (1828–1910) is one of the immortal geniuses of European literature. He and Feodor Dostoyevsky have, in their novels, given us matchless pictures of Russian life in the nineteenth century. In his youth, Tolstoy served in the Czar's army, seeing action as the commander of a battery in the Crimean War (1854–56). He retired to his family's estates, and began his career as a writer. His masterpiece, *War and Peace*, was published in 1866. It is a panoramic story of Russian life and thought during the great struggle of Russia against Napoleon.

In 1876, Tolstoy underwent a profound spiritual conversion to a form of Russian Orthodox Christianity that emphasized the virtues of the simple life and hard, physical labor. He worked alongside the peasants in the fields of his estates, while continuing to write novels and essays. Among the works of this later period in his life are Anna Karenina, which was begun before his conversion and completed in 1877; *The Death of Ivan Ilyich*; and the essay on the nature of art from which the selection in this book is taken.

elist Leo Tolstoy. You have all heard of Tolstoy's immortal novel, *War and Peace*, though in all likelihood very few of you have plowed your way through that immensely long book. Tolstoy is an extraordinary figure in literature and philosophy. He was born, in 1828, into the Russian aristocracy, and served in the army as a young man. When he was only thirty-eight, he published *War and Peace*, his great novel of Russian life and thought during the period of the Napoleonic Wars. Some time later, he underwent a deep religious conversion, and adopted a life of poverty and peasant simplicity. Out of his conversion emerged a new, simplified Christian faith and a rejection of the cultivated aesthetic sensibilities which he himself had contributed to in his earlier writings. Thirty years after the publication of *War and Peace*, in 1896, Tolstoy gave formal philosophical expression to his new conception of art and life in an essay entitled *What Is Art?*

Tolstoy argues that there are two basic means by which human beings communicate with one another. The first is speech, by which men communicate their *thoughts*; the second is art, by which men communicate their *feelings*. Each of us has the capacity to communicate feelings by arousing them in others. We not only tell our listeners that we are sad, we actually arouse feelings of sadness in them, sometimes by reporting what it is that has made us sad, sometimes by the tone of our voice, sometimes by looks, gestures, or other means of expression. Feelings are in-

175

fectious. When one person laughs, others laugh too. When one cries, others cry. Tolstoy describes art in this way:

> To evoke in oneself a feeling one has experienced, and having evoked it in oneself, then, by means of movements, lines, colors, sounds, or forms expressed in words, so to transmit that feeling that others may experience the same feeling—this is the activity of art.
>
> Art is a human activity consisting in this, that one man consciously, by means of certain external signs, hands on to others feelings he has lived through, and that other people are infected by these feelings and also experience them.

The stronger the degree of infectiousness of art, the better the art is, Tolstoy maintains. And the fundamental source of infectiousness—the quality in the artist which enables him or her to spark a contagion of feeling in the audience—is not reason nor imaginative brilliance, nor metaphysical insight, nor extraordinary creativity, but simply *sincerity*. Honesty of feeling is directly apprehended and responded to by an artist's audience.

So far as the content of the work of art is concerned. Tolstoy—as you

Folk art.

High art.

might expect—turns the usual canons of aesthetic judgment upside down. Common subjects are best, for they will enable the artist to reach the largest audience. The purpose of art (Tolstoy is an instrumentalist, remember) is to unite humanity through shared feeling. Art that relies on specialized knowledge or highly refined taste will exclude rather than include, divide rather than unite. If men and women can respond emotionally to a work of art only after long training and cultivation, then it will mark off the few from the many and place obstacles in the way of a union of all mankind.

If sincerity and universality of emotional appeal are the criteria of greatness in art, then obviously some so-called artistic "masterpieces" are going to get pretty low marks. Sure enough, Tolstoy downgrades some of the works of music, literature, and painting that had been held up for generations as perfect examples of great art, and in their place offers peasant stories, folk music, and other arts of the common people.

There is one last element in Tolstoy's aesthetic theory which we have not yet mentioned—namely, the *religious* dimension of art. In the following selection from *What Is Art*, Tolstoy draws upon his analysis of art as a means for the communication of feeling and as an instrument for uniting human beings in a universal brotherhood, in order to lay the foundations for a religious justification of art.

177

In every period of history, and in every human society, there exists an understanding of the meaning of life which represents the highest level to which men of that society have attained, an understanding defining the highest good at which that society aims. And this understanding is the religious perception of the given time and society. And this religious perception is always clearly expressed by some advanced men, and more or less vividly perceived by all the members of the society. Such a religious perception and its corresponding expression exists always in every society. If it appears to us that in our society there is no religious perception, this is not because there really is none, but only because we do not want to see it. And we often wish not to see it because it exposes the fact that our life is inconsistent with that religious perception.

Religious perception in a society is like the direction of a flowing river. If the river flows at all, it must have a direction. If society lives, there must be a religious perception indicating the direction in which, more or less consciously, all its members tend. . . .

I know that according to an opinion current in our times religion is a superstition which humanity has outgrown, and that it is therefore assumed that no such thing exists as a religious perception, common to us all, by which art, in our time, can be evaluated. I know that this is the opinion current in the pseudo-cultured circles of today. People who do not acknowledge Christianity in its true meaning because it undermines all their social privileges, and who, therefore, invent all kinds of philosophic and aesthetic theories to hide from themselves the meaninglessness and wrongness of their lives, cannot think otherwise. These people intentionally, or sometimes unintentionally, confusing the conception of a religious perception think that by denying the cult they get rid of religious perception. But even the very attacks on religion and the attempts to establish a life-conception contrary to the religious perception of our times most clearly demonstrate the existence of a religious perception condemning the lives that are not in harmony with it.

If humanity progresses, i.e., moves forward, there must inevitably be a guide to the direction of that movement. And religions have always furnished that guide. All history shows that the progress of humanity is accomplished not otherwise than under the guidance of religion. But if the race cannot progress without the guidance of religion—and progress is always going on, and consequently also in our own times—then there must be a religion of our times. So that, whether it pleases or displeases the so-called cultured people of today, they must admit the existence of religion—not of a religious cult, Catholic, Protestant, or another, but of religious perception—which, even in our times, is the guide always present where there is any progress. And if a religious perception exists among us, then our art should be appraised on the basis of that religious perception; and, as has always and every-where been the case, art transmitting feelings flowing from the religious perception of our time should be chosen from all the indifferent art, should be acknowledged, highly esteemed, and encouraged, while art running counter to that perception should be condemned and despised, and all the remaining indifferent art should neither be distinguished nor encouraged. . . .

Christian art, i.e., the art of our time, should be catholic in the original meaning of the word, i.e., universal, and therefore it should unite all men. And only two kinds of feeling do unite all men: first, feelings flowing from the perception of our sonship to God and of the brotherhood of man; and next, the simple feelings of common life, accessible to every one without exception—such as the feeling of merriment, of pity, of cheerfulness. of tranquillity, etc. Only these two kinds of feelings can now supply material for art good in its subject matter. . . .

Beethoven's *Ninth Symphony* is considered a great work of art. To verify its claim to be such, I must first ask myself whether this work transmits the highest religious feeling. I reply in the negative, for music in itself cannot transmit those feelings; and therefore I ask myself next, Since this work does not belong to the highest kind of religious art, has it the other characteristic of the good art of our time—the quality of uniting all men in one common feeling: does it rank as Christian universal art? And again I have no option but to reply in the negative; for not only do I not see how the feelings transmitted by this work could unite people not specially trained to submit themselves to its complex hypnotism, but I am unable to imagine to myself a crowd of normal people who could understand anything of this long, confused, and artificial production, except short snatches which are lost in a sea of what is incomprehensible. And therefore, whether I like it or not, I am compelled to conclude that this work belongs to the rank of bad art. It is curious to note in this connection that attached to the end of this very symphony is a poem of Schiller's which (though somewhat obscurely) expresses this very thought, namely, that feeling (Schiller speaks only of the feeling of gladness) unites people and evokes love in them. But though this poem is sung at the end of the symphony, the music does not accord with the thought expressed in the verses; for the music is exclusive and does not unite all men, but unites only a few, dividing them off from the rest of mankind.

And just in this same way, in all branches of art, many and many works considered great by the upper classes of our society will have to be judged. By this one sure criterion we shall have to judge the celebrated *Divine Comedy* and *Jerusalem Delivered*, and a great part of Shakespeare's and Goethe's works, and in painting every representation of miracles, including Raphael's "Transfiguration," etc.

Whatever the work may be and however it may have been extolled, we have first to ask whether this work is one of real art or a counterfeit. Having acknowledged, on the basis of the indication of its infectiousness even to a small class of people, that a certain production belongs to the realm of art, it is necessary, on the basis of the indication of its accessibility, to decide the next question. Does this work belong to the category of bad, exclusive art, opposed to religious perception, or to Christian art uniting people? And having acknowledged an article to belong to real Christian art, we must then, according to whether it transmits the feelings flowing from love to God and man, or merely the simple feelings uniting all men, assign it a place in the ranks of religious art or in those of universal art.

Only on the basis of such verification shall we find it possible to select from the whole mass of what in our society claims to be art those works which form real, important, necessary spiritual food, and to separate them from all the harmful and useless art and from the counterfeits of art which surround us. Only on the basis of such verification shall we be able to rid ourselves of the pernicious results of harmful art and to avail ourselves of that beneficent action which is the purpose of true and good art and which is indispensable for the spiritual life of man and of humanity.

VI Plato says that art is negative, disruptive, antirational, and therefore that it ought to be banned from the good society. Aristotle, Wordsworth, and Tolstoy all in their different ways say that good art is positive, constructive, and ought to play an important role in social life. Wilde, Bell, and the art-for-art's-sake movement insist that art is intrinsically, rather than instrumentally valuable, and therefore deserves a central place in human life regardless of its consequences. You might think that we had exhausted the possibilities so far as the function of art is concerned, but our last theory of art puts these elements together in a startling, apparently contradictory way. Herbert Marcuse argues that great art is negative, destructive, irrational, and *therefore* is a valuable element in human life! Why on earth would anyone praise art for having precisely the qualities that other philosophers have considered worthy of condemnation? To put the question in its most paradoxical form, what is positive about being negative?

Marcuse begins his argument with a puzzle that doesn't at first seem to have anything to do with art. Why is it that the most dramatic, out-

Herbert Marcuse.

rageous, powerful words and ideas so rapidly become domesticated and acceptable in America today, *without changing anything along the way?* Radicals call America imperialist, and decent people everywhere are horrified. Several years later, Senator J. William Fulbright refers in passing to America's imperialist foreign policy on a television interview program and none of the newsmen thinks it worth commenting on. Black militants shout "Power to the people!" and "nice folks" cringe in their beds. Next season, "Power to the people!" is a liberal Democratic campaign slogan, and soon thereafter a Richard Nixon campaign promise. Avantgarde artists violate every canon of artistic sensibility in a last-ditch effort to repudiate the plastic culture of Madison Avenue capitalism, and Madison Avenue reproduces their most outrageous productions as decorations for its advertisements. Woodstock begins as a cry of protest against middle America, and ends as the name of a bird in *Peanuts.* How can this be? Is nothing sacrilegious? Can modern American society absorb anything into itself without changing? Must every protest turn into this year's fad and next year's ancient history?

181

To answer these questions, Marcuse draws on the psychological theory of the origins of the ego and of civilization which Sigmund Freud set forth in *Civilization and its Discontents,* and which Marcuse revised and developed in *Eros and Civilization.* Freud argued that the objective, "ungetoverable" constraints of the real world force each infant to, as he put it, substitute the reality principle for the pleasure principle. Because the physical world just won't always fit itself to our desires, and also because we all inevitably get into interpersonal conflicts, particularly those fueled by sexual desire, we are forced to regulate or deny entirely some of our strongest desires. The psychic means for this regulation, Freud suggested, are repression, sublimation, and fantasy, of which repression is the first and most important. Thus is generated the realm of the "unconscious," populated by wishes, impulses, desires, loves, and hatreds which cannot be expressed and acted out in the real world. "Where id was, let ego be!" Freud said, making it clear that repression was the price of that necessary substitution. Civilization itself, the organized collective life of man, rests upon a foundation of repression, for not even the most miraculous technical wonders or the most flexible social arrangements can gratify the infantile wishes that lie beneath the conscious surface in every adult man and woman.

Two features of the content and structure of the unconscious are crucial to Marcuse's analysis. First, the unconscious is timeless. The thwarted desires and fears which reside there retain their power across decades of real-world time, returning again and again irrespective of changes in the world which originally thwarted them. A mother who loses her child grieves, mourns, and eventually becomes reconciled to the loss. Time heals her wounds, and the objective passage of events places the loss further and further behind her. The child whose mother dies before he or she can cope with the loss may repress the grief and anger, so that half a century later, the anger at the mother's desertion will recur as strongly, albeit in transmuted forms. In particular, all of us carry with us unrelinquished infantile desires for the sorts of total, immediate, ecstatic satisfaction which as tiny babies we imagined we could, in our omnipotence, command.

Second, the content of the unconscious has a thoroughly ambivalent character. That content is whatever reality (either natural or social) has decreed to be bad, inefficient, worthless, dirty, ugly, hostile, shameful. But the wishes and desires that fill the unconscious retain their power, even though they have been denied fulfillment. Part of the self—the part that identifies with society, reality, adulthood, and the world—hates, loathes, feels shame for that which is repressed. That is the part of the self that cannot acknowledge a fascination with its own feces, or sexual desire for objects deemed socially inappropriate, or laziness, or messiness, or the urge to inflict pain and suffering. But another part of the self secretly delights in the content of the repressed. And what is more, it delights in the repressed *because* it is repressed. So we have the men and women who can only enjoy illicit sex; or, rather less dramatically, we find the familiar folk-character of the perpetual child who refuses to grow up—Pan, Til Eulen-spiegel, Peter Pan.

Marcuse accepts Freud's fundamental claim that repression is essential to civilization. But in a brilliant deployment of one of Marx's key notions, he revises Freud's theory of repression by introducing a distinction between necessary repression and surplus repression. Necessary repression is simply that kind and amount of repression that is required at any stage of social development in order to carry on the struggle for existence. It involves, for example, denying ourselves part of the harvest even when we are hungry so that we have seed for the next planting; it involves forcing ourselves to continue laboring at painful tasks because of our rational recognition that hunger, disease, danger, and death may result if we let up too soon. But some repression, Marcuse argues, is not required by the objective constraints of reality. Rather, it is required by the specific system of domination and submission that exists in society at that moment in history. In short, some repression serves only to protect the favored position of the rulers by restraining the subjects from rising up and over-throwing their masters. That repression is "surplus repression," and human progress consists in eliminating surplus repression while simultaneously decreasing the amount of necessary repression through technological advance. Indeed, Marcuse argues, at a time when our technology should permit us considerably to relax the bonds of necessary repression, through the shortening and lightening of the workday, through the relaxation of work discipline, and so forth, surplus repression grows greater and greater so that the total burden of repression suffered by modern industrial man is not appreciably lighter than that suffered by his technically less advanced predecessors. The purpose of that ever-increasing sector of surplus repression is, Marcuse claims, to maintain the ever more manifestly unjustifiable dominance of the ruling sectors of our society.

The concept of surplus repression is one of those brilliant insights which are too often rejected by hard-headed social scientists because they prove difficult to quantify or operationalize. How would we measure the relative proportions of necessary and surplus repression in an individual psyche? Indeed, how could we ever show of a single instance of repression that it was unnecessary, and hence surplus? I don't know the answer to these questions, but I remain convinced that Marcuse has his finger on a fundamental fact here, and that to the extent that it is fuzzy or imprecise, we should struggle to clarify it rather than use the unclarity as an excuse for rejecting it.

Now, with the notion of surplus repression, and the theory of the unconscious, we can sketch Marcuse's theory of the function of negative thinking and thereby approach his analysis of the function of art. Briefly, his position is this: The repressed content of the unconscious in all of us exists as a permanent psychic pool or source of opposition to the established order of society. We all construct powerful defenses against this repressed content within ourselves, using such familiar mechanisms as denial, projection, and transference. When a rebellious member of society violates some taboo, by uncovering a part of his body that is supposed to be concealed, or by using, in public, language that is supposed only to be used in private, or by defying canons of dress, decorum, or deference, he provokes a response that is exaggerated all out of proportion. The rest of us recoil from the temporary and perhaps insignificant breach of the rules of repression because it provokes the ever-present desire within us to liberate ourselves from the same rules, and we can control that desire only by clamping down on the transgressor. A struggle over bare nipples or long hair or even an insolent, slouching way of standing becomes a struggle between the repressed content and the forces of civilization.

Now, if all the actual repression were necessary repression, then it would be clear that the rebel should be contained, however sympathetically we might acknowledge that he speaks for a part of each of us. But Marcuse's claim is precisely that not all of the repression is necessary, that some of it is surplus, unnecessary, and that in the interest of human happiness it ought to be eliminated. But—and this is the key to his entire theory, so far as I can see—in order to generate sufficient emotional energy in enough people to conquer the surplus repression inflicted by our society, it is necessary to tap the ubiquitous, irrational, infantile desire for a release from all repression. To put it bluntly, you must promise men an impossible liberation from necessary repression in order to get them to struggle for the elimination of the merely surplus repression. To get men to the barricades, it is not enough to say, "Workers of the world, unite! After the revolution you shall suffer only necessary repression." Instead, you must say, "Workers of the world, unite! After the revolution you shall be free." And each projects his own fantasy of absolute freedom, a daydream both inevitable and unfulfillable.

The revolutionary role of negative, oppositional styles of artistic expression is precisely to tap the reservoir of repressed desires, to draw on the permanent opposition within us to necessary repression, and thereby to fuel the fight against surplus repression. The artist's image of liberation is necessary, and illusory. The particular content of the rebellion against the established order of aesthetic canons is not crucial. In one social setting, the expletive "damn" will have as much effect as total nudity in another. The point is that no matter what is permitted, there remains both a repressed content that is denied and a longing to express it that can be tapped. The fight always appears to be about the particular artistic rule that has been broken, but it is always really about the existence of repression itself. If the rebellion is successful, surplus repression is reduced, but that success is always perceived as a failure by the participants themselves, because they must sooner or later relinquish their fantasy of total liberation.

The social function of art is thus to keep alive the possibility of what Marcuse calls "transcendence." By transcendence, he does not mean, as Plato or Wordsworth might, the passing from this world of space, time, and objects to a higher, eternal realm of forms or ideal entities. Rather, he means the imaginative leap beyond the given social world, with its repressions, oppressions, and reality-oriented sacrifices, to the conception of possible future social orders in which some of the repressed libidinal energy has been liberated. In thus adding a second "dimension" to our existence, Marcuse claims, art helps us to escape the one-dimensionality of present society. But it is not art's job to draw us blueprints of the future. It must simply keep alive those repressed dreams of liberation and gratification whose energies, stopped but not diminished, will fuel the revolutions that reduce surplus repression and bring us closer to conditions of genuine human happiness.

In this last selection of the chapter, we listen to Marcuse talking about the "negative" function of great art. Despite the difficulty of his philosophical language, I think you will be able to see here some of the themes I have been discussing in the last few pages.

> The achievements and the failures of this society invalidate its higher culture. The celebration of the autonomous personality, of humanism, of tragic and romantic love appears to be the ideal of a backward stage of the development. What is happening now is not the deterioration of higher culture into mass culture but the refutation of this culture by the reality. The reality surpasses its culture. Man today can do *more* than the culture heros and half-gods; he has solved many insoluble problems. But he has also betrayed the hope and destroyed the truth which were preserved in the sublimations of higher culture. To be sure, the higher culture was always in contradiction with social reality, and only a privileged minority enjoyed its blessings and represented its ideals. The two antagonistic spheres of society have always coexisted; the higher culture has always been accommodating, while the reality was rarely disturbed by its ideals and its truth.
>
> Today's novel feature is the flattening out of the antagonism between culture and social reality through the obliteration of the opposi-

tional, alien, and transcendent elements in the higher culture by virtue of which it constituted *another dimension* of reality. This liquidation of *two-dimensional* culture takes place not through the denial and rejection of the "cultural values," but through their wholesale incorporation into the established order, through their reproduction and display on a massive scale.

In contrast to the Marxian concept, which denotes man's relation to himself and to his work in capitalist society, the *artistic alienation* is the conscious transcendence of the alienated existence—a "higher level" or mediated alienation. The conflict with the world of progress, the negation of the order of business, the anti-bourgeois elements in bourgeois literature and art are neither due to the aesthetic lowliness of this order nor to romantic reaction—nostalgic consecration of a disappearing stage of civilization. "Romantic" is a term of condescending defamation which is easily applied to disparaging avant-garde positions. just as the term "decadent" far more often denounces the genuinely progressive traits of a dying culture than the real factors of decay. The traditional images of artistic alienation are indeed romantic in as much as they are in aesthetic incompatibility with the developing society. This incompatibility is the token of their truth. What they recall and preserve in memory pertains to the future: images of a gratification that would dissolve the society which suppresses it.

The tension between the actual and the possible is transfigured into an insoluble conflict, in which reconciliation is by grace of the oeuvre as *form:* beauty as the "promesse de bonheur." In the form of the oeuvre, the actual circumstances are placed in another dimension where the given reality shows itself as that which it is. Thus it tells the truth about itself; its language ceases to be that of deception, ignorance, and submission. Fiction calls the facts by their name and their reign collapses; fiction subverts everyday experience and shows it to be mutilated and false. But art has this magic power only as the power of negation. It can speak its own language only as long as the images are alive which refuse and refute the established order.

Whether ritualized or not, art contains the rationality of negation. In its advanced positions, it is the Great Refusal—the protest against that which is. The modes in which man and things are made to appear, to sing and sound and speak, are modes of refuting, breaking, and recreating their factual existence. But these modes of negation pay tribute to the antagonistic society to which they are linked. Separated from the sphere of labor where society reproduces itself and its misery, the world of art which they create remains, with all its truth, a privilege and an illusion.

In this form it continues, in spite of all democratization and popularization, through the nineteenth and into the twentieth century. The "high culture" in which this alienation is celebrated has its own rites and its own style. The salon, the concert, opera, theater are designed to create and invoke another dimension of reality. Their attendance requires festive-like preparation; they cut off and transcend everyday experience.

Now this essential gap between the arts and the order of the day, kept open in the artistic alienation, is progressively closed by the advancing technological society. And with its closing, the Great Refusal is in turn refused; the "other dimension" is absorbed into the prevailing state of affairs. The works of alienation are themselves incorporated into this society and circulate as part and parcel of the equipment which adorns and psychoanalyzes the prevailing state of affairs. Thus they become commercials—they sell, comfort, or excite.

HERBERT MARCUSE, *One-Dimensional Man*

SØREN KIERKEGAARD (1813–1855) was the founder and most brilliant spokesman of the style of philosophizing known as "existentialism." His life was devoted to an unending inward reflection on man's existence and the terror and uncertainty which each of us experiences in the face of his own death. Kierkegaard was deeply religious, though he rejected what he felt to be the superficial, self-satisfied Lutheranism of his native Denmark. In a series of books, some on philosophical topics, others more directly religious in their focus, he redefined the nature of faith, making it radically subjective and totally alien to the processes of ordinary systematic reason.

Kierkegaard was a witty, brilliantly provocative writer. His works abound in complex ironies which are challenges to the reader. He seems always to seek to unsettle the reader, to put him off balance and thereby force him to examine his life as Kierkegaard had examined his own. One of his many literary devices to achieve this was the practice of publishing his books under pseudonyms. The *Philosophical Fragments*, for example, was published with the author listed as "Johannes Climacus." Further down on the page, there appeared the statement, "Responsible for publication: S. Kierkegaard." By this and other devices, Kierkegaard hoped to block any attempt by his readers to classify his position and pigeon-hole him, for Kierkegaard was convinced that such techniques of systematic professional philosophy were merely ways of defusing a book and making it safe.

As he pessimistically predicted, Kierkegaard has fallen into the hands of professors and systematizers, and even his challenge to established philosophy has itself come to be treated merely as one more philosophy, namely Existentialism. Kierkegaard would have laughed, or perhaps he would have wept, to see his struggle with death and eternity reduced to an "ism."

Philosophy of Religion 6

Søren Kierkegaard was born in 1813 to a father fifty-six and a mother forty-four. His early life and education were very closely supervised by his father, who demanded both a scholarly mastery of classical languages and a highly charged imaginative appreciation of the literature his young son read. The young Soren had laid upon him the full weight of the guilt which extreme Pietist Protestantism so often inflicted upon its communicants. Although Kant and Kierkegaard thus had roughly the same sort of religious upbringing, Kierkegaard completely lacked Kant's quiet inner confidence and peace. He reacted first against the torment of his religious training by plunging himself into a life of physical self-indulgence, eating, drinking, dressing the dandy. But these distractions could not free him from the black gloom which hung over him, and he decided finally to return to his studies and become a pastor.

The dramatic turning point in Kierkegaard's private life was his engagement, and then the breaking of it, to seventeen-year-old Regine Olson. Kierkegaard wrote endlessly of his feelings for Regine, of the philosophical significance of marriage, love, and the problems of such a life commitment, but one cannot help thinking that she was more important to him as a subject for meditation than as a real, live woman. After pouring out a

189

series of essays and books on aesthetic, moral, and religious topics, Kierkegaard died at the relatively early age of forty-two.

Kierkegaard's inner emotional life, his lifelong struggle with religious faith, and his reaction to the dominant Hegelian philosophy of his day are all so intimately intertwined that it is very difficult to speak of any one without immediately bringing in all three. There is hardly space in an introductory text of this sort to explore the subject fully, but a few systematic remarks may be helpful to you. I especially want you to develop an interest in Kierkegaard, because in my opinion, he is, after the immortal Plato, the most gifted artist among all the important philosophers who have come down to us in the Western tradition. If you pick up one of his books, many of which are easily available in paperback editions, you will find him profound, troubling, witty, touching, and in the end deeply rewarding.

The passionate center of Kierkegaard's thought and life is his confrontation with the ever-present terror of existential dread—the obsessive, unavoidable fact of my own impending death, the infinity of the universe and the meaninglessness of my own brief life in comparison. Every man, woman, and child faces these terrible, fundamental facts of the human condition. We may deny them, flee from them, repress them, distract ourselves to escape from them, but always they are there, at the edge of consciousness, waiting to return in the darkness of night. The first lesson Kierkegaard teaches us, both in his books and by his life, is that this dread of death and meaninglessness must be faced, confronted, not shoved aside again and again. If I may speak personally—and the greatest honor we can pay to Kierkegaard is precisely to be honest, each one of us, about our own encounter with the fear of death—I first came face to face with this dread as a teenager. I was obsessed with fears of death, and the more I thrust them from my mind, the more intensely they returned. In my case, the fear was not of pain, or age, or sickness, but simply of nonbeing. The more I turned the thought over in my mind, the closer my own eventual death seemed to come, until finally I would seize any distraction to divert my attention from what was, and of course still is, an unavoidable fate.

For Kierkegaard, the dread of death was both heightened and complicated by the hope of eternal life which the religion of his fathers held out to him. All of you have heard the expression, "Trust in the Lord." But how many of you have actually asked yourselves what it means to "trust in the Lord?" What does it mean to "believe in" God, to have faith in Him?

Well, what it *doesn't* mean is believing *that* God exists! In our increasingly nonreligious society, when a person says that he "believes in God," we automatically assume that he means that he believes there is such a thing as God. But in the Judeo-Christian religious tradition, par-

The Old Testament doctrine of God's
promise to man.

ticularly in the extreme individualistic Protestant sort of Christianity that
was Kierkegaard's heritage, the phrase "belief in God" has quite a different
meaning. To believe in God, to trust in Him, to have faith in Him, means to
believe that He will keep His promise to man; it is to have faith that He
will keep the pact, or covenant, that He made with man. That pact is
testified to first in what we call the Old Testament, and then again, in a
renewed form in the New Testament.

The promise, of course, is the promise of salvation, of a life after death,
of true happiness, of fruitfulness, of a union of the soul with God. (Needless to say, long books could be written on the various interpretations that
Jews, Christians, and Muslims have placed upon this notion of a covenant
between man and God. The version I am summarizing here is something
like what Kierkegaard would have learned and brooded upon.) According
to the Old Testament, God made a promise to Noah, He repeated it to
Abraham, He renewed it again and again, despite man's repeated failures
to keep His Law and follow His commands. Finally, God embodied that
Law (or Word or Logos) in the Person of Jesus Christ, in order that His
offer of salvation might be made to man once more. With the birth, suffering, and death of Jesus, God sealed his free gift of eternal life. As the
price of that blessedness, He asked only faith, an unstinting, unconditioned, unqualified belief by man that He would keep His promise of this
free gift.

191

Other Christian traditions had emphasized the role of right behavior, or "good works," either as part of the price of salvation or else as worldly evidence of one's true belief. But the pietist strain of Protestantism placed a very heavy emphasis upon the pure possession of that unconditioned faith in God. So it was that for Kierkegaard, the central religious problem quite naturally became the problem of *faith*.

You might think, on first reflection, that the Christian message would be a very welcome message indeed! After all, life is short, bedeviled by suffering, terminated by the absolute finality of unavoidable death. It was good enough news to be told, in the Old Testament, that God would grant life everlasting to those who kept His commandments. But we are weak, imperfect creatures, and it soon became clear that doing God's bidding was a task too hard for man, even with the promise of salvation to lead us on. So He took upon Himself, in the Person of His Son, the atonement for *our* sins, and offered to us the priceless pearl of salvation for the merest asking. All we need do was believe that we would receive it. What could possibly be better news than that? Small wonder that this message was called the Gospel, which means "good news." Small wonder too that those who spread the message were called Evangelists, which means "bringers of good news."

But strange to tell, the glad tidings of God's free gift have brought fear, dread, doubt, torment, and tortured self-examination to countless hearers, among them Søren Kierkegaard. The gift is so great, the price so small—and yet, the price of faith must be paid freely, unhesitatingly, without doubts or second thoughts. Therein lie the seeds of terror. Do I truly believe? Is my faith pure? Can I trust in the Lord, or is there lurking deep within my heart a doubt that so great a gift will be conferred on so undeserving a creature as myself? Out of this inner hell Kierkegaard tore the writings by which we remember him. His doubts and fears concerned his very *existence* as an individual, mortal creature longing to believe in God's promise, not the abstract, impersonal logical relationships among disembodied forms, or "essences." Hence, Kierkegaard's way of thinking has come to be called *existentialist*. Indeed, Kierkegaard is universally acknowledged to be the first true existentialist philosopher. Whether he would have appreciated such a categorization and sterilization of his inner torment is of course not so clear.

In his lifelong struggle with the problem of faith, Kierkegaard did battle with three enemies, against whom he turned not only his considerable philosophical and theological gifts, but also a brilliant, convoluted, ironic wit. The first of his enemies was the established Christianity of his own day, the solid, comfortable, Sunday-sermon Lutheranism of nineteenth-century Denmark. Like so many passionate prophets before him, Kierkegaard accused the established church of mouthing empty formulae

A bourgeoisie couple
in nineteenth century France
as the painter Toulouse-Lautrec saw them

which were neither lived nor understood. Sin, redemption, damnation, salvation, all were the subjects of elegant sermons and pious attitudes which did not for a moment interfere with the secular, weekday activities of this world. Kierkegaard once observed that just as it is harder to jump up in the air and land exactly on the spot from which one began, so too it is harder to become a Christian when one has been born a Christian. He meant that those who were born into Christianity, who were baptized, confirmed, and raised in the official emptiness of its dogmas and rituals, might actually find it more difficult to take the message of Christianity seriously than would a pagan to whom the divine promise came as wonderful, terrible, astonishing news. Kierkegaard devoted many of his books to a sustained effort to breathe new existential significance into the familiar phrases and concepts of Christian theology.

His second enemy was the complacent middle-class culture of his society, the "bourgeois" culture of solid tradesmen and lawyers; sound, self-confident people who disdained anyone so odd, so passionate, so disruptive as Kierkegaard. The word "bourgeois" has drifted into our vocabulary these days as a catch-all term for what we in America call "middle-class" life, but in the nineteenth century in Europe, it had a much richer,

193

"You seem troubled, Brother Timothy.
Is anything worrying you?
I mean besides the sins of the world,
*the vanities of man-kind, and that sort of thing."**

more resonant set of associations. Historically, a "bourgeois," or a "burger," is simply a resident of a "bourg" or "burg," which in the late Middle Ages was a walled city. By extension, the word came to mean a member of the urban merchant class, and also a "freeman" or citizen of one of the cities whose charter came from the king rather than from the feudal aristocracy. The burghers of the European cities were men of substance, solid citizens, true to their word in business deals, extremely conservative in their family relationships, jealous of their rights as city leaders, forward-looking in commerce, and quite often supporters of a strong monarchy against the ancient and dispersed powers of the landed aristocracy. For the burghers of Copenhagen, religion was first of all a matter of propriety, of respectability, and only then a matter of conscience or salvation. One dressed in one's finest clothes on Sunday and went as a family to church; one sat in a front pew, purchased at great expense, where one was seen by one's neighbours. One listened piously to the sermon, which, though heavy on damnation, was conveniently light on social responsibility, and then one returned to one's substantial townhouse for a good Sunday dinner.

As you can imagine, the unthinking religiosity, the self-satisfied complacency of the solid citizens of Denmark made Kierkegaard furious.

*Drawing by Stevenson; © 1960 The New Yorker Magazine, Inc.

Many of his most spectacular literary tricks and devices, and particularly his extremely heavy irony, are aimed at puncturing that complacency and somehow reaching the real human beings behind those masks.

The final enemy was the official philosophy of Kierkegaard's day, the vast, pompous, elaborate philosophical systems constructed by the disciples and followers of the great German philosopher Georg Hegel. The Hegelian philosophy, as it was expounded by the professors of Europe, put itself forward as the objective, impersonal, purely rational, totally systematic, absolutely final truth about just about everything. It was turgid, jargon-filled, and completely self-confident. It claimed to wrap up space, time, eternity, being, history, man, the state, and God in one vast metaphysical synthesis that simultaneously answered all our questions about the universe and also—rather conveniently—demonstrated the superiority of precisely the social and religious system then dominant in European society.

In short, Kierkegaard's three enemies were really one and the same enemy in different disguises. The Christianity of his day was bourgeois Christianity, buttressed and justified by the official philosophical system. The burghers were Establishment Christians, who—though they knew precious little philosophy—were justified and rationalized by that same philosophy. And the philosophy, though it claimed to be the purest product of reason, was a thoroughgoing justification of the reign of the burghers and the ascendency of their religion.

Karl Marx, facing this very same union of religion, philosophy, and the ascendent bourgeoisie, turned his attack on the social and economic consequences, for Marx was a secular man, concerned with this—worldly issues of justice, poverty, and work. Kierkegaard, before all else a man of God, attacked the same union of forces on its religious front. He cared nothing at all for worldly happiness or misery. Rather, he brushed all secular considerations aside and instead demanded that the good Christians of Denmark begin to pay to eternal life as much attention as they regularly gave to a daily profit.

Kierkegaard's onslaught was complex, subtle, and hence is impossible to summarize in a few paragraphs. Two ideas lie at the heart of his religio-philosophical message, and we can at least take a first step toward understanding them. These notions are the inwardness, or subjectivity, of truth, and the irrational, unarguable "leap of faith." Now, that sounds more like a Hegelian mouthful than a bit of biting wit, so let us take a look at each.

The Hegelian philosophers put their doctrines forward as *rational* and *objective*. They were, in a way, like today's scientists. All of you have noticed, I imagine, that there is a very big difference in the teaching style and approach of science professors as compared with professors in literature or philosophy. In a literature class, you are encouraged to express your own "interpretation" of Dickens or Mailer or Shakespeare. In a philosophy class—I hope!—you are prompted to think out your own position, to develop your own arguments, and to defend whatever point of view you think closest to the truth. But nobody teaches calculus or physics that way! Can you imagine a physics quiz with questions like "Write a ten-minute essay on your impressions of Boyle's Law," or "Take a position for or against relativity and defend it—in your answer, make reference to the text" Hardly! Scientists quite confidently assume that their knowledge is objective, and that what they teach is a matter neither of "opinion" nor of personality. In the same way, the Hegelian philosophers represented themselves as objective, rational discoverers of the truth. Their private fears, hopes, terrors, and joys were no more a part of their philosophy, they thought, than would a modern biochemist's neuroses be a part of his theory of DNA. To be sure, readers might be curious, in a gossipy way, about the personal lives of the great philosophers, just as we today like to read stories about Albert Einstein. But no one would suppose for a moment that there was any important scientific connection between those delightful or depressing glimpses into the scientist's private life and the scientific truth of his theories!

In a total reversal of the received philosophical-scientific opinion of his day, Kierkegaard argued that Truth is Subjectivity. In other words, he denied the objective impersonality of truth, and insisted instead that all truth must be inward, dependent upon the subject, particular rather than universal, personal rather than interpersonal or impersonal.

When Kierkegaard says that Truth is Subjectivity, he is denying the ancient philosophical doctrine that the truth of an idea or a statement consists in its conformity to an independent object. When I say, "That is a very good picture of Jim," I mean that the picture looks like Jim, that it resembles, or copies, or conforms to the objective nature of Jim's body. When I say, "It is true that Sacramento is the capital of California," I mean that the real world—California, in this case—actually has the characteristics that my statement says it has. In other words, truth is conformity to the objective state of things in the world. Or, Truth is Objectivity. If this familiar conception of truth is correct, then the truth of a statement or belief depends only on the relationship between the statement or belief and the world, *not* on the relationship between the statement or belief and the person who thinks it. If Truth is Objectivity, then it doesn't matter, so far as truth is concerned, whether I believe Sacramento to be the capital of California passionately, calmly, tentatively, with all my heart, or simply because a friend told me so.

Kierkegaard doesn't care about the capitals of states or nations, of course. He cares about salvation, the Christian message. And when it comes to salvation, *how* you believe is as important as *what* you believe, he thought. The Hegelian system-builders wanted to treat the Christian message as though it were merely one subpart of their grand structure of objective knowledge. So "Jesus died for my sins" would be treated by them as more or less on a par with "Space is three-dimensional and homogeneous." Each statement would be true if it corresponded correctly to the objective state of things, false otherwise. But that treatment of the promise of salvation as "objective" was precisely wrong, Kierkegaard insisted. Truth does not consist in the proper relationship between the belief and the *object*; rather, it consists in the proper relationship between the belief and the *subject*, the individual human being who holds that belief. *How* he holds it is the criterion of its truth. In order for the belief to be true, it must be held passionately, unconditionally, absolutely without inner reservation or doubt.

But—and here we come to the second of Kierkegaard's great ideas, the "leap of faith." That belief in God's promise of eternal life can have no rational justification, no evidence, no proof. Theologians since the time of Aristotle had sought to *prove* the existence of God, to prove the truth of this or that religious doctrine. Sometimes they used evidence of their senses—what they could see, hear, and touch. At other times, they erected abstract arguments of pure logic, deducing the absolute, objective truth of Christianity (or Islam, or Judaism). But Kierkegaard believed that all such attempts at rational justification were doomed to total failure. The absolute gap between finite man and infinite God made any rational bridge-building between the two on man's part futile. God might reach down to man, though how He could manage that was beyond our comprehension. But man could no more reason his way into the presence of God than a mathematician, by doggedly adding unit to unit, could calculate his way to infinity.

Because reason was inadequate to the task of supporting our belief in God's promise, Kierkegaard said, our only hope was an absolutely irrational, totally unjustifiable leap of faith. I must take the plunge and say, with all my heart, Credo—I believe.

Couldn't we perhaps look for a little bit of support from reason? Mightn't reason at least show that God's promise is probable? That the weight of the evidence inclines us toward God's promise? That a reasonable man, as they say in the law courts, could tend to believe God's promise?

Not a bit of it! That is just what a fat, solid, smug merchant or a pompous, self-important professor would say. Can't you just imagine the two of them sitting in front of the fire, the burgher after a long day at the counting house, the professor after a day of serious, important lectures. The burgher leans back in his comfortable chair, puffs a bit on his pipe (one wouldn't want to speak too quickly on such matters—it might show a lack of seriousness), and then asks, "Is it your opinion that the weight of the evidence, objectively and impartially considered, inclines us to the view that God has promised us eternal life rather than eternal death?" The professor takes a sip of beer, strokes his beard thoughtfully, and answers, "Well, on the one hand, Hegel, in the *Phenomenology of Mind*, seems to suggest that God does make such a promise; but on the other hand, Kant, in the *Critique of Pure Reason*, argues that we cannot know with certainty that such a promise has been made. In the light of recent research which I understand has been reported in the latest issue of the Berlin *Journal of Metaphysics*, I would judge professionally that the answer is a qualified yes."

Both the subjectivity of truth and the leap of faith are central to the work from which I have selected our reading in Kierkegaard. The *Philosophical Fragments*, as it is called, deals with the contrast between secular truth and religious truth, between the objective and the subjective, between reason and faith, between wisdom and salvation. Kierkegaard imagines all these contrasts as gathered together into the person of Socrates, who is the greatest of all Teachers, and Jesus, who is not a teacher in the rational sense, but the Saviour. Kierkegaard's argument in the body of the text goes like this (yes indeed, Kierkegaard uses arguments to show us that arguments cannot be used in matters of faith! I leave it to you to determine whether there is a contradiction in his mode of procedure). Secular knowledge of morality is something that can be learned through rational self-reflection. Teachers like Socrates help us to bring our moral knowledge to consciousness by probing questions that force us to justify our beliefs. But since in some sense this moral knowledge already lies within each of us, a teacher—even so great a teacher as Socrates—is merely helpful; if we had to, we could get along without one. As philosophers say, a teacher is "accidental" rather than "essential." But salvation is a matter of the fate of my soul. It is a matter of my *existence*, not merely of my state of knowledge. And salvation is not something I can acquire on my own if I am forced to do so. Salvation requires that God reach down and lift me up to His Kingdom. Somehow, the gulf between myself and God must be crossed. Thus salvation is totally different from the acquisition of wisdom, for there is no gulf to be crossed on the road to wisdom. I need only look carefully and critically enough inside myself.

Jesus is God's instrument for bridging the gulf between Himself and myself. Jesus is the Saviour. And since salvation concerns my *existence*, the actual, historical reality of Jesus is all-important. You see, it doesn't really matter to me whether Socrates ever actually lived. Once I have learned from Plato's Dialogues how to engage in Socratic questioning, it would make no difference if I were to discover that the Dialogues were a hoax, and that there never had been any Socrates. But if God never actually became Man in the form of Jesus Christ; if Christ never died for my sins; then I am damned rather them saved. The mere Idea of the Saviour isn't enough. I need to be absolutely certain that Jesus actually existed, that He really died for my sins, that God did renew His free gift to man through His only begotten Son.

But just because I need so deperately to know that Jesus really lived, I am hopelessly at a loss for evidence or argument sufficient to my need. Can I rest comfortably in the belief that I have been promised eternal life, when the evidence for my belief is merely probable, merely the sort of evidence that an historian or a philosopher can produce? No, too much is at stake: salvation is everything, it is eternity of life rather than death. I am reduced by my terror and my need to infinite concern for something that defies rational grounding. In short, I am reduced to an absolute *leap of faith*.

The preface to the *Philosophical Fragments* is an extraordinary piece of comic writing about the most serious of all subjects. The writing is through and through ironic. The first, or superficial audience is of course the Hegelian professors and the serious burghers of Denmark. To them, Kierkegaard says, "Here is my little effort. It is an essay of no importance whatsoever; it does not contribute in the slightest to your magnificent efforts to construct a total system of objective knowledge. I don't want you even to take notice of it to the extent of writing a book review of it. Just allow it to slip into town, as it were, without fanfare." We, the readers, are the real audience, and to us Kierkegaard is saying, "This little book is about salvation, which is not merely the most important subject, but the only subject. It is not objective, because the truth is not objective. It makes no contribution to the System, because the System is worthless. I make none of the usual claims for it, such as that it is the best book of this month, or that it deserves a prize, or that I should be given a professorship for it, because prizes and professorships are as dust beneath my feet in comparison with the Gift of eternal life for which I am gambling my soul." But all the while, Kierkegaard is laughing, with that wonderful sense of humor that only deeply serious people can possess. Here is his Preface. I hope it provokes you to get a copy of the *Fragments* from the library and read the whole book.

The present offering is merely a piece, *proprio Marte, propriis auspiciis, proprio stipendio*. It does not make the slightest pretention to share in the philosophical movement of the day, or to fill any of the various rôles customarily assigned in this connection: transitional, intermediary, final, preparatory, participating, collaborating, volunteer follower, hero, or at any rate relative hero, or at the very least absolute trumpeter. The offering is a piece and such it will remain, even if like Holberg's *magister* I were *volente Deo* to write a sequel in seventeen pieces, just as half-hour literature is half-hour literature even in folio quantities. Such as it is, however, the offering is commensurate with my talents, since I cannot excuse my failure to serve the System after the manner of the noble Roman, *merito magis quam ignavia*; I am an idler from love of ease, *ex animi sententia*, and for good and sufficient reasons. Nevertheless, I am unwilling to incur the reproach of απραγμοσυνη, at all times an offense against the State, and especially so in a period of ferment; in ancient times it was made punishable by death. But suppose my intervention served merely to increase the prevailing confusion, thus making me guilty of a still greater crime, would it not have been better had I kept to my own concerns? It is not given to everyone to have his private tasks of meditation and reflection so happily coincident with the public interest that it becomes difficult to judge how far he serves merely himself and how far the public good. Consider the example of Archimedes, who sat unperturbed in the contemplation of his circles while Syracuse was being taken, and the beautiful words he spoke to the Roman soldier who slew him: *nolite perturbare circulos meos*. Let him who is not so fortunate look about him for another example. When Philip threatened to lay seige to the city of Corinth, and all its inhabitants hastily bestirred themselves in defense, some polishing weapons, some gathering stones, some repairing the walls, Diogenes seeing all this hurriedly folded his mantle about him and began to roll his tub zealously back and forth through the streets. When he was asked why he did this he replied that he wished to be busy like all the rest, and rolled his tub lest he should be the only idler among so many industrious citizens. Such conduct is at any rate not sophistical, if Aristotle be right in describing sophistry as the art of making money. It is certainly not open to misunderstanding; it is quite inconceivable that Diogenes should have been hailed as the saviour and benefactor of the city. And it seems equally impossible that anyone could hit upon the idea of ascribing to a piece like the present any sort of epoch-making significance, in my eyes the greatest calamity that could possibly befall it. Nor is it likely that anyone will hail its author as the systematic Solomon Goldkalb so long and eagerly awaited in our dear royal residential city of Copenhagen. This could happen only if the guilty person were by nature endowed with extraordinary stupidity, and presumably by shouting in antistrophic and antiphonal song every time someone persuaded him that now was the beginning of a new era and a new epoch, had howled his head so empty of its original *quantum satis* of common sense as to have attained a state of ineffable bliss in what might be called the howling madness of the higher lunacy, recognizable by such symptoms as convulsive shouting; a constant reiteration of the words "era," "epoch," "era and epoch," "epoch and era," "the System"; an irrational exaltation of the spirits as if each day were not merely a quadrennial leap-year day, but one of those extraordinary days that come only once in a thousand years; the concept all the while like an acrobatic clown in the current circus season, every moment performing these everlasting dog-tricks of flopping over and over, until it flops over the man himself. May a kind Heaven preserve me and my piece from such a fate! And may no noise-making busybody interfere to snatch me out of my carefree content as the author of a little piece, or prevent a kind and benevolent reader from examining it at his leisure, to see if it contains anything that he can use. May I escape the tragi-comic predicament of being forced to laugh at my own misfortune, as must have been the case with the good people of Fredericia, when they awoke one morning to read in the newspaper an account of a fire in their town, in which it was described how "the drums beat the alarm, the fire-engines rushed through the streets"—although the town of Fredericia boasts of only one fire-engine and not much more than one street; leaving it to be inferred that this one engine, instead of making for the scene of the fire, took time to execute important maneuvers and flanking movements up and down the street. However, my little piece is not very apt to suggest the beating of a drum, and its author is perhaps the last man in the world to sound the alarm.

But what is my personal opinion of the matters herein discussed? ... I could wish that no one would ask me this question; for next to knowing whether I have any opinion or not, nothing could very well be of less importance to another than the knowledge of what that opinion might be. To have an opinion is both too much and too little for my uses. To have an opinion presupposes a sense of ease and security in life, such as is implied in having a wife and children; it is a privilege not to be enjoyed by one who must keep himself in readiness night and day, or is without assured means of support. Such is my situation in the realm of the spirit. I have disciplined myself and keep myself under discipline, in order that I may be able to execute a sort of nimble dancing in the service of Thought, so far as possible also to the honor of God, and for my own satisfaction. For this reason I have had to resign the domestic happiness, the civic respectability, the glad fellowship, the *communio bonorum*, which is implied in the possession of an opinion.—Do I enjoy any reward? Have I permission, like the priest at the altar, to eat of the sacrifices? ... That must remain my own affair. My master is good for it, as the bankers say, and good in quite a different sense from theirs. But if anyone were to be so polite as to assume that I have an opinion, and if he were to carry his gallantry to the extreme of adopting this opinion because he believed it to be mine, I should have to be sorry for his politeness, in that it was bestowed upon so unworthy an object, and for his opinion, if he has no other opinion than mine. I stand ready to risk my own life, to play the game of thought with it in all earnest; but another's life I cannot jeopardize. This service is perhaps the only one I can render to Philosophy. I who have no learning to offer her, "scarcely enough for the course at one drachma,. to say nothing of the great course at fifty drachmas" (*Cratylus*). I have only my life, and the instant a difficulty offers I put it in play. Then the dance goes merrily, for my partner is the thought of Death, and is indeed a nimble dancer; every human being, on the other hand, is too heavy for me. Therefore I pray, *per deos obsecro*: Let no one invite me, for I will not dance.

NOTES

Page 199. *proprio Marte*, etc.) on its own errand, under its own auspices, for its own sake.

Page 200. Holberg's *magister*) Stygotius, in *Jacob von Thyboe*, Act III Scene v, remarks: "when *volente Deo* I intend to present myself for my disputation. . . . The title [of my thesis] is *De alicubitate*, and the subject will be continued in five other essays."

Page 200. the philosophical movement) in Denmark, efforts dominated by Hegelian ideas to complete and perfect, or to expound, the System.

Page 200. the noble Roman) Sallust, in *The War with Jugurtha*, IV 4, speaking of his retirement form public life to devote himself to the writing of histories, says that his readers may be assured that he does this "rather from justifiable motives than from indolence."

Page 200. *ex animi sententia*) from inclination.

Page 200. απραγμοσυνη) aloofness from public affairs.

Page 200. *nolite perturbate*, etc) do not disturb my circles.

Page 200. Aristotle) *De sophisticis elenchis*, Chapter 1, near the end,

Page 200. Solomon Goldkalb) In J.L. Heiberg's comedy, *King Colomon and Jörgen the Hatmaker*, a wealthy philanthropist and entrepreneur from Copenhagen, tensely expected in the village of Korsör. The enthusiastic welcome prepared for him is actually extended to an old clothes' dealer from Hamburg bearing the same name, who happens to arrive at the critical juncture.

Page 200. *quantum satis*) sufficient quantity.

Page 201. dog-tricks of flopping over) a reference to the Hegelian dialectic, in which concepts logically pass over into their opposites.

Page 201. *communio bonorum*) community of goods.

Page 202. *per deos obsecro*) I adjure you by the gods.

II When students are introduced to the study of philosophy, one of the standard moves is to go through what are usually referred to as the "proofs of the existence of God." This is a set of arguments developed over the past 2000 years by many different philosophers which purport to demonstrate that there is, or exists, an infinite, omnipotent, omniscient, benevolent creator of the universe who goes by the name of God. When I teach an introduction to philosophy, I try to slip the proofs for the existence of God in just before Christmas in the fall semester, and just before Easter in the spring semester. It seems fitting, somehow.

Is anyone ever convinced by the proofs? Well you may ask! I have, from time to time, started off my presentation of them by asking how many members of the class believe in God. I mean by that, of course, how many believe that there is a God, not how many believe that He will keep His promise to us of eternal life. Anyway, I count the hands, and then I present one of the proofs. Usually, I try out what is called the Cosmological Argument, and sometimes I go right into the real number one proof, which is called the Ontological Argument. (We'll get to these in a minute. Don't despair!) After running through the proof, I ask whether there are any objections or criticisms. Usually there aren't any (how many students are going to tell their professors that they think he is crazy?). Then I ask for another show of hands on those who believe in God. Now, it is the most peculiar thing, but even though no one ever objects to my proofs or raises any doubts, not a single person is ever converted to the faith by them! I don't think I have convinced a single, solitary nonbeliever in all the years I have been proving the existence of God. Next I run through the standard refutations for the proofs. (In philosophy, there is an argument against just about everything that there is an argument for.) Same result. I never make agnostics out of the believers, any more than I have made believers out of the agnostics.

When you stop and think about it, there is really something wonderful and mad about a finite, mortal man or woman undertaking to *prove* that God exists. It is as though the philosopher rears up on his hind legs and says, "God! You may be out there, You may exist, but unless You fit into my syllogisms, unless You follow from premises, unless You are a theorem in my system, I won't acknowledge Your existence!" When it comes to sheer effrontery, to what the Greeks called *hubris* and the Jews call *chutzpah*, there just isn't anything to match it.

Philosophers have never been known for their humility, and a fair number of the great ones have had a shot at proving the existence of God. Aristotle tried it, and so did St. Thomas Aquinas. Occam had a proof, Descartes had several, Spinoza came up with some, and even William James, the American pragmatist, offered his own rather odd version of reasons for believing in the existence of God. In this section, we are going to take a close look at the three most famous proofs. These aren't all the proofs, by any means, but they will give you a good idea of some of the different tactics that philosophers have used over the ages. The three proofs are called the *Argument from Design*, the *Cosmological*

Proof, and the *Ontological Proof*. We will examine the version of the Argument from Design offered by the eighteenth-century English philosopher William Paley, the Cosmological Argument as it was set forth by the great medieval theologian St. Thomas, and the Ontological Argument in its original version as stated by the man who thought it up, the eleventh-century logician St. Anselm. Since David Hume and Immanuel Kant are the two best proof-for-existence-of-God-refuters who have ever lived, we will look at their refutations together with the proofs. Here we go. Don't be surprised if you hear Kierkegaard laughing at us along the way!

William Paley: The Argument from Design

Our first proof for the existence of God is at once the most obvious, the most natural, the most ancient, the most persuasive, the easiest to understand, and—alas—the philosophically weakest! The *Argument from Design* is quite simple. We observe that certain man-made objects exhibit an internal purposive organization, a fitting of parts to the function of the whole. In a watch, to take the example that Paley himself uses, the various springs and pins and hands are all made precisely to serve the purpose of keeping and telling time. This rational, purposive order in the watch is the direct result of the conscious, rational, purposive activity of its creator, the watchmaker. From the character of the watch, we naturally infer the existence of a watchmaker, whether we actually know him or not. If you show me a watch (or a chair or a painting or even a simple stone axe) and say, It is so old that no one can remember who made it, I would never dream of saying, Perhaps no one made it. The intelligence of its creation inheres in its internal organization. The watch is, if you will permit a bad pun, intelligently produced on the face of it. Well, Paley argues (and so have countless other theologians and philosophers over the ages), nature is more wonderfully organized than the most subtle contrivance of man. The human eye far exceeds a camera in sensitivity and fidelity of reproduction; the human brain cannot be duplicated by the most sophisticated computer; the merest one-celled microscopic organism exhibits a biochemical complexity and adaptation that taxes the analytic powers of all science. Who can doubt for a moment that nature has its Creator, an intelligent, purposeful, all-powerful Maker, who in His infinite

WILLIAM PALEY (1743–1805) was an English churchman whose writings in defense of Christianity were widely read and much admired in the eighteenth and nineteenth centuries. Paley was a defender of utilitarianism in moral philosophy and of the truths of revelation in theology (a position known as *theism*). His book, *Natural Theology*, was a systematic presentation of the so-called "argument from design" for the existence of God, an argument which David Hume had vigorously attacked in his *Dialogues Concerning Natural Religion*.

wisdom has adjusted means to ends, part to whole, organ to organism, throughout the whole of space and time?

The technical name for this is an *argument from analogy*. You have probably encountered ratios or proportions in high school math—problems like: "Eight is to four as six is to *x*. Solve for *x*." When I was in school, the way to state that mathematically was either like this: 8:4::6:*x*, or else like this: $\frac{8}{4} = \frac{6}{x}$. The solution, of course, is *x* = 3. The same sort of "analogy" turns up in aptitude tests. "Fire engine is to fire department as _____ is to police department." The answer is "police car." The point is that if we already know the relationship between one pair of things (such as the numbers 8 and 4, or a fire engine and the fire department), then when we are presented with only one member of another pair, we may be able to figure out what the other member of the pair is (3 in the math example, or a police car in the other case). Now all this may seem like baby talk to you, but philosophers frequently build very powerful arguments from what look like very simple pieces.

Paley and the other arguers from design draw up two sorts of analogies. The first is between a man-made object and its human maker on the one hand, and a particular organism or bit of natural organization and its divine Creator on the other. So we get:

Watch is to watchmaker as the human eye is to *x*.   *x* = God.

The other analogy is between a man-made object and its human maker on the one hand, and the whole universe and its divine Creator on the other. So this time we get:

Watch is to watchmaker as the universe is to *x*.   *x* = God.

Here is Paley's own statement of the argument. Because he tends to be rather wordy, I have edited it down to the bare bones.

In crossing a heath, suppose I pitched my foot against a *stone*, and were asked how the stone came to be there, I might possibly answer, that for any thing I knew to the contrary it had lain there for ever; nor would it, perhaps, be very easy to show the absurdity of this answer. But suppose I had found a *watch* upon the ground, and it should be inquired how the watch happened to be in that place, I should hardly think of the answer which I had before given, that for any thing I knew the watch might have always been there. Yet why should not this answer serve for the watch as well as for the stone;

why is it not as admissible in the second case as in the first? For this reason, and for no other, namely, that when we come to inspect the watch, we perceive—what we could not discover in the stone—that its several parts are framed and put together for a purpose, *e.g.* that they are so formed and adjusted as to produce motion, and that motion so regulated as to point out the hour of the day; that if the different parts had been differently shaped from what they are, or placed after any other manner or in any other order than that in which they are placed, either no motion at all would have been carried on in the machine, or none which would have answered the use that is now served by it. . . .

. . . This mechanism being observed—it requires indeed an examination of the instrument, and perhaps some previous knowledge of the subject, to perceive and understand it; but being once, as we have said, observed and understood, the inference we think is inevitable, that the watch must have had a maker—that there must have existed, at some time and at some place or other, an artificer or artificers who formed it for the purpose which, we find it actually to answer, who comprehended its construction and designed its use. . . .

Were there no example in the world of contrivance except that of the *eye*, it would be alone sufficient to support the conclusion which we draw from it, as to the necessity of an intelligent Creator. It could never be got rid of, because it could not be accounted for by any other supposition which did not contradict all the principles we possess of knowledge—the principles according to which things do, as often as they can be brought to the test of experience, turn out to be true or false. . . .

. . . If other parts of nature were inaccessible to our inquiries, or even if other parts of nature presented nothing to our examination but disorder and confusion, the validity of this example would remain the same. If there were but one watch in the world, it would not be less certain that it had a maker. If we had never in our lives seen any but one single kind of hydraulic machine, yet if of that one kind we understood the mechanism and use, we should be as perfectly assured that it proceeded from the hand and thought and skill of a workman, as if we visited a museum of the arts, and saw collected there twenty different kinds of machines for drawing water, or a thousand different kinds for other purposes. Of this point each machine is a proof independently of all the rest. So it is with the evidences of a divine agency. The proof is not a conclusion which lies at the end of a chain of reasoning, of which chain each instance of contrivance is only a link, and of which, if one link fail, the whole falls; but it is an argument separately supplied by every separate example. An error in stating an example affects only that example. The argument is cumulative, in the fullest sense of that term. The eye proves it without the ear; the ear without the eye. The proof in each example is complete; for

> when the design of the part, and the conduciveness of its structure to that design is shown, the mind may set itself at rest; no future consideration can detract any thing from the force of the example.
>
> WILLIAM PALEY, Natural Theology

This argument has an antique sound, of course. It was written 175 years ago, after all. But the principle underlying it is one we use today in interplanetary exploration. When men first walked on the moon, they looked of course for evidences of intelligent life, though they didn't really expect to find such evidences on an atmosphereless body. Now how on earth (or elsewhere) could they possibly tell what would *be* evidence of intelligent life? Having no advance knowledge of the sorts of creatures that might inhabit other parts of the universe, by what signs could the astronauts infer their existence and presence? The answer is obvious. Any sort of device, or instrument, or machine, that exhibited some purposive internal organization, and that seemed not to grow naturally in that environment, would permit them to infer by analogy the existence of some (presumably) nonhuman intelligent maker.

Anyone who has been enraptured, bemused, or awestruck by the wonder of nature will appreciate the psychological force of the Argument from Design. Can the order of planets, stars, and galaxies, the underlying simplicity and regularity of natural forces, the exquisitely delicate adjustment of part to part in living things really just *be*? Must there not be some intelligence directing, organizing, creating this vast interconnected universe?

Well, maybe so, but the Argument from Design won't prove it! There are basically two things wrong with the Argument from Design. First of all, even if it is correct, it doesn't prove what Paley and most other Christian, Jewish, or Muslim theologians want it to prove. And second, it doesn't really prove much of anything at all. The first point is liable to slip by us because we are so mesmerized by the word "God." In the great Western religions, God is conceived as an infinite, eternal, omnipotent (infinitely powerful), omniscient (all-knowing) creator of the universe. But the most that the Argument from Design can prove, even if it is sound, is that there is a *very* long-lived (not eternal), very powerful (not omnipotent), very wise (not omniscient) world-organizer who has worked up the raw materials of space, time, and matter into a reasonably well-integrated machinelike universe. After all, the watchmaker does not create his materials, he merely fashions them to his purposes. And the human eye is not infinitely complex, it is just a good deal more complex than a camera. So if the analogy is taken strictly, we can at best demonstrate the existence of a conscious, purposeful, powerful, very knowledgeable, very old world-maker. But if we label that world-maker "God," then we may mistakenly slip into identifying him, or it, with the God of the Old and New Testaments, the God of the great Western religions, the God who lays down commandments, punishes the wicked, offers the free gift of eternal life, and so forth. And absolutely nothing in the analogy justifies any of those conclusions!

But the argument isn't even very sound, as David Hume pointed out in one of his most brilliant works, the *Dialogues Concerning Natural Religion*. Hume actually wrote the dialogues in the 1750s, twenty years before his death in 1776, but he was prevailed upon by his friends (including the economist and philosopher Adam Smith) to withhold them from publication, because the forcefulness of their attack on received religious opinions would open Hume to condemnation. Eventually, they were brought out posthumously in 1779 by his nephew. The work is a three-person discussion of all the principal arguments for the existence of God, in which first one character and then another comes to the fore. In the subtlety of their development and pacing, the *Dialogues* have something of the quality of a Baroque trio, and I think it may fairly be said that Hume is the only great philosopher after Plato to use the dialogue form to its full literary effect. The work is in twelve parts, and this selection comes from Part Two.

In reality, CLEANTHES, continued he, there is no need of having recourse to that affected scepticism, so displeasing to you, in order to come at this determination. Our ideas reach no farther than our experience: We have no experience of divine attributes and operations: I need not conclude my syllogism: You can draw the inference yourself. And it is a pleasure to me (and I hope to you too) that just reasoning and sound piety here concur in the same conclusion, and both of them establish the adorably mysterious and incomprehensible nature of the supreme Being. . . .

What I chiefly scruple in this subject, said PHILO, is not so much, that all religious arguments are by CLEANTHES reduced to experience, as that they appear not to be even the most certain and irrefragable of that inferior kind. That a stone will fall, that fire will burn, that the earth has solidity, we have observed a thousand and a thousand times; and when any new instance of this nature is presented, we draw without hesitation the accustomed inference. The exact similarity of the cases gives us a perfect assurance of a similar event; and a stronger evidence is never desired nor sought after. But wherever you depart, in the least, from the similarity of the cases, you diminish proportionably the evidence; and may at last bring it to a very weak *analogy*, which is confessedly liable to error and uncertainty. After having experienced the circulation of the blood in human creatures, we make no doubt that it takes place in Titius and Maevius: But from its circulation in frogs and fishes, it is only a presumption, though a strong one, from analogy, that it takes place in men and other animals. The analogical reasoning is much weaker, when we infer the circulation of the sap in vegetables from our experience that the blood circulates in animals; and those, who hastily followed that imperfect analogy, are found, by more accurate experiments, to have been mistaken.

If we see a house, CLEANTHES, we conclude, with the greatest certainty, that it had an architect or builder; because this is precisely that species of effect, which we have experienced to proceed from that species of cause. But surely you will not affirm, that the universe bears such a resemblance to a house, that we can with the same certainty infer a similar cause, or that the analogy is here entire and perfect. The dissimilitude is so striking, that the utmost you can here pretend to is a guess, a conjecture, a presumption concerning a similar cause; and how that pretension will be received in the world, I leave you to consider. . . .

Were a man to abstract from every thing which he knows or has seen, he would be altogether incapable, merely from his own ideas, to determine what kind of scene the universe must be, or to give the preference to one state or situation of things above another. For as nothing, which he clearly conceives, could be esteemed impossible or implying a contradiction, every chimera of his fancy would be upon an equal footing; nor could he assign any just reason, why he adheres to one idea or system, and rejects the others, which are equally possible.

Again; after he opens his eyes, and contemplates the world, as it really is, it would be impossible for him, at first, to assign the cause of any one event; much less, of the whole of things or of the universe. He might set his fancy a rambling; and she might bring him in an infinite variety of reports and representations. These would all be possible; but being all equally possible, he would never, of himself, give a satisfactory account for his preferring one of them to the rest. Experience alone can point out to him the true cause of any phenomenon.

Although Hume's refutation stands pretty well on its own feet, it also draws upon the more fundamental criticisms which Hume developed of causal reasoning of all sorts. In Chapter Seven, we will have another opportunity to examine the reasons for his skepticism concerning any attempt to infer causes from effects or effects from causes.

St. Thomas Aquinas: The Cosmological Argument

Christian theologians derive their beliefs about God from two sources. The first is *revelation*, consisting of those truths which God has revealed

ST. THOMAS AQUINAS (1225–1274) is the greatest intellectual figure of the high medieval culture
that flourished in Europe during the thirteenth
century. Aquinas was an Italian theologian and
philosopher who spent his life in the Dominican
Order, teaching and writing. His writings, which
run to many volumes, set forth in extremely
systematic form a full-scale theory of God, man,
and the universe. The official dogma of the
Church, as established by revelation and interpretation of holy scriptures, was combined by
Aquinas with the secular metaphysical doctrines
of Aristotle and the post-Aristotelian Greek and
Roman philosophers.

Aquinas' philosophical synthesis of philosophy
and theology became the accepted teaching of
the Roman Catholic Church. It is known today as
Thomism, and in various forms continues to exercise a profound intellectual influence both on
Church doctrine and on the philosophical work
of Catholic and non-Catholic thinkers.

to man through the holy writings of the Old and New Testaments or
through his miraculous appearance to particular individuals. Revelation
must of course be interpreted, and therein lies the origin of many learned
disputes and bloody wars. But everyone agrees that the *fact* of revelation
is simply a miracle, to be taken on faith. The second source is *reason*,
our natural human power of analysis, argument, observation, and inference. Man must wait for revelation. He cannot make it happen, and
he cannot predict when or where God will reveal Himself. But reason
is man's own instrument, and he can deploy it at will to seek out
the origins of the universe and the existence and nature of a Creator. The
greatest of all the rational theologians, by universal agreement, is the
thirteenth-century Christian philosopher St. Thomas Aquinas. His elab-
oration and codification of the rational metaphysical basis for Christian
theology remains to this day the dominant intellectual influence in the
Roman Catholic Church. The philosophy known as Thomism is an enduring monument of medieval intellectual architecture, as impressive in
its way as the great Cathedral of Notre Dame in Paris.

Aquinas actually offers five separate proofs for the existence of God
in his most important work, the *Summa Theologica*. The first three of
these are variations of the same argument, and we shall examine them
all together. In each case, Aquinas begins with some fact about the world:
The first argument takes off from the fact that things *move* in the world
around us; the second from the fact that every event that is observed to
take place is made to happen, or caused, by something else that precedes
it; the third from the fact that there are at least some things in the world

whose existence is not necessary, which are, in metaphysical language, "possible." Aquinas then reasons that the observed motion, or event, or possible thing, is the last in a chain of motions or causes or possible things, and he asserts that such a chain cannot reach back endlessly to prior motions, to earlier causes, to other possible things on which this possible thing depends for its existence. Somewhere, the chain must end, with a mover that is not itself also moved by something else, with a cause which is not itself caused by yet another cause, with a being whose existence is not merely possible but necessary. That first mover, first cause, or necessary being, is God.

If the task of proving the existence of God weren't such a serious business, we might say that the cosmological argument is a very sophisticated answer to the four-year-old's question, "Where did I come from, Mommy?" Now a straight answer would be, "You came from inside mommy's womb." And after a few more details have been added, that answer usually satisfies a four-year-old. Eventually, the obvious follow-up question will occur to a six- or seven-year-old, namely, "Where did you come from, mommy?" A somewhat longer story about grandma and grandpa should handle that one. But sooner or later, a bright teenager is going to start brooding on the *real* problem. Maybe I came from mom and dad, each of whom came in turn from a mother and father; maybe the earliest human mothers and fathers evolved through a combination and mutation and selection from prehuman mammals, who in turn evolved from reptiles, or what have you; and maybe life itself sprang up spontaneously through chance rearrangements of amino-acidlike compounds, which in turn emerged from the stuff of which the earth was formed, but *damn it*, somewhere the buck has got to stop! If there weren't anything that was *first*, then how can there be anything at all? If the existence of each particular thing is to be explained by saying that it came from some preceding thing, then we have no explanation at all. We just have a chain that leads so far back into the misty past that finally we get tired of asking, and mistake our fatigue for an answer. In short, an "infinite regress" is no answer at all. We might just as well have answered the very first question by saying, "Shut up and don't ask silly questions!"

So we might summarize Aquinas' proofs by saying that if the universe makes any sense at all, if it is through and through rational, then there must be a necessary being, a first mover, a first cause. Here are the three proofs as Aquinas stated them. Notice that he doesn't waste any words! He proves the existence of God three times in the space it takes Plato to introduce one of the characters in a dialogue.

> . . . The existence of God can be proved in five ways.
> The first and more manifest way is the argument from motion. It is certain, and evident to our senses, that in the world some things are

in motion. Now whatever is moved is moved by another, for nothing can be moved except it is in potentiality to that towards which it is moved; whereas a thing moves inasmuch as it is in act. For motion is nothing else than the reduction of something from potentiality to actuality. But nothing can be reduced from potentiality to actuality, except by something in a state of actuality. Thus that which is actually hot, as fire, makes wood, which is potentially hot, to be actually hot, and thereby moves and changes it. Now it is not possible that the same thing should be at once in actuality and potentiality in the same respect but only in different respects. For what is actually hot cannot simultaneously be potentially hot; but it is simultaneously potentially cold. It is therefore impossible that in the same respect and in the same way a thing should be both mover and moved, *i.e.*, that it should move itself. Therefore, whatever is moved must be moved by another. If that by which it is moved be itself moved, then this also must needs be moved by another, and that by another again. But this cannot go on to infinity, because then there would be no first mover, and, consequently, no other mover, seeing that subsequent movers move only inasmuch as they are moved by the first mover; as the staff moves only because it is moved by the hand. Therefore it is necessary to arrive at a first mover, moved by no other; and this everyone understands to be God.

The second way is from the nature of efficient cause. In the world of sensible things we find there is an order of efficient causes. There is no case known (neither is it, indeed, possible) in which a thing is found to be the efficient cause of itself; for so it would be prior to itself, which is impossible. Now in efficient causes it is not possible to go on to infinity, because in all efficient causes following in order, the first is the cause of the intermediate cause, and the intermediate is the cause of the ultimate cause, whether the intermediate cause be several, or one only. Now to take away the cause is to take away the effect. Therefore, if there be no first cause among efficient causes, there will be no ultimate, nor any intermediate, cause. But if in efficient causes it is possible to go on to infinity, there will be no first efficient cause, neither will there be an ultimate effect, nor any intermediate efficient causes; all of which is plainly false. Therefore it is necessary to admit a first efficient cause, to which everyone gives the name of God.

The third way is taken from possibility and necessity, and runs thus. We find in nature things that are possible to be and not to be, since they are found to be generated, and to be corrupted, and consequently, it is possible for them to be and not to be. But it is impossible for these always to exist, for that which can not-be at some time is not. Therefore, if everything can not-be, then at one time there was nothing in existence. Now if this were true, even now there would be nothing in existence, because that which does not exist begins to exist only through something already existing. Therefore, if at one time nothing was in existence, it would have been impossible for anything to have begun to exist; and thus even now nothing would be in existence—which is absurd. Therefore, not all beings are merely possible, but there must exist something the existence of which is necessary. But every necessary thing either has its necessity caused by another, or not. Now it is impossible to go on to infinity in necessary things which have their necessity caused by another, as has been already proved in regard to efficient causes. Therefore we cannot but admit the existence of some being having of itself its own necessity, and not receiving it from another, but rather causing in others their necessity. This all men speak of as God.

SAINT THOMAS AQUINAS, Summa Theologica

Hume has an answer to these arguments as well as to the argument from design. In Part IX of his *Dialogues*, he considers a version which reasons from cause and effect to the existence of a first cause, whose existence must therefore be necessary. It is thus a combination of the second and third of Aquinas' proofs. Hume's refutation, put this time into the mouth of the character named Cleanthes, begins with a paragraph that is also a refutation of the third great proof, the ontological argument. More of that a little later.

I shall begin with observing, that there is an evident absurdity in pretending to demonstrate a matter of fact, or to prove it by any arguments a *priori*. Nothing is demonstrable, unless the contrary implies a contradiction. Nothing, that is distinctly conceivable, implies a contradiction. Whatever we conceive as existent, we can also conceive as non-existent. There is no Being, therefore, whose non-existence implies a contradiction. Consequently there is no Being, whose existence is demonstrable. I propose this argument as entirely decisive, and am willing to rest the whole controversy upon it.

It is pretended that the Deity is a necessarily existent Being; and this necessity of his existence is attempted to be explained by asserting that, if we knew his whole essence or nature, we should perceive it to be as impossible for him not to exist as for twice two not to be four. But it is evident, that this can never happen, while our faculties remain the same as at present. It will still be possible for us, at any time, to conceive the non-existence of what we formerly conceived to exist; nor can the mind ever lie under a necessity of supposing any object to remain always in being: in the same manner as we lie under a necessity of always conceiving twice two to be four. The words, therefore, *necessary existence*, have no meaning; or, which is the same thing, none that is consistent.

But farther; why may not the material universe be the necessarily existent Being, according to this pretended explication of necessity? We dare not affirm that we know all the qualities of matter; and for aught we can determine, it may contain some qualities, which, were they known, would make its non-existence appear as great a contradiction as that twice two is five. I find only one argument employed to prove, that the material world is not the necessarily existent Being; and this argument is derived from the contingency both of the matter and the form of the world. "Any particle of matter," it is said, "may be *conceived* to be annihilated; and any form may be *conceived* to be altered. Such an annihilation or alteration, therefore, is not impossible." But it seems a great partiality not to perceive, that the same argument extends equally to the Deity, so far as we have any conception of him; and that the mind can at least imagine him to be nonexistent, or his attributes to be altered. It must be some unknown, inconceivable qualities, which can make non-existence appear impossible, or his attributes unalterable: And no reason can be assigned, why these qualities may not belong to matter. As they are altogether unknown and inconceivable, they can never be proved incompatible with it.

Add to this, that in tracing an eternal succession of objects, it seems absurd to inquire for a general cause or first Author. How can any thing, that exists from eternity, have a cause, since that relation implies a priority in time and a beginning of existence?

In such a chain too, or succession of objects, each part is caused by that which preceded it, and causes that which succeeds it. Where then is the difficulty? But the WHOLE, you say, wants a cause. I answer, that the uniting of these parts into a whole, like the uniting of several distinct counties into one kingdom, or several distinct members into one body, is performed merely by an arbitrary act of the mind, and has no influence on the nature of things. Did I show you the particular causes of each individual in a collection of twenty particles of matter, I should think it very unreasonable, should you afterwards ask me, what was the cause of the whole twenty. This is sufficiently explained in explaining the cause of the parts.

DAVID HUME, *Dialogues Concerning Natural Religion*

St. Anselm: The Ontological Argument

Here it is, the most famous, the most mystifying, the most outrageous and irritating philosophical argument of all time! Read it carefully and see what you think.

> *Truly there is a God, although the fool hath said in his heart, There is no God.*

And so, Lord, do thou, who dost give understanding to faith, give me, so far as thou knowest it to be profitable, to understand that thou art as we believe; and that thou art that which we believe. And, indeed, we believe that thou art a being than which nothing greater can be conceived. Or is there no such nature, since the fool hath said in his heart, there is no God? (Psalms xiv. 1). But, at any rate, this very fool, when he hears of this being of which I speak—a being than which nothing greater can be conceived—understands what he hears, and what he understands in his understanding; although he does not understand it to exist.

SAINT ANSELM (1033–1109) was born in Italy, and was trained there for the priesthood. In 1093, he was appointed Archbishop of Canterbury in England by the Norman king William Rufus. His most important philosophical work is the *Proslogion*, in which he set forth a startling and radically new proof for the existence of God. The proof, known now as the "ontological argument," has been defended over the past nine centuries by Descartes, Spinoza, and others. St. Thomas Aquinas, on the other hand, claimed that it was not a valid proof, and he rejected it.

For, it is one thing for an object to be in the understanding, and another to understand that the object exists. When a painter first conceives of what he will afterwards perform, he has it in his understanding, but he does not yet understand it to be, because he has not yet performed it. But after he has made the painting, he both has it in his understanding, and he understands that it exists, because he has made it.

Hence, even the fool is convinced that something exists in the understanding, at least, than which nothing greater can be conceived. For, when he hears of this, he understands it. And whatever is understood, exists in the understanding. And assuredly that, than which nothing greater can be conceived, cannot exist in the understanding alone. For, suppose it exists in the understanding alone: then it can be conceived to exist in reality; which is greater.

Therefore, if that, than which nothing greater can be conceived, exists in the understanding alone, the very being, than which nothing greater can be conceived, is one, than which a greater can be conceived. But obviously this is impossible. Hence, there is no doubt that there exists a being, than which nothing greater can be conceived, and it exists both in the understanding and in reality.

And it assuredly exists so truly, that it cannot be conceived not to exist. For, it is possible to conceive of a being which cannot be conceived not to exist; and this is greater than one which can be conceived not to exist. Hence, if that, than which nothing greater can be conceived, can be conceived not to exist, it is not that, than which nothing is greater can be conceived. But this is an irreconcilable contradiction. There is, then, so truly a being than which nothing greater can be conceived to exist, that it cannot even be conceived not to exist; and this being thou art, O Lord, our God.

So truly, therefore, dost thou exist, O Lord, my God, that thou canst not be conceived not to exist; and rightly. For, if a mind could conceive of a being better than thee, the creature would rise above the Creator; and this is most absurd. And, indeed, whatever else there is, except thee alone, can be conceived not to exist. To thee alone, therefore, it belongs to exist more truly than all other beings, and hence in a higher degree than all others. For, whatever else exists does not exist so truly, and hence in a less degree it belongs to it to exist. Why, then, has the fool said in his heart, there is no God (Psalms xiv. 1), since it is so evident, to a rational mind, that thou dost exist in the highest degree of all? Why, except that he is dull and a fool?

ST. ANSELM, *Proslogion*

Whenever I read the Ontological Argument, I have the same feeling that comes over me when I watch a really good magician. Nothing up this sleeve; nothing up the other sleeve; nothing in the hat; presto! A big, fat rabbit. How can Anselm pull God out of an idea? At least the Argument from Design and Cosmological Arguments start from some actual fact about the world, whether it is the apparently purposeful organization of living things, or the motion of bodies in space, or whatever. But the Ontological Argument starts from a mere idea in the mind of the philosopher and undertakes to prove, from that idea alone, that there must actually be something corresponding to the idea. The argument makes no use at all of facts that might be gathered by observation or analysis of the world. Philosophers call an argument of this sort an *a priori* argument. Propositions that can be known to be true without consideration of factual support, merely from an analysis of the concepts involved in the judgments, are called propositions *knowable a priori*, or simply *"a priori* propositions."

Now, philosophers have for a long time known that there were *a priori* propositions, or propositions whose truth can be known merely from a consideration of their meaning. For example, consider the proposition, "If an aardvark is a mammal, then it bears its young live." Is that true? Well, your first reaction might be to ask yourself whether you know what an aardvark is, or maybe to look it up in the encyclopedia. But stop and think about it for a moment. A mammal is an animal that bears its young live rather than laying eggs. That is what we *mean* when we call something a mammal. That is part of the definition of the word "mammal." So if anything is to be classified as a mammal, it will have to be the sort of thing that bears its young live. Otherwise, we wouldn't call it a mammal; we would call it something else, or even just say that we don't have a word for it. If you think about it, you will realize that you can decide about the truth of my proposition without knowing anything about aardvarks, indeed without ever having heard the word "aardvark" before. Whatever aardvarks are, "If an aardvark is a mammal, then it bears its young live." In short, you can know the truth of the proposition *a priori*, or even more briefly, it is an *a priori* proposition.

But are there any aardvarks? Ah well, that is quite another question. My *a priori* proposition only tells me that if there are any, and if they are mammals, then they bear their young live. It doesn't tell me whether there are any. Indeed, it doesn't even tell me whether aardvarks are mammals. It just says, *if* there are aardvarks and they are mammals, then they bear their young live. Propositions that can be known to be true merely on the basis of the meanings of the words used in them are called *tautologies*, and you can make up tautologies all day long, with no more material to work with than the English language.

The Ontological Argument seems to depend on a tautology too. First Anselm *defines* the word "God" as meaning "a being than which nothing greater can be conceived." Then he argues that this concept, of a greatest being, must include the notion that the being cannot be conceived not to exist. In other words, he argues that when we spell out the definition of "God" as "a being than which nothing greater can be conceived," we will find that the definition includes the characteristic "necessarily existing," just as when we spell out the definition of "mammal," we find that it includes the notion "bearing its young live."

Well, "Mammals bear their young live" is a tautology; it is true by definition; we can know it to be true merely by understanding the words used in the statement. It follows from the definition. So too, Anselm claims, "God necessarily exists" is a tautology; it too is true by definition; it too can be known merely through an understanding of the words used in the statement. But there is one enormous difference. The statement about mammals, and all the other ordinary tautologies that have ever been thought up, say nothing about whether something *exists*. Ordinary tautologies just tell us that *if* there are any things fitting a certain definition, *then* they have the following characteristics. If there are mammals, then they bear their young live; if there are any bachelors, then they are unmarried (because "bachelor" means "unmarried man"); if there are any triangles, then they have three angles; and so forth. The Ontological Argument is the only case in which a tautology is used to prove that something —namely, God—exists.

Now, of course philosophers who use the Ontological Argument are perfectly well aware that this is a very special and peculiar sort of tautology. If they can prove the existence of God this way, why can't I use the same trick to prove the existence of a perfect horse, or a necessarily existent ox, or a mosquito than which none greater can be conceived? Their answer is that God is different from all the other beings in or out of the universe, and that God's existence is a different sort of existence from the existence of every created thing. God is infinite, all other things are finite; God's existence is necessary, the existence of every other thing is merely contingent; God is perfect, all else is imperfect; and God's existence follows *a priori* from His definition, whereas the existence of every other thing, since it depends ultimately on God and not on itself alone, follows *not* from its own definition but only from God's act of creation.

The Ontological Argument remains to this day one of the most controversial arguments in all of philosophy. Some very devout theologians, including St. Thomas Aquinas, have believed that it was wrong, invalid, a confusion. Several of the greatest philosophers of the seventeenth century, including Descartes and Spinoza, thought it was valid, and developed their own versions of it. In his great *Critique of Pure Reason*, Immanuel Kant offered an elaborate refutation of the argument which for more than a hundred years was thought to have permanently laid it to rest. Just recently, however, there has been a revival of philosophical interest in the Ontological Argument, and philosophers like myself, who grew up thinking that Kant had once and for all finished it off, now find the technical journals full of new versions of the Ontological Argument, in which the latest tools of formal logic are used to give the old warhorse some new life.

Let us wind up this discussion of proofs for the existence of God with Kant's refutation of the Ontological Argument. This is a difficult passage, harder even than the argument itself, which was no breeze. Please don't expect to understand everything Kant is saying. I have been studying Kant for twenty-five years, and I am not sure what he means sometimes. But read through this selection two or three times, with the aid of your professor. Kant always repays hard work, and his treatment of the Ontological Argument is one of his most brilliant efforts.

> Notwithstanding all these general considerations, in which every one must concur, we may be challenged with a case which is brought forward as proof that in actual fact the contrary holds, namely, that there is one concept, and indeed only one, in reference to which the not-being or rejection of its object is in itself contradictory, namely, the concept of the *ens realissimum*. It is declared that it possesses all reality, and that we are justified in assuming that such a being is possible (the fact that a concept does not contradict itself by no means proves the possibility of its object: but the contrary assertion I am for the moment willing to allow). Now 'all reality' includes existence; existence is therefore contained in the concept of a thing that is possible. If, then, this thing is rejected, the internal possibility of the thing is rejected—which is self-contradictory.
>
> My answer is as follows. There is already a contradiction in intro-

ducing the concept of existence—no matter under what title it may be disguised—into the concept of a thing which we profess to be thinking solely in reference to its possibility. If that be allowed as legitimate, a seeming victory has been won: but in actual fact nothing at all is said: the assertion is a mere tautology. We must ask: Is the proposition that *this* or *that thing* (which, whatever it may be, is allowed as possible) *exists*, an analytic or a synthetic proposition? If it is analytic, the assertion of the existence of the thing adds nothing to the thought of the thing; but in that case either the thought, which is in us, is the thing itself, or we have presupposed an existence as belonging to the realm of the possible, and have then, on that pretext, inferred its existence from its internal possibility—which is nothing but a miserable tautology. The word "reality," which in the concept of the thing sounds other than the word "existence" in the concept of the predicate, is of no avail in meeting this objection. For if all positing (no matter what it may be that is posited) is entitled reality, the thing with all its predicates is already posited in the concept of the subject, and is assumed as actual; and in the predicate this is merely repeated. But if, on the other hand, we admit, as every reasonable person must, that all existential propositions are synthetic, how can we profess to maintain that the predicate of existence cannot be rejected without contradiction? This is a feature which is found only in analytic propositions, and is indeed precisely what constitutes their analytic character.

I should have hoped to put an end to these idle and fruitless disputations in a direct manner, by an accurate determination of the concept of existence, had I not found that the illusion which is caused by the confusion of a logical with a real predicate (that is, with a predicate which determines a thing) is almost beyond correction. Anything we please can be made to serve as a logical predicate; the subject can even be predicated of itself; for logic abstracts from all content. But a *determining* predicate is a predicate which is added to the concept of the subject and enlarges it. Consequently, it must not be already contained in the concept.

"*Being*" is obviously not a real predicate; that is, it is not a concept of something which could be added to the concept of a thing. It is merely the positing of a thing, or of certain determinations, as existing in themselves. Logically, it is merely the copula of a judgment. The proposition, "God is omnipotent," contains two concepts, each of which has its object—God and omnipotence. The small word "is" adds no new predicate, but only serves to posit the predicate *in its relation* to the subject. If, now, we take the subject (God) with all its predicates (among which is omnipotence), and say "God is," or "There is a God," we attach no new predicate to the concept of God, but only posit the subject in itself with all its predicates, and indeed posit it as being an *object* that stands in relation to my *concept*. The content of both must be one and the same; nothing can have been added to the concept, which expresses merely what is possible, by my thinking its object (through the expression "it is") as given absolutely. Otherwise stated, the real contains no more than the merely possible. A hundred real thalers do not contain the least coin more than a hundred possible thalers. For as the latter signify the concept, and the former the object and the positing of the object, should the former contain more than the latter, my concept would not, in that case, express the whole object, and would not therefore be an adequate concept of it. My financial position is, however, affected very differently by a hundred real thalers than it is by the mere concept of them (that is, of their possibility). For the object, as it actually exists, is not analytically contained in my concept, but is added to my concept (which is a determination of my state) synthetically; and yet the conceived hundred thalers are not themselves in the least increased through thus acquiring existence outside my concept.

IMMANUEL KANT, *Critique of Pure Reason*

III   Kierkegaard concentrated entirely on *faith*, on the inner passionate concern with the truth of the Christian message. He scorned all rational evidences and arguments as radically inadequate to his religious needs. Anselm, Aquinas, and Paley, together with thousands of other rational theologians and religious philosophers, have looked to *reason* to support their faith, either through *a priori* arguments for the existence of God, or through *a posteriori* arguments founded upon His effects in the world He created. But for Kierkegaard, Anselm, Aquinas, Paley and all the rest, there can be no real human doubt about the truth and centrality of religion. Even Kant was, in his personal life, a devoted, practicing Christian.

To some men and women, however, religion has seemed to be a fraud, a sham, a delusion foisted by man upon himself, or else foisted by priests and holy men on the common people. Karl Marx, angered by the tendency of popular Christianity to make the working class resigned to its poverty, called religion the "opiate of the masses." He believed that the proletarian revolution would eliminate established religious institutions along with all the other instruments by which ruling classes have oppressed mankind. Eventually, religion, like the state, would wither away, leaving a society thoroughly secular and thoroughly rational.

Quite apart from formal attacks on religion by philosophers or social reformers, there has been a dramatic decline in the religiosity of Western society during the last century and a half. Even in such countries as Italy, which maintains official ties with the Roman Catholic Church, the influence of religious belief on the everyday lives of men and women has declined. In the United States, religion plays virtually no part in the public affairs of the nation, and despite a fair amount of Sunday church-going, only a small portion of the American people place their religious beliefs at the center of their private lives in the way that almost all people did two centuries ago. This progressive secularization of Western society seems to be related to industrialization, to urbanization, to the gradual rise to dominance of scientific modes of relating to the world, rather than to changes in philosophical arguments. Periodically, religious revivals sweep the country, apparently reversing the tide of secularization. But when the waves recede, the level of religiosity settles at a new low, and the process continues.

One of the most powerful attacks on religious belief comes not from a philosopher but from the father of modern psychoanalytic theory, Sigmund Freud. Freud is famous for the discovery of the unconscious, for his theory of infant sexuality, and for his invention of the method of psychoanalysis. "Lying on the couch" and "going to the shrink" have entered into our language as slang for receiving the treatment which Freud developed for emotional problems. Because of his emphasis on the irra-

SIGMUND FREUD (1856–1939) was the founder of the branch of medicine and psychological theory known as psychoanalysis. Freud was born in Austria, where he was trained as a neurologist. Through his clinical work on problems of hysterical paralysis, he became interested in the possibility of unconscious mental processes. Working first with the techniques of hypnosis and later with techniques of dream interpretation and word association which he invented, Freud made major discoveries about the workings of the mind. His studies of the unconscious and his emphasis on the central importance of sexuality in the mental life of adults and of children aroused great controversy and brought down on Freud considerable criticism both from the medical community and from the general public. Freud had many pupils and disciples who carried on his research and developed the therapeutic techniques he had devised. Though only a portion of modern-day psychiatrists and psychoanalysts describe themselves as "Freudians," virtually every branch of psychiatry is deeply indebted to Freud's work. In the last years of his life Freud was forced to leave Austria to escape persecution by the Nazis. He died in England.

tional components in the human personality, Freud is sometimes thought of as an enemy of rationalism. Certainly, he was an enemy of the facile and comfortable belief that man is a rational animal, and that reason can without much trouble establish control over the nonrational forces in the soul. But in a deeper sense, Freud was a rationalist through and through. He believed, as Plato did, that human beings suffer great unhappiness when the irrational elements in the soul control and manipulate the rational elements. He believed too, as Plato did, that self-knowledge was the cure for that unnecessary unhappiness. But Freud parted company with Plato, and with many other students of the human condition as well, in his pessimistic conviction that even a healthy personality would necessarily suffer pain and misery. The problem, as Freud saw it, was that the human condition is fundamentally compromised by disease, by death, and by the unbridgeable gap between the deep desires we all have for erotic gratification and the limited opportunities we have in the real world for the satisfaction of those desires.

Faced with frustration and death, Freud argued, we systematically fool ourselves with fairy tales, dreams, fantasies, and illusions. The greatest of those illusions is religion, and its hold on us is so strong that we persist in believing even in the face of the most powerful negative evidence. We believe in heaven, in God, in a life after death, in reward for virtue and punishment for sin, not because there is the slightest evidence for our beliefs, but because we *want* so much to believe. Religion is indeed an opiate, as Marx said, but for all mankind, not merely for the working class. To those who ask Freud what he offers in place of religion, he can answer only, the hard truth, however painful it is to face.

Here is Freud's statement of his conception of religion. Notice that even if Freud is right, the issue is not settled, for though we believe because we want to believe rather than because evidence or reasoning justifies our belief, our belief might still be true!

> ... religious ideas ... which profess to be dogmas, are not the residue of experience or the final result of reflection; they are illusions, fulfilments of the oldest, strongest and most insistent wishes of mankind; the secret of their strength is the strength of these wishes.
>
> When I say that they are illusions, I must define the meaning of the word. An illusion is not the same as an error, it is indeed not necessarily an error. Aristotle's belief that vermin are evolved out of dung, to which ignorant people still cling, was an error; so was the belief of a former generation of doctors that *tabes dorsalis* was the result of sexual excess. It would be improper to call these errors illusions. On the other hand, it was an illusion on the part of Columbus that he had discovered a new sea-route to India. The part played by

his wish in this error is very clear. One may describe as an illusion the statement of certain nationalists that the Indo-Germanic race is the only one capable of culture, or the belief, which only psycho-analysis destroyed, that the child is a being without sexuality. It is characteristic of the illusion that it is derived from men's wishes; in this respect it approaches the psychiatric delusion, but it is to be distinguished from this, quite apart from the more complicated structure of the latter. In the delusion we emphasize as essential the conflict with reality; the illusion need not be necessarily false, that is to say, unrealizable or incompatible with reality. For instance, a poor girl may have an illusion that a prince will come and fetch her home. It is possible; some such cases have occurred. That the Messiah will come and found a golden age is much less probable; according to one's personal attitude one will classify this belief as an illusion or as analogous to a delusion. Examples of illusions that have come true are not easy to discover, but the illusion of the alchemists that all metals can be turned into gold may prove to be one. The desire to have lots of gold, as much gold as possible, has been considerably damped by our modern insight into the nature of wealth, yet chemistry no longer considers a transmutation of metals into gold as impossible. Thus we call a belief an illusion when wish-fulfilment is a prominent factor in its motivation, while disregarding its relations to reality, just as the illusion itself does.

If after this survey we turn again to religious doctrines, we may reiterate that they are all illusions, they do not admit of proof, and no one can be compelled to consider them as true or to believe in them. Some of them are so improbable, so very incompatible with everything we have laboriously discovered about the reality of the world, that we may compare them—taking adequately into account the psychological differences—to delusions. Of the reality value of most of them we cannot judge; just as they cannot be proved, neither can they be refuted. We still know too little to approach them critically. The riddles of the universe only reveal themselves slowly to our enquiry, to many questions science can as yet give no answer; but scientific work is our only way to the knowledge of external reality.

SIGMUND FREUD, The Future of an Illusion

RENÉ DESCARTES (1596–1650) is universally recognized among philosophers as the first great figure of the modern age. Born in a small town in Touraine, France, Descartes was educated by the Jesuits, and he remained throughout his life a devoted Catholic. His early interest was principally in mathematics and physics, fields in which exciting new work was being done by many continental and English thinkers. In his early twenties, perhaps as the result of a dramatic trio of dreams, Descartes conceived the grandiose plan of formulating an entirely new system of science founded upon mathematics. Though he never accomplished this impossible task, his contributions to mathematics and physics place him in the forefront of seventeenth century science.

Descartes' primary concern throughout his life was with problems of methodology, justification, and certainty. His first work was entitled *Rules for the Direction of the Mind*, and in it he sought to establish the proper procedures by which a question could be investigated without danger of error or confusion. His most famous work, *Meditations on First Philosophy*, was immediately recognized as a dramatic challenge to all established philosophy and science. It was circulated widely throughout Europe, and provoked a series of objections, to which Descartes wrote extended replies. In these objections and replies we can see a number of profound and dramatic debates unfolding, in which such famous thinkers as Hobbes, Gassendi, and Arnauld locked horns with Descartes.

Although Descartes was deeply influenced by the scholastic philosophy which had preceded him, the problems he posed, the questions he raised, and the demands he made for absolute subjective certainty in knowledge, served to undermine the influence of the 2000-year-old tradition of Aristotelian philosophizing. Virtually all the great philosophy written during the 150 years following Descartes' death can be seen as an attempt to answer the questions raised by the brilliant, iconoclastic Frenchman.

Theory of Knowledge 7

I If you have been working your way through this book carefully, reading and thinking, discussing the problems it raises with your teacher and your fellow students, you should by now be getting some feel for what philosophy is and how philosophers think. And if I have been at all successful, then philosophy ought to seem a fairly sensible sort of business to you. Perhaps philosophical questions aren't exactly what your mind would turn to if you had a few spare moments caught in a traffic jam or if you couldn't sleep late at night, but at least it is easy enough to understand how reasonable men and women might get genuinely worked up about them. What rules should I use to decide the hard moral choices that life poses for me? How should the wealth of a society be divided up among its members? Do I have an obligation to obey the state, even when I believe that its laws are unjust? What place should painting and poetry, music and fiction play in a good society? Is there a God? Can I trust Him to keep his promise of eternal life? These may not be everyone's questions, but they are surely questions worth asking. Some of them even get asked in political campaigns, in hospital emergency wards, in law courts, or in the front lines of a war.

In this chapter, the situation changes dramatically. We are going to

225

take a look at philosophical attempts to deal with questions that some of you may think are just plain crazy. Suppose a friend of yours asks whether you and he really did go to the movies last night or whether he just dreamed it. A little odd, perhaps, but people do have very lifelike dreams; I have myself on a couple of occasions had dreams so real that afterwards I wasn't entirely sure whether they had actually happened or not. You wouldn't think your friend was being *philosophical*, but on the other hand you wouldn't think he was crazy either. Suppose he went on to wonder, in absolute seriousness, whether everything that had ever happened to him was a dream, whether his childhood, his adolescence, his school days, his fights with his parents, his first romance, his first trip away from home, his coming to college, and his standing right there in front of you were *all just dreams*. If he was really dead serious, not just kidding around or trying to get a rise out of you, then about now you would start edging toward the phone, trying to figure out how you could call the school psychiatrist without getting your friend too upset. People who really aren't sure whether their whole lives have been dreams "need help," as the saying goes.

Suppose another friend said, as the two of you were waiting for an elevator, that she couldn't really be sure that she needed an elevator to get back down to the first floor. Maybe if she stepped out of the window, she would be able simply to fly down. Suppose, indeed, that she expressed doubt about whether she could ever tell what would happen next—whether she would drown if she held her head under water, whether her finger would burn if she held it in a flame, whether her books would fall down or up if she let go of them. She might even admit that she wasn't sure there was anyone else in the whole world besides herself, though of course there might be a lot of human-looking bodies that made speechlike noises and acted in peoplelike ways. Well, once again, you would probably think that either the whole act was a put-on, or your friend was in the midst of a bad trip, or else that it was time for the shrink. You certainly wouldn't think that she was simply doing philosophy!

From the beginning of the seventeenth century until the present day, some of the most brilliant men ever to grace the cultural and intellectual life of Western civilization have devoted their best philosophical efforts to just such questions as the ones we have been imagining your friends to be asking. And though I would be the first to admit that philosophers have suffered their share of mental illness, there is no reason at all to suspect that any of these great thinkers was mentally unsound when he wrote his philosophy. (Rousseau, as we have seen, was more than a little odd, but we won't be talking about him in this chapter.) The greatest challenge any teacher of philosophy faces is to present the epistemological theories of the seventeenth- and eighteenth-century theorists of knowledge in such a way that students not only understand the arguments but also understand why in heaven's name sane men worried about such peculiar problems.

Why not just leave the theory of knowledge out of an introductory course—or book—altogether? After all, physicists don't try to teach the most sophisticated wrinkles of particle physics or quantum theory to beginning students. Mathematicians save ring topology for math majors. Couldn't we just sort of skip over the theory of knowledge? The answer is no, for two reasons. First of all, the theory of knowledge is the heart and soul of the philosophy that has been written since the beginning of the seventeenth century. All of the most important philosophers—Descartes, Leibniz, Locke, Berkeley, Hume, Kant—set epistemological investigations at the center of their work. If we cannot understand what made them take so seriously the questions that seem odd to us today, then we cannot really understand philosophy as it has been done during the past four centuries. In the second place, the strange-seeming problems of the modern theory of knowledge (in philosophy, anything since 1600 is called "modern") connect up directly with one of the dominant cultural and intellectual developments of the post-medieval world—namely, the steady movement toward a radical individualism in religion, in politics, in art, and in literature, as well as in philosophy. Though the epistemological puzzles of seventeenth- and eighteenth-century philosophy seem bizarre or unintuitive on first inspection, they have deeply influenced the way painters painted, the way poets wrote, the way theologians reinterpreted the Word of God, and even the way economists, political scientists, and sociologists have explained our collective social life. So like it or not, we are in for some complicated philosophy in this chapter.

By common agreement, the man who started the new theory of knowledge on its way in philosophy was a Frenchman, born in 1596, named René Descartes. Indeed, though Descartes wrote a number of important works during his fifty-four years, in which mathematics, physics, and other subjects as well as philosophy were discussed, we can even name the precise piece of philosophy that marks the beginning of modern philosophy as we study it today. That honor clearly belongs to a seventy-page work entitled *Meditations on First Philosophy*, published by Descartes in 1641.

The seventeenth century was an age of scientific giants, and among the truly great thinkers whose efforts created what we know today as modern science, only the German Gottfried Leibniz and the Englishman Isaac Newton can stand with Descartes. You have probably already met Descartes, or at least spent some time working with one of his contributions to knowledge, for it was he who invented what is called analytic geometry. (That is why, when you draw a graph and plot points on it, you are said to be using "Cartesian" coordinates.) In Chapter Eight, we will be talking about some of the metaphysical problems which were raised by the new science, but now we shall concentrate on Descartes' revolutionary transformation of our understanding of knowledge itself. In short, we shall look at Descartes' *theory of knowledge*.

Descartes was born in 1596, three-quarters of a century after Martin Luther had begun the Protestant Reformation by nailing his famous theses to the church door in Wittenberg. Descartes himself was, and remained throughout his life, a Roman Catholic, and his early education was received from the Jesuits. Nevertheless, if the essence of the Protestant Reformation was the rejection of the religious authority of the institution of the Church and the emphasis on the primacy of individual conscience, then it is clear that Descartes was, intellectually and emotionally, an extreme protestant. The keynote of his life work was a thoroughgoing rejection of received opinion, established doctrine, and the authority of the ancients, and a thoroughly individualistic insistence upon accepting only those truths which his own reason could certify to be correct.

In his early twenties, Descartes' interest turned to mathematics and physics, fields which at that time were dominated by concepts and methods almost 2000 years old. Exciting new work was being done in both areas, and Descartes, like many young scientific geniuses, moved immediately to the scientific frontier. On the night of November 10, 1619, the

23-year-old Descartes had a series of three dreams which seem to have transformed his life. He spoke and wrote of them ever after as the turning point in his career. I am not going to try my hand at armchair dream interpretation. As Freud made very clear when he first described the psychoanalytic method of interpreting dreams, you cannot figure out what a dream meant to the person who had it unless you can get that person actually to talk to you about the dream. There isn't any code book of dream symbols in which you can look up the meaning of falling, or a mirror, or whatever. But Descartes himself interpreted his dreams as a sign that he was to spend his life establishing a new, unified theory of the universe based upon mathematics—what we today would call mathematical physics.

The important part of Descartes' plan, for our purposes, is not the new science he developed, but his conception of the *method* by which he was to proceed. Descartes devoted a great deal of thought to problems of intellectual and scientific method, and his contributions in this field are, if anything, more revolutionary than his actual mathematical and scientific work itself. Descartes published nothing while he was young, despite the fact that he had made a number of important discoveries in his twenties and thirties. In 1637, when he was past forty, he brought out his first published work, appropriately titled "Discourse on the Method of Rightly Conducting the Reason and Seeking for Truth in the Sciences." In this partly autobiographical, partly philosophical work, he lays down a set of four rules which he claims are sufficient to guide the mind in whatever inquiry it may undertake. Here are the rules, as Descartes stated them:

> The first of these was to accept nothing as true which I did not clearly recognize to be so: that is to say, carefully to avoid precipitation and prejudice in judgements, and to accept in them nothing more than what was presented to my mind so clearly and distinctly that I could have no occasion to doubt it.
>
> The second was to divide up each of the difficulties which I examined into as many parts as possible, and as seemed requisite in order that it might be resolved in the best manner possible.
>
> The third was to carry on my reflections in due order, commencing with objects that were the most simple and easy to understand, in order to rise little by little, or by degrees, to knowledge of the most complex, assuming an order, even if a fictitious one, among those which do not follow a natural sequence relatively to one another.
>
> The last was in all cases to make enumerations so complete and reviews so general that I should be certain of having omitted nothing.
>
> RENÉ DESCARTES, *Discourse on Method*

They don't seem like much when you first read them, do they? Avoid prejudice, don't take anything on faith, be careful, tackle questions a step at a time, be orderly, and so forth. It sounds more like instructions to an army filing clerk or the directions for assembling an outdoor barbecue grill than a great revolution in philosophy. Indeed, Leibniz once remarked rather sarcastically that Descartes' famous "method" boiled down to saying, "take what you need, and do what you should, and you will get what you want." But first impressions are often wrong (as Descartes himself pointed out), and in this case Leibniz was being more clever than wise.

The real importance of Descartes' method lies in *two* of its features, and a consequence that follows from those two. Since what follows may be easier to understand if you have some labels to attach to it, let me start by telling you that Descartes' method is both a *method of inquiry* and a *method of doubt,* and that the combined consequence of these two methods is to set in motion a philosophical transformation known as the *epistemological turn.* Now, if you have carefully underlined these three terms in red or yellow or blue, we can try to make some sense out of them.

First of all, Descartes' method is a *method of inquiry.* In other words, it is a method for finding things out and making sure that you get them right; it is not a method for proving what you already know, or for setting forth your knowledge in the most systematic way. Think for a moment about traditional Euclidean geometry. On the first page of a geometry book (at least this was so when I went to school) you find definitions, axioms, and postulates. These are the simplest, or the most fundamental part of the geometric theory, but they are hardly the first things that a real mathematician would think up if he were doing geometry. Then come the theorems, each one neatly set forth, step by step, from the axioms or previously proved theorems down to what is to be proved, Q.E.D. That may be the way Euclid rearranged his proofs once he had thought them up, but it surely isn't the way he discovered them! Most likely, when he wanted to prove something (say, the theorem that the line bisecting the apex of an isosceles triangle is perpendicular to the base), he drew a diagram, fiddled around with the lines, looked to see whether there was anything that was equal to anything else, worked his way up from the conclusion and down from the premises, until the proof finally fell into place. So his *method of inquiry*—his way of finding something out—was very different from his method of proof or exposition. Descartes' rules for the mind are obviously intended as guides for someone who is trying to solve a problem or analyze a phenomenon. In other words (and this is going to turn out to be very important indeed), he adopts the point of view of someone who does not yet know anything, but is trying by the use of his intelligence to discover something, rather than the point of view of a teacher or expert who is quite sure he knows something, and is simply trying to explain it to someone else.

Second, Descartes' method is a *method of doubt*. His first rule is "to accept nothing as true which I do not clearly recognize to be so." Just how radical this rule will be depends on how we interpret the phrase "clearly recognize." If Descartes merely wants us to stop and think before we say we are sure, as a quiz show contestant might pause before answering the jackpot question, then obviously that rule is not going to produce any great intellectual revolution. But as you shall see in a few pages, when you read part of the *Meditations on First Philosophy*, Descartes had much more in mind. When he tells us not to accept anything unless we can "clearly recognize" it as true, he means that we should refuse to accept anything, however sure we once were of it, however many people believe it, however obvious it seems, unless we can be *absolutely certain that it is one hundred percent right*. If there is the slightest, the wildest, the farthest out chance that it just might be false, then we are not to accept it. Now that opens up quite a can of worms! For example, I am quite sure that Washington, D.C. is the capital of the United States of America. If you ask me how I can be so sure, I will tell you that I have read it in history and government books, that I have heard Washington referred to a thousand times on television as "our nation's capital," that I have visited Washington and actually sat for a day in the visitor's gallery of the Senate, and so forth. But does that make it absolutely, one hundred percent certain? Couldn't I be wrong? It isn't likely that I am wrong, but is it logically possible? Maybe the books were wrong; maybe the television commentators were wrong; maybe I was actually in Philadelphia when I thought I was in Washington; indeed, maybe there is a giant conspiracy afoot to fool me into thinking that Washington is the capital. I can't imagine why anyone would go to all that trouble, but it *is* possible. Put it this way: I could write a science fiction story about such a conspiracy, and although you might say it wasn't very plausible, you couldn't say that the story was a total impossibility.

Well, you protest, if Descartes is going to interpret "clearly recognize" like that, then just about everything anyone has ever believed will go out the window! I might as well doubt that there is even a United States, or an earth, or a human race, or space and time and the universe. If I am going to refuse to accept things like that, then maybe I ought to start doubting that two plus two is four. After all, if a giant conspiracy might be underway to trick me into believing that Washington is the capital of the United States, then maybe some mysterious, evil, powerful demon is reaching into my mind and tricking me into thinking that two plus two is four when really it is five. Maybe every time I take two objects and place them next to two more, that demon sneaks one of them away, so that as I count them up, I get only four instead of five, which is the right number!

Strange as it may sound, this is just what Descartes has in mind. When he says accept *nothing* that isn't certain, he means *nothing*. But, you object, that is madness! We have to start somewhere. Why, if I am going to doubt everything that has even the most minute bit of possible uncertainty attached to it, then I might even have to doubt my own existence! Perhaps I don't exist either; maybe that evil demon is fooling me about myself as well as about simple arithmetic! No, says Descartes, with one of the most dramatic reversals in all philosophical literature. Doubt all else, but you cannot doubt your own existence. That, and nothing but that, is the true foundation, the unshakable first principle, the rock on which all the rest of your knowledge shall be raised up. How does he manage to prove that I cannot rationally doubt my own existence, when he has erected a standard of certainty so strict that literally everything else that I have ever believed fails to meet it? You shall see when you read the *Meditations*. I do not want to spoil the effect of the argument by giving it away. Descartes' proof of his own existence is one of the high points in the history of philosophy. It is also, in a way, the high point of unbridled individualism in Western civilization. Imagine a philosopher who proposes to base the entire edifice of scientific, mathematical, and religious knowledge *not* on the collective learning and wisdom of mankind, *not* on the evidence of the laboratory, *not* on the existence of God, *not even* on the first principles of logic, *but simply on the fact of his own existence!*

When the method of inquiry is combined with the method of doubt, a transformation in the central nature of philosophy is begun. That transformation, which I am calling the *epistemological turn*, took a century and a half to complete. Not until Kant's *Critique of Pure Reason* was the epistemological turn brought to its end; thereafter, all philosophy was so changed that the very questions philosophers asked, as well as the answers they gave, looked little like what was written before the *Meditations*. The epistemological turn is a very simple, but tricky, notion. Even after you have it, you find it slipping away from you. Like Einstein's notion of relativity, or a Picasso painting, it makes you see familiar things in an entirely new way.

The heart of the E.T. (philosophers these days like to abbreviate things, so let's use E.T. for *epistemological turn*) is a simple reversal in the order of two basic questions. From the ancient pre-Socratic cosmologists up to the time of Descartes, philosophers put questions about what exists, about the nature of the universe, before questions about what I can know to exist, about what I can know the nature of the universe to be. That is to say, philosophers considered questions of *being* to take precedence over questions of *knowing*. Aristotle, for example, called the essays in which he discussed questions of being "essays on first philosophy." He didn't mean that these very difficult, very abstract essays were the first sorts of philosophy a student should read. He meant that questions about the nature of being were the logically first, or most fundamental, or most basic questions to be dealt with.

To be sure, Aristotle and many of his predecessors and followers discussed the nature of knowledge. They talked about the nature of the mind, the role of the senses (sight, hearing, touch, and so forth) in knowledge, the role of reasoning, the limits of human knowledge, and countless other topics. But they considered these *epistemological* questions to be secondary, less important than questions about the nature of God, the reality of space and time, and all the other topics dealt with in "first philosophy," or as we call it today, in metaphysics. So we can sum up philosophy prior to Descartes by saying that in it, *metaphysics took precedence over epistemology.*

Descartes' two methods—the method of inquiry and the method of doubt—had the effect of reversing this order of precedence. Properly understood and carried out with a consistency and rigor which Descartes himself never achieved, these two methods forced philosophers to set questions of being aside until they had dealt with the questions of knowing. And that fact in turn changed the meaning of the questions about being, so that by the time the revolution begun by Descartes had run its course, old-style metaphysics was finished, and new-style epistemology had taken its place as "first philosophy." Let us see how Descartes' two methods began this transformation.

First, as we have noted, the method of inquiry tells us to adopt the point of view of someone who is ignorant but is trying to learn, rather than the point of view of someone who knows something and is trying to explain. What is more, it teaches us to take questions in an orderly manner, not moving on to the next until we have settled the first. There is an old case in the English Common Law, going back to the Middle Ages, which illustrates the hidden force of Descartes' rule. Jones sued Smith for damages, claiming that Smith had borrowed a water jug from him and had returned it broken. Smith's defense was a classic of what we now call "stonewalling." First of all, he argued, the jug does not exist; second I didn't borrow it; third, it was whole when I returned it; and fourth, it was cracked when I borrowed it. Smith wasn't out of his mind. He was simply saying to Jones, Before I am going to pay you any money, you are going to have to prove every single item in your story. You must prove that the jug even exists; then you must prove that I borrowed it; then you must prove that I didn't return it whole; and then you must prove that it wasn't cracked when I borrowed it, but was cracked when I returned it.

Now the legal point of this story is that proving one of these points might be a good deal harder than proving another, and Jones must prove them all in order to collect damages. If he threw the jug away after it was returned broken, then he may have trouble proving that it ever existed. Even if he kept the pieces, he may have trouble proving that it wasn't already cracked when he lent it to Smith. And so on. When the defense in a court case agrees not to dispute some assertion by the prosecution about the facts of the case, it is called "stipulating." Descartes' first rule tells us not to stipulate anything!

For example, at the beginning of his book entitled *Physics*, Aristotle says that the subject matter of physics is motion, or rather things in motion. If anyone wants to deny that there is motion in the world (as some philosophers in fact had denied), then a book on physics is not the right place to argue with him. "We physicists," Aristotle writes, "must take for granted that the things that exist by nature are, either all or some of them, in motion. . . . No man of science is bound to solve every kind of difficulty that may be raised, but only as many as are drawn falsely from the principles of the science." But Descartes adopts the opposite view. Before we can do physics, we must prove that there are bodies in motion in space. Once we have established that, we can appeal to the experiments and observations, deductions and proofs, which scientists have developed in their study of nature. But until we have shown that nature exists—until we have, like Jones, proved that there is a jug—we must set aside such investigations. We shall not stipulate the universe.

The second half of Descartes' method—the method of doubt—makes things ten times worse, of course. Having refused to stipulate anything, even the existence of the world, Descartes now insists that the standard of proof be absolute certainty. In a court of law, the jury is asked whether the case has been proved "beyond a reasonable doubt." There is a whole lot of difference between absolute certainty and beyond a reasonable doubt. I am pretty sure that my car won't turn into a boa constrictor and squeeze me to death while I am putting on my seat belt. I am sure enough of it to bet my life on it every day when I drive somewhere. My conviction goes way beyond any reasonable doubt. But if Descartes asks me whether I can be *certain* that my car won't turn into a boa, I must answer that of course I cannot rule it out as absolutely impossible. I can, after all, imagine some weird planet across the galaxy in which cars turn into boa constrictors. In a way, that isn't much stranger than the fact that caterpillars turn into butterflies!

Combining the two methods seems to drive us into the corner which philosophers call "skepticism." If we can't move on to point B until we have proved point A, and if in order to prove point A, we must establish it with absolute certainty, then it looks as though we will have a very hard time proving any point at all. Instead of wandering all over the universe, studying the stars, the planets, the origins of life, the workings of the human body, the laws of society, or the movement of the tides, we are going to be huddled in a corner, trying to figure out how to take step A, so that we can take step B. Now, if your car is working, you go on trips and look at the scenery. But if your car won't run, you open the hood and inspect the motor. So too, if your logical engine is in good working order, then you cruise through the world of knowledge, looking at one interesting field after another; but if your logical engine breaks down—if your rules of inquiry and proof don't permit you to move with ease from one truth to another, then you stop, raise the lid on your mind (which is, after all, your logical engine), and take a good hard look to see what is wrong. In short, you start analyzing and examining the process by which you come to know anything. Epistemology is the study of the way in which we know, the rules by which we reason, the limits of what we can know, and the criteria or standards we use for judging whether a supposed piece of knowledge really is knowledge. If we follow Descartes' rules, we cannot take a scientific or metaphysical trip through the universe until we have checked out our means of transportation—our knowing process itself—and made sure that it will take us where we want to go.

Descartes himself never realized the full magnitude of the revolution that his two methods were to produce. He thought of himself as laying the basis for a new, unified system of scientific knowledge free of all reliance on tradition, the wisdom of the ancients, or the old concepts of Aristotelian metaphysics. But he seems still to have supposed that questions of being would take precedence over questions of knowing. In the *Meditations*, after the section which you are about to read, he went on to offer "proofs" for the existence of God, of the physical universe, and of all the other things he had so carefully doubted at the beginning of the essay. It remained for later philosophers, both on the continent of Europe and in Great Britain, to draw out the deeper implications of the process which Descartes started.

Here now are selections from the First and Second Meditation.

MEDITATION I

It is now some years since I detected how many were the false beliefs that I had from my earliest youth admitted as true and how doubtful was everything I had since constructed on this basis; and from that time I was convinced that I must once for all seriously undertake to rid myself of all the opinions which I had formerly accepted, and commence to build anew from the foundation, if I wanted to establish any firm and permanent structure in the sciences.

Now for this object it is not necessary that I should show that all of these are false—I shall perhaps never arrive at this end. But inasmuch as reason already persuades me that I ought no less carefully to with-hold my assent from matters which are not entirely certain and in-dubitable than from those which appear to me manifestly to be false, if I am able to find in each one some reason to doubt, this will suffice to justify my rejecting the whole. And for that end it will not be requisite that I should examine each in particular, which would be an endless undertaking; for owing to the fact that the destruction of the foundations of necessity brings with it the downfall of the rest of the edifice, I shall only in the first place attack those principles upon which all my former opinions rested.

All that up to the present time I have accepted as most true and certain I have learned either from the senses or through the senses; but it is sometimes proved to me that these senses are deceptive, and it is wiser not to trust entirely to any thing by which we have once been deceived.

But it may be that although the senses sometimes deceive us con-cerning things which are hardly perceptible, or very far away, there are yet many others to be met with as to which we cannot reasonably have any doubt, although we recognise them by their means. For ex-ample, there is the fact that I am here, seated by the fire, attired in a dressing gown, having this paper in my hands and other similar matters. And how could I deny that these hands and this body are mine, were it not perhaps that I compare myself to certain persons, devoid of sense, whose cerebella are so troubled and clouded by the violent vapours of black bile, that they constantly assure us that they think they are kings when they are really quite poor, or that they are clothed in purple when they are really without covering, or who imagine that they have an earthenware head or are nothing but pumpkins or are made of glass. But they are mad, and I should not be any the less insane were I to follow examples so extravagant.

At the same time I must remember that I am a man, and that con-sequently I am in the habit of sleeping, and in my dreams represent-ing to myself the same things or sometimes even less probable things, than do those who are insane in their waking moments. How often has it happened to me that in the night I dreamt that I found myself in this particular place, that I was dressed and seated near the fire, whilst in reality I was lying undressed in bed! At this moment it does indeed seem to me that it is with eyes awake that I am looking at this paper; that this head which I move is not asleep, that it is deliberately and of set purpose that I extend my hand and perceive it; what hap-pens in sleep does not appear so clear nor so distinct as does all this. But in thinking over this I remind myself that on many occasions I have in sleep been deceived by similar illusions, and in dwelling care-fully on this reflection I see so manifestly that there are no certain indications by which we may clearly distinguish wakefulness from sleep that I am lost in astonishment. And my astonishment is such that it is almost capable of persuading me that I now dream.

Now let us assume that we are asleep and that all these particulars, e.g. that we open our eyes, shake our head, extend our hands, and so on, are but false delusions; and let us reflect that possibly neither our hands nor our whole body are such as they appear to us to be. At the same time we must at least confess that the things which are represented to us in sleep are like painted representations which can only have been formed as the counterparts of something real and true, and that in this way those general things at least, i.e. eyes, a head, hands, and a whole body, are not imaginary things, but things really existent. For, as a matter of fact, painters, even when they study with the greatest skill to represent sirens and satyrs by forms the most strange and extraordinary, cannot give them natures which are entirely new, but merely make a certain medley of the members of different animals; or if their imagination is extravagant enough to invent something so novel that nothing similar has ever before been seen, and that then their work represents a thing purely fictitious and absolutely false, it is certain all the same that the colours of which this is composed are necessarily real. And for the same reason, although these general things, to wit, [a body], eyes, a head, hands, and such like, may be imaginary, we are bound at the same time to confess that there are at least some other objects yet more simple and more universal, which are real and true; and of these just in the same way as with certain real colours, all these images of things which dwell in our thoughts, whether true and real or false and fantastic, are formed.

To such a class of things pertains corporeal nature in general, and its extension, the figure of extended things, their quantity or magnitude and number, as also the place in which they are, the time which measures their duration, and so on.

That is possibly why our reasoning is not unjust when we conclude from this that Physics, Astronomy, Medicine and all other sciences which have as their end the consideration of composite things, are very dubious and uncertain; but that Arithmetic, Geometry and other sciences of that kind which only treat of things that are very simple and very general, without taking great trouble to ascertain whether they are actually existent or not contain some measure of certainty and an element of the indubitable. For whether I am awake or asleep, two and three together always form five, and the square can never have more than four sides, and it does not seem possible that truths so clear and apparent can be suspected of any falsity [or uncertainty].

Nevertheless I have long had fixed in my mind the belief that an all-powerful God existed by whom I have been created such as I am. But how do I know that He has not brought it to pass that there is no earth, no heaven, no extended body, no magnitude, no place, and that nevertheless [I possess the perceptions of all these things and that] they seem to me to exist just exactly as I now see them? And, besides, as I sometimes imagine that others deceive themselves in the things which they think they know best, how do I know that I am not deceived every time that I add two and three, or count the sides of a square, or judge of things yet simpler, if anything simpler can be imagined? But possibly God has not desired that I should be thus deceived, for He is said to be supremely good. If, however, it is contrary to His goodness to have made me such that I constantly deceive myself, it would also appear to be contrary to His goodness to permit me to be sometimes deceived, and nevertheless I cannot doubt that He does permit this.

I shall then suppose, not that God who is supremely good and the fountain of truth, but some evil genius not less powerful than deceitful, has employed his whole energies in deceiving me; I shall consider that the heavens, the earth, colours, figures, sound, and all other external things are nought but the illusions and dreams of which this genius has availed himself in order to lay traps for my credulity; I shall consider myself as having no hands, no eyes, no flesh, no blood, nor any senses, yet falsely believing myself to possess all these things; I shall remain obstinately attached to this idea, and if by this means it is not in my power to arrive at the knowledge of any truth, I may at least do what is in my power [i.e. suspend my judgment], and with firm purpose avoid giving credence to any false thing, or being imposed upon by this arch deceiver, however powerful and deceptive he may be. . . .

MEDITATION II

The Meditation of yesterday filled my mind with so many doubts that it is no longer in my power to forget them. And yet I do not see in what manner I can resolve them; and, just as if I had all of a sudden fallen into very deep water, I am so disconcerted that I can neither make certain of setting my feet on the bottom, nor can I swim and so support myself on the surface. I shall nevertheless make an effort and follow anew the same path as that on which I yesterday entered, i.e. I shall proceed by setting aside all that in which the least doubt could be supposed to exist, just as if I had discovered that it was absolutely false; and I shall ever follow in this road until I have met with something which is certain, or at least, if I can do nothing else, until I have learned for certain that there is nothing in the world that is certain. Archimedes, in order that he might draw the terrestrial globe out of its place, and transport it elsewhere, demanded only that one point should be fixed and immoveable; in the same way I shall have the right to conceive high hopes if I am happy enough to discover one thing only which is certain and indubitable.

I suppose, then, that all the things that I see are false; I persuade myself that nothing has ever existed of all that my fallacious memory represents to me. I consider that I possess no senses; I imagine that body, figure, extension, movement and place are but the fictions of my mind. What, then, can be esteemed as true? Perhaps nothing at all, unless that there is nothing in the world that is certain.

But how can I know there is not something different from those things that I have just considered, of which one cannot have the slightest doubt? Is there not some God, or some other being by whatever name we call it, who puts these reflections into my mind? That is not necessary, for is it not possible that I am capable of producing them myself? I myself, am I not at least something? But I have already denied that I had senses and body. Yet I hesitate, for what follows from that? Am I so dependent on body and senses that I cannot exist without these? But I was persuaded that there was nothing in all the world, that there was no heaven, no earth, that there were no minds, nor any bodies: was I not then likewise persuaded that I did not exist? Not at all; of a surety I myself did exist since I persuaded myself of something [or merely because I thought of something]. But there is some deceiver or other, very powerful and very cunning, who ever employs his ingenuity in deceiving me. Then without doubt I exist also if he deceives me, and let him deceive me as much as he will, he can never cause me to be nothing so long as I think that I am something. So that after having reflected well and carefully examined all things, we must come to the definite conclusion that this proposition: I am, I exist, is necessarily true each time that I pronounce it, or that I mentally conceive it.

But I do not yet know clearly enough what I am, I who am certain that I am; and hence I must be careful to see that I do not imprudently take some other object in place of myself, and thus that I do not go astray in respect of this knowledge that I hold to be the most certain and most evident of all that I have formerly learned. That is why I shall now consider anew what I believed myself to be before I embarked upon these last reflections; and of my former opinions I shall withdraw all that might even in a small degree be invalidated by the reasons which I have just brought forward, in order that there may be nothing at all left beyond what is absolutely certain and indubitable.

RÉNE DESCARTES, *Meditations on First Philosophy*

II When Descartes summarized his proof for his own existence in Latin, he used the phrase, *Cogito, ergo sum,* which means "I think, therefore I am." So his proof has come to be known in philosophical shorthand as the Cogito argument. Now, if you read the selection from the *Medita- tions* carefully, you will realize that "I think, therefore I am" is not exactly what Descartes says. Instead, he says something slightly but very significantly different; namely, "The proposition, I exist, is necessarily true each time I pronounce it." Pronouncing or asserting the proposition is crucial, because it is the asserting that guarantees its truth. The point is that if the proposition is being *asserted*, then someone must be doing the asserting, and if I am asserting it, then that someone must be me. Need- less to say, I cannot use this proof to establish the existence of anyone else. Suppose, for example, that I try to prove my wife's existence by saying, "The proposition, She exists, is necessarily true each time I pronounce it." Well, that just won't work. The fact that I pronounce or assert that she exists in no way guarantees that she does. But it does guarantee that I exist! In fact, my asserting any proposition, true or false, about myself or about anything else, guarantees that *I* exist, because I am the subject, the asserter, the conscious thinker of the proposition. And—this is the key point—propositions or assertions or statements cannot simply hang in midair with no one asserting them. A proposition is an assertion, and therefore it must be asserted *by* someone.

Incidentally, I hope you realize that Descartes' Cogito argument only proves his existence to him; it doesn't prove his existence to you or to me. "The proposition, Descartes exists, is necessarily true everytime I pro- nounce it" doesn't hold water at all. Descartes can use his new argument to prove his existence to himself, I can use his argument to prove my existence to myself, and each of you can use his argument to prove your own existence to yourself. But no one can use the argument to prove someone else's existence. This fact about the Cogito argument has two important consequences for subsequent epistemology. First, it drives each philosopher into the position called *solipsism*: that is, the individual sub- ject knows his own existence prior to, and better than, anything else, and perhaps knows the existence of nothing but himself. Second, it turns the attention of philosophers away from the *objects* of knowledge, the things that we know about, and toward the *subject* of knowledge, the mind that does the knowing. Later in this chapter, we shall see that this pair of implications of the Cogito argument is used by Kant in his effort to find a way out of the skepticism and solipsism of the Cartesian position.

Descartes got himself, and us, into the skeptical solipsist box in the First Meditation by doubting everything that was not known with cer- tainty. He proceeded, you will recall, by adopting a criterion of certainty so strict that in the end, nothing save the assertion of his own existence could meet its requirements. In surveying the multitude of his beliefs, furthermore, Descartes divided them into two major groups: those which he thought he knew on the basis of the evidence of his own senses, and those which he thought he knew on the basis of reasoning with general concepts. In this way, two central problems are raised by the argument in the First Meditation. The first is the problem of *certainty*. What criterion of truth should we adopt as the standard against which to measure our various knowledge claims? The second is the problem of the sources of knowledge. Insofar as we know anything, is our knowledge based upon the evidence of the senses, upon abstract reasoning, or upon some combination of the two? The philosophy of the 150 years following the publication of the *Meditations* was very largely a series of variations on these two themes.

Descartes himself offered preliminary answers to the questions of certainty and the sources of knowledge in the latter part of the Second Meditation. Before taking our leave of him, and moving on to survey the attempts of his successors to deal with the problems he had raised, perhaps we ought to see what he had to say about them. On the problem of certainty, he offered two criteria, two tests of the certainty of an assertion. Here is what he says:

> . . . I am certain that I am a thing which thinks; but do I not then likewise know what is requisite to render me certain of a truth? Certainly in this first knowledge there is nothing that assures me of its truth, excepting the clear and distinct perception of that which I state, which would not indeed suffice to assure me that what I say is true, if it could ever happen that a thing which I conceived so clearly and distinctly could be false; and accordingly it seems to me that already I can establish as a general rule that all things which I perceive very clearly and very distinctly are true.

Clearness and distinctness aren't much as a hedge against the farreaching skepticism fostered by the method of doubt. How can I be sure that I really perceive a proposition clearly or distinctly? It is no good saying that it really, truly *seems* clear and distinct to me. After all, it really, truly seems to me that I am awake, but as Descartes himself pointed out, I might nonetheless be mistaken. Later on, after using the clearness and distinctness test to prove the existence of God, Descartes turns around and uses the goodness of God as a proof that clearness and distinctness are adequate criteria of certainty. A good God, he argues, would not deceive me! Well, that is about as obvious a case of arguing in a circle as you will find in the writings of great philosophers, and I think we can agree that having posed the problem of certainty, Descartes didn't really have a solution to it.

As for the sources of our knowledge, Descartes came down foursquare on the side of reason rather than the senses. That is what you would expect from someone whose dream it was to create a mathematical physics. In place of observation and the collecting of data from sight, smell, hearing, and touch, Descartes wanted a universal system of science derived from logical and mathematical premises and proved by rigorous deduction. In order to persuade his readers of the primacy of reason in our acquiring of knowledge, Descartes uses what is called a "thought experiment." That is, he asks us to imagine with him a situation—in this case, that he is sitting near his fire with a piece of wax in his hand—and then he tries to get us to see, through an analysis of the situation, that our methods of reasoning or of acquiring knowledge must have a certain character. Philosophers frequently argue in this way when they are trying to establish some general proposition rather than to prove a particular fact. The thought experiment isn't supposed to be evidence, in the modern scientific sense. Rather, it is merely a device for exploring the logical or conceptual relationships between different ideas. Here is Descartes' thought experiment to show that our knowledge comes from understanding or reason or the mind, rather than through the senses.

> Let us begin by considering the commonest matters, those which we believe to be the most distinctly comprehended, to wit, the bodies which we touch and see; not indeed bodies in general, for these general ideas are usually a little more confused, but let us consider one body in particular. Let us take, for example, this piece of wax: it has been taken quite freshly from the hive, and it has not yet lost the sweetness of the honey which it contains; it still retains somewhat of the odour of the flowers from which it has been culled; its colour, its figure, its size are apparent; it is hard, cold, easily handled, and if you strike it with the finger, it will emit a sound. Finally all the things which are requisite to cause us distinctly to recognise a body, are met with in it. But notice that while I speak and approach the fire what remained of the taste is exhaled, the smell evaporates, the colour alters, the figure is destroyed, the size increases, it becomes liquid, it heats, scarcely can one handle it, and when one strikes it, no sound is emitted. Does the same wax remain after this change? We must confess that it remains; none would judge otherwise. What then did I know so distinctly in this piece of wax? It could certainly be nothing of all that the senses brought to my notice, since all these things which fall under taste, smell, sight, touch, and hearing, are found to be changed, and yet the same wax remains.
>
> Perhaps it was what I now think, viz. that this wax was not that sweetness of honey, nor that agreeable scent of flowers, nor that particular whiteness, nor that figure, nor that sound, but simply a body

which a little while before appeared to me as perceptible under these forms, and which is now perceptible under others. But what, precisely, is it that I imagine when I form such conceptions? Let us attentively consider this, and, abstracting from all that does not belong to the wax, let us see what remains. Certainly nothing remains excepting a certain extended thing which is flexible and movable. But what is the meaning of flexible and movable? Is it not that I imagine that this piece of wax being round is capable of becoming square and of passing from a square to a triangular figure? No, certainly it is not that, since I imagine it admits of an infinitude of similar changes, and I nevertheless do not know how to compass the infinitude by my imagination, and consequently this conception which I have of the wax is not brought about by the faculty of imagination. What now is this extension? Is it not also unknown? For it becomes greater when the wax is melted, greater when it is boiled, and greater still when the heat increases; and I should not conceive [clearly] according to truth what wax is, if I did not think that even this piece that we are considering is capable of receiving more variations in extension than I have ever imagined. We must then grant that I could not even understand through the imagination what this piece of wax is, and that it is my mind alone which perceives it. I say this piece of wax in particular, for as to wax in general it is yet clearer. But what is this piece of wax which cannot be understood excepting by the [understanding or] mind? It is certainly the same that I see, touch, imagine, and finally it is the same which I have always believed it to be from the beginning. But what must particularly be observed is that its perception is neither an act of vision, nor of touch, nor of imagination, and has never been such although it may have appeared formerly to be so, but only an intuition of the mind, which may be imperfect and confused as it was formerly, or clear and distinct as it is at present according as my attention is more or less directed to the elements which are found in it, and of which it is composed.

DESCARTES, *Meditations*

The debate over Descartes' problems soon resolved itself into a conflict between two more or less unified schools of thought, the continental rationalists and the British empiricists. (Since this makes it sound a bit like an international soccer match, let me explain that those are labels we put on the two groups today; they themselves did not go about wearing T-shirts saying "Continental Rationalist" or "British Empiricist.") The rationalists accepted Descartes' demand for certainty, agreed with his view that logic and mathematics were the model for all true knowledge, and sought to discover ways of establishing the principal propositions of science and metaphysics with as much certainty as the truths of the syllogism or geometry possessed. They sought proofs for the existence of God (using some that had been around for quite a while, such as the cosmological and ontological proofs that we have already examined); they offered demonstrations of the fundamental principles of the new physics; and they pursued Descartes' dream of a universal system of knowledge. Like Descartes, they downgraded the senses as a source of knowledge, and instead claimed that all valid knowledge-claims must rest upon the operations of reason.

The empiricists also accepted Descartes' demand for certainty, but in progressively more sweeping attacks on the knowledge-claims of the rationalists, they argued that nothing could meet that demand. David Hume, the most brilliant and thoroughgoing of the empiricists, produced devastating proofs that neither the theorems of science nor the beliefs of common sense could possibly qualify as knowledge when measured against Descartes' own standard of certainty.

The empiricists also challenged the rationalists' reliance upon reason as the sole source of knowledge. First John Locke, in his *Essay Concerning the Human Understanding,* and then Hume, in the *Treatise of Human Nature,* insisted that all the ideas in the human mind must ultimately be derived from the sights, sounds, smells, feels, and tastes of our sense organs. Reason, they argued, could do no more than rearrange and sort the materials provided to the mind by sensation. This subordination of reason to the senses was one of the most powerful weapons in the empiricists' assault on the systems of science and metaphysics erected by the rationalist philosophers.

If you have managed to follow our discussion of epistemology thus far, it should be obvious to you that there is much more to be discussed in the theory of knowledge than we can hope to touch on in the remainder of this chapter. Rather than mentioning everyone and everything without explaining anything, therefore, I shall limit myself to *three* areas only. First, we shall take a brief look at Gottfried Leibniz's attempt to deal with the criteria of certainty, and his very important distinction between what he calls truths of reasoning and truths of fact. Then we shall examine David Hume's attempt to reduce all the contents of the mind to data of the senses, and his analysis of the criterion of certainty, so that we can understand the full force of his skeptical attack on the claims of science and common sense. And finally, I will try to explain how Immanuel Kant sought to overcome the division between the rationalists and the empiricists by compromising their dispute over the sources of knowledge and the criteria of certainty. If you can get all that under your belts, then you will have had quite enough philosophy for one chapter!

III Descartes' tests of certainty were clearness and distinctness. These essentially psychological criteria tell us very little about the structure of knowledge, about the kinds of knowledge claims that can meet the test of certainty and the kinds that cannot. After all, any belief might, upon inspection, turn out to be conceived clearly and distinctly, or at least it might seem to be. I think I clearly and distinctly apprehend that two things added to two things make a total of four things; but I also think I clearly and distinctly apprehend that I am seated now at a desk in my office, with a typewriter in front of me and a chair under me.

In place of Descartes' psychological tests, Leibniz offered logical criteria of truth and certainty. All truths, he proposed, could be divided into two sorts. The first are truths that can be known merely by application of a fundamental principle of logic called the *law of contradiction*. When we state some truth, we do so by making an assertion. "Two plus two equals four" is an assertion; "Washington, D.C. is the capital of the United States" is an assertion; "$E = mc^2$" is an assertion. Any declarative statement in its ordinary usage makes an assertion. If I have one assertion, I can make another, opposite assertion simply by denying the first. So from "Two plus two equals four" I can make "It is not the case that two plus two equals four." From "Washington D.C. is the capital of the United States" I can make "It is not the case that Washington, D.C. is the capital of the United States." The denial of an assertion is called its *negation*, and since "It is not the case that" is a little clumsy to keep repeating, philosophers and logicians shorten it to "not." The negation of "Two plus two equals four" would thus be "Not two plus two equals four," and so on.

If you think about it for a moment, you will see that an assertion and its negation cannot both be true. Maybe Washington is our capital, maybe it isn't, but there is just no way that it can both be and not be our capital. Logicians express this in very general form by saying that for any assertion, it cannot be the case that both the assertion and its negation are true. Because two assertions are said to "contradict" one another if they cannot both be true, this general principle about assertions and their negations is called the law of contradiction. There is another law of logic which usually goes along with the law of contradiction, according to which for any assertion, either it is true or else its negation is true. There is no third possibility, no middle ground. This law is called the *law of the excluded middle*. So logic teaches us that no matter what assertion we are thinking about, either it is true or its negation is true, but not both.

According to Leibniz, truths of reasoning are those assertions which we can know to be true merely by using the law of contradiction (and the law of the excluded middle, although he doesn't mention it). For example, suppose a fast-talking door-to-door salesman tries to push a fifteen-

245

volume encyclopedia on you. "This encyclopedia is absolutely free," he says. "You only pay ten dollars per volume." Now you don't have to know anything about encyclopedias to be certain that he isn't telling you the truth. All you have to do is whip out your trusty law of contradiction, and perform the following process of reasoning:

> Number one, you say this encyclopedia is absolutely free.
>
> Number two, you say I must pay ten dollars per volume for it.
>
> But "free" means "I don't have to pay."
>
> So you are saying that I don't have to pay, and I do have to pay.
>
> Or, as we logicians put it,
>
> I do have to pay and not I do have to pay.

And that violates the law of contradiction, so it must be false. What is more, with a quick application of the law of the excluded middle, I can draw the absolutely certain conclusion that

> Either I have to pay or I do not have to pay, so stop the fast talk and tell me which it is.

Truths of reasoning are nice, because we can know them to be certain merely by application of these two simple laws, but they leave a good deal to be desired. Thus, my bit of reasoning doesn't tell me whether I have to pay. It just tells me that either I have to or I don't, but not both. Truths that cannot be certified by appeal to the laws of logic are called *truths of fact* by Leibniz. They include most of what we ordinarily call *knowledge*, and to establish their truth, we must appeal to a quite different principle, which Liebniz labeled the *principle of sufficient reason*. Here is the passage from his short summary work, *The Monadology*, in which he defined and distinguished the two sorts of truths.

> Our reasoning is based upon two great principles: first, that of Contradiction, by means of which we decide that to be false which involves contradiction and that to be true which contradicts or is opposed to the false.
>
> And second, the principle of Sufficient Reason, in virtue of which we believe that no fact can be real or existing and no statement true unless it has a sufficient reason why it should be thus and not otherwise. Most frequently, however, these reasons cannot be known by us.
>
> There are also two kinds of Truths: those of Reasoning and those

of Fact. The Truths of Reasoning are necessary, and their opposite is impossible. Those of Fact, however, are contingent, and their opposite is possible. When a truth is necessary, the reason can be found by analysis in resolving it into simpler ideas and into simpler truths until we reach those which are primary. . . .

There are finally simple ideas of which no definition can be given. There are also the Axioms and Postulates or, in a word, the primary principles which cannot be proved and, indeed, have no need of proof. These are identical propositions whose opposites involve express contradictions.

But there must be also a sufficient reason for contingent truths or truths of fact; that is to say, for the sequence of the things which extend throughout the universe of created beings, where the analysis into more particular reasons can be continued into greater detail without limit because of the immense variety of the things in nature and because of the infinite division of bodies. There is an infinity of figures and of movements, present and past, which enter into the efficient cause of my present writing, and in its final cause there are an infinity of slight tendencies and dispositions of my soul, present and past.

And as all this detail again involves other and more detailed contingencies, each of which again has need of a similar analysis in order to find its explanation, no real advance has been made. Therefore, the sufficient or ultimate reason must needs be outside of the sequence or series of these details of contingencies, however infinite they may be.

It is thus that the ultimate reason for things must be a necessary substance, in which the detail of the changes shall be present merely potentially, as in the fountain-head, and this substance we call God.

As you can see, Leibniz thought that when it came to truths of fact, such as the laws of physics or the facts of history, we could only certify them by an indirect appeal to God. The skeptical opponents of the rationalists had very little faith in the proofs for the existence of God, so you can imagine that they were not much impressed by this sort of justification for scientific theories. (Take a look back at Chapter Five for Hume's objections to some of those proofs.)

IV   The first major assault on the continental rationalists was launched by the Englishman John Locke, whose theory of the social contract you have already encountered. Locke hit upon a simple but very powerful strategy for attacking the claims by Descartes and others that reason alone could provide us with knowledge. Instead of examining our knowledge claims directly, Locke suggested, let us instead ask from what source we derive the ideas which we use in stating these knowledge claims. Scientists and metaphysicians had been accustomed to express their theories by statements using terms like "matter," "space," "time," "substance," "cause," "necessary," "possible," "object," and "self." In addition, of course, they used more familiar terms like "red," "hard," "round," and "sweet." If our knowledge claims make any sense at all, Locke argued, then these words must correspond to ideas in our minds. Otherwise, we will simply seem to be saying something, but really we won't be asserting anything at all. (That is what humorists do when they write nonsense verse. Lewis Carroll, the author of *Alice in Wonderland*, wrote a poem that begins, "Twas brillig, and the slithy toves did gyre and gimbel in the wabe." That sounds as though it ought to mean something, but it doesn't, because "words" like "brillig" and "toves" don't correspond to any ideas in our minds.)

According to Locke, the mind is a blank when we are born. He compares it to a piece of white paper on which experience writes. Here, from his *Essay Concerning Human Understanding* (Book II, Chapter 1), is his statement of this famous doctrine:

> Let us then suppose the mind to be, as we say, white paper, void of all characters, without any ideas:—How comes it to be furnished? Whence comes it by that wide store which the busy and boundless fancy of man has painted on it with almost endless variety? Whence has it all the *materials* of reason and knowledge? To this I answer, in one word, EXPERIENCE. In that all our knowledge is founded; and from it ultimately derives itself.

That doesn't sound like such a brilliant philosophical strategy when you first hear it. Indeed, it sounds positively obvious. But in the hands of Locke, of George Berkeley, and especially of David Hume, it turned out to be a crusher. To see why this is so, think for a moment about all the assertions that philosophers and theologians have made over the ages about God. Every one of those assertions uses the idea of God somehow. For example, one assertion is that God exists; a second is that God is omnipotent; a third is that God has promised man eternal life if only man will obey His laws; and so forth. If we follow Locke's suggestion, instead of asking directly what evidence there is for these assertions, we will instead ask, Is there an *idea* of God in our minds corresponding to the word "God" which is used in each of the assertions? And following Locke's theory of the blank white paper, we will ask whether the idea of God has come to us through our eyes, our ears, our fingertips, our noses, or our other sense organs. As soon as you put the question that way, it

GEORGE BERKELEY (1685–1753) was an Irish philosopher and cleric who is remembered as the defender of a philosophical position known as "idealism." Berkeley's most important philosophical works, including his *Treatise Concerning the Principles of Human Knowledge* and *Three Dialogues Between Hylas and Philonus*, were all written before his thirtieth birthday. Berkeley defended the view that the only things that could be known to exist are human minds, the ideas in these minds, and God. This doctrine is opposed to the view, defended by Hobbes and others, that physical bodies are the only things that exist ("materialism").

Berkeley spent three years in the New World, seeking to found a college in the Bermudas. Though his plans never were carried out, he did leave his philosophical library to the recently founded Yale College in New Haven, Connecticut.

is obvious that we couldn't have derived the idea of God from any sensory sources. God is supposed to be infinite, but we can only see, hear, feel, and taste finite things. God is supposed to be eternal, but we cannot see or hear or feel something that exists outside time, or even something that exists in time forever and ever. God is supposed to be omnipotent, but the most our senses could ever show us is something very powerful, not something infinitely powerful. So it would seem to follow simply and directly from Locke's strategy that *we do not really have an idea of God at all!* We have the word "God," and we make up what we think are meaningful assertions using it, but all that talk about God turns out to have no more meaning than Lewis Carroll's poem about slithy toves. (Incidentally, Locke himself did not draw this antireligious conclusion from his theory of ideas, and would have been horrified by it!)

Since that last paragraph may have whipped by a bit fast, let's stop a moment and be sure that we understand what the argument is really saying. Lewis Carroll's poem isn't *false*; it is *meaningless*, because it uses "words" which don't correspond to ideas in our minds, and hence have no meaning. An assertion has to mean something before we can ask whether it is true or false. Philosophical books are full of arguments about the truth or falsehood of various theological, metaphysical, and scientific theories. But Locke's attack cuts these arguments off at the knees. Before two philosophers can even begin to argue about the existence of God, they must show that their words have meaning, and according to Locke, that means showing that the words correspond to ideas in our minds which have been derived from the senses. So by his strategy of looking to the sources of our ideas, together with his doctrine of the mind as a blank sheet of paper written on by experience, Locke shifted the whole debate into a new channel.

Locke's weapon, incidentally, is a double-edged sword. If the theory proves that we do not even have a coherent idea of God, then one possible conclusion is that all our talk about God is nonsense, and all our theories of religion meaningless. But another possible conclusion is that since his theory implies such a ridiculous notion, it must itself be false! It comes down to deciding which is harder to believe. If I do have an idea of God, then it cannot have come through my senses, so I am going to have to explain how the mind can acquire ideas which it does not derive from sense experience; on the other hand, if all my ideas are derived from sense experience, then I cannot have an idea of God, so I am going to have to explain why so many apparently reasonable people firmly believe that they have such an idea, and why people who talk about God think they are making sense and not nonsense.

The empiricist who carried Locke's strategy to its logical conclusion was David Hume. As you will recall from Chapter One, Hume conceived the plan, when still a very young man, of writing a full-scale theory of the human mind along the lines of Isaac Newton's enormously successful theory of the physical universe. In the very opening pages of the *Treatise of Human Nature*, Hume adopts Locke's strategy and stakes out his own version of the "white paper" principle. In the following selection, remember that Hume uses the word "perception" to mean any content of the mind. He then divides perceptions into those which come directly from our senses and those which we form from our impressions by copying, rearranging, and otherwise altering them.

ALL the perceptions of the human mind resolve themselves into two distinct kinds, which I shall call IMPRESSIONS and IDEAS. The difference betwixt these consists in the degrees of force and liveliness with which they strike upon the mind, and make their way into our thought or consciousness. Those perceptions, which enter with most force and violence, we may name *impressions*; and under this name I comprehend all our sensations, passions and emotions, as they make their first appearance in the soul. By *ideas* I mean the faint images of these in thinking and reasoning; such as, for instance, are all the perceptions excited by the present discourse, excepting only, those which arise from the sight and touch, and excepting the immediate pleasure or uneasiness it may occasion. I believe it will not be very necessary to employ many words in explaining this distinction. Every one of himself will readily perceive the difference betwixt feeling and thinking. The common degrees of these are easily distinguished; tho' it is not impossible but in particular instances they may very nearly approach to each other. Thus in sleep, in a fever, in madness, or in any very violent emotions of soul, our ideas may approach to our impressions: As on the other hand it sometimes happens, that our impressions are so faint and low, that we cannot distinguish them from our ideas. But notwithstanding this near resemblance in a few instances, they are in general so very different, that no-one can make a scruple to rank them under distinct heads, and assign to each a peculiar name to mark the difference.

There is another division of our perceptions, which it will be convenient to observe, and which extends itself both to our impressions and ideas. This division is into SIMPLE and COMPLEX. Simple perceptions or impressions and ideas are such as admit of no distinction nor separation. The complex are the contrary to these, and may be distinguished into parts. Tho' a particular colour, taste, and smell are qualities all united together in this apple, 'tis easy to perceive they are not the same, but are at least distinguishable from each other.

Having by these divisions given an order and arrangement to our objects, we may now apply ourselves to consider with the more accuracy their qualities and relations. The first circumstance, that strikes my eye, is the great resemblance betwixt our impressions and ideas in every other particular, except their degree of force and vivacity. The one seem to be in a manner the reflexion of the other; so that all the perceptions of the mind are double, and appear both as impressions and ideas. When I shut my eyes and think of my chamber, the ideas I form are exact representations of the impressions I felt; nor is there any circumstance of the one, which is not to be found in the other. In running over my other perceptions, I find still the same resemblance and representation. Ideas and impressions appear always to correspond to each other. This circumstance seems to me remarkable, and engages my attention for a moment.

Upon a more accurate survey I find I have been carried away too far by the first appearance, and that I must make use of the distinction of perceptions into *simple and complex*, to limit this general decision, *that all our ideas and impressions are resembling*. I observe, that many of our complex ideas never had impressions, that corresponded to them, and that many of our complex impressions never are exactly copied in ideas. I can imagine to myself such a city as the *New Jerusalem*, whose pavement is gold and walls are rubies, tho' I never saw any such. I have seen *Paris*; but shall I affirm I can form such an idea of that city, as will perfectly represent all its streets and houses in their real and just proportions?

I perceive, therefore, that tho' there is in general a great resemblance betwixt our *complex* impressions and ideas, yet the rule is not universally true, that they are exact copies of each other. We may next consider how the case stands with our *simple* perceptions. After the most accurate examination, of which I am capable, I venture to affirm, that the rule here holds without any exception, and that every simple idea has a simple impression, which resembles it; and every simple impression a correspondent idea. That idea of red, which we form in the dark, and that impression, which strikes our eyes in sun-shine, differ only in degree, not in nature. That the case is the same with all our simple impressions and ideas, 'tis impossible to prove by a particular enumeration of them. Every one may satisfy himself in this point by running over as many as he pleases. But if any one should deny this universal resemblance, I know no way of convincing him, but by desiring him to shew a simple impression that has not a correspondent idea, or a simple idea, that has not a correspondent impression. If he does not answer this challenge, as 'tis certain he cannot, we may from his silence and our own observation establish our conclusion.

Thus we find, that all simple ideas and impressions resemble each other; and as the complex are formed from them, we may affirm in general, that these two species of perception are exactly correspondent. Having discover'd this relation, which requires no farther examination, I am curious to find some other of their qualities. Let us consider how they stand with regard to their existence, and which of the impressions and ideas are causes, and which effects.

The *full* examination of this question is the subject of the present treatise; and therefore we shall here content ourselves with establishing one general proposition. *That all our simple ideas in their first appearance are deriv'd from simple impressions, which are correspondent to them, and which they exactly represent.*

Hume's style is not nearly as technical or forbidding as that of Aristotle, Descartes, Leibniz, or Kant, but you mustn't be misled into supposing that his arguments are therefore less powerful. The few simple principles which he lays down in the opening pages of the *Treatise* turn out to be more than enough to destroy some of the most impressive systems built up by his philosophical predecessors. There are three key points to notice in the passage you have just read. The first, of course, is Hume's adoption of the "white paper" theory. The second is what is sometimes called the *copy theory* of ideas. According to Hume, all our ideas are either straight copies of sense impressions or combinations and rearrangements of copies of sense impressions. When we are confronted with some metaphysical assertion, therefore, we need not ask immediately whether it is true or false. Instead, we may simply examine the words in which it is expressed and ask whether they correspond to ideas in our minds. If we do have such ideas, then either they will be copies of sense impressions or they will be constructed out of copies of sense impressions by combinations and rearrangements. We have already seen what a blow this doctrine can be to the claim that we have an idea of God. The third important point is that Hume has an "atomic" theory of the contents of the mind. That is to say, he conceives of the mind as containing little indivisible "atomic" bits of sensation, plus indivisible copies of those bits of sensation, plus what we might call "molecular" combinations of atomic sensations. But unlike chemical molecules, the combinations of atomic sensations don't have any properties that the atomic components lack.

Since all the contents of the mind can be divided into atomic units, it follows that we can always distinguish one unit from another. In addition, Hume says, the mind has the power to "separate" two units of sensation from one another by imagining one away while keeping the other in mind. For example, when I look at a horse, I can distinguish my visual perception of its head from my visual perception of its body. Therefore, I can at least *imagine* the head without the body, or the body without the head. That power of "separating" impressions in imagination, and then recombining the parts in new ways, is of course what we all do when we imagine giants, or unicorns, or little green men, or anything else we have not actually seen. Hume summarizes this third point, a bit later on in the *Treatise*, in two principles:

1. Whatever objects are different are distinguishable.
2. Whatever objects are distinguishable are separable by the thought and imagination.

By means of these two principles, which follow directly from his copy theory of ideas and his atomic theory of the contents of the mind,

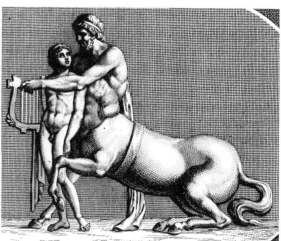

The mind combines the head and torso
of a man with the body of a horse,
to form an image of something it has never seen.

Hume constructs an argument which at one blow wipes out all metaphysics, all natural science, and just about all our common-sense beliefs
about the world. Here is the entire argument, as it appears in the *Treatise*.

'Tis a general maxim in philosophy, that *whatever begins to exist,
must have a cause of existence.* This is commonly taken for granted
in all reasonings, without any proof given or demanded. 'Tis suppos'd
to be founded on intuition, and to be one of those maxims, which
tho' they may be deny'd with the lips, 'tis impossible for men in
their hearts really to doubt of. But if we examine this maxim by the
idea of knowledge above-explain'd, we shall discover in it no mark
of any such intuitive certainty; but on the contrary shall find, that
'tis of a nature quite foreign to that species of conviction.

All certainty arises from the comparison of ideas, and from the
discovery of such relations as are unalterable, so long as the ideas
continue the same. These relations are *resemblance, proportions in
quantity and number, degrees of any quality, and contrariety;* none
of which are imply'd in this proposition, W*hatever has a beginning
has also a cause of existence.* That proposition therefore is not intuitively certain. At least any one, who wou'd assert it to be intuitively
certain, must deny these to be the only infallible relations, and must
find some other relation of that kind to be imply'd in it; which it will
then be time enough to examine.

But here is an argument, which proves at once, that the foregoing proposition is neither intuitively nor demonstrably certain. We
can never demonstrate the necessity of a cause to every new existence,
or new modification of existence, without shewing at the same time
the impossibility there is, that any thing can ever begin to exist without some productive principle; and where the latter proposition cannot be prov'd, we must despair of ever being able to prove the former.
Now that the latter proposition is utterly incapable of a demonstra-
tive proof, we may satisfy ourselves by considering, that as all distinct
ideas are separable from each other, and as the ideas of cause and
effect are evidently distinct, 'twill be easy for us to conceive any
object to be non-existent this moment, and existent the next, without
conjoining to it the distinct idea of a cause or productive principle. The
separation, therefore, of the idea of a cause from that of a beginning
of existence, is plainly possible for the imagination; and consequently
the actual separation of these objects is so far possible, that it implies
no contradiction nor absurdity; and is therefore incapable of being
refuted by any reasoning from mere ideas; without which 'tis impossible to demonstrate the necessity of a cause.

Accordingly we shall find upon examination, that every demonstra-
tion, which has been produc'd for the necessity of cause, is fallacious
and sophistical. All the points of time and place, say some philosophers, in which we can suppose any object to begin to exist, are in
themselves equal; and unless there be some cause, which is peculiar
to one time and to one place, and which by that means determines

and fixes the existence, it must remain in eternal suspence; and the object can never begin to be, for want of something to fix its beginning. But I ask; Is there any more difficulty in supposing the time and place to be fix'd without a cause, than to suppose the existence to be determin'd in that manner? The first question that occurs on this subject is always, *whether* the object shall exist or not: The next, *when* and *where* it shall begin to exist. If the removal of a cause be intuitively absurd in the one case, it must be so in the other: And if that absurdity be not clear without a proof in the one case, it will equally require one in the other. The absurdity, then, of the one supposition can never be a proof of that of the other; since they are both upon the same footing, and must stand or fall by the same reasoning.

The second argument, which I find us'd on this head, labours under an equal difficulty. Every thing, 'tis said, must have a cause; for if any thing wanted a cause, *it* wou'd produce *itself*; that is, exist before it existed; which is impossible. But this reasoning is plainly unconclusive; because it supposes, that in our denial of a cause we still grant what we expressly deny, *viz.* that there must be a cause; which therefore is taken to be the object itself; and *that*, no doubt, is an evident contradiction. But to say that any thing is produc'd, or to express myself more properly, comes into existence, without a cause, is not to affirm, that 'tis itself its own cause; but on the contrary in excluding all external causes, excludes a *fortiori* the thing itself which is created. An object, that exists absolutely without any cause, certainly is not its own cause; and when you assert, that the one follows from the other, you suppose the very point in question, and take it for granted, that 'tis utterly impossible any thing can ever begin to exist without a cause, but that upon the exclusion of one productive principle, we must still have recourse to another.

'Tis exactly the same case with the third argument, which has been employ'd to demonstrate the necessity of a cause. Whatever is produc'd without any cause, is produc'd by *nothing*; or in other words, has nothing for its cause. But nothing can never be a cause, no more than it can be something, or equal to two right angles. By the same intuition, that we perceive nothing not to be equal to two right angles, or not to be something, we perceive, that it can never be a cause; and consequently must perceive, that every object has a real cause of its existence.

I believe it will not be necessary to employ many words in shewing the weakness of this argument, after what I have said of the foregoing. They are all of them founded on the same fallacy, and are deriv'd from the same turn of thought. 'Tis sufficient only to observe, that when we exclude all causes we really do exclude them, and neither suppose nothing nor the object itself to be the causes of the existence; and consequently can draw no argument from the absurdity of these suppositions to prove the absurdity of that exclusion. If every thing must have a cause, it follows, that upon the exclusion of other causes we must accept of the object itself or of nothing as causes. But 'tis the very point in question, whether every thing must have a cause or not; and therefore, according to all just reasoning, it ought never to be taken for granted.

They are still more frivolous, who say, that every effect must have a cause, because 'tis imply'd in the very idea of effect. Every effect necessarily pre-supposes a cause; effect being a relative term, of which cause is the correlative. But this does not prove, that every being must be preceded by a cause; no more than it follows, because every husband must have a wife, that therefore every man must be marry'd. The true state of the question is, whether every object, which begins to exist, must owe its existence to a cause; and this I assert neither to be intuitively nor demonstratively certain, and hope to have prov'd it sufficiently by the foregoing arguments.

DAVID HUME, A Treatise of Human Nature

It doesn't take much imagination to see how deeply Hume's argument cuts. We can hardly get out of bed in the morning without implicitly relying on a host of causal beliefs. I believe that when I swing my legs over the side of the bed, they will naturally fall down toward the floor. (As astronauts have discovered, that is a belief which turns out to be false once we get away from the gravitational pull of the earth.) I believe that when I take a drink of water, it will cause my thirst to be abated. I believe that when I push the light switch, it will cause the lights to go on. The simplest propositions of physics, chemistry, and biology either are, or else depend upon, causal judgments. Needless to say, the proofs for the existence of God are invalid if we cannot infer causes from effects or effects from causes.

Hume himself did not believe that it was psychologically possible for human beings to suspend their belief in causal judgments for very long. Although he was absolutely convinced that no adequate justification could ever be found for our beliefs, he also thought that we were naturally so constituted that we believed anyway. In a much-quoted passage from the end of the First Book of the *Treatise*, Hume tells us how he disperses the clouds of gloom and doubt that settle over him when he follows out the logical conclusions of his powerful arguments.

Most fortunately it happens, that since reason is incapable of dispelling these clouds, nature herself suffices to that purpose, and cures me of this philosophical melancholy and delirium, either by relaxing this bent of mind, or by some avocation, and lively impression of my senses, which obliterate all these chimeras. I dine, I play a game of back-gammon, I converse, and am merry with my friends; and when after three or four hours' amusement, I wou'd return to these speculations, they appear so cold, and strain'd, and ridiculous, that I cannot find in my heart to enter into them any farther.

V But Immanuel Kant was not content to flee from the skepticism into which Hume had plunged philosophy by his wholesale destruction of causal beliefs. If Hume's arguments were accepted, then I could not even be sure that anything at all existed outside my own mind. Descartes' fanciful notion that his whole life was a mere dream might be true, as far as philosophers could prove. It was, Kant said, a "scandal to philosophy and to human reason in general that the existence of things outside us . . . must be accepted merely on *faith*, and that if anyone thinks good to doubt their existence, we are unable to counter his doubts by any satisfactory proof." So Kant decided to return to Descartes' starting point, the Cogito, or "I think." He wanted to see whether he could derive directly from that fundamental premise an argument that would avoid the skepticism and solipsism that seemed to be implied by the powerful attacks of the British empiricists.

As we have seen, Descartes' philosophical investigations raised two basic problems: the problem of certainty and the problem of the sources of knowledge. But Kant realized that the Cogito argument raised an even more fundamental issue which both the rationalists and the empiricists had tended to ignore. The conclusion of Descartes' argument, you will recall, was the following:

> This proposition: I am, I exist, is necessarily true each time that I pronounce it, or that I mentally conceive it.

On the basis of this conclusion, Descartes went on to argue that he was essentially a "thing that thinks." Descartes' successors concentrated on the criteria to be used in judging the truth of what the mind thinks, and they concentrated on the sources of the ideas with which the mind thinks, but they paid much less attention to the central fact that the mind, in thinking, is *conscious*. Trees are not conscious, rocks are not conscious, even calculating machines (which Descartes and the others did not know about) are not conscious, but the mind is. It occurred to Kant that perhaps a proof of our scientific beliefs in the existence of physical objects and in causal connections between them could be based on the mere fact of consciousness. Such a proof would certainly be very hard to find, for the mere fact of consciousness isn't much to go on in proving anything as large-scale as the truth of science. But if he could find such a proof, Kant would have an answer to anyone who wanted to challenge the claims of reason, even someone prepared to go as far in the direction of skepticism as David Hume.

Descartes had simply accepted consciousness as an indisputable, directly observable, inexplicable fact. I know that I am conscious because I can think about my own thoughts and become aware of myself thinking about them. This self-awareness or self-consciousness is clearly central to the mind's operation; what is more, it is directly self-confirming. Even an evil demon could not trick me into thinking I was conscious when I wasn't, because if I thought anything at all, it would have to be the case that I was conscious. So instead of the premise "I think" as the starting point of all philosophy, Kant instead adopted the slightly different premise "I am conscious." But introspection reveals, and logical analysis confirms, that my consciousness has a certain basic structure or characteristic: it is unified into a *single* consciousness. All the thoughts, impressions, beliefs, expectations, hopes, and doubts that I have are *my* thoughts, etc. They occur in *my* consciousness, and that consciousness is a single consciousness, or—to put it somewhat differently—the consciousness of a single subject, a single center of thought. Kant described this fundamental fact as the *unity of consciousness*. In order to show the connection between what he was doing and what Descartes had done, Kant invoked Descartes' language when he stated his own basic premise. In the central section of the *Critique of Pure Reason*, as he started the argument which he hoped would refute the skeptics and reinstate science as objectively justified, Kant stated his premise in the following way:

> It must be possible for the "I think" to accompany
> all my representations.

This was his way of saying that all the contents of my consciousness are bound up in a unity of consciousness.

Kant argued that the *unity* of my thoughts and perceptions could not be a given fact of my experience. The individual thoughts and impressions might just be brute facts of consciousness, but their unity could only be explained by some unifying act of the mind itself. Kant claimed that when my mind unifies its various thoughts and perceptions, when it holds them all together in a single consciousness and thinks of them all as *my* thoughts, it follows a certain set of *rules*. These rules are rules for holding thoughts together in the mind, and he gave them the technical name "categories." The only way in which I can think all of my thoughts as unified in a single consciousness is by following the rules or categories for holding thoughts together. Kant claimed that the categories were innate in the human mind; we are all born with them, he said, and we cannot change them.

What are these rules, or categories? Well, it turns out—if Kant is right—that they are just exactly those crucial concepts which play so large a role in the metaphysics, mathematics, and physics that Hume and the skeptics were attacking. Among the categories are such central concepts as substance, cause and effect, unity, plurality, possibility, necessity, and reality.

It may not look as though Kant moved very far toward an answer to Hume, but stop and reflect for a moment on what he is saying. Descartes claimed I could be conscious of my own thoughts, and even conscious of their unity *as* my thoughts, without knowing whether they were really accurate or truthful thoughts about substances, causation, and a world independent of my mind. In other words, Descartes admitted that my subjective knowledge of my own thoughts was better established than any claims I might make about a world of objects. Locke, Hume, and other critics of the rationalists accepted Descartes' starting point—they agreed that I could know the contents of my own mind—but they threw doubt on all Descartes' attempts to move from that purely subjective knowledge to anything further.

Kant turned the whole argument around by denying Descartes' first premise. I cannot know the contents of my own mind unless I first unify them into a single consciousness, he said. And that means that I must first have applied the categories to them, for those categories are the rules for unifying contents of consciousness. Now the categories are precisely the concepts (substance, cause, etc.) which we use in making objective judgments about the world outside the mind. So Kant concluded that I could not even be subjectively conscious, a la Descartes, unless I had first put my thoughts and perceptions together in ways that would allow me to make objective judgments about them. Descartes' nightmare of life as an endless dream is an epistemological impossibility, Kant argued.

But Kant paid a price for his solution to the problem of skepticism. It might very well be that my objective concepts were guaranteed to apply to my experiences—it might, in short, be a sure thing that I would encounter substances related to one another causally—but such knowledge as I obtained through the use of the categories would not and could not be knowledge of the world as it really is in itself. Rather, my knowledge must be merely of a world of things as they appear to me.

We have already encountered the distinction between appearance and reality in the philosophy of Plato, you will recall. But Plato claimed that we could, by the use of our reason, gain knowledge of true reality. Kant, by contrast, insists that we can only obtain knowledge of appearance, even though such knowledge is real knowledge, and not—as the skeptics claimed—error or unfounded belief.

The dispute between the rationalists and the empiricists was changed by Kant's new theory of the unity of consciousness. Even though many subsequent philosophers rejected his distinction between appearance and reality, they continued to ponder the problem of the nature of consciousness, a problem that Descartes had discovered and that Kant had substantially deepened by his arguments.

GOTTFRIED LEIBNIZ (1646–1716) was the most original and brilliant rationalist metaphysician of the modern era. Born in Germany, he was very early recognized as an enormously gifted thinker. His efforts to work out a coherent metaphysical foundation for the new science of the seventeenth century led him to the discovery of a form of the differential calculus. This discovery occurred at roughly the same time that Isaac Newton in England was developing a different form of the same branch of mathematics. For years thereafter, a dispute raged between the Leibnizeans and the Newtonians over which thinker deserved credit for having made the discovery first.

Leibniz chose to affiliate himself with the courts of the elector of Mainz and the Duke of Brunswick, rather than to hold the position of professor which he was offered. His mathematical, scientific, and philosophical theories were set forth in essays, treatises, and letters which to this day have not been adequately edited and collected. Leibniz's theories of space, time, substance, force, motion, and causation were a subtle interweaving of traditional philosophical concepts with radically new scientific and mathematical ideas.

Although he is remembered now for his work in metaphysics, mathematics, and science, Leibniz was also deeply concerned with problems of religious doctrine. In his book on *Theodicy*, he sought to make the absolute goodness of God compatible with the apparent existence in the world of various evils. Leibniz's conclusion, that the actually existing world is, contrary to appearances, the best of all possible worlds, provoked a brilliant satirical attack from the French philosopher Voltaire. In *Candide*, Voltaire *painted* a hilarious portrait of a Leibnizean pundit whose repeated catchphrase of mindless optimism was, "All is for the best in the best of all possible worlds."

Metaphysics 8

I Some years ago, there appeared a listing in the Yellow Pages of the Manhattan telephone book, between "Metals" and "Meteorologists," for "Metaphysician." A gentleman who shall remain nameless had hung out his shingle in Greenwich Village, and was apparently prepared to offer his metaphysical services for a fee to all comers. The listing has disappeared from subsequent editions of the Yellow Pages, but I continue to wonder just what services he offered, and what his clients imagined they were going to get when they sought him out.

What *is* metaphysics? Or should we ask, What *are* metaphysics? The term itself is a sheer historical accident. As you already know, Aristotle wrote a set of essays on fundamental problems concerning the most basic classifications or categories of being, and the most general concepts by means of which we can think about what is. He called his discussions *First Philosophy*, not because they were about things most easily understood, but because they were about fundamentals. Several centuries after Aristotle's death, when other philosophers commented on Aristotle's arguments, they found that the essays on *first philosophy* came after the book on physics in the edition or manuscript with which they worked. Because the essays had no name, they were referred to in Greek as "*ta*

261

meta ta physika biblia," which is to say "the books which come after the physics." Eventually this was shortened to *The Metaphysics,* and the topics dealt with under this title were dubbed "metaphysics." Unfortunately, over the centuries the prefix "meta" has acquired the bogus sense of "super" or "going beyond" or "transcending sense perception." So metaphysics is thought somehow to deal with what transcends physics, with what is supernatural, occult, mysterious. Perhaps that is what our Greenwich Village metaphysician's clients expected—a touch of the beyond.

In philosophy, metaphysics is not really a single field or discipline, but rather a catch-all for a number of problems whose scope and significance are so broad that they seem to have implications for virtually every other field of philosophy. Let me mention just a few of the questions that are dealt with by philosophers under the heading of "metaphysics." You will very quickly see why this branch of philosophy is considered truly fundamental.

First, there is the basic question, What sorts of things are there? What are the categories into which whatever is can be sorted? Physical bodies in space? Minds? Properties of things, such as size, shape, color, smell, hardness, and taste? Events, such as the moving of a body from one place to another, or the growth of a tree from a seed, or the change in color of a leaf as it dies and browns? Ideas in a mind, thoughts, feelings, sense perceptions? How many different categories are there? Can some of these sorts of things be reduced to instances of other sorts? Is there one correct set of general categories for classifying things? What shall we say of peculiar things, like the number three, which doesn't seem to *exist,* in any ordinary sense, but on the other hand can hardly be said not to exist? (It would certainly sound odd to say there is no such thing as the number three!)

Then there are more particular questions: What is space, and what is time? Are they dimensions? containers in which things exist and happen? relations among things? forms of our perception of things? Can there be space in which nothing exists—a void, as it is called by philosophers and scientists? Can there be a stretch of time in which absolutely nothing happens? Could there be totally empty time, in which nothing happens and nothing even exists? What sense does it make to speak of "empty" time and "empty" space, as though they were huge boxes waiting to be filled up?

Is there such a thing as a soul? Is it made out of physical matter, and if not, what then is it? Is the soul the same as the mind? Can a soul exist without relation to a body? How? Do souls continue to exist after the body dies? Did they exist before they were associated with, or planted in, bodies? What *is* the relationship of the soul to the body? Is the mind the same as the brain? Is the body just an idea in the mind?

Does the past exist? If not, then does nothing exist save whatever there is right now at this very moment? If the past does exist, then where is it? Is there some other universe of past things? What about future things as well? Is there a whole assortment of possible worlds alongside this actual one that we live in? Does it make any sense at all to say that something has *possible* existence?

Are all my actions absolutely causally determined by what has gone before, or am I free in some sense to choose among a variety of alternative actions available to me? If I am determined to act as I do, then can I also consider myself responsible for what I do? If I am free, what is the nature of my freedom? What sort of thing am I, that I should have this strange capacity to act freely?

Why is there anything at all in the universe? Why is there in general something and not nothing? Is the universe fundamentally absurd, or does it make some sort of rational sense? Was it created? Has it existed from all eternity? Can I even imagine a satisfactory *reason* for the universe? Does the universe stretch infinitely away from me in space? Will it go on existing forever?

And last, but of course hardly least, the question we have already examined: Is there an infinite, omnipotent, omniscient creator of all that is—a God?

Well, no one can accuse metaphysics of wasting its time on trivia! But how are we to get a handle on a field this vast in the confines of a single chapter? I propose to adopt a three-stage strategy for imposing some manageable order on the field of metaphysics. Following the practice of previous chapters, we shall begin by focusing on the life and thought of a single great philosopher, Gottfried Leibniz, whose philosophical writings constitute one of the enduring monuments to systematic metaphysical investigation. Our primary concern will be the connections between Leibniz's metaphysical theories of space, time, substance, and God on the one hand, and his interpretation of the new science of the seventeenth century on the other. At one point, we shall look at a famous debate which Leibniz carried on with Samuel Clarke, a follower and defender of the foremost scientist of the century, Sir Isaac Newton. Through the medium of this debate, we shall see how theological questions, metaphysical questions, epistemological questions, mathematical questions, and questions of the latest experimental data got bound up together in a complex dispute going to the foundations of modern science and philosophy.

In the second part of the chapter, we shall choose a single metaphysical topic, the vexing issue of the relationship between the mind and the body, and examine some of the ways philosophers have attempted to deal with it. Since the issue is not settled yet, we shall have the opportunity to look at some contemporary work in metaphysics as well as at some of the theories from the past several centuries.

Finally, we shall broaden our scope once more, and ask a question about method rather than about substance: What sort of discipline should metaphysics be? What kinds of questions should it ask, and how should it judge whether it has found answers? We shall consider four different answers to this question, by which time, if your head is not reeling, you will have some idea what to expect should you ever see a sign outside an office reading "metaphysician."

II   Gottfried Wilhelm Leibniz was born in 1646 in the city of Leipzig, in what is now Germany. He was a precocious child, the son of a professor and the grandson, through his mother, of another professor. (In Germany, the title of "professor" is reserved for a very small number of the most distinguished members of a university faculty. Professors in a German university are treated roughly in the way four-star generals are treated in the army.) Very early, Leibniz distinguished himself in his studies, first at the University of Leipzig and then at Altdorf, where he was actually offered a professorship. Rather than taking up the vocation of professor, Leibniz chose instead to affiliate himself with, or enter the service of, a series of rulers in the various principalities, duchies, and electorates of the area now unified as Germany. It was quite common for artists, composers, and men of learning to join the courts of these little independent territories, serving sometimes as performers at court, sometimes as tutors to the royal children, sometimes simply as confidantes or wise men in residence. Some of you may have heard a series of six concerti for orchestra called the "Brandenburg Concerti." These were written by Johann Sebastian Bach at the request of the Elector of Brandenburg (though never played in Bach's lifetime!) Until the nineteenth century, much of the financial support for artistic and intellectual work took the form of aristocratic or royal patronage. It is a bit difficult to imagine some man or woman being named "philosopher in residence to the governor of Kansas," but it was not at all odd for Leibniz to serve in effect as resident philosopher to the Duke of Hanover.

Leibniz was a man of the most extraordinarily broad interests. You can get some idea of his brilliance and his breadth if I tell you that he invented a version of the calculus, conceived the idea of a universal encyclopedia of human knowledge, worked out a philosophical explanation for the apparent existence of evil in a world created by an infinitely powerful, infinitely good God, and developed a scheme for sending Jesuits to convert the Chinese!

Today, learned men and women communicate their discoveries to one another by publishing articles in scholarly journals. In Leibniz's day, however, it was much more common for such communication to take the form of long letters. These were not your "Having wonderful time, wish you were here" sorts of things, The writer, after a few courtesies at the beginning, would launch into page after page of technical mathematics, physics, philosophy, or theology. Much of Leibniz's important work was "published" in this form, and it was therefore extremely difficult for several centuries to get a systematic overview of his theories. Only in recent years has anything like a complete edition of the works of Leibniz become available. A bit later on in this section, we shall read excerpts from a series of letters exchanged by Leibniz and Samuel Clarke. The exchange began with a letter from Leibniz to Caroline, Princess of Wales! Can you imagine Albert Einstein setting forth his most important work on the theory of relativity in a letter to the king of England?

Leibniz's metaphysical theory revolves around his conception of the nature of what philosophers call *substance*. This is a technical term that was introduced by Aristotle and has since become one of the key terms in metaphysical disputes. In order to explain what it means, let me do what Aristotle himself did, and take a detour through some facts about language. In English, and many other languages as well, sentences can be put together by combining a subject-term and a predicate-term, using the connector or copula "is." For example, I can make the sentence "Iron is hard" by using "iron" as the subject, "hard" as the predicate, and "is" as the copula or connector. Sometimes, instead of using "is, I just use a verb, as in the sentence "Ice melts." Now, in English and other languages, I can frequently turn a word that has been used as a predicate into a word usable as a subject, simply by adding an ending or altering its form a bit. I can turn the predicate "hard" into a subject by adding -ness to get "hardness." Then I can make the sentence "Hardness is a property of iron." I can also turn the verb "melt" into a subject by adding -ing. Then I can make the sentence, "Melting is what ice does."

It occurred to Aristotle that although many words can be used as both subject and predicate, with appropriate grammatical shifting around, there are some words which can be the subjects of sentences, but cannot also serve as predicates, no matter how they are altered grammatically. For example, I can say, "The earth is round," but there is no way I can change "The earth" into a predicate. Of course, there is the adjective "earthy," but that doesn't do the trick; and there is the rather fancy term "terrestrial," but that means "having to do with, or pertaining to, or existing on, the earth." "Earthness" and "earthing" just don't mean anything.

In short, some terms are ultimate subjects, in the sense that they can be the subjects of predication but cannot themselves be predicated of anything else. The things these terms name or refer to, Aristotle said, are *substances*. The characteristics, states, activities, or features which predicates name or refer to are called *attributes* by Aristotle. So a substance is anything that can have attributes predicated of it, but which itself cannot be predicated as an attribute of any other thing. The most obvious examples of substances, of course, are just ordinary physical objects. A tree is a substance, and the word "tree" is an ultimate grammatical subject. Tallness is an attribute, and so are greenness and leafiness and life. So I can say of a tree that it is green, leafy, and alive. In short, I can attribute greenness, leafiness, and life to a tree. But I cannot "attribute" treeness to anything else. So a tree is a bearer of attributes which is not itself an attribute of any other thing, which is to say that it is a *substance*.

Attributes are characteristics *of* substances, so they cannot exist unless the substance exists. Even though the famous cheshire cat in *Alice in Wonderland* is supposed to have faded slowly away until nothing was left of it but the smile, in real life you cannot have a smile without a face, nor can you have intelligence without a mind, or color without a body. Philosophers express this by saying that attributes must *inhere* in a substance, which is said to "support" them. But substances, Aristotle said, do not inhere in anything, nor do they require the existence of anything other than themselves. A substance can exist without this or that particular property (though it obviously cannot exist without any properties at all), but there are no properties that can exist without being the properties of some substance.

The fundamental idea of Aristotle's theory of "first philosophy"—an idea that persisted into the seventeenth century and beyond, influencing Leibniz and many other philosophers—was that we could get a systematic grasp of the universe by conceiving it in terms of the *substances* that make it up, together with a classification of all the properties or attributes that characterize those substances. Because substances are the sorts of things that can exist without depending on something else, they must be the most real, the most basic things. Aristotle used the linguistic insight which we sketched a few pages ago as a way of linking his theory of the universe with his theory of the way we know the universe. Put simply, the idea was that there is a parallelism of language, thought, and being. In the world, there are substances and their attributes; in our minds, there are concepts of substances and concepts of attributes; and in our language, corresponding to our concepts, there are subject terms that cannot serve as predicates (i.e., the names of substances) and predicate terms (the names of the attributes). So the universe is through and through rational, because its structure is mirrored in the structure of our thought and the structure of our language. A good deal of philosophy since Aristotle has devoted itself either to defending this view of a rational universe mirrored in the mind of man or to attacking it by arguing that man's mind is not rational, or that the universe is not rational, or that we cannot ever *know* whether our concepts adequately mirror reality.

What sorts of substances is the universe made up of? Philosophers have given many answers to this fundamental question of metaphysics, but they have tended to focus on one or more of three candidates. The ancient cosmologists known as "atomists" argued that tiny, indivisible, simple bits of matter called *atoms* are the building blocks of the universe. They pointed out that complex or composite bodies, because they are made up out of atoms, are in a sense dependent upon their component parts. But the component parts are not dependent upon the whole of which they are parts. A piece of rock cannot exist unless its atomic parts exist, but the individual parts can perfectly well exist even though the rock, as a rock, does not (the atoms go on existing after the rock is broken up or worn away). So the atoms must be the substances of the universe, and any larger bodies, or properties of those larger bodies, are merely dependent complexes or attributes.

A number of philosophers, including Descartes, claimed that minds are substances. This raises all sorts of questions, some of which we shall try to explore in the next section. Minds, Descartes held, are not material —they do not occupy space, they do not have shapes, or sizes, or density. They are "immaterial substances," which just means that they are "not matter," and still leaves us trying to figure out what they are. Philosophers have found two important reasons for insisting on the substantiality of minds, even though such a view is hard to explain. First, Christian doctrine teaches that the soul continues to exist after the death and breakup of the material body, so the soul must be a substance. It seems natural to identify the soul with the mind, and to conclude that the mind is a nonmaterial substance. Second (this is Descartes' reason), consciousness is an absolutely undeniable fact, and consciousness is apparently a feature or characteristic or attribute of minds rather than of bodies. Now if consciousness is an attribute, then it must inhere in some substance, and if it doesn't seem to be the sort of attribute that could inhere in bodies, then the mind must be a different sort of substance.

Finally, many philosophers from Aristotle onward have claimed that God is a special, one-of-a-kind substance. Obviously God meets the requirements for "substance-hood." He can exist independently of other things, and attributes can be predicated of Him. But if God is a substance, and if God created the universe of nondivine substances, then it would seem that He is the *only* substance, for everything else depends for its existence on Him. Some philosophers handled this difficulty by distinguishing *created substances* from *uncreated substance* (God), but at least one philosopher—the seventeenth-century Jewish metaphysician Baruch Spinoza—drew the natural conclusion from the definition of substance and asserted that God is the only substance. Everything else, he said, is merely an attribute of God. Believe it or not, this doctrine led people to accuse Spinoza of being an atheist!

The dispute over the nature and categories of substance has been shaped by different philosophical motivations in different ages. Sometimes, the problems philosophers wanted to deal with by means of a theory of substance were religious or theological; at other times, the problems were mainly logical. But in the seventeenth century, when Leibniz developed his metaphysical theory, the primary motivation was a desire to find an adequate theoretical foundation for the new science, in particular for the physical theories of motion which Galileo, Kepler, Newton, and others were advancing. Four questions at least had to be answered by any philosophical theory adequate to the new science:

First: What is the nature of the substances whose behavior is described by scientific laws of motion?

Second: What is the nature of the space and time in which substances exist, interact, and change in accordance with scientific laws?

Third: What is the nature of the interactions between substances? What forces, or causal influences, connect the behavior of one substance with the behavior of another?

Fourth: What is the relationship, if any, between the universe of spatially located substances governed by the laws of motion, and the God who —at least in the seventeenth century—was agreed on all sides to be the Creator of that universe?

Leibniz's unique and startling theory of *monads* was designed to answer all four of these questions in a manner that permitted the latest scientific discoveries, the most advanced developments in mathematics, and orthodox Christian doctrine all to fit together into a consistent metaphysics.

In 1714, only two years before his death, Leibniz wrote out a short, systematic statement of his metaphysical theory. *The Monadology*, as it is called, remains the best introduction to his philosophy, and in the selection that follows, you will find his answers to several of the four questions we have just articulated. Since this is a summary rather than a full-scale defense, Leibniz's arguments are rather sketchy, but you should be able to form a preliminary notion of his theory from what is presented here.

The Monad, of which we will speak here, is nothing else than a simple substance, which goes to make up composites; by simple, we mean without parts.

There must be simple substances because there are composites; for a composite is nothing else than a collection or *aggregatum* of simple substances.

Now, where there are no constituent parts there is possible neither extension, nor form, nor divisibility. These Monads are the true Atoms of nature, and, in fact, the Elements of things.

Their dissolution, therefore, is not to be feared and there is no way conceivable by which a simple substance can perish through natural means.

For the same reason there is no way conceivable by which a simple substance might, through natural means, come into existence, since it can not be formed by composition.

We may say then, that the existence of Monads can begin or end only all at once, that is to say, the Monad can begin only through creation and end only through annihilation. Composites, however, begin or end gradually.

There is also no way of explaining how a Monad can be altered or changed in its inner being by any other created thing, since there is no possibility of transposition within it, nor can we conceive of any internal movement which can be produced, directed, increased or diminished there within the substance, such as can take place in the case of composites where a change can occur among the parts. The Monads have no windows through which anything may come in or go out. The Attributes are not liable to detach themselves and make an excursion outside the substance, as could *sensible species* of the Schoolmen. In the same way neither substance nor attribute can enter from without into a Monad.

Still Monads must needs have some qualities, otherwise they would not even be existences. And if simple substances did not differ at all in their qualities, there would be no means of perceiving any change in things. Whatever is in a composite can come into it only through its simple elements and the Monads, if they were without qualities, since they do not differ at all in quantity, would be indistinguishable one from another. For instance, if we imagine *a plenum* or completely filled space, where each part receives only the equivalent of its own previous motion, one state of things would not be distinguishable from another.

Each Monad, indeed, must be different from every other. For there are never in nature two beings which are exactly alike, and in which it is not possible to find a difference either internal or based on an intrinsic property.

I assume it as admitted that every created being, and consequently the created Monad, is subject to change, and indeed that this change is continuous in each.

It follows from what has just been said, that the natural changes of the Monad come from an internal principle, because an external cause can have no influence upon its inner being.

Now besides this principle of change there must also be in the Monad a manifoldness which changes. This manifoldness constitutes, so to speak, the specific nature and the variety of the simple substances.

This manifoldness must involve a multiplicity in the unity or in that which is simple. For since every natural change takes place by degrees, there must be something which changes and something which remains unchanged, and consequently there must be in the simple substance a plurality of conditions and relations, even though it has no parts.

Let us consider in turn each of our four questions, and see how Leibniz's theory of monads answers them. First of all, the created universe consists of an infinity of simple, nonmaterial spiritual substances, or minds. Each of these minds is conscious, and its attributes or states are the thoughts and perceptions, desires and feelings in its consciousness. Monads, as Leibniz calls his simple substances, are created by God, who has—as we shall see—arranged their inner natures according to a rather complex divine plan.

The monad I am best acquainted with, of course, is myself, my own mind. I am not only conscious; I am also self-conscious, as Descartes pointed out. But Leibniz does not think that self-consciousness is necessarily a characteristic of every monad in the universe. Indeed, there is a sort of hierarchy of monads, rising from those monads whose consciousness is so feeble as barely to occur at all, through clear consciousness not combined with self-consciousness, on through the sort of self-aware or reflexive consciousness human beings have, up to the consciousness of angels (if there are any), and finally to God's consciousness, which we mortals can hardly imagine.

What then is a body? Well, bodies are not substances, for substances are simple and bodies are divisible into parts, hence complex. Substances are conscious and bodies are not. Bodies are, as Leibniz puts it, "colonies" of monads. We can think of a body as a set of monads that bear certain relationships to one another. But if this set of monads is broken up, divided, or redistributed, so that the body as such ceases to exist, the monads go right on existing. Each monad can be thought of as occupying a dimensionless point in space (a point has no length, breadth, or depth; it is merely a location, mathematically speaking). So monads, as nonmaterial substances, have no spatial extension, no size or shape. This sounds odd, of course, but it sounds even odder to suggest that the human mind is triangular, or six feet long, or two inches thick. Minds simply aren't the sorts of things to take up space, and monads are fundamentally minds.

Monads have two sorts of properties, internal and external. The internal properties of a monad are all the contents or states of its own consciousness, all the things that happen inside it. The external properties of a monad are its relationships to other monads. For example, if I see a squirrel run across a branch outside my window, and then feel a twinge of pain where I bumped myself yesterday, that visual perception and that twinge are events in my mind (according to Leibniz); they are internal to me, and as such are part of the life of the monad which is my self or soul. On the other hand, my physical distance from the squirrel is a fact about the relationships between two monads—namely, myself or mind or soul and the self or the mind of the squirrel (assuming, for the moment, that there is some consciousness associated with the body I call a squirrel). That is an external relationship or property both of myself and of the squirrel.

Space, according to Leibniz, is the totality or system of the external relations of monads to one another at a single moment of time. Because this is an extremely important part of Leibniz's philosophy, and also a very confusing notion, we had better linger over it a while. There seem to be two basically opposed ways of conceiving of space. Either we can think of it as an independently existing container, or volume, or thereness, *into which* things can move or be placed, and out of which they can be taken again; or else we can think of space as some property or characteristic of independently existing things, such that without them, there is no space. Most of us probably think of space more in the first way than the second, insofar as we think about the subject at all, but the more you try to figure out how there can be empty space that is independent of what is in it, the stranger the notion becomes. Is space something? Presumably it isn't any sort of substance, because if it were, there wouldn't be any room *in* it for things. Well, if it isn't something, then it must be nothing, right? But if it is nothing, then how can I put something in it? The very idea of totally empty space boggles the mind, once you really start puzzling over it.

On the other hand, if there isn't any empty space—what philosophers since ancient times have called *the void*—then how does anything move around? We intuitively understand physical movement as a body's going from some place that it is in to some other place that is either empty or else is made empty by the arrival of the body (as when a billiard ball pushes another ball out of the way to make room for itself). Do you know those pocket puzzles which consist of fifteen little numbered squares in a bigger square that has room for sixteen? The problem is to use the one empty square to move the others around until you get them in the right order. There is no way to do the puzzle unless one of the squares is empty. Well, the world would seem to be in the same fix. Unless there are some empty spaces, it is hard to see how anything can move at all.

Nevertheless, Leibniz claimed that space is simply a characteristic of

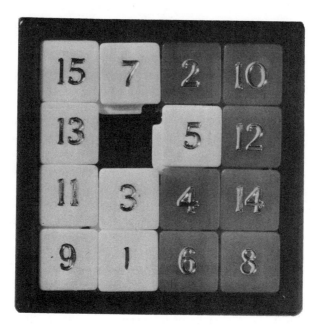

Mathematical pocket puzzle.

things that exist (namely monads), not an independently existing place or volume or something into which monads can move. This helped him to explain the nature of space, but it left him with the conclusion that there is no void.

The two opposed theories of space which we have been discussing are sometimes called the *absolute theory* and the *relational theory.* The key difference between them is that according to the absolute theory, it makes sense to talk about the absolute position or location or dimensions of a body in space, whereas according to the relational theory it only makes sense to talk about the position or location or dimensions or size of a body relative to the rest of the system of other bodies. An example from horse-racing may make this a bit clearer. Suppose you have gone to the race-track with a friend, and have gotten yourself stuck behind a pillar where you can't see the track; so you must rely on your friend's reports of the progress of the horses. In the fifth race, there are six horses, and you bet on number four. As the race begins, you hear a roar, and ask your friend where number four is. He says, "Number four is roughly two hundred yards from the starting gate." He has given you number four's absolute position on the track. But you want to know number four's *relative* position—is he first, second, third, fourth, fifth, or last? Now the peculiar thing about relative, as opposed to absolute, position is that while your friend

272

can perfectly well tell you your horse's absolute position without mentioning the other horses or even knowing where they are, he cannot give you its relative position unless he also knows the relative positions of all six horses. What is more, the absolute position of your horse wouldn't be altered by the sudden, mysterious disappearance of the other five horses from the track; but its relative position might go from sixth to first by virtue of such a disappearance. That is why a disqualification by the judges can't change the time in which your horse ran the race, but can change whether he won or lost.

Time presents many of the same problems as space, and both Leibniz and his philosophical opponents tended to give analyses of time that followed all the main points of their theories of space. Again, there are absolute and relative conceptions of time. The absolute conception characterizes time as an independently existing dimension, stretching from creation to the end of eternity, within which events take place. The relative conception, which Leibniz held, characterizes time as the relationship among a set of things—in this case, the relationship among all the internal events of consciousness. As in the case of space, so in the case of time, the absolute theory implies the possibility of empty time and the relational theory implies the impossibility of empty time. The absolute theory seems to say that an event has a time location—a date—independently of the occurrences or locations of any other events. The relational theory asserts that the date of an event is determined entirely by its relative occurrence before or after or at the same time as other events. The defenders of the theory of absolute time have the same problem explaining what time is that they have explaining what space is. It can't be a substance, but it can't be nothing either. And if it is an attribute of substance, then the relational theory must be right.

Leibniz and Isaac Newton were absolutely at loggerheads about the nature of space and time. Leibniz was committed to the relational theory, while Newton was equally committed to a theory of absolute space and time. Since the absolute theory seems to commit you to such a peculiar conception of space and time, as neither something nor nothing, why on earth would a man as brilliant as Newton defend that point of view?

The answer can be found in a fascinating argument and counterargument appearing in the Leibniz-Clarke correspondence. Leibniz, in arguing for his relational theory of space, pointed out that the absolute theory of space had certain peculiar implications over and above its inability to explain exactly what space was. If space is absolute, then as we have seen there can be empty space. And if there can be empty space, then it must make sense to ask whether the entire physical universe could be moved (by God, presumably) three feet to the left, or half a mile up, or whether perhaps the universe as a whole could be rotated a quarter-

Relative motion.

turn clockwise. Now these questions are sheerly meaningless, Leibniz said, because there is no conceivable way that any of us inside the universe could tell that such a change in position or orientation had taken place. In a passage that anticipates what came to be known in the twentieth century as the "verification theory of meaning," Leibniz claimed that a statement has meaning only if there is some possible observation or evidence by means of which we could determine whether it was true or false.

But Clarke was ready for this argument, and in his reply, he appealed to the Newtonian notions of inertia and acceleration to refute Leibniz. On straight scientific grounds, Clarke argued that the relational theory of space must be wrong, and that Newton's absolute theory, however difficult to understand, was the right one. Here is the exchange, as it appears in the letters between Leibniz and Clarke.

Clarke: If the world be finite in dimensions, it is moveable by the power of God and therefore my argument drawn from that moveableness is conclusive. Two places, though exactly alike, are not the same place. Nor is the motion or rest of the universe, the same state; any more than the motion or rest of a ship, is the same state, because a man shut up in the cabin cannot perceive whether the ship sails or not, so

274

long as it moves uniformly. The motion of the ship, though the man perceives it not, is a real different state, and has real different effects; and, upon a sudden stop, it would have other real effects; and so likewise would an indiscernible motion of the universe. To this argument, no answer has ever been given. It is largely insisted on by Sir Isaac Newton in his *Mathematical Principles*, (Definit. 8.) where, from the consideration of the properties, causes, and effects of motion, he shows the difference between real motion, or a body's being carried from one part of space to another; and relative motion, which is merely a change of the order or situation of bodies with respect to each other. This argument is a mathematical one; showing, from real effects, that there may be real motion where there is none relative; and relative motion, where there is none real: and is not to be answered, by barely asserting the contrary.

Leibniz: In order to prove that space, without bodies, is an absolute reality; the author objected, that a finite material universe might move forward in space. I answered, it does not appear reasonable that the material universe should be finite; and, though we should suppose it to be finite; yet 'tis unreasonable it should have motion any otherwise, than as its parts change their situation among themselves; because such a motion would produce no change that could be observed, and would be without design. 'Tis another thing, when its parts change their situation among themselves; for then there is a motion in space; but it consists in the order of relations which are changed. The author replies now, that the reality of motion does not depend upon being observed; and that a ship may go forward, and yet a man, who is in the ship, may not perceive it. I answer, motion does not indeed depend upon being observed; but it does depend upon being possible to be observed. There is no motion, when there is no change that can be observed. And when there is no change that can be observed, there is no change at all. The contrary opinion is grounded upon the supposition of a real absolute space, which I have demonstratively confuted by the principle of the want of a sufficient reason of things.

Clarke: My argument here, for the motion of space being really independent upon body, is founded on the possibility of the material universe being finite and moveable: 'tis not enough therefore for this learned writer to reply, that he thinks it would not have been wise and reasonable for God to have made the material universe finite and moveable. He must either affirm, that 'twas impossible for God to make the material world finite and moveable; or else he must of necessity allow the strength of my argument, drawn from the possibility of the world's being finite and moveable. Neither is it sufficient barely to repeat his assertion, that the motion of a finite material universe would be nothing, and (for want of other bodies to compare it with) would produce no discoverable change: unless he could disprove the instance which I gave of a very great change that would happen; viz. that the parts would be sensibly shocked by a sudden acceleration, or stopping of the motion of the whole: to which instance, he has not attempted to give any answer.

The Leibniz-Clarke Correspondence

So we have before us now Leibniz's answers to the first two questions. What is the nature of substances? They are nonmaterial, conscious monads. What is the nature of space and time? Space is the order of the external relations among monads and time is the order of the internal relations or attributes of monads. Let us turn to the third question: What is the nature of the interactions between monads? What forces or causal influences connect the behavior of one substance with the behavior of others?

Leibniz's answer to this central question of science and metaphysics is strange, unexpected, and quite astonishing. Indeed, it ranks as one of the oddest views ever expressed on a major philosophical question by a great philosopher. Before telling you what that view is, however, I want you to reflect for a moment on just how peculiar Newton's view was on this subject of the nature of causal connections between substances. Newton is of course famous for making the force of *gravity* central to his system. According to classical physics, those of you who have taken some physics will remember, each body in the universe, each star, planet, comet, or cloud of intergalactic dust exerts a force on each other body, no matter where the two are located. This force of gravity, as we call it, pulls the two bodies together, and according to the Newtonian formula, the force pulling them together is directly proportional to the product of their masses and inversely proportional to the square of the distance between them.

We don't care, here, about the precise formula, which no one but a physicist or astronomer need carry around with him in his head. The crucial thing about this theory of gravity is that, according to Newton, each body exerts such a pull on each other body, no matter how far apart they are from one another! Have you ever stopped to wonder how on earth (or in the heavens) such a long-distance pull could possibly occur? Philosophers traditionally call this sort of thing "action at a distance," and they usually consider it nonsense. We can understand easily enough how one body can move another when they are touching. It pushes it. And we can also understand how one body can indirectly move another when there is a series of bodies in between the two, connecting one to the other. The first body moves the one just next to it, which in turn moves the one next to it, and so forth, until the next-to-last body moves its neighbor. But Newton claimed that one body could move another at a distance, with nothing whatsoever in between them but empty space!

Newton had no idea how this could be. Indeed, he explicitly refused to speculate on the question. "I make no hypotheses," he said, meaning that he offered no metaphysical guesses as to how action at a distance might be possible. But the theory of universal gravitation fit the facts, he claimed, and it fit with the rest of his physical theory as well, so it could be adopted by scientists even though it was philosophically incomprehensible. In other words, Newton took the same line on gravity that he took on the absolute nature of space and time.

What was Leibniz's view of the interactions between substances in nature? Early in his life, he devoted some effort to working out a version of the theory that Descartes had offered. Briefly, Descartes held that there was no void, that the physical universe was completely filled with matter, and that whirlpools or "vortices" of this stuff communicated motion from one heavenly body to another. This hypothesis was extremely complicated to work out in any scientific detail, as compared with the elegant simplicity of Newton's universal gravitation, but it had the philosophical virtue of basing physical interactions on direct contact, rather than on any sort of action at a distance.

Eventually, however, Leibniz came to the extraordinary conclusion that substances do *not* interact with one another at all, despite what would seem to be overwhelming evidence to the contrary. It was his view that each monad, each simple immaterial substance, was complete and self-sufficient unto itself. None of the inner perceptions or states of consciousness of one monad were actually *caused* by the action of any other monad. As he put it in the selection from the *Monadology* which you read earlier, "The Monads have no windows through which anything may come in or go out."

But something is very wrong here! Leibniz is not a skeptic. He does not say that he can have no knowledge of anything save the inner states of his own mind at any given moment. He claims that his thoughts and perceptions accurately represent the world around him, just as they purport to do. Now, if my visual perception of the typewriter in front of me is *caused* by the typewriter, by the light coming from the typewriter into my eyes and affecting the retina, etc., then I can perhaps understand how that perception might accurately represent some aspect of the typewriter. But if nothing outside my mind can affect my mind in any way; if no other substance can cause thoughts or perceptions in my mind; if, in Leibniz's colorful phrase, my mind has no windows; then what conceivable grounds can I possess for supposing that the thoughts in my mind bear any regular relationship at all to the characteristics, events, states, or relations of other substances?

Leibniz's answer provides us at the same time with his reply to the fourth question, concerning the relationship between God and the universe of created substances. According to Leibniz, there is no *secular* ground for supposing that my thoughts adequately reflect the world beyond the walls of my mind. If there were no God, or if God did not see fit to arrange things in a special way, my internal thoughts would give me no clue at all as to things outside of my own inner consciousness. But God is good, and he is all-powerful, and so, Leibniz claims, he has systematically fitted the internal nature of each monad to the totality of the rest, so that the thoughts in any single monad correspond in some way, more or less perfectly, to the universe they purport to represent. This systematic fitting is described by Leibniz as a "pre-established harmony." It is *pre*-established because God builds into each monad, when He creates it, the whole succession of thoughts and perceptions which shall pass through that monad's consciousness as time goes on. It is a *harmony* because the subjective thoughts of each monad are, by divine arrangement, fitted to or harmonized with the rest of the monads.

In order to get a notion of what Leibniz means by this odd doctrine, imagine that you have been locked up in a dark room and strapped to a chair facing a wall. Suddenly, a window *seems* to open in the wall, and you see the people, the cars, the trucks on the street outside. But in fact there is no window! Instead, your mysterious captor is using the wall as a screen, and projecting onto it a *movie* of the street beyond the wall. Now, this mysterious captor is very rich and rather eccentric, so he hires actors to drive and walk on the street at exactly the moment, and in exactly the way, that perfectly similar characters are walking or driving in the movie he is showing on the wall of your cell. There is no direct causal connection, of course, between the pictures in the movie and the people outside. The movie was made before you were ever thrown into the room, and the "cause" of the pictures on the wall is simply the passing of light through the film in the projector behind you. But thanks to the careful planning of your captor, there is a pre-established harmony between the movie and the events on the street.

Roughly speaking, this peculiar arrangement is what Leibniz claims to be the actual relationship between my perceptions and the rest of the universe. They correspond to one another because of God's infinitely careful plan, but there is no actual causal connection between them. In philosophical language, the correspondence is *virtual* rather than *actual*.

Why would God go to all this trouble? God's ways are traditionally said to be mysterious to men, but this does seem to be carrying mystery a bit far! The truth, I think, is that Leibniz has got himself into a metaphysical box with his theory of simple monads, and he just doesn't know

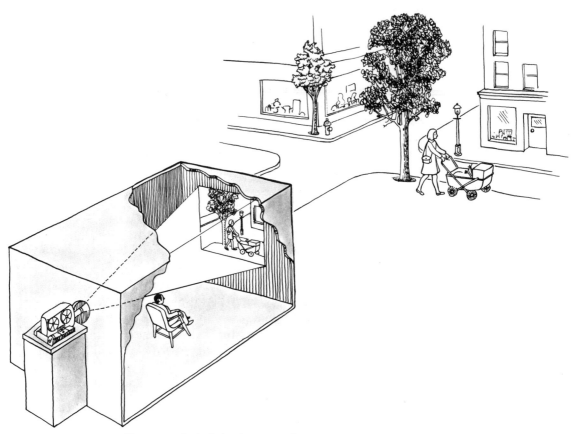

The concept of windowless monads.

how to get out. The theory of monads is useful for some purposes, including an explanation of the nature of space and time and an account of the nature of force in physics (we haven't talked about this last point). But it compels Leibniz to put forward the implausible notion of a pre-established harmony, and to that extent is clearly an inadequate basis for either metaphysics or science.

Lest you think that Leibniz was just being needlessly silly, let me assure you that the problem he was dealing with—namely, the relationship between the subjective contents of the mind and the physical objects they supposedly represent—was a problem as well for virtually all of the metaphysicians of the seventeenth and eighteenth centuries. Indeed, in the next section, we shall see that it continues to stir up philosophical disagreement today.

279

III One of the characteristic symptoms of the mental illness known as schizophrenia is a sense on the part of the patient of being divorced from his own body. The patient's foot, or hand, or torso seems to him to be an alien or independent entity. The patient may say that he doesn't know whether he really has a body; he may wonder whether he can move his hand should he choose to do so; he may speak of his body as not being *his*. Psychiatrists aren't sure just how to treat schizophrenia, but they have no doubt that it *is* a form of mental disorder or disease. We may perhaps be forgiven for wondering, therefore, whether philosophers for the past three and a half centuries have been suffering from some weird intellectual form of schizophrenia, for Descartes, Berkeley, Hume, and others say some pretty strange things about minds and bodies. In this section, in addition to sketching several theories of the relation of mind to body that have been put forward in the literature of modern philosophy, I shall try to suggest what legitimate concerns have led philosophers to focus so much attention on the so-called mind-body problem.

The physical theories developed by Aristotle, and refined by countless philosophers during the many centuries following, placed great emphasis upon the purposive order of nature. Aristotle himself conceived of nature as exhibiting an inherent purpose that need not be traced to the conscious intentions of a divine creator. Later philosophers in the Christian tradition tended to appeal, at some point in their arguments, to such a divine purpose. But whether religiously based or not, physical theories relied heavily upon notions of goal, end, purpose, and rational order usually associated with the operations of conscious agents. As we saw in the last chapter, Descartes focused his attention entirely on the self-conscious self or mind at the outset of his philosophical deliberations. But when he came to develop his theory of the physical universe, he rejected entirely any appeal to properties, concepts, or modes of explanation associated with the mental or the conscious. The material universe, he argued, was characterized by such properties as extension and motion. All explanation in science must be couched in terms of size, shape, density, velocity, and the like.

This exclusion of the mental from the sphere of physical explanation was prompted by the fact that extension and motion could be quantified and treated mathematically whereas purpose, end, goal, intention, or rational order could not be. The tools of arithmetic and analytic geometry were inapplicable to the notions that Aristotle and his followers had employed in their physical explanations. So it was the search for a mathematical science which led Descartes to exclude all "mentalistic" characteristics from his physical theories. But having thus shunted aside the mental, Descartes was forced to ask himself what relationship there was between the physical realm of extension and motion to which the new science applied, and the realm of thought, purpose, and reason. For Descartes, the problem was especially pressing because his method of doubt had focused attention as never before on the sphere of consciousness.

Drawing on metaphysical theories already in circulation, Descartes put forward a relatively simple but ultimately unworkable theory of the relationship between the realms of consciousness and physics. He argued that there are two kinds of created substances, minds and bodies. Minds are immaterial, unextended, simple conscious substances, and bodies are material, extended, composite, nonconscious substances. A human being is thus a combination of a material substance—the body—and a spiritual substance—the mind.

But in the traditional theory of substance, a substance (or "essence") of one sort can only interact with or influence another substance of the same sort. A mind can interact with a mind, a body can interact with a body. But minds cannot interact with bodies, because there is no way in which a nonmaterial, unextended substance can be touched, moved, altered, or affected by a material, extended substance. And there is no way in which a simple, unextended, conscious substance can touch, move, alter, or affect an extended, material substance. So having excluded the mind from the arena of mathematical physics, Descartes finds himself with no satisfactory way to reintroduce mind back into the world.

The problem is compounded, of course, by Descartes' search for inner subjective certainty. Beginning as he did with the self's conscious awareness of its own existence, he was forced to ask how such a self-aware self could ever come to know the existence and nature of nonconscious bodies external to it. So for some of Descartes' contemporaries and successors,

the "mind-body" problem consisted in finding a place in physical, mathematically describable nature for a nonphysical, nonquantitative mind; while for others, the problem consisted in showing that a mind could acquire well-established knowledge of bodies in space. These two forms of the problem intermingled with one another, as philosophers puzzled over them, so that sometimes the scientific-metaphysical aspect was dominant, and at other times the epistemological aspect took precedence.

There are countless metaphysical solutions to the problem of the nature and relationship of mind and body, some of which are enormously subtle and suggestive, but in an introductory text of this sort, it would be madness to try to lay them all out for you. *Three* positions have dominated the history of this debate, and you have actually encountered two of them in this chapter already. The three major theories of the relation of mind to body are the *two-substance theory*, which asserts that minds and bodies are fundamentally different sorts of beings or substances; the *one-substance theory*, which states that everything in the universe is a mind, and that bodies are to be analyzed as collections of, or aspects of, or thoughts in, minds; and the *one-substance theory*, which states that everything in the universe is a body, and minds are to be analyzed as collections of, or aspects of, or configurations of, bodies. The two-substance theory is called *dualism,* the everything-is-a-mind theory is called *idealism,* (not to be confused with a belief in high principles or the flag), and the everything-is-a-body theory is called *materialism* (also not to be confused with an excessive desire for money).

Descartes was a *dualist,* as you know. Leibniz was an *idealist* of a certain sort. He held that there were many minds in the universe, and that bodies were collections or colonies of those minds. Other idealists, such as George Berkeley, developed their theory of mind and body out of epistemological considerations. They argued that bodies could only be collections of perceptions or ideas in the mind of a conscious self, for such perceptions and ideas are the only things that we, as minds, can know anything about. To suggest that there are things outside our minds about which we can know nothing is simply to use words without meaning anything. How, after all, could we even imagine a way of testing such an assertion?

The materialist position is one of the oldest in philosophy, and also one of the most current. The ancient atomists whom you met in the first chapter—Democritus, Epicurus, Lucretius—were materialists. They explicitly stated that the mind is made up of very small, very fine atoms, rather like the atoms which make up air. They saw no problem in explaining the relationship of mind to body, for the mind on their view *is* body, and the interaction of mind-atoms with other atoms was just like the interaction between any atoms at all.

In Descartes' own day, the most famous defenders of the materialist position were the witty French philosopher Pierre Gassendi and the Englishman Thomas Hobbes. You may have encountered Hobbes in other courses, for he is the author of a book called *Leviathan*, which is one of the classics of political philosophy. Hobbes claimed that sense perception, ideas, imagination, deliberation, reasoning, desire, love, hatred, and all the other "mental" events, activities, and traits were really just motions of tiny atomic particles in the sense organs or the nervous system. For him, as for the ancient Greek atomists, there was no difficulty in explaining the interaction of "mind" and "body." Atomic particles strike the sense organs and set up vibrations in our nervous system, which of course also consists of atomic particles. The internal motions of the particles of the nervous system constitute perception, imagination, memory, and deliberation. Desire is merely the tendency of the body to move physically toward some external object, while aversion is the tendency to move away from such an object. When the internal motions in the nervous system build up to such a point that the muscles and bones are moved one way or the other, Hobbes said, then "thought" produces "action," and we say that the mind has caused the body to do something. But actually, of course, all that has happened is that the motion imparted to the particles of the nervous system by bodies striking on them from elsewhere has been trans-

THOMAS HOBBES (1588–1679) is one of the major figures in what has come to be called the "social contract" school of political theory. Deeply moved by the social chaos of the English civil war (1640–1660), and persuaded of the necessity for a strong, authoritative central government as the only defense against man's natural *destructive* tendencies, Hobbes argued in his most famous book, *Leviathan*, for a state founded upon an agreement among all men to give up their natural liberty and submit to the commands of the sovereign.

Hobbes was a materialist; he believed that physical atoms in motion are the only real things. He combined this metaphysical doctrine with a psychological theory that each human being acts always to satisfy his desires and increase his power. In *Leviathan*, he attempted to deduce his theory of the social contract from these two fundamental propositions. Hobbes was both an acute observer of human behavior and an elegant stylist of English prose. *Leviathan* is the single most impressive piece of political philosophy written in English.

mitted through a chain of internal collisions to other bodies once more external to what we call "the" body—i.e., the human body. Here are some selections from the opening chapters of *Leviathan* in which Hobbes lays out some of the basic definitions and theses of his one-substance materialism.

Concerning the thoughts of man, I will consider them first singly, and afterwards in train, or dependence upon one another. Singly, they are every one a *representation* or *appearance*, of some quality, or other accident of a body without us, which is commonly called an *object*. Which object worketh on the eyes, ears, and other parts of a man's body; and by diversity of working, produceth diversity of appearances.

The original of them all, is that which we call SENSE, for there is no conception in a man's mind, which hath not at first, totally, or by parts, been begotten upon the organs of sense. The rest are derived from that original. . . .

The cause of sense, is the external body, or object, which presseth the organ proper to each sense, either immediately, as in the taste and touch; or mediately, as in seeing, hearing, and smelling; which pressure, by the mediation of the nerves, and other strings and membranes of the body, continued inwards to the brain and heart, causeth there a resistance, or counter-pressure, or endeavour of the heart to deliver itself, which endeavour, because *outward*, seemeth to be some matter without. And this *seeming*, or *fancy*, is that which men call *sense*; and consisteth, as to the eye, in a *light*, or *colour figured*; to the ear, in a *sound*; to the nostril, in an *odour*; to the tongue and palate, in a *savour*; and to the rest of the body, in *heat, cold, hardness, softness*, and such other qualities as we discern by *feeling*. All which qualities, called *sensible*, are in the object, that causeth them, but so many several motions of the matter by which it presseth our organs diversely. Neither in us that are pressed, are they any thing else, but divers motions; for motion produceth nothing but motion. But their appearance to us is fancy, the same waking, that dreaming. And as pressing, rubbing, or striking the eye, makes us fancy a light; and pressing the ear, produceth a din; so do the bodies also we see, or hear, produce the same by their strong, though unobserved action. For if those colours and sounds were in the bodies, or objects that cause them, they could not be severed from them, as by glasses, and in echoes by reflection, we see they are; where we know the thing we see is in one place, the appearance in another. And though at some certain distance, the real and very object seem invested with the fancy it begets in us; yet still the object is one thing, the image or fancy is another. So that sense, in all cases, is nothing else but original fancy, caused, as I have said, by the pressure, that is, by the motion, of external things upon our eyes, ears, and other organs thereunto ordained. . . .

That when a thing lies still, unless somewhat else stir it, it will lie still for ever, is a truth that no man doubts of. But that when a thing is in motion, it will eternally be in motion, unless somewhat else stay it, though the reason be the same, namely, that nothing can change itself, is not so easily assented to. For men measure, not only other men, but all other things, by themselves; and because they find themselves subject after motion to pain, and lassitude, think every thing else grows weary of motion, and seeks repose of its own accord; little considering, whether it be not some other motion, wherein that desire of rest they find in themselves consisteth. From hence it is, that the schools say, heavy bodies fall downwards, out of an appetite to rest, and to conserve their nature in that place which is most proper for them; ascribing appetite, and knowledge of what is good for their conservation, which is more than man has, to things inanimate, absurdly.

When a body is once in motion, it moveth, unless something else hinder it, eternally; and whatsoever hindreth it, cannot in an instant, but in time, and by degrees, quite extinguish it; and as we see in the water, though the wind cease, the waves give not over rolling for a long time after: so also it happeneth in that motion, which is made in the internal parts of a man, then, when he sees, dreams, &c. For after the object is removed, or the eye shut, we still retain an image of the thing seen, though more obscure than when we see it. And this is it, the Latins call *imagination*, from the image made in seeing; and apply the same, though improperly, to all the other senses. But the Greeks call it *fancy*; which signifies *appearance*, and is as proper to one sense, as to another. *Imagination* therefore is nothing but *decaying sense*; and is found in men, and many other living creatures, as well sleeping as waking. . . .

There be in animals, two sorts of *motions* peculiar to them: one called *vital*; begun in generation, and continued without interruption through their whole life; such as are the *course* of the *blood*, the *pulse*, the *breathing*, the *concoction, nutrition, excretion*, &c., to which motions there needs no help of imagination: the other is *animal motion*, otherwise called *voluntary motion*; as to *go*, to *speak*, to *move* any of our limbs, in such manner as is first fancied in our minds. That sense is motion in the organs and interior parts of man's body, caused by the action of the things we see, hear, &c.; and that fancy is but the relics of the same motion, remaining after sense, has been already said in the first and second chapters. And because *going, speaking*, and the like voluntary motions, depend always upon a precedent thought of *whither, which way*, and *what*; it is evident, that the imagination is the first internal beginning of all voluntary motion. And although unstudied men do not conceive any motion at all to be there, where the thing moved is invisible; or the space it is moved in is, for the shortness of it, insensible; yet that doth not hinder, but that such motions are. For let a space be never so little, that which is moved over a greater space, whereof that little one is part, must first be moved over that. These small beginnings of motion, within the body of man, before they appear in walking, speaking, striking, and other visible actions, are commonly called ENDEAVOUR.

This endeavour, when it is toward something which causes it, is called APPETITE, or DESIRE; the latter being the general name; and the other oftentimes restrained to signify the desire of food, namely *hunger* and *thirst*. And when the endeavour is fromward something, it is generally called AVERSION. These words, *appetite* and *aversion*, we have from the Latins; and they both of them signify the motions, one of approaching, the other of retiring. . . .

That which men desire, they are also said to LOVE: and to HATE those things for which they have aversion. So that desire and love are the same thing; save that by desire, we always signify the absence of the object; by love, most commonly the presence of the same. So also by aversion, we signify the absence; and by hate, the presence of the object. . . .

And because the constitution of a man's body is in continual mutation, it is impossible that all the same things should always cause in him the same appetites, and aversions: much less can all men consent, in the desire of almost any one and the same object.

But whatsoever is the object of any man's appetite or desire, that is it which he for his part calleth *good:* and the object of his hate and aversion, *evil*; and of his contempt, *vile* and *inconsiderable*. For these words of good, evil, and contemptible, are ever used with relation to the person that useth them: there being nothing simply and absolutely so; nor any common rule of good and evil, to be taken from the nature of the objects themselves. . . .

When in the mind of man, appetites, and aversions, hopes, and fears, concerning one and the same thing, arise alternately; and divers good and evil consequences of the doing, or omitting the thing propounded, come successively into our thoughts; so that sometimes we have an appetite to it; sometimes an aversion from it; sometimes hope to be able to do it; sometimes despair, or fear to attempt it; the whole sum of desires, aversions, hopes and fears continued till the thing be either done, or thought impossible, is that we call DELIBERATION.

Therefore of things past, there is no *deliberation*; because manifestly impossible to be changed: nor of things known to be impossible, or thought so; because men know, or think such deliberation vain. But of things impossible, which we think possible, we may deliberate; not knowing it is in vain. And it is called *deliberation*; because it is a putting an end to the *liberty* we had of doing, or omitting, according to our own appetite, or aversion.

This alternate succession of appetites, aversions, hopes and fears, is no less in other living creatures than in man: and therefore beasts also deliberate.

Every *deliberation* is then said to *end,* when that whereof they deliberate, is either done, or thought impossible; because till then we retain the liberty of doing, or omitting; according to our appetite, or aversion.

Materialism handles the problem of mind-body interaction easily enough, and it also explains quite clearly what place there is for minds in a physical universe of bodies. Minds *are* bodies, so there is no reason why the two should not interact, and as bodies they have a natural place in the physical world. But materialists have a really tough time accounting for the existence and nature of *consciousness.* You remember that Descartes considered consciousness to be *the* distinctive characteristic of the mind. What is more, self-consciousness served as the logical starting point for his search for certainty. There was no conceivable way, he said, in which a self-conscious mind could doubt its own existence. But if the mind is a collection of atoms, if perception is one movement of those atoms, reasoning another movement of those atoms, and desire, aversion, love, hatred, deliberation, and choice yet other movements, then what becomes of consciousness?

My thoughts may be associated in some way with the motions of the atoms of my body, to be sure. There may be some close causal connection which modern techniques of brain surgery, neurophysiology, and the like can discover. But the most that a brain surgeon can prove, surely, is that when he puts an electrode in my brain and sends a little current through it, then I feel or hear or see or taste something. Does that show that my feeling, hearing, seeing, or tasting *is* the movement of the electricity along my nerve paths?

A number of very shrewd and sophisticated philosophers have argued quite recently that the answer is yes. The arguments are complex, as you might imagine, but you can get some sense of them from the selections with which we shall close this section. The principal selection is a portion of a 1963 article by the Australian philosopher J. J. C. Smart (1920–   ), who has taken the lead in defending the modern version of materialism. The brief criticism that follows is by the well-known American philosopher Norman Malcolm (1911–   ), who teaches at Cornell University.

Smart: First of all let me try to explain what I mean by "materialism." I shall then go on to try to defend the doctrine. By "materialism" I mean the theory that there is nothing in the world over and above those entities which are postulated by physics (or, of course, those entities which will be postulated by future and more adequate physical theories). Thus I do not hold materialism to be wedded to the billiard-ball physics of the nineteenth century. The less visualizable particles of modern physics count as matter. Note that energy counts as matter for my purposes: indeed in modern physics energy and matter are not sharply distinguishable. Nor do I hold that materialism implies determinism. If physics is indeterministic on the micro-level, so must be the materialist's theory. I regard materialism as compatible with a wide range of conceptions of the nature of matter and energy. For example, if matter and energy consist of regions of special curvature of an absolute space-time, with "worn holes" and what not, this is still compatible with materialism: we can still argue that in the last resort the world is made up entirely of the ultimate entities of physics, namely space-time points. . . . [M]y definition will in some respects be narrower than those of some who have called themselves "materialists." I wish to lay down that it is incompatible with materialism that there should be any irreducibly "emergent" laws or properties, say in biology or psychology. According to the view I propose to defend, there are no irreducible laws or properties in biology, any more than there are in electronics. Given the "natural history" of a superheterodyne (its wiring diagram), a physicist is able to explain, using only laws of physics, its mode of behavior and its properties (for example, the property of being able to receive such and such a radio station which broadcasts on 25 megacycles). Just as electronics gives the physical explanation of the workings of superheterodynes, etc., so biology gives (or approximates to giving) physical and chemical explanations of the workings of organisms or parts of organisms. The biologist needs natural history just as the engineer needs wiring diagrams, but neither needs nonphysical laws.

It will now become clear why I define materialism in the way I have done above. I am concerned to deny that in the world there are nonphysical entities and nonphysical laws. In particular I wish to deny the doctrine of psychophysical dualism. (I also want to deny any theory of "emergent properties," since irreducibly nonphysical properties are just about as repugnant to me as are irreducibly nonphysical entities.)

Popular theologians sometimes argue against materialism by saying that "you can't put love in a test tube." Well you can't put a gravitational field in a test tube (except in some rather srained sense of these words), but there is nothing incompatible with materialism, as I have defined it, in the notion of a gravitational field.

Similarly, even though love may elude test tubes, it does not elude materialistic metaphysics, since it can be analyzed as a pattern of bodily behavior or, perhaps better, as the internal state of the human organism that accounts for this behavior. (A dualist who analyzes love as an internal state will perhaps say that it is a soul state, whereas the materialist will say that it is a brain state. It seems to me that much of our ordinary language about the mental is neither dualistic nor materialistic but is neutral between the two. Thus, to say that a locution is not materialistic is not to say that it is immaterialistic.)

But what about consciousness? Can we interpret the having of an after-image or of a painful sensation as something material, namely, a brain state or brain process? We seem to be immediately aware of pains and after-images, and we seem to be immediately aware of them as something different from a neurophysiological state or process. For example, the after-image may be green speckled with red, whereas the neurophysiologist looking into our brains would be unlikely to see something green speckled with red. However, if we object to materialism in this way we are victims of a confusion which U. T. Place has called "the phenomenological fallacy." To say that an image or sense datum is green is not to say that the conscious experience of having the image or sense datum is green. It is to say that it is the sort of experience we have when in normal conditions we look at a green apple, for example. Apples and unripe bananas can be green, but not the experiences of seeing them. An image or a sense datum can be green in a derivative sense, but this need not cause any worry, because, on the view I am defending, images and sense data are not constituents of the world, though the processes of having an image or a sense datum are actual processes in the world. The experience of having a green sense datum is not itself green; it is a process occurring in grey matter. The world contains plumbers, but does not contain the average plumber; it also contains the having of a sense datum, but does not contain the sense datum. . . .

It may be asked why I should demand of a tenable philosophy of mind that it should be compatible with materialism, in the sense in which I have defined it. One reason is as follows. How could a non-physical property or entity suddenly arise in the course of animal evolution? A change in a gene is a change in a complex molecule which causes a change in the biochemistry of the cell. This may lead to changes in the shape or organization of the developing embryo. But what sort of chemical process could lead to the springing into existence of something nonphysical? No enzyme can catalyze the production of a spook! Perhaps it will be said that the nonphysical comes into existence as a by-product: that whenever there is a certain complex physical structure, then, by an irreducible extraphysical law, there is also a nonphysical entity. Such laws would be quite outside normal scientific conceptions and quite inexplicable: they would be, in Herbert Feigl's phrase, "nomological danglers." To say the very least, we can vastly simplify our cosmological outlook if we can defend a materialistic philosophy of mind. . . .

J. J. C. SMART, *Materialism*

Malcolm: I wish to go into Smart's theory that there is a contingent identity between mental phenomena and brain phenomena. If such an identity exists, then brain phenomena must have all the properties that mental phenomena have, with the exception of intentional and modal properties. I shall argue that this condition cannot be fulfilled.

a. First, it is not meaningful to assign spatial locations to some kinds of mental phenomena, e.g., thoughts. Brain phenomena have spatial location. Thus, brain phenomena have a property that thoughts do not have. Therefore, thoughts are not identical with any brain phenomena.

b. Second, any thought requires a background of circumstances ("surroundings"), e.g., practices, agreements, assumptions. If a brain event were identical with a thought, it would require the same. The circumstances necessary for a thought cannot be described in terms of the entities and laws of physics. According to Smart's scientific materialism, everything in the world is "explicable in terms of physics." But if the identity theory were true, not even those brain events which are identical with thoughts would be "explicable in terms of physics." Therefore, the identity theory and scientific materialism are incompatible.

3. According to the identity theory, the identity between a thought and a brain event is contingent. If there is a contingent identity between *A* and *B*, the identity ought to be empirically verifiable. It does not appear that it would be empirically verifiable that a thought was identical with a brain event. Therefore, if a thought and a brain event are claimed to be identical, it is not plausible to hold that the identity is contingent.

NORMAN MALCOLM, *Scientific Materialism and the Identity Theory*

Let me give a brief explanation of one point that underlies the position Smart is defending. Smart's key claim, of course, is that states of consciousness just identically *are* states of the brain. You might think that you could test a claim like that immediately and conclusively, merely by examining the meanings of the words used in making it. After all, when I say "John Smith identically is John Smith," I can tell that that is true merely from the logical fact that in general anything is identical to itself. By the same token, when I say "Bachelors just identically are unmarried men," I can tell that that is true by examining the words used and realizing that "bachelor" means "unmarried man." So if states of consciousness really are just identically brain states, then I should be able to tell that that is true forthwith. But although this seems natural enough, it turns out not to be true. The reason is that two words or phrases may refer to one and the same thing, even though that fact is not revealed by their meanings. Let me give you a simple example that has become famous in recent philosophy. It is originally from the influential German mathematician and philosopher Gottlob Frege. As some of you may have noticed, it is sometimes possible to see what looks like a very bright star in the heavens just before sunset. From ancient times, that body has been referred to as "the evening star." It is also sometimes possible to see what looks like a very bright star in the heavens just after sunrise. That has long been called "the morning star." The ancients did not know exactly what those two visible bodies were, and because they appeared in different parts of the skies (one in the east, the other in the west), it was assumed that they were different bodies. We now know that both the evening star and the morning star are the planet Venus, which is large enough and close enough to be faintly visible in daylight at certain times in its movements around the sun.

Now think what this means. If a medieval astronomer had said, "The evening star is just identically the morning star," he would have been exactly right, but he would not have been able to prove that he was right without telescopes and other modern astronomical instruments. One of his fellow astronomers might have said, "If they are identical, then you ought to be able to tell that they are just by examining the meanings of the words in your assertion." But plausible though that would have sounded, it would have been wrong. The object named by the phrase "morning star" is identical with the object named by the phrase "evening star," but that fact must be discovered by science; it cannot be deduced merely from the meanings of the words. Philosophers refer to this as a *contingent identity*. J. J. C. Smart claims that the phrase "state of consciousness" names identically the same object or state of affairs as the phrase "brain state," but he says that the identity is a contingent one, and hence must be discovered by science, rather than merely deduced from the meanings of those phrases.

IV Metaphysicians and politicians are popularly considered to be long-winded, and sure enough this chapter has already run on for quite a time. Nevertheless, before closing our discussion of metaphysics, I should like to sketch for you a number of the broad conceptions of the subject which various philosophers have held over the ages. There are at least four different sorts of intellectual enterprises that have gone under the title "metaphysics" since philosophy began two and a half millennia ago.

The first in point of time is speculation on the origins, structure, composition, and nature of the universe. In Chapter One, we learned that the very first people in the Western world to do anything resembling philosophy were speculative cosmologists who engaged in this sort of enterprise. As our scientific understanding of the physical universe has progressed. thoughtful men and women have sought to extend that understanding by speculations about space, time, the stars, and the origins of the universe as a whole. Sometimes these speculations are no more than advanced scientific hypotheses, put forward as proposals to be tested against available evidence. At other times, the speculation reaches so far beyond current science that it seems to cut itself loose altogether from any empirical base. Some philosophers have argued strenuously that there is no validity to any cosmology that cannot be firmly grounded in the data and theories of the physical sciences, but it seems safe to say that as long as human beings are born, live, and die under the sun and the stars, some of them will speculate about the nature of our universe.

The second philosophical enterprise which goes under the name of metaphysics is the search for a rational, *a priori* proof of very general propositions about the universe and perhaps about God as well. Both Leibniz and Descartes engaged in this sort of search, as we have seen. Indeed, for much of the past two and a half thousand years, metaphysics as the rational knowledge of the first principles of the universe has been the heart and soul of philosophy. The proofs for the existence of God, the theory of substance, the analysis of space and time, the definition of the self, all are a part of metaphysics as rational *a priori* knowledge of first principles. Philosophers who engage in the search for rational *a priori* knowledge of being tend, by and large, to accept the Aristotelian assumption that the universe is fundamentally rational, and that there is a parallel between the workings of human reason and the structure of the universe. Such metaphysicians as Aristotle and St. Thomas Aquinas claim that the order of the universe is "teleological" or purposive; they claim also that man's power of reason is derived from the same source as the order of nature. Hence they consider man's admittedly limited reason to be capable of grasping at least a portion of the universal order written in things. If a philosopher has doubts about either of these assumptions— that is to say, if he doubts either that the universe is fundamentally rational or that man's reasoning processes parallel the natural order—then it is hard to see how he could expect the search for *a priori* rational knowledge of first principles to turn up anything at all.

A third conception of metaphysics was advanced by Immanuel Kant in the *Critique of Pure Reason*. Kant thought that rational metaphysics was doomed to failure, and he devoted more than half of his great book to refuting the arguments of previous metaphysicians. But he did believe that philosophers could critically examine the mind's own powers of knowledge—its cognitive faculties, as they were called—and thereby arrive at some general idea of the sorts of things that could possibly be known, and the sorts of things that the mind, by virtue of its inherent characteristics, could not ever hope to know. He called this investigation of the mind's own powers a "transcendental inquiry," and his philosophy has consequently come to be known as *transcendental philosophy*. "Transcendental" sounds as though it has something to do with "transcending" the limits of perception or reason or what have you, and when you encounter the word today, it is usually in such phrases as "transcendental meditation." But by "transcendental," Kant really meant just what we today mean by "epistemological," so Kant's idea was that metaphysics should merely be the foundational part of the theory of knowledge. As you will recall from Chapter Seven, this subordination of metaphysics to epistemology is called the *epistemological turn*.

Kant believed that his transcendental philosophy could lay a firm foundation for mathematics and science, but he also thought it would destroy the claims of theology, rational metaphysics. and speculative cosmology. Consequently, although Kant thought of himself as doing a kind of metaphysics, modern readers of Kant frequently view him as having been an opponent of metaphysics.

The fourth and most recent conception of metaphysics is that it is, or ought to be, a systematic laying out of the basic categories and concepts which we all use in our thinking about the world and its contents. This laying out can be called *descriptive* because it simply describes the way we already think. It does not tell us how we ought to think. It makes no claims to new discoveries, and it certainly does not try to defend strange and counter-intuitive theses, such as that I am the only being in the universe, or that there are no minds, or that bodies are merely colonies of simple minds. If metaphysics is truly descriptive, then when man's basic ways of thinking change, so will metaphysics. Sure enough, defenders of descriptive metaphysics admit that their assertions are to be taken only as descriptions of the way men and women think now, not as truths chiseled in marble for all times and all places.

The most forceful modern defender of this conception of metaphysics is the English philosopher Peter Strawson (1919–   ), the Waynflete Professor of Metaphysical Philosophy at Oxford University in England. As you will see from the following selection, which is taken from the introduction of his best-known book, *Individuals*, Strawson thinks that a number of famous philosophers have actually engaged in descriptive metaphysics, even though they themselves would not have said so. Among this number he includes Kant, surprisingly enough. My own view is that Strawson is wrong about Kant, but that is a matter better pursued in scholarly journals than in an introductory text! Here is Strawson's account of descriptive metaphysics.

Metaphysics has been often revisionary, and less often descriptive. Descriptive metaphysics is content to describe the actual structure of our thought about the world, revisionary metaphysics is concerned to produce a better structure. The productions of revisionary metaphysics remain permanently interesting, and not only as key episodes in the history of thought. Because of their articulation, and the intensity of their partial vision, the best of them are both intrinsically admirable and of enduring philosophical utility. But this last merit can be ascribed to them only because there is another kind of metaphysics which needs no justification at all beyond that of inquiry in general. Revisionary metaphysics is at the service of descriptive metaphysics. Perhaps no actual metaphysician has ever been, both in intention and effect, wholly the one thing or the other. But we can distinguish broadly: Descartes, Leibniz, Berkeley are revisionary, Aristotle and Kant descriptive. Hume, the ironist of philosophy, is more difficult to place. He appears now under one aspect, now under another.

The idea of descriptive metaphysics is liable to be met with scepticism. How should it differ from what is called philosophical, or logical, or conceptual analysis? It does not differ in kind or intention, but only in scope and generality. Aiming to lay bare the most general features of our conceptual structure, it can take far less for granted than a more limited and partial conceptual inquiry. Hence, also, a certain difference in method. Up to a point, the reliance upon a close examination of the actual use of words is the best, and indeed the only sure way in philosophy. But the discriminations we can make, and the connexions we can establish, in this way, are not general enough and not far-reaching enough to meet the full metaphysical demand for understanding. For when we ask how we use this or that expression, our answers, however revealing at a certain level, are apt to assume, and not to expose, those general elements of structure which the metaphysician wants revealed. The structure he seeks does not readily display itself on the surface of language, but lies submerged. He must abandon his only sure guide when the guide cannot take him as far as he wishes to go.

The idea of a descriptive metaphysics might be assailed from another direction. For it might be held that metaphysics was essentially an instrument of conceptual change, a means of furthering or registering new directions or styles of thought. Certainly concepts do change, and not only, though mainly, on the specialist periphery; and even specialist changes react on ordinary thinking. Certainly, too, metaphysics has been largely concerned with such changes, in both the suggested ways. But it would be a great blunder to think of metaphysics only in this historical style. For there is a massive central core of human thinking which has no history—or none recorded in histories of thought; there are categories and concepts which, in their most fundamental character change not at all. Obviously these are not the specialities of the most refined thinking. They are the commonplaces of the least refined thinking; and are yet the indispensable core of the conceptual equipment of the most sophisticated human beings. It is with these, their interconnexions, and the structure that they form, that a descriptive metaphysics will be primarily concerned.

Metaphysics has a long and distinguished history, and it is consequently unlikely that there are any new truths to be discovered in descriptive metaphysics. But this does not mean that the task of descriptive metaphysics has been, or can be, done once for all. It has constantly to be done over again. If there are no new truths to be discovered, there are old truths to be rediscovered. For though the central subject-matter of descriptive metaphysics does not change the critical and analytical idiom of philosophy changes constantly. Permanent relationships are described in an impermanent idiom, which reflects both the age's climate of thought and the individual philosopher's personal style of thinking. No philosopher understands his predecessors until he has re-thought their thought in his own contemporary terms; and it is characteristic of the very greatest philosophers, like Kant and Aristotle, that they, more than any others, repay this effort of re-thinking.

An Ending and –
Perhaps –
A Beginning

9

When doctors want to protect us against a dangerous disease, they develop what they call a *vaccine*. It works something like this: first, they give the disease to a suitable animal (a horse, maybe). Then they take some serum from the animal containing the disease-causing organisms, and weaken it until it can only cause a mild case of the disease. When they put a little of the weakened serum under someone's skin (i.e., vaccinate him), he comes down with a very mild case of the disease. His body develops antibodies to fight the disease, and in the act of curing him, it makes him immune to any further attacks. If you vaccinate enough people, especially when they are young, you can just about wipe out the disease.

I sometimes think we professors of philosophy operate on a public health or immunization theory of education. We treat philosophy as a dangerous disease, a bad case of which might be fatal. So we take a bit of weakened philosophy and give our students a mild case of Socratic doubt. By the end of a semester, they have gotten over the infection, and their minds have built up a permanent resistance to any further attacks of philosophy. If you ask a college graduate about philosophy, he is liable to say, "Oh yeah; I had that," just as he might say he "had" measles or

297

mumps. His tone suggests that having had philosophy once, there is precious little chance that he will ever get it again!

In writing a textbook like this one, I very much fear I may be contributing to the stamping out of philosophy, no matter how hard I struggle against that tendency. As you move, chapter by chapter, through the several fields of philosophy—social philosophy, ethics, metaphysics, theory of knowledge, and the rest—you may mentally check each one off, thinking to yourself, "All right. Now I've had that." How can I counteract this natural reaction in these few closing pages? How can I encourage you to keep philosophy alive in your thoughts and actions, and not merely to read a little bit of weakened philosophy every few years (like getting a booster shot to keep up your immunity)?

There are plenty of gimmicks I might try, but the best method is undoubtedly to be honest with you about the reasons why I find philosophy alive in my own existence, putting to one side of course that it is the way in which I earn my living. Now, that sounds like the opening line of a rather dull graduation speech, so instead of offering you some inspiring and uplifting thoughts about the unworthiness of the unexamined life, I am going to talk with you for a while about a single great philosophical idea which makes its debut in the writings of Plato, reappears in countless forms in the midst of the most varied philosophical debates throughout the history of western philosophy, and is still today the conceptual key to an understanding of urgent political, social, ethical, aesthetic, and religious issues in our own lives. I am referring to the distinction between *appearance* and *reality*. My own philosophical work at this moment is an attempt to follow out the implications of that distinction in the area of politics and social theory. I will try to show you that when you argue about whether to take mind-altering drugs, when you wonder whether there is any real difference between the Democrats and the Republicans, when you claim that American advertisers brainwash consumers and manipulate their desires (or when you deny that claim), in all these and countless other real world situations, you are using the philosophical distinction between appearance and reality. Many of the philosophers you have read about in this book were exploring that same appearance/reality distinction. If you think intelligently and critically about drugs, about politics, about the right career, about how best to spend your lives, then you are carrying on the activity of philosophy, keeping it alive. Perhaps then this book will have helped you to contract a life-long "case" of philosophy, one from which you will never completely recover.

Back in 1955, a very imaginative social psychologist named Solomon Asch did an experiment with college students that is still, after all this time, a classic study of the effects of group pressure on individual opinion. Asch hired some students, telling them that they were going to be subjects in an experiment on visual judgment. (That was, as we say now, a "cover story.") Each subject was put in a room (equipped with one of those one-way windows psychologists always seem to have in their little rooms) along with seven or eight other supposed subjects who were really stooges working with Asch. Then pairs of cards were passed around the room, Card B containing several lines and Card A, a single line. Each subject was asked to pick out the line on Card B which matched in length the single line on Card A. The real subject didn't know it but the stooges were all primed to give the same obviously wrong answer. The idea was to see whether the real subject would stand his ground in the face of unanimous group disagreement, or whether he would perhaps go along with the crowd by picking out a line which he could perfectly well see wasn't the right answer.

After a while, Asch varied the experiment. Sometimes he had one of the stooges give the right answer before the subject's turn came up. Sometimes (rather fiendishly), he had a stooge give the right answer for several sets of cards and then "desert" the subject by going back to giving wrong answers.

Well, perhaps it doesn't surprise you—and I guess it doesn't even surprise me, though it certainly depresses me—but an awful lot of intelligent, strong-minded, independent college students went along with the group and picked out the wrong answer from the three lines, even when Asch made the wrong lines *so* wrong that nobody would possibly miss. Asch admits that this was just a simple experiment with lines on a card, from which we can't draw too much in the way of conclusions. But his summation of his results indicates how deeply troubled he was by the behavior of some of his subjects. Here is what he had to say at the end of an article written for the popular journal *Scientific American:*

> Life in society requires consensus as an indispensable condition. But consensus, to be productive, requires that each individual contribute independently out of his experience and insight. When consensus comes under the dominance of conformity, the social process is polluted and the individual at the same time surrenders the powers on which his functioning as a feeling and thinking being depends. That we have found the tendency to conformity in our society so strong that reasonably intelligent and well-meaning young people are willing to call white black is a matter of concern. It raises questions about our ways of education and about the values that guide our conduct.
>
> (SA, Nov. 1955, p. 34)

Asch's experiment illustrates some of the many different ways in which we can use the distinction between appearance and reality as a

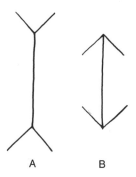

A   B

tool of philosophical analysis and social theory. The entire experiment is obviously built on the familiar distinction between the *real* length of a line and the *apparent* length of a line. Most of you are familiar already with the optical illusion shown in the diagram. Line A and line B are actually exactly the same length, but Line A appears longer because of the effect on us of the extra lines.

None of us could make it through a single day without using this sort of distinction between appearance and reality a thousand times. But even a little thought will reveal that the distinction is trickier than it looks. (That's just another example of the difference between appearance and reality!) After all, suppose you try that optical illusion on a friend and he refuses to believe that A and B are really the same length. How can you prove it to him? Easy. You take out a ruler and measure them. That means you lay the ruler down next to each line, and ask him to take a look. But he might be clever enough (and stubborn enough) to answer: they just *appear* to be the same length. You fooled me a minute ago; how do we know we aren't both being fooled now? Well, you measure the lines again, and maybe you get a neutral friend to have a look, and if something really big depends on it (such as winning a big bet), you may even set up elaborate, expensive scientific measuring equipment to triple check your measurement with the ruler. But no matter what you do, it all comes down to checking one appearance against another. Even if you haul in a computer and an electron microscope, you must still look at the results and judge what they appear to be. So the simple, familiar distinction between the real and the merely apparent length of a line begins to appear more and more complicated. (But is this too only an appearance, a philosophical trick, or is the distinction *really* complicated? Plato, Descartes, and Kant, among other great philosophers, thought the distinction really is complicated; Wittgenstein, and many other modern philosophers of the "analytic" school, disagree.)

The same sort of experiment has been used to study the influence on our attitudes and judgments of sex prejudice. For example, a group of students were handed a brief essay on a fairly complicated economic question and asked to give their opinion of the clarity, forcefulness, intelligence, and persuasiveness of the argument in the essay. Half of the students had copies listing the author as "John Miller," and the other half had identical copies listing the author as "Joan Miller." Even though the words actually printed on the page were exactly the same on all copies, except for the name, the students with the copies signed "John Miller" rated the selection much higher. Because of the student's preexisting expectations about the intelligence and persuasiveness of men as compared with women, words signed with a male name appeared more intelligent, clearer, and more persuasive than exactly the same words signed with a female name. In Asch's experiment, the subjects could see that the lines were unequal, but they went along with the dominant opinion in order not to cause trouble. In this case, however, the social pressure had been internalized before the experiment began. The subjects didn't merely go along; they really *thought* they were judging the words fairly and objectively.

But the two experiments have one very important feature in common. Leaving sophisticated philosophical doubts to one side, most of us would agree that both Asch and the scientists who did the second experiment were able to determine the *real* truth of the situation which they had set up as the basis for their tests. Surely Asch knows how to measure lines, we would all agree. And equally certainly, a scientist can inspect copies of a statement to make sure that they are identical save for the name of the author. (The experiment would be a flop if it turned out that the statements signed "John" were different from those signed "Joan.")

However, suppose that a political scientist, impressed by these experiments, decided to investigate the "curious fact" that American voters perceive Republicans as different from Democrats, even though "every sensible, intelligent person can see that there is not the slightest difference between them!" Wait a minute! we would say. Maybe you don't think there is any difference between Democrats and Republicans, but a lot of knowledgeable people disagree. You can go ahead and try to convince us of your belief, but you can't just make it one of the assumptions of a study of "distortions in the perception of political reality" because your belief is one of the claims about "reality" that reasonable men and **women** debate.

Once again, we find that the distinction between appearance and reality is both fundamental and highly debatable. In politics, Democrats and Republicans look pretty much indistinguishable to a dedicated defender of traditional laissez-faire capitalism. They are all big-spending, big-government types. And to a socialist, there may appear to be no difference between a middle-of-the-road Republican and a right-wing conservative, despite what those two themselves believe. To a defender of absolute monarchy, of course (if there are any left in the world), the whole political spectrum from left to right might just as well be collapsed into a single point, for radicals, liberals and conservatives all look alike to him.

If there is so much disagreement about political "reality," (never mind any problems we might have over physical "reality"), then why not just scrap the distinction? What use is it, anyway? We might draw a sort of medical analogy here. The more powerful a drug is, the more dangerous are its side-effects, and the more careful doctors must be in prescribing it. In much the same way, the more powerful a tool of analysis is, the more controversial it will be, and the more difficult it is to use it wisely and fruitfully. The distinction between appearance and reality is a tremendously powerful tool of philosophical analysis and argument. To give it up would be to give up much of philosophy itself. Let me give you several extended examples of its use, so that you can see for yourself some of the ways in which you might strengthen your own thinking by means of it.

Consider first the familiar charge that advertising brainwashes consumers into buying things they do not really want—flashy new cars, automatic garbage compacters, electric toothbrushes, and all the rest. This is an old argument, going all the way back at least to Plato's complaints about the popular Greek politician Pericles, but recently the concern about the environmental effects of waste, pollution, and endless growth in production have given the claim a new lease on life.

The argument begins in a very simple, straightforward manner. If you point a gun at me and threaten to kill me unless I buy a new car, that is pretty clearly coercion. I don't want to spend all my money (and then some) for the car, but I want less to be killed. So I sign on the dotted line, and find myself with an expensive new item and three years of payments. But forcing people to buy cars at the point of a gun is against the law, and besides it isn't really very efficient (after a while, people start getting their own guns, and then you have to pay the salesmen battle pay, and the whole procedure becomes quite expensive). So instead, you advertise. First, of course, you just tell people what a wonderful car you make, how well it runs, how long it lasts, and you hope that they will be moved *by the desires they already have* to buy your car. In other words, you accept the consumers' desires as given, and adjust yourself to them. If they want red cars and you have blue cars, you repaint your cars. If they want small cars and you have big cars, then you retool, and start making small cars. The consumer is king.

After a while, you have sold a car to everyone who already wanted one, and you still have that factory turning out new cars. So now you try to change people's desires! You tell the consumer that a new car is more than an efficient means of transportation: it is a symbol of sexual attractiveness, a modern substitute for war, a fulfiller of fantasies, a dream machine. You try to *create* a desire to fit your product, instead of creating a product to fit the consumer's desire. But since it is still against the law to hold people up with guns, or force them into psychological conditioning laboratories, or stick electrodes into their brains, you must somehow change people's desires without letting them know that you are doing it. In short, you must let the consumers *think* that they are still sovereign, while covertly taking away their freedom to decide what it is that they really want.

Can advertising do this to us? There are three possible answers. (Actually there are more than three, but it would take forever to mention them all.) Some people say, yes, it is theoretically possible to manipulate men's desires, but as a matter of practical fact, advertising just isn't powerful enough to accomplish anything like the science-fiction effects that the "brainwash" story claims. Others, such as Herbert Marcuse, the economist John Kenneth Galbraith, and Plato, say yes, it is theoretically possible to manipulate people's desires, and what is more, it really does happen, even to those of us who are aware of the threat. The third possible answer is that the very notion of manipulating desires is incoherent, meaningless, because it assumes that someone could think he desires something when in fact he doesn't. But, these philosophers insist (Bentham is among them, for example), a desire is a conscious, directly discoverable fact of the mind. I cannot be wrong about whether I desire something, any more than I can be wrong about whether I am in pain. If a consumer *thinks* that he desires a new car, then he *does* desire a new car. Of course, he may be wrong to think that a new car will make him supremely happy. But even Bentham would grant that the satisfaction of my desires might not make me as happy as I had hoped.

The key to this argument, which many of you have no doubt heard already in one form or another, is our old friend, the distinction between appearance and reality. Starting with Plato, philosophers and social critics have argued that I can appear to have a desire, even though I don't really have it; that an experience can seem pleasurable even though it isn't; that I can think I am happy while actually being unhappy. Plato, Marx, Freud, and countless other thinkers have maintained that ordinary, intelligent, adult men and women can be profoundly mistaken about their own inner psychological states, about their desires, their pleasures, their pains, their happiness or unhappiness, about love, about hatred, about what they want out of life and even about whether they are truly happy once they get what they think they want.

Is there a legitimate distinction between apparent happiness and real happiness? Can someone believe he has everything in life and yet be totally wrong? Religious teachers certainly say so. Both western and eastern religions have taught for thousands of years that true happiness comes from rejecting the merely apparent happiness of worldly things. Those who declare themselves to be reborn in Christ, or to have found inner peace through meditation, frequently say that they now realize the emptiness of the pleasures they used to think they enjoyed.

This ancient debate resurfaced in recent years when mind-altering drugs were reintroduced into our culture. (I say "reintroduced" because such drugs, in one form or another, have been used by many cultures for countless thousands of years.) When you take LSD or some other hallucinogen, do you retreat from the *real* world into a private mental realm of mere appearances? Or is it really the other way around—do the drugs turn your mind away from the merely apparent realm of the senses to a higher, more real realm that transcends the senses? Hard-headed, practical types will insist that drug trips are mere fantasies, nothing more. To prove their claim, they will point out that the experiences cannot be shared publicly by other observers, that they cannot be reproduced experimentally in a laboratory, that they cannot be measured and quantified. But that is just a very complicated way of saying that drug experiences are not like nondrug experiences. It doesn't settle the dispute about which experience reveals *reality* and which experience reveals mere appearance. In order to back up your opinion about the reality of drug-experienced worlds, you would have to go rather deeply into metaphysics, for in the end, the issue comes down to your theory of the categories or kinds of reality.

The same sort of argument about what's real and what isn't turns up in the abstract reaches of theoretical physics, of all places. You will recall from Chapter One that the very earliest philosophers in the western tradition were speculative cosmologists who puzzled about the basic building blocks of the universe. One group of them, called atomists, claimed that the ordinary, visible objects which we encounter in the world are really made up of countless tiny atoms, too small to be seen by the eye. What looks like a solid, indivisible rock is really a sort of colony of little atoms which can break away, move about, come and go without our being able to see them. (The philosophers who took this line were Democritus, Epicurus, and Lucretius.) The modern theory of the atom tells us things that are even stranger and less common-sensical. If physicists are correct, what looks like a solid table is really mostly empty space, for the atoms and molecules which make up the wood of the table are themselves composed of sub-atomic particles held together by powerful forces. I can still remember my physics professor in college telling the class that if all the known matter in the universe were jammed together into an absolutely solid mass, it would make a great big neutron about one yard wide. Everything else in all the stars and planets we know about is empty space!

In fact, we might describe science as one long assault on common sense. Objects seem solid, but they are mostly empty space. Ordinary pond water looks clear, but under a microscope it turns out to be positively full of living organisms. Glass looks like a solid, but it is really a super-cooled liquid. The earth seems to be standing still but is really moving around the sun. I think I am making a free, unconstrained choice when I get married but really I am acting out unconscious fantasies which first took hold of me when I was a tiny baby. The list goes on and on!

In social philosophy, as we have already seen, the distinction between appearance and reality plays a central role. For the past two centuries, critics of industrial society have attempted to get some independent perspective on their world by contrasting what they could see all around them—social appearances—with the true, underlying good for man, rooted in his basic human nature—human reality. Burke and the conservative critics of the French revolution used this contrast to argue that the changes of the early industrial era were destructive of the truths embodied in social traditions. Marx and the socialist critics of capitalism used the same contrast to argue that capitalism alienated man from himself, from his real human nature, and from his fellow workers. Later, Freud employed a different version of the distinction to expose the real unconscious roots of motivation, and dissolve the surface appearances which concealed the repressed causes of human suffering.

Each of us must draw the line between appearance and reality for himself, but that is not to say that each of us will draw it correctly. If philosophy has taught us anything over the past two millennia, it is that in the end, self-deception is the most destructive form of ignorance. When Socrates turned away from scientific speculations, choosing instead to look inward for a self-conscious, critical, reflective knowledge of himself, he expressed by that life choice the conviction that has driven men and women into philosophical reflection ever since. The unexamined life, he told us in his final speech before the Athenian court, is not worth living. As you close this book, I hope you will take from it a renewed desire to attempt a reasoned, critical examination of your beliefs. your principles, and your life plans. And I hope, too, that this book will have helped you to carry out that examination philosophically.